Anonymous

Check-list of North American birds

Anonymous

Check-list of North American birds

ISBN/EAN: 9783337717131

Printed in Europe, USA, Canada, Australia, Japan

Cover: Foto ©ninafisch / pixelio.de

More available books at **www.hansebooks.com**

CHECK-LIST

OF

NORTH AMERICAN BIRDS

PREPARED BY A COMMITTEE

OF THE

American Ornithologists' Union

SECOND AND REVISED EDITION

Zoölogical Nomenclature is a means, not an end, of Zoölogical Science

NEW YORK
AMERICAN ORNITHOLOGISTS' UNION
1895

Copyright, 1895,
By American Ornithologists' Union.

Cambridge, Mass.:
Press of Edward W. Wheeler.

PREFACE TO THE FIRST EDITION.

AT the first Congress of the American Ornithologists' Union, held in New York, September 26-29, 1883, the following resolution was adopted: —

"*Resolved*, That the Chairman appoint a Committee of five, including himself, to whom shall be referred the question of a Revision of the Classification and Nomenclature of the Birds of North America."

In pursuance of this resolution the following Committee was appointed: Messrs. Coues, Allen, Ridgway, Brewster, and Henshaw.

The Committee, having held numerous sessions in Washington and New York, presented its Report at the second Congress of the Union, held in New York, Sept. 30 to Oct. 2, 1884, when the following resolution was adopted: —

"*Resolved*, That the Report of the Committee on the Revision of the Nomenclature and Classification of North American Birds be accepted and adopted, and that it be recommitted to the Committee, with instructions to complete and submit it to the Council as soon as practicable; and that the Council be empowered and instructed to accept and adopt the Report as finally rendered, with such modifications as they may deem necessary, and to publish the same, copyrighted, in part or in whole, and in one or more forms, in the name and under the auspices of the American Ornithologists' Union."

The Committee, having continued its sessions, presented its final report to the Council at a meeting held in Washington on the 21st of April, 1885, when the Report of the Committee was accepted and adopted, and was referred again to the Committee for publication, the Committee to exercise such editorial revison as might seem necessary.

Pursuant to the foregoing resolutions of the Union and Council, the Committee now offers to the public, in the name and on behalf of the Union, the result of its labors, consisting of a List of North American Birds, preceded by the Code of Rules adopted by the Committee for its guidance in the preparation of the List.

The Committee ventures to hope that the new Code will find favor, not only with ornithologists, but among zoölogists generally.

ELLIOTT COUES.
J. A. ALLEN.
ROBERT RIDGWAY.
WILLIAM BREWSTER.
H. W. HENSHAW.

PREFACE TO THE SECOND EDITION.

AT the Eleventh Congress of the American Ornithologists' Union, held in Cambridge, Mass., November 20-23, 1894, it was voted to publish, as early as practicable, a new edition of the Union's Check-List of North American Birds, to include the numerous additions and nomenclatural changes made in the several Supplements[1] to the Check-List since the publication of the original edition, together with a revision of the 'habitats' of the species and subspecies, but omitting the Code of Nomenclature.[2] The original Com-

---

[1] Supplement | to the | Code of Nomenclature and Check-List | of | North American Birds | adopted by the American Ornithologists' Union | Prepared by | a Committee of the Union | — | New York | American Ornithologists' Union | 1889. — 8vo, pp. 23.

Second Supplement to the American Ornithologists' Union Check-List of North American Birds. *The Auk*, VII, Jan. 1890, pp. 60-66. Also separate.

Third Supplement to the American Ornithologists' Union Check-List of North American Birds. *The Auk*, VIII, Jan. 1891, pp. 83-90. Also separate.

Fourth Supplement to the American Ornithologists' Union Check-List of North American Birds. *The Auk*, IX, Jan. 1892, pp. 105-108. Also separate.

Fifth Supplement to the American Ornithologists' Union Check-List of North American Birds. *The Auk*, X, Jan. 1893, pp. 59-63. Also separate.

Sixth Supplement to the American Ornithologists' Union Check-List of North American Birds. *The Auk*, XI, Jan. 1894, pp. 46-51. Also separate.

Seventh Supplement to the American Ornithologists' Union Check-List of North American Birds. *The Auk*, XII, April, 1894, pp. 163-169. Also separate.

Check-List | of | North American Birds | according to the Canons of Nomenclature | of the | American Ornithologists' Union | — | Abridged Edition | Revised | — | Published by the American Ornithologists' Union | 1889. — 8vo, pp. 71. Includes the additions to the original Check-List made in the first Supplement.

[2] Republished separately in 1892 as a pamphlet of 72 pages with the following title: The | Code of Nomenclature | adopted by the | American Ornithologists' Union | — | Zoölogical Nomenclature is a means, not an end, of Zoölogical Science | — | New York | American Ornithologists' Union | 1892.

mittee on Classification and Nomenclature of North American Birds was reappointed[1] to take charge of the work. The Committee held sessions in Washington, D. C., January 15-19, 1894, and February 12, 13, 1895, to outline the work and to rule on the questions involved in the publication of the revised List. The revision of the matter relating to the geographic distribution of the species and subspecies was undertaken by the Committee as a whole, each member in turn taking it in hand, while the incorporation of typographic and other rectifications made during the sessions of the Committee,[2] and the final preparation of the manuscript for the printer, was referred to a subcommittee consisting of the Editor of 'The Auk,' to whom was also assigned the general editorial supervision of the work.

The following extracts from the Introduction to the Code of Nomenclature (pp. 14, 15) will serve to explain the scope and plan of the Check-List, including the method of incorporating additions.

"1. That the term 'North American,' as applied to the proposed List of Birds, be held to include the continent of North America north of the present United States and Mexican boundary, and Greenland; and the peninsula of Lower California, with the islands naturally belonging thereto.

"2. That species be numbered consecutively, and that subspecies be enumerated by affixing the letters *a*, *b*, *c*, etc., to the number borne by their respective species; provided, that any subspecies of a species not included in the North American Fauna shall be separately numbered as if a species.

"3. That stragglers or accidental visitors, not regarded as components of the North American Fauna, be distinguished by having their respective numbers in brackets.

---

[1] With the exception of Mr. H. W. Henshaw, who was unable to serve, and Dr. C. Hart Merriam was appointed in his stead.

[2] The Committee desires to here acknowledge valuable assistance received, especially in the preparation of the geographic portions of the list, from Major Charles Bendire, Mr. Frank M. Chapman, Dr. Walter Faxon, Dr. A. K. Fisher, Mr. Gerrit S. Miller, Jr., and Dr. T. S. Palmer. The Committee is further indebted to Dr. Palmer for numerous corrections in the citations of original references.

"4. That any subsequent additions to the list be interpolated in systematic order, and bear the number of the species immediately preceding, with the addition of a figure (1, 2, etc., as the case may require), separated from the original number by a period or decimal point, thus giving the interpolated number a decimal form (*e. g.*, 243.1, etc.), in order that the original numbers may be permanent.

* * * * * * *

"6. That Giraud's at present unconfirmed species of Texan birds be included in the List on Giraud's authority.

"7. That species and subspecies the zoölogical status of which cannot be satisfactorily determined, like, *e. g.*, *Regulus cuvieri* and *Spiza townsendi* of Audubon, be referred to a hypothetical list, in each case with a brief statement of the reasons for such allocation.

"8. That a list of the fossil species of North American birds be added as an Appendix to the List proper.

"9. That the names of subgeneric and supergeneric groups of North American birds be included in the List in systematic order, to the end that the List may represent a classification as well as a nomenclature of the birds.

"10. That references be given to the original description of the species, and to the publication where the name as adopted in the List was first used; that the number borne by each species and sub-species in the Lists of Baird, 1858, of Coues, 1873, of Ridgway, 1880, and of Coues, 1882, be bracketed in chronological order after the synonymatic references.

"11. That a summary statement of the habitat of each species and subspecies, with special reference to its North American range, be included in the List.

"12. That the name of each bird shall consist of its generic without its subgeneric name, and of its specific with its subspecific name, if it have one, without the intervention of any other term.

* * * * * * *

"14. That every technical name be followed by a vernacular name, selected with due regard to its desirability.

"15. That the name of each species and subspecies be followed by the name of the original describer of the same, to be enclosed in parentheses when it is not also the authority for the name adopted.

"16. That all specific and subspecific names shall begin with a lower-case letter.

"17. That the sequence in classification followed in previous Lists be reversed, the List to begin with the lowest or most generalized type, and end with the highest or most specialized."

ELLIOTT COUES.
J. A. ALLEN.
WILLIAM BREWSTER.
C. HART MERRIAM.
ROBERT RIDGWAY.

TABLE OF CONTENTS.

	PAGE
PREFACE TO FIRST EDITION	iii
PREFACE TO SECOND EDITION	v
CHECK-LIST	1
I. PYGOPODES	1
a. Podicipedes	1
1. Podicipidæ	1
b. Cepphi	3
2. Urinatoridæ	3
3. Alcidæ	5
II. LONGIPENNES	13
4. Stercorariidæ	13
5. Laridæ	15
6. Rynchopidæ	27
III. TUBINARES	28
7. Diomedeidæ	28
8. Procellariidæ	29
IV. STEGANOPODES	39
9. Phaëthontidæ	39
10. Sulidæ	39
11. Anhingidæ	41
12. Phalacrocoracidæ	42
13. Pelecanidæ	45
14. Fregatidæ	46
V. ANSERES	47
15. Anatidæ	47
VI. ODONTOGLOSSÆ	66
16. Phœnicopteridæ	66
VII. HERODIONES	66
c. Ibides	66
17. Plataleidæ	66
18. Ibididæ	67

		PAGE
d. Ciconiæ		68
19. Ciconiidæ		68
e. Herodii		69
20. Ardeidæ		69
VIII. PALUDICOLÆ		75
f. Grues		75
21. Gruidæ		75
g. Ralli		76
22. Aramidæ		76
23. Rallidæ		76
IX. LIMICOLÆ		82
24. Phalaropodidæ		82
25. Recurvirostridæ		83
26. Scolopacidæ		84
27. Charadriidæ		98
28. Aphrizidæ		103
29. Hæmatopodidæ		104
30. Jacanidæ		105
X. GALLINÆ		106
h. Phasiani		107
31. Tetraonidæ		107
32. Phasianidæ		117
i. Penelopes		119
33. Cracidæ		119
XI. COLUMBÆ		119
34. Columbidæ		119
XII. RAPTORES		124
j. Sarcorhamphi		124
35. Cathartidæ		124
k. Falcones		126
36. Falconidæ		126
l. Striges		142
37. Strigidæ		142
38. Bubonidæ		142
XIII. PSITTACI		152
39. Psittacidæ		152
XIV. COCCYGES		153
m. Cuculi		153
40. Cuculidæ		153
n. Trogones		156
41. Trogonidæ		156
o. Alcyones		156
42. Alcedinidæ		156

	PAGE
XV. Pici	157
43. Picidæ	157
XVI. Macrochires	168
p. Caprimulgi	168
44. Caprimulgidæ	168
q. Cypseli	171
45. Micropodidæ	171
r. Trochili	173
46. Trochilidæ	173
XVII. Passeres	179
s. Clamatores	179
47. Cotingidæ	179
48. Tyrannidæ	179
t. Oscines	191
49. Alaudidæ	191
50. Corvidæ	194
51. Sturnidæ	202
52. Icteridæ	202
53. Fringillidæ	211
54. Tanagridæ	254
55. Hirundinidæ	256
56. Ampelidæ	260
57. Laniidæ	261
58. Vireonidæ	262
59. Cœrebidæ	267
60. Mniotiltidæ	268
61. Motacillidæ	288
62. Cinclidæ	291
63. Troglodytidæ	291
64. Certhiidæ	303
65. Paridæ	304
66. Sylviidæ	313
67. Turdidæ	316
HYPOTHETICAL LIST	325
THE FOSSIL BIRDS OF NORTH AMERICA	335
INDEX	347

CHECK-LIST.

Order PYGOPODES. Diving Birds.
Suborder PODICIPEDES. Grebes.
Family PODICIPIDÆ. Grebes.
Genus ÆCHMOPHORUS Coues.

Æchmophorus Coues, Pr. Ac. Nat. Sci. Phila. April, 1862, 229. Type, *Podiceps occidentalis* Lawr.

1. **Æchmophorus occidentalis** (Lawr.).
    Western Grebe.

    Podiceps occidentalis Lawr. in Baird's B. N. Am. 1858, 894.
    Æchmophorus occidentalis Coues, Pr. Ac. Nat. Sci. Phila. 1862, 229.
    [B 704, C 608, R 729, C 845.]

    Geographic Distribution.—Western North America, eastward to Manitoba, south to central Mexico.

Genus COLYMBUS Linnæus.

Colymbus Linn. S. N. ed. 10, I. 1758, 135. Type, by elimination, *Colymbus cristatus* Linn.

Subgenus COLYMBUS.

2. **Colymbus holbœllii** (Reinh.).
    Holbœll's Grebe.

    Podiceps holbœllii Reinh. Vid. Med. 1853, 76.
    Colymbus holbœllii Ridgw. Water B. N. Am. II. 1884, 428.

[B 702, C 610, R 731, C 847.]

GEOG. DIST.— North America at large, including Greenland. Also eastern Siberia, and southward to Japan. Breeds in high latitudes, migrating south in winter.

SUBGENUS **DYTES** KAUP.

Dytes KAUP, Sk. Ent. Eur. Thierw. 1829, 41. Type, *Colymbus auritus* LINN.

3. **Colymbus auritus** LINN.
    Horned Grebe.

Colymbus auritus LINN. S. N. ed. 10, I. 1758, 135.

[B 706, C 611, R 732, C 848.]

GEOG. DIST.— Northern hemisphere. Breeds from the northern United States northward.

4. **Colymbus nigricollis californicus** (HEERM.).
    American Eared Grebe.

Podiceps californicus HEERM. Pr. Ac. Nat. Sci. Phila. 1854, 179.
Colymbus nigricollis californicus RIDGW. Pr. U. S. Nat. Mus. VIII. 1885, 356.

[B 707, C 612, R 733*a*, C 850.]

GEOG. DIST.— Northern and western North America, from the Mississippi Valley westward, southward to Guatemala.

SUBGENUS **PODICEPS** LATHAM.

Podiceps LATH. Ind. Orn. II. 1790, 780. Type, by elimination, *Colymbus fluviatilis* TUNST.

5. **Colymbus dominicus** LINN.
    St. Domingo Grebe.

Colymbus dominicus LINN. S. N. ed. 12, I. 1766, 223.

[B 708*a*, C 613, R 734, C 851.]

GEOG. DIST.— Southern Texas and Lower California southward through tropical America to Paraguay, including the West Indies.

Genus **PODILYMBUS** Lesson.

Podilymbus Less. Traité, I. 1831, 595.   Type, *Colymbus podiceps* Linn.

6. Podilymbus podiceps (Linn.).
Pied-billed Grebe.

Colymbus podiceps Linn. S. N. ed. 10, I. 1758, 136.
Podilymbus podiceps Lawr. in Baird's B. N. Am. 1858, 898.

[B 709, C 614, R 735, C 852.]

Geog. Dist.— British Provinces southward to Brazil, Argentine Republic, and Chili, including the West Indies and Bermuda, breeding nearly throughout its range.

Suborder CEPPHI.   Loons and Auks.

Family **URINATORIDÆ**.   Loons.

Genus **URINATOR** Cuvier.

Urinator Cuv. Anat. Comp. I. 1800, tabl. ii.   Type, *Colymbus imber* Gunn.

7. Urinator imber (Gunn.).
Loon.

Colymbus imber Gunnerus, Trondh. Selsk. Skr. I. 1761, pl. iii.
Urinator imber Stejn. Orn. Expl. Kamchat. 1885, 313.

[B 698, C 605, R 736, C 840.]

Geog. Dist.— Northern part of northern hemisphere. In North America breeds from the northern tier of States northward; ranges in winter south to the Gulf of Mexico and Lower California.

8. **Urinator adamsii** (GRAY).
Yellow-billed Loon.

Colymbus adamsii GRAY, P. Z. S. 1859, 167.
Urinator adamsii STEJN. Pr. U. S. Nat. Mus. V. 1882, 43.

[B—, C 605a, R 737, C 841.]

GEOG. DIST.— Arctic America, west of Hudson Bay, and northeastern Asia. Casual in northern Europe.

9. **Urinator arcticus** (LINN.).
Black-throated Loon.

Colymbus arcticus LINN. S. N. ed. 10, I. 1758, 135.
Urinator arcticus STEJN. Pr. U. S. Nat. Mus. V. 1882, 43.

[B 699, C 606, R 738, C 842.]

GEOG. DIST.— Northern part of the northern hemisphere. In North America of casual occurrence in autumn and winter in the northern United States east of Rocky Mountains.

10. **Urinator pacificus** (LAWR.).
Pacific Loon.

Colymbus pacificus LAWR. in BAIRD'S B. N. Am. 1858, 889.
Urinator pacificus STEJN. Pr. U. S. Nat. Mus. V. 1882, 43.

[B 700, C 606a, R 739, C 843.]

GEOG. DIST.— Pacific coast of North America, south in winter to Cape St. Lucas and Guadalupe Island.

11. **Urinator lumme** (GUNN.).
Red-throated Loon.

Colymbus lumme GUNN. Trond. Selsk. Skr. I. 1761, pl. ii. fig. 2.
Urinator lumme STEJN. Pr. U. S. Nat. Mus. V. 1882, 43.

[B 701, C 607, R 740, C 844.]

GEOG. DIST.— Northern part of northern hemisphere, migrating southward in winter nearly across the United States.

FAMILY **ALCIDÆ**. AUKS, MURRES, AND PUFFINS.

SUBFAMILY **FRATERCULINÆ**. PUFFINS.

GENUS **LUNDA** PALLAS.

Lunda PALL. Zoog. Rosso-As. II. 1826, 363. Type, *Alca cirrhata* PALL.

12. **Lunda cirrhata** PALL.
Tufted Puffin.

Alca cirrhata PALL. Spic. Zool. V. 1769, 7, pl. i., pl. ii. figs. 1-3.
Lunda cirrhata PALL. Zoog. Rosso-As. II. 1826, 363, pl. 82.

[B 712, 716, C 619, R 745, C 856.]

GEOG. DIST. — Coasts and islands of the North Pacific from the Santa Barbara Islands, California, to Alaska, and from Japan to Bering Strait. Accidental on the coast of Maine.

GENUS **FRATERCULA** BRISSON.

Fratercula BRISS. Orn. VI. 1760, 81. Type, *Alca arctica* LINN.

13. **Fratercula arctica** (LINN.).
Puffin.

Alca arctica LINN. S. N. ed. 10, I. 1758, 130.
Fratercula arctica SCHÄFFER, Mus. Orn. 1789, 61.

[B 715, C 618, R 743, C 854.]

GEOG. DIST. — Coasts and islands of the North Atlantic, breeding on the North American coast from the Bay of Fundy northward. South in winter to Long Island, and casually further.

13 *a*. **Fratercula arctica glacialis** (TEMM.).
Large-billed Puffin.

Fratercula glacialis STEPHENS, Gen. Zool. Aves, XIII. pt. 1, 1826, 40.
Fratercula arctica β *glacialis* BLASIUS, List B. Europ. 1862, 24.

[B 714, C 618a, R 743a, C 855.]

GEOG. DIST.— Coasts and islands of the Arctic Ocean, from Spitzbergen to northern and western Greenland.

14. Fratercula corniculata (NAUM.).
Horned Puffin.

Mormon corniculata NAUM. Isis, 1821, 782, pl. vii. figs. 3, 4.
Fratercula corniculata BRANDT, Bull. Ac. St. Pétersb. II. 1837, 348.

[B 713, C 617, R 744, C 853.]

GEOG. DIST.— Coasts and islands of the North Pacific, from the Kuril Islands to British Columbia.

SUBFAMILY **PHALERINÆ**. AUKLETS, MURRELETS, GUILLEMOTS.

GENUS **CERORHINCA** BONAPARTE.

Cerorhinca BONAP. Ann. Lyc. N. Y. 1828, 427. Type, *C. occidentalis* BP. = *Alca monocerata* PALL.

15. Cerorhinca monocerata (PALL.).
Rhinoceros Auklet.

Alca monocerata PALL. Zoog. Rosso-As. II. 1826, 362.
Cerorhina monocerata CASS. in BAIRD'S B. N. Am. 1858, 905.

[B 717, 718, C 620, R 746, C 857.]

GEOG. DIST.— Coasts and islands of the North Pacific, breeding southward (formerly) to the Farallones; in winter southward to Lower California and Japan.

GENUS **PTYCHORAMPHUS** BRANDT.

Ptychoramphus BRANDT, Bull. Ac. St. Pétersb. II. 1837, 347. Type, *Uria aleutica* PALL.

ORDER PYGOPODES.

16. **Ptychoramphus aleuticus** (PALL.).
    Cassin's Auklet.

    Uria aleutica PALL. Zoog. Rosso-As. II. 1826, 370.
    Ptychoramphus aleuticus BRANDT, Bull. Ac. St. Pétersb. II. 1837, 347.

    [B 724, C 625, R 751, C 862.]

    GEOG. DIST.— Pacific coast of North America, from the Aleutian Islands to Lower California, breeding southward to San Geronimo Island (Lat. 30°).

GENUS **CYCLORRHYNCHUS** KAUP.

Cyclorrhynchus KAUP, Sk. Ent. Eur. Thierw. 1829, 155. Type, *Alca psittacula* PALL.

17. **Cyclorrhynchus psittaculus** (PALL.).
    Paroquet Auklet.

    Alca psittacula PALL. Spic. Zool. V. 1760, 13, pl. ii., pl. v. figs. 4–6.
    Cyclorhynchus psittaculus STEJN. Pr. U. S. Nat. Mus. VII. Aug. 5, 1884, 216.

    [B 725, C 621, R 747, C 858.]

    GEOG. DIST.— Coasts and islands of the North Pacific, from Sitka and the Kuril Islands northward.

GENUS **SIMORHYNCHUS** MERREM.

SUBGENUS **SIMORHYNCHUS**.

Simorhynchus MERREM, in ERSCH & GRUBER's Encycl. 1 sect. II. 1819, 405. Type, *Alca cristatella* PALL.

18. **Simorhynchus cristatellus** (PALL.).
    Crested Auklet.

    Alca cristatella PALL. Spic. Zool. V. 1769, 20, pl. iii., pl. v. figs. 7–9.
    Simorhynchus cristatellus BONAP. Compt. Rend. XLII. 1856, 774.

[B 719, 720, C 622, R 748, C 859.]

GEOG. DIST.—Coasts and islands of the North Pacific, from Kadiak and Japan northward.

SUBGENUS **PHALERIS** TEMMINCK.

Phaleris TEMM. Man. Orn. 1820, p. cxii. Type, by elimination, *Alca pygmæa* GMEL.

19. **Simorhynchus pygmæus** (GMEL.).
Whiskered Auklet.

Alca pygmæa GMEL. S. N. I. ii. 1788, 555.
Simorhynchus pygmæus BRANDT, Mél. Biol. VII. 1869, 222.

[B 721, C 623, R 749, C 860.]

GEOG. DIST.—Coasts and islands of the North Pacific, from Unalaska through the Aleutian chain to Kamchatka.

SUBGENUS **CICERONIA** REICHENBACH.

Ciceronia REICH. Syst. Av. 1852, p. iii. Type, *Phaleris microceros* BRANDT = *Uria pusilla* PALL.

20. **Simorhynchus pusillus** (PALL.).
Least Auklet.

Uria pusilla PALL. Zoog. Rosso-As. II. 1826, 373, pl. 70.
Simorhynchus pusillus COUES, Pr. Ac. Nat. Sci. Phila. 1862, 324.

[B 722, 723, C 624, R 750, C 861.]

GEOG. DIST.—Coasts and islands of the North Pacific, from Sitka and Japan northward to Bering Strait.

GENUS **SYNTHLIBORAMPHUS** BRANDT.

Synthliboramphus BRANDT, Bull. Ac. St. Pétersb. II. 1837, 347. Type, *Alca antiqua* GMEL.

21. **Synthliboramphus antiquus** (GMEL.).
Ancient Murrelet.

Alca antiqua GMEL. S. N. I. ii. 1788, 554.
Synthliboramphus antiquus BRANDT, Bull. Ac. St. Pétersb. II. 1837, 347.

[B 734, 736, C 627, R 753, 759, C 864, 870.]

GEOG. DIST.—Coasts and islands of the North Pacific, from southern Vancouver Island and Japan northward. Accidental in Wisconsin.

GENUS **BRACHYRAMPHUS** BRANDT.

Brachyramphus BRANDT, Bull. Ac. St. Pétersb. II. 1837, 346.
Type, *Colymbus marmoratus* GMEL.

23. **Brachyramphus marmoratus** (GMEL.).
    Marbled Murrelet.

Colymbus marmoratus GMEL. S. N. I. ii. 1788, 583.
Brachyramphus marmoratus BRANDT, Bull. Ac. St. Pétersb. II. 1837, 346.

[B 732, 733, C 629, R 755, C 866.]

GEOG. DIST.—Coasts and islands of the North Pacific; on the American coast from San Diego northward, and breeding as far south as Vancouver Island.

24. **Brachyramphus kittlitzii** BRANDT.
    Kittlitz's Murrelet.

Brachyramphus kittlitzii BRANDT, Bull. Ac. St. Pétersb. II. 1837, 346.

[B 735, C 630, R 756, C 867.]

GEOG. DIST.—Northern Japan, Kamchatka and Aleutian Islands, east to Unalaska.

25. **Brachyramphus hypoleucus** XANTUS.
    Xantus's Murrelet.

Brachyrhamphus hypoleucus XANTUS, Pr. Ac. Nat. Sci. Phila., Nov. 1859, 299.

[B —, C —, R 757, C 868.]

GEOG. DIST.—Coasts of southern and Lower California, from Santa Barbara Island to Cape St. Lucas.

26. Brachyramphus craveri (SALVAD.).
   Craveri's Murrelet.

Uria craveri SALVAD. Atti Soc. It. Sc. Nat. VIII. 1866, Estr. p. 17.
Brachyrhamphus craverii COUES, Pr. Ac. Nat. Sci. Phila., 1868, 66.

[B—, C—, R 758, C 869.]

GEOG. DIST.— Both coasts of Lower California, from Cape St. Lucas northward to Espiritu Santo Island in the Gulf of California, and to Natividad Island (lat. 28°) on the Pacific side.

GENUS **CEPPHUS** PALLAS.

Cepphus PALL. Spic. Zool. V. 1769, 33. Type, *C. lacteolus* PALL. = *C. grylle*, albino.

27. Cepphus grylle (LINN.).
   Black Guillemot.

Alca grylle LINN. S. N. ed. 10, I. 1758, 130.
Cepphus grylle BREHM, Handb. Vög. Deutschl. 1831, 987.

[B 726, *part*, C 631, *part*, R 760, *part*, C 871, *part*.]

GEOG. DIST.— Coasts of northern Europe, south to Denmark and the British Islands. Newfoundland and coast of Maine, south in winter to Philadelphia.

28. Cepphus mandtii (LICHT.).
   Mandt's Guillemot.

Uria mandtii LICHT. in MANDT'S Obs. Itin. Dissert. 1822, 30.
Cepphus mandtii BP. Cat. Parzud. 1856, 12.

[B 726, *part*, C 631, *part*, R 760, *part*, C 871, *part*.]

GEOG. DIST.— Arctic regions of both continents; south on the Atlantic coast of North America, in winter, to Massachusetts, breeding south to Hudson Bay and Labrador; Alaskan coast, south, in winter, to Norton Sound.

29. **Cepphus columba** PALL.
Pigeon Guillemot.

Cepphus columba PALL. Zoog. Rosso-As. II. 1826, 348.

[B 727, C 632, R 761, C 872.]

GEOG. DIST.—Coasts and islands of the North Pacific, southward from Bering Strait to northern Japan and the Santa Barbara Islands, California.

SUBFAMILY **ALCINÆ**. AUKS AND MURRES.

GENUS **URIA** BRISSON.

Uria BRISS. Orn. VI. 1760, 70. Type, by elimination, *Colymbus troile* LINN.

30. **Uria troile** (LINN.).
Murre.

Colymbus troile LINN. Faun. Suec. ed. 1761, 52; S. N. ed. 12, I. 1766, 220.
Uria troile LATH. Ind. Orn. II. 1790, 796.

[B 729, 730, C 634, R 763, C 874.]

GEOG. DIST.—Coasts and islands of the North Atlantic, southward on the coast of North America, in winter, to southern New England; breeding from the Magdalen Islands northward.

30 *a*. **Uria troile californica** (BRYANT).
California Murre.

Catarractes californicus BRYANT, Pr. Bost. Soc. VIII. 1861, 11, figs. 3, 5.
Uria troile californica RIDGW. Water B. N. Am. II. 1884, 483.

[B—, C—, R 763*a*, C 875.]

GEOG. DIST.—Coasts and islands of the North Pacific, breeding from California north to the Pribilof Islands.

31. Uria lomvia (LINN.).
Brünnich's Murre.

Alca lomvia LINN. S. N. ed. 10, I. 1758, 130.
Uria lomvia BRYANT, Proc. Bost. Soc. N. H. VIII. May, 1861, 75.

[B. 731, C 635, R 764a, C 876.]

GEOG. DIST.— Coasts and islands of the North Atlantic and eastern Arctic Oceans; south to the lakes of northern New York and the coast of New Jersey. Breeding from the Gulf of St. Lawrence northward.

31 a. Uria lomvia arra (PALL.).
Pallas's Murre.

Cepphus arra PALL. Zoog. Rosso-As. II. 1826, 347.
Uria lomvia arra RIDGW. Water B. N. Am. II. Sept. 1884, 485.

[B —, C —, R 764, C —.]

GEOG. DIST.— Coasts and islands of the North Pacific and western Arctic Oceans, south to Kadiak and Kamchatka.

GENUS **ALCA** LINNÆUS.

Alca LINN. S. N. ed. 10, I. 1758, 130. Type, by elimination, *Alca torda* LINN.

32. Alca torda LINN.
Razor-billed Auk.

Alca torda LINN. S. N. ed. 10, I. 1758, 130.

[B 711, C 616, R 742, C 877.]

GEOG. DIST.— Coasts and islands of the North Atlantic, south in winter on the North American coast casually to North Carolina, breeding from eastern Maine northward.

GENUS **PLAUTUS** BRÜNNICH.

Plautus BRÜNN. Zool. Fund. 1772, 78. Type, *Alca impennis* LINN.

33. **Plautus impennis** (LINN.).
   Great Auk.

Alca impennis LINN. S. N. ed. 10, I. 1758, 130.
Plautus impennis STEENSTR. Vid. Med. Nat. For. Kjøb. 1855, 114.

[B 710, C 615, R 741, C 878.]

GEOG. DIST.— Formerly the coasts and islands of the North Atlantic, from Massachusetts and Ireland northward nearly to the Arctic Circle. Now extinct.

SUBFAMILY **ALLINÆ**. DOVEKIES.

GENUS **ALLE** LINK.

Alle LINK, Beschr. Nat. Samml. Univ. Rostock, I. 1806, 17. Type, *Alca alle* LINN.

34. **Alle alle** (LINN.).
   Dovekie.

Alca alle LINN. S. N. ed. 10, I. 1758, 131.
Alle alle STEJNEGER, Stand. Nat. Hist. IV, 1885, 69.

[B 738, C 626, R 752, C 863.]

GEOG. DIST.— Coasts and islands of the North Atlantic and eastern Arctic Oceans; in North America south in winter to New Jersey; breeds in high northern latitudes. Accidental in Michigan.

ORDER LONGIPENNES. LONG–WINGED SWIMMERS.

FAMILY **STERCORARIIDÆ**. SKUAS AND JAEGERS.

GENUS **MEGALESTRIS** BONAPARTE.

Megalestris BONAP. Cat. Parzudaki, 1856, 11. Type, *Catharacta skua* BRÜNN.

35. **Megalestris skua** (BRÜNN.).
Skua.

Catharacta skua BRÜNN. Orn. Bor. 1764, 33.
Megalestris skua RIDGW. Pr. U. S. Nat. Mus. III. Sept. 4, 1880, 208.

[B 652, C 539, R 696, C 764.]

GEOG. DIST.— Coasts and islands of the North Atlantic, chiefly northward. South to Spain and North Carolina. Apparently rare on the coast of North America.

GENUS **STERCORARIUS** BRISSON.

Stercorarius BRISS. Orn. V. 1760, 149. Type, *Larus parasiticus* LINN.

36. **Stercorarius pomarinus** (TEMM.).
Pomarine Jaeger.

Larus pomarinus TEMM. Man. d'Orn. 1815, 514.
Stercorarius pomarinus VIEILL. Nouv. Dict. XXXII. 1819, 158.

[B 653, C 540, R 697, C 765.]

GEOG. DIST.— Seas and inland waters of northern portions of the northern hemisphere, south in winter to Africa, Australia, and probably South America.

37. **Stercorarius parasiticus** (LINN.).
Parasitic Jaeger.

Larus parasiticus LINN. S. N. ed. 10, I. 1758, 136.
Stercorarius parasiticus SCHÄFF. Mus. Orn. 1789, 62, pl. 37.

[B 654, C 541, R 698, C 766.]

GEOG. DIST.— Northern part of northern hemisphere, southward in winter to South Africa and South America. Breeds in high northern districts, and winters from New York and California southward to Brazil.

38. **Stercorarius longicaudus** VIEILL.
    Long-tailed Jaeger.

Stercorarius longicaudus VIEILL. Nouv. Dict. XXXII. 1819, 157.

[B 655, C 542, R 699, C 767.]

GEOG. DIST.— Northern part of northern hemisphere, breeding in high northern districts; south in winter to the Gulf of Mexico.

FAMILY **LARIDÆ**. GULLS AND TERNS.

SUBFAMILY **LARINÆ**. GULLS.

GENUS **GAVIA** BOIE.

Gavia BOIE, Isis, 1822, 563. Type, *Larus eburneus* PHIPPS = *Larus albus* GUNN.

39. **Gavia alba** (GUNN.).
    Ivory Gull.

Larus albus GUNN. in LEEM's Beskr. Finm. Lapp. 1767, 285.
Gavia alba STEJN. Pr. U. S. Nat. Mus. V. 1882, 39.

[B 676, 677, C 550, R 657, C 785.]

GEOG. DIST.— Arctic Seas, south in winter on the Atlantic coast of North America to Labrador and Newfoundland, casually to New Brunswick, and on the Pacific side to Bering Sea.

GENUS **RISSA** STEPHENS.

Rissa STEPHENS, Gen. Zool. XIII. 1825, 180. Type, *Larus tridactylus* LINN.

40. **Rissa tridactyla** (LINN.).
    Kittiwake.

Larus tridactylus LINN. S. N. ed. 10, I. 1758, 136.
Rissa tridactyla BONAP. Comp. List, 1838, 62.

[B 672, C 552, R 658, C 782.]

GEOG. DIST.— Arctic regions, south in eastern North America in winter to the Great Lakes and the Middle States.

40 a. Rissa tridactyla pollicaris RIDGW.
Pacific Kittiwake.

Rissa tridactyla pollicaris "STEJN. MS." RIDGW. Water B. N. Am. II. 1884, 202.

[B —, C 552a, R 658a, C 783.]

GEOG. DIST.— Coasts of North Pacific and Bering Sea, south in winter casually to southern California.

41. Rissa brevirostris (BRUCH).
Red-legged Kittiwake.

Larus brevirostris BRUCH, J. f. O. 1853, 103.
Rissa brevirostris LAWR. in BAIRD'S B. N. Am. 1858, 855.

[B 674, 675, C 553, R 659, C 784.]

GEOG. DIST.— Coasts and islands of Bering Sea.

GENUS **LARUS** LINNÆUS.

Larus LINN. S. N. ed. 10, I. 1758, 136. Type, by elimination, *L. canus* LINN.

42. Larus glaucus BRÜNN.
Glaucous Gull.

Larus glaucus BRÜNN. Orn. Bor. 1764, 44.

[B 656, C 543, R 660, C 768.]

GEOG. DIST.— Arctic regions, south in winter in North America to the Great Lakes and Long Island.

42.1. Larus barrovianus RIDGW.
Point Barrow Gull.

Larus barrovianus RIDGW. Auk, III. July, 1886, 330.

ORDER LONGIPENNES.

[B—, C—, R—, C—.]

GEOG. DIST.— Bering Sea and contiguous waters; northeastward to Point Barrow, southwestward to Japan.

43. **Larus leucopterus** FABER.
    Iceland Gull.

Larus leucopterus FABER, Prodr. Isl. Orn. 1822, 91.

[B 658, C 544, R 661, C 769.]

GEOG. DIST.— Arctic regions, south in winter in North America to Massachusetts and the Great Lakes, occasionally much further south.

44. **Larus glaucescens** NAUM.
    Glaucous-winged Gull.

Larus glaucescens NAUM. Naturg. Vög. Deutschl. X. 1840, 351.

[B 657, 659, C 545, R 662, C 770.]

GEOG. DIST.— Pacific coast of North America, from Alaska south to California; on the Asiatic side south to Japan.

45. **Larus kumlieni** BREWST.
    Kumlien's Gull.

Larus kumlieni BREWST. Bull. Nutt. Orn. Club, VIII. 1883, 216.

[B—, C—, R—, C—.]

GEOG. DIST.— North Atlantic coast of North America, breeding in Cumberland Gulf; south in winter to the coast of the Middle States.

46. **Larus nelsoni** HENSH.
    Nelson's Gull.

Larus nelsoni HENSH. Auk, I. July, 1884, 250.

[B—, C—, R—, C—.]

GEOG. DIST.— Coast of Norton Sound, Alaska.

47. Larus marinus LINN.
Great Black-backed Gull.

Larus marinus LINN. S. N. ed. 10, I. 1758, 136.

[B 660, C 546, R 663, C 771.]

GEOG. DIST.— Coasts of the North Atlantic; south in winter to Long Island and Italy.

48. Larus schistisagus STEJN.
Slaty-backed Gull.

Larus schistisagus STEJN. Auk, I. July, 1884, 231.

[B —, C —, R —, C —.]

GEOG. DIST.— North Pacific, chiefly on the Asiatic side; Herald Island, Arctic Ocean, and Alaskan coast of Bering Sea.

49. Larus occidentalis AUD.
Western Gull.

Larus occidentalis AUD. Orn. Biog. V. 1839, 320.

[B 662, C 547*b*, R 664, C 774.]

GEOG. DIST.— Pacific coast of North America, breeding from Lower California northward to British Columbia.

[50.] **Larus affinis** REINH.
Siberian Gull.

Larus affinis REINH. Vid. Med. 1853, 78.

[B —, C —, R 665, C 776.]

GEOG. DIST.— Northern Asia and Europe, southward in winter to northern Africa. Accidental in Greenland.

51. Larus argentatus BRÜNN.
Herring Gull.

Larus argentatus BRÜNN. Orn. Bor. 1764, 44.

[B —, C 547, R 666, C 772.]

GEOG. DIST.— Old World, south to the Azores; Cumberland Sound; occasional on the eastern coast of the United States.

ORDER LONGIPENNES.

51 a. **Larus argentatus smithsonianus** Coues.
   American Herring Gull.

   Larus smithsonianus Coues, Pr. Ac. Nat. Sci. Phila. 1862, 296.
   Larus argentatus var. *smithsonianus* Coues, Check-List, 1873, no. 547a.

   [B 661, C 547a, R 666a, C 773.]

   Geog. Dist.— North America generally, breeding from Maine, northern New York, the Great Lakes, and Minnesota northward; in winter south to Cuba and Lower California.

52. **Larus vegæ** (Palmén).
   Vega Gull.

   Larus argentatus var. *vegæ* Palm. Bidr. Sibirisk. Vega Exp. 1887, 370.
   Larus vegæ Stejn. Auk, V. July, 1888, 310.

   [B —, C —, R 667, C 775.]

   Geog. Dist.— Bering Sea and adjacent waters, south in winter to California and Japan.

53. **Larus californicus** Lawr.
   California Gull.

   Larus californicus Lawr. Ann. Lyc. N. Y. VI. 1854, 79.

   [B 663, C 548a, R 668, C 777.]

   Geog. Dist.— Western North America, chiefly in the interior, from Alaska to Mexico.

54. **Larus delawarensis** Ord.
   Ring-billed Gull.

   Larus delawarensis Ord, Guthrie's Geog. 2d Am. ed. 1815, 319.

   [B 664, C 548, R 669, C 778.]

   Geog. Dist.— North America at large; south in winter to Cuba and Mexico.

55. Larus brachyrhynchus RICH.
Short-billed Gull.

Larus brachyrhynchus RICH. F. B. A. II. 1831, 421.

[B 665, 673, C 549, R 670, C 780.]

GEOG. DIST.— Arctic America and Pacific coast, south in winter to southern California.

[**56.**] **Larus canus** LINN.
Mew Gull.

Larus canus LINN. S. N. ed. 10, I. 1758, 136.

[B —, C —, R 671, C 779.]

GEOG. DIST.— Europe and Asia; accidental in Labrador?

57. Larus heermanni CASS.
Heermann's Gull.

Larus heermanni CASS. Pr. Ac. Nat. Sci. Phila. VI. 1852, 187.

[B 666, C 551, R 672, C 781.]

GEOG. DIST.— Pacific coast of North America, from British Columbia to Panama.

58. Larus atricilla LINN.
Laughing Gull.

Larus atricilla LINN. S. N. ed. 10, I. 1758, 136.

[B 667, C 554, R 673, C 786.]

GEOG. DIST.— Atlantic and Gulf coasts of the United States, north to Maine and Nova Scotia; south in winter through West Indies, Mexico (both coasts), Central America, and northern South America (Atlantic side) to the Lower Amazon.

59. Larus franklinii SW. & RICH.
Franklin's Gull.

Larus franklinii SW. & RICH. F. B. A. II. 1831, 424, pl. 71.

[B 668, 669, C 555, R 674, C 787.]

Geog. Dist.— Interior of North America, chiefly west of the Mississippi River and east of the Rocky Mountains, breeding from Iowa northward; south in winter through Mexico and Central America to Peru.

60. **Larus philadelphia** (Ord).
Bonaparte's Gull.

Sterna philadelphia Ord, Guthrie's Geog. 2d Am. ed. II. 1815, 319.
Larus philadelphia Gray, List Brit. B. 1863, 235.

[B 670, C 556, R 675, C 788.]

Geog. Dist.— Whole of North America, breeding mostly north of the United States. Not yet recorded from south of the United States, though reported from the Bermudas.

[60.1.] **Larus minutus** Pall.
Little Gull.

Larus minutus Pall. Reis. Russ. Reichs. III. App. No. 35, 1771, 702.

[B—, C—, R—, C—.]

Geog. Dist.— Europe and parts of Asia and Africa; accidental in Bermuda and on Long Island.

Genus **RHODOSTETHIA** Macgillivray.

Rhodostethia Macgil. Man. Brit. Orn. II. 1842, 253. Type, *Larus roseus* Macgil.

61. **Rhodostethia rosea** (Macgil.).
Ross's Gull.

Larus roseus Macgil. Mem. Wern. Soc. V. 1824, 249.
Rhodostethia rosea Bonap. Rev. Crit. Orn. Eur. Degland, 1850, 201.

[B 678, C 557, R 676, C 789.]

GEOG. DIST.— Arctic regions; south in autumn and winter to Kamchatka, Point Barrow, Alaska, and Disco Bay, Greenland. Casual in England, Faroes, Helgoland, etc.

GENUS **XEMA** LEACH.

Xema LEACH, Ross's Voy. App. 1819, p. lvii. Type, *Larus sabinii* SAB.

62. Xema sabinii (SAB.).
Sabine's Gull.

Larus sabinii J. SAB. Trans. Linn. Soc. XII. 1818, 520, pl. 29.
Xema sabini LEACH, App. Ross's Voy. Baff. Bay. 4to ed. 1819, lvii.

[B 680, C 558, R 677, C 790.]

GEOG. DIST.— Arctic regions; in North America south in winter to New York, the Great Lakes, and Great Salt Lake; casual in Kansas, Bahama, and on coast of Peru.

SUBFAMILY **STERNINÆ**. TERNS.

GENUS **GELOCHELIDON** BREHM.

Gelochelidon BREHM, Isis, 1830, 994. Type, *G. meridionalis* BREHM = *Sterna nilotica* HASSELQ.

63. Gelochelidon nilotica (HASSELQ.).
Gull-billed Tern.

Sterna nilotica HASSELQ. Reise nach Pal. Deutsche Ausg. 1762, 325.
Gelochelidon nilotica STEJN. Auk, I. Oct. 1884, 366.

[B 681, C 560, R 679, C 792.]

GEOG. DIST.— Nearly cosmopolitan; in North America chiefly along the Atlantic and Gulf coasts of the United States, breeding north to southern New Jersey, and wandering casually to Long Island and Massachusetts; in winter both coasts of Mexico and Central America and south to Brazil.

Genus **STERNA** Linnæus.

Subgenus **THALASSEUS** Boie.

Thalasseus Boie, Isis, 1822, 563. Type, *Sterna caspia* Pall. = *S. tschegrava* Lepech.

64. Sterna tschegrava Lepech.
   Caspian Tern.
   Sterna tschegrava Lepech. Nov. Comm. Petrop. XIV. 1770, 500, pl. 13, fig. 2.
   [B 682, C 561, R 680, C 793.]

Geog. Dist.— Nearly cosmopolitan; in North America breeding southward to Virginia, Lake Michigan, Texas, Nevada, and California.

Subgenus **ACTOCHELIDON** Kaup.

Actochelidon Kaup, Sk. Ent. Eur. Thierw. 1829, 31. Type, *Sterna cantiaca* Gmel. = *S. sandvicensis* Gmel.

65. Sterna maxima Bodd.
   Royal Tern.
   Sterna maxima Bodd. Tabl. P. E. 1783, 58.
   [B 683, C 562, R 681, C 794.]

Geog. Dist.— Tropical America, and warmer parts of North America, casually northward to Massachusetts, the Great Lakes, and California. West coast of Africa, north to Tangiers.

66. Sterna elegans Gamb.
   Elegant Tern.
   Sterna elegans Gamb. Pr. Ac. Nat. Sci. Phila. IV. 1848, 129.
   [B 684, C 563, R 682, C 795.]

Geog. Dist.— Pacific coast of America, from California to Chili.

67. **Sterna sandvicensis acuflavida** (Cabot).
Cabot's Tern.

Sterna acuflavida Cabot, Pr. Boston Soc. N. H. II. 1847, 257.
Sterna sandvicensis acuflavida Ridgw. Water B. N. Am. II. 1884, 288.

[B 685, C 564, R 683, C 796.]

Geog. Dist.—South Atlantic and Gulf coasts of the United States, north, casually, to southern New England; south, in winter, to Central America (both coasts) and West Indies.

Subgenus **STERNA**.

Sterna Linn. S. N. ed. 10, I. 1758, 137. Type, by elimination, *S. hirundo* Linn.

[68.] **Sterna trudeaui** Aud.
Trudeau's Tern.

Sterna trudeaui Aud. Orn. Biog. V. 1839, 125, pl. 409.

[B 687, C 571, R 684, C 802.]

Geog. Dist.— Southern South America. Casual, or accidental, on the Atlantic coast of the United States (New Jersey, Long Island).

69. **Sterna forsteri** Nutt.
Forster's Tern.

Sterna forsteri Nutt. Man. II. 1834, 274.

[B 691, 686, C 566, R 685, C 798.]

Geog. Dist.— North America generally, breeding from Manitoba southward to Virginia, Illinois, Texas, and California; in winter southward to Brazil.

70. **Sterna hirundo** Linn.
Common Tern.

Sterna hirundo Linn. S. N. ed. 10, I. 1758, 137.

[B 689, C 565, R 686, C 797.]

GEOG. DIST.— Greater part of the northern hemisphere and Africa. In North America chiefly east of the Plains, breeding from the Arctic coast, somewhat irregularly, to Florida, Texas, and Arizona, and wintering northward to Virginia. Also coast of Lower California.

71. Sterna paradisæa BRÜNN.
Arctic Tern.

Sterna paradisæa BRÜNN. Orn. Bor. 1764, 46.

[B 690, 693, C 567, 568, R 687, C 799.]

GEOG. DIST.— Northern hemisphere; in North America breeding from Massachusetts to the Arctic regions, and wintering southward to Virginia and California.

72. Sterna dougalli MONTAG.
Roseate Tern.

Sterna dougalli MONTAG. Orn. Dict. Suppl. 1813, —.

[B 692, C 569, R 688, C 800.]

GEOG. DIST.— Temperate and tropical regions; north on the Atlantic coast of North America to Massachusetts, and casually to Maine and Nova Scotia.

73. Sterna aleutica BAIRD.
Aleutian Tern.

Sterna aleutica BAIRD, Tr. Chicago Ac. Nat. Sci. I. 1869, 321, pl. 31, fig. 1.

[B —, C 572, R 689, C 803.]

GEOG. DIST.— Coast of Alaska from Kadiak to Norton Sound.

SUBGENUS **STERNULA** BOIE.

Sternula BOIE, Isis, 1822, 563. Type, *Sterna minuta* LINN.

74. Sterna antillarum (Less.).
   Least Tern.

   Sternula antillarum Less. Descr. Mam. et Ois. 1847, 256.
   Sterna antillarum Coues, Pr. Ac. Nat. Sci. Phila. 1862, 552.

   [B 694, C 570, R 690, C 801.]

   Geog. Dist.— Northern South America, northward to California, Minnesota, and New England, and casually to Labrador, breeding nearly throughout its range.

   Subgenus **HALIPLANA** Wagler.

   Haliplana Wagl. Isis, 1832, 1224. Type, *Sterna fuliginosa* Gmel.

75. Sterna fuliginosa Gmel.
   Sooty Tern.

   Sterna fuliginosa Gmel. S. N. I. ii. 1788, 605.

   [B 688, C 573, R 691, C 804.]

   Geog. Dist.— Tropical and subtropical coasts of the globe. In America from Chili to western Mexico and the Carolinas, and casually to New England.

[**76.**] **Sterna anæthetus** Scop.
   Bridled Tern.

   Sterna anæthetus Scop. Del. Faun. et Flor. Ins. II. 1786, no. 72, 92.

   [B —, C 574, R 692, C 805.]

   Geog. Dist.— Tropical regions generally. Casual in Florida.

   Genus **HYDROCHELIDON** Boie.

   Hydrochelidon Boie, Isis, 1822, 563. Type, *Sterna nigra* Linn.

77. Hydrochelidon nigra surinamensis (Gmel.).
   Black Tern.

   Sterna surinamensis Gmel. S. N. I. ii. 1788, 604.
   Hydrochelidon nigra surinamensis Stejn. Pr. U. S. Nat. Mus. 1882, 40.

[B 695, C 575, R 693, C 806.]

GEOG. DIST.—Temperate and tropical America. From Alaska and the Fur Countries to Brazil and Chili, breeding from the middle United States, west of the Alleghanies, northward.

[78.] **Hydrochelidon leucoptera** (MEISN. & SCHINZ).
   White-winged Black Tern.
Sterna leucoptera MEISN. & SCHINZ, Vög. Schweiz, 1815, 264.
Hydrochelidon leucoptera BOIE, Isis, 1822, 563.

[B —, C 575 *bis*, R 694, C 807.]

GEOG. DIST.—Eastern hemisphere, accidental in North America (Lake Koshkonong, Wisconsin).

GENUS **ANOUS** STEPHENS.

Anous STEPH. Gen. Zool. XIII. pt. i. 1826, 139. Type, *Sterna stolida* LINN.

79. **Anous stolidus** (LINN.).
   Noddy.
Sterna stolida LINN. S. N. ed. 10, I. 1758, 137.
Anous stolidus GRAY, List Gen. B. 1841, 100.

[B 696, C 576, R 695, C 808.]

GEOG. DIST.—Tropical and subtropical regions; in America from Brazil and Chili north to the Gulf and South Atlantic States.

FAMILY **RYNCHOPIDÆ**. SKIMMERS.

GENUS **RYNCHOPS** LINN.

Rynchops LINN. S. N. ed. 10, I. 1758, 138. Type, *R. nigra* LINN.

80. **Rynchops nigra** LINN.
   Black Skimmer.
Rynchops nigra LINN. S. N. ed. 10, I. 1758, 138.

[B 697, C 577, R 656, C 809.]

GEOG. DIST.—Warmer parts of America, north on the Atlantic coast to New Jersey, and casually to the Bay of Fundy.

Order TUBINARES. Tube-nosed Swimmers.

Family DIOMEDEIDÆ. Albatrosses.

Genus DIOMEDEA Linnæus.

Diomedea Linn. S. N. ed. 10, I. 1758, 132. Type, *D. exulans* Linn.

81. Diomedea nigripes Aud.
Black-footed Albatross.

Diomedea nigripes Aud. Orn. Biog. V. 1839, 327.

[B—, C 579, R 700, C 811.]

Geog. Dist.— North Pacific, including west coast of North America.

82. Diomedea albatrus Pall.
Short-tailed Albatross.

Diomedea albatrus Pall. Spic. Zool. V. 1769, 28.

[B 631, C 578, R 701, C 810.]

Geog. Dist.— Pacific Ocean, including western coast of America, northward to Bering Sea.

Genus THALASSOGERON Ridgway.

Thalassogeron Ridgw. Water B. N. Am. II. 1884, 357. Type, *Diomedea culminata* Gould.

[83.] Thalassogeron culminatus (Gould).
Yellow-nosed Albatross.

Diomedea culminata Gould, P. Z. S. 1843, 107.
Thalassogeron culminatus Ridgw. Water B. N. Am. II. 1884, 358.

[B 632, C —, R 702, C —.]

GEOG. DIST.— Indian and South Pacific Oceans; casual off the coast of Oregon; accidental in the Gulf of St. Lawrence.

GENUS **PHŒBETRIA** REICHENBACH.

Phœbetria REICH. Syst. Av. 1852, p. v. Type, *Diomedea fuliginosa* GMEL.

84. **Phœbetria fuliginosa** (GMEL.).
Sooty Albatross.

Diomedea fuliginosa GMEL. S. N. I. ii. 1788, 568.
Phœbetria fuliginosa REICH. Syst. Av. 1852, p. v.

[B 633, C 580, R 703, C 812.]

GEOG. DIST.— Oceans of the southern hemisphere, northward to the coast of Oregon.

FAMILY **PROCELLARIIDÆ**.   FULMARS AND SHEARWATERS.

SUBFAMILY **PROCELLARIINÆ**. FULMARS.

GENUS **OSSIFRAGA** HOMBRON & JACQUINOT.

Ossifraga HOMB. & JACQ. Compt. Rend. XVIII. 1844, 356. Type, *Procellaria gigantea* GMEL.

[85.] **Ossifraga gigantea** (GMEL.).
Giant Fulmar.

Procellaria gigantea GMEL. S. N. I. ii. 1788, 563.
Ossifraga gigantea REICH. Syst. Av. 1852, p. iv.

[B 634, C 581, R 704, C 813.]

GEOG. DIST.— Southern Oceans; casual off the coast of Oregon.

GENUS **FULMARUS** STEPHENS.

SUBGENUS **FULMARUS**.

Fulmarus STEPHENS, Gen. Zool. XIII. pt. i. 1826, 233. Type, *Procellaria glacialis* LINN.

86. Fulmarus glacialis (LINN.)
Fulmar.

Procellaria glacialis LINN. Faun. Suec. 2d ed. 1761, 51 ; S. N. ed. 12, I. 1766, 213.
Fulmarus glacialis STEPH. Gen. Zool. XIII. pt. i. 1826, 234, pl. 27.

[B 635, C 582, R 705, C 814.]

GEOG. DIST.— North Atlantic, south on the American coast to Massachusetts, casually to New Jersey.

86 *a*. Fulmarus glacialis minor (KJÆRBŒLLING).
Lesser Fulmar.

Procellaria minor KJÆRB. Danm. Fugle, 1852, 324.
Fulmarus glacialis b. *minor* BONAP. Consp. II. 1856, 187.

[B —, C —, R —, C —.]

GEOG. DIST.— North Atlantic, south on American side to coast of Massachusetts.

86 *b*. Fulmarus glacialis glupischa STEJN.
Pacific Fulmar.

Fulmarus glacialis glupischa STEJN. Auk, I. July, 1884, 234.

[B 636, C 582*a*, R 705*a*, C 815.]

GEOG. DIST.— North Pacific, south on the American coast to Mexico.

86 *c*. Fulmarus glacialis rodgersii (CASS.).
Rodgers's Fulmar.

Fulmarus rodgersii CASS. Pr. Ac. Nat. Sci. Phila. 1862, 290.
Fulmarus glacialis var. *rodgersi* COUES, Key, 1872, 327.

ORDER TUBINARES.

[B —, C 582*b*, R 705*b*, C 816.]

GEOG. DIST.— Bering Sea and adjacent parts of the North Pacific.

SUBGENUS **PRIOCELLA.** HOMBRON & JACQUINOT.

Priocella HOMB. & JACQ. Compt. Rend. XVIII. 1844, 357. Type, *P. garnoti* HOMB. & JACQ. = *Procellaria glacialoides* SMITH.

87. Fulmarus glacialoides (SMITH).
Slender-billed Fulmar.

Procellaria glacialoides SMITH, Illustr. S. Afr. B. 1840, t. 51.
Fulmarus glacialoides STEJN. Auk, 1884, p. 233.

[B 637, C 583, R 706, C 817.]

GEOG. DIST.— Seas of the southern hemisphere, and northward along Pacific coast of North America to Washington.

GENUS **PUFFINUS** BRISSON.

Puffinus BRISS. Orn. VI. 1760, 131. Type, *Procellaria puffinus* BRÜNN.

88. Puffinus borealis CORY.
Cory's Shearwater.

Puffinus borealis CORY, Bull. Nutt. Orn. Club, VI. April, 1881, 84.

[B —, C —, R —, C 888.]

GEOG. DIST.— Known only from off the coasts of Massachusetts, Rhode Island, and Long Island.

89. Puffinus major FABER.
Greater Shearwater.

Puffinus major FABER, Prodr. Isl. Orn. 1822, 56.

[B 647, C 597, R 709, C 832.]

GEOG. DIST.— Atlantic Ocean, from Cape Horn and Cape of Good Hope northward to the Arctic Circle.

[90.] **Puffinus puffinus** (Brünn.).
  Manx Shearwater.

Procellaria puffinus Brünn. Orn. Bor. 1764, 29.
Puffinus puffinus Licht. Nomencl. Mus. Berol. 1854, 100.

[B 649, C 599, R 711, C 834.]

Geog. Dist.— North Atlantic, chiefly on the eastern side; accidental in Greenland, and rare or casual off the North American coast (?).

91. **Puffinus creatopus** Coues.
  Pink-footed Shearwater.

Puffinus creatopus "Cooper, MS.," Coues, Pr. Ac. Nat. Sci. Phila. April, 1864, 131.

[B —, C 598, R 710, C 833.]

Geog. Dist.— Pacific Ocean; on the American coast from California to Juan Fernandez Islands.

92. **Puffinus auduboni** Finsch.
  Audubon's Shearwater.

Puffinus auduboni Finsch, P. Z. S. 1872, 111.

[B 650, C 600, R 712, C 835.]

Geog. Dist.— Warmer parts of the Atlantic, north casually to New Jersey and Long Island.

93. **Puffinus gavia** (Forst.).
  Black-vented Shearwater.

Procellaria gavia Forst. Descr. An. 1844, 148.
Puffinus gavia Finsch, J. f. O. 1872, 256.

[B —, C 601, R 713, C 836.]

Geog. Dist.— Pacific Ocean, chiefly southward; coast of Lower California, north to Santa Cruz, Cal.

94. **Puffinus stricklandi** Ridgw.
  Sooty Shearwater.

Puffinus stricklandi Ridgw. Water B. N. Am. II. 1884, 390.

[B 648, C 602, R 714, C 837.]

Geog. Dist.—Atlantic Ocean, breeding in the southern hemisphere; a summer visitor off our coast, from South Carolina northward.

95. Puffinus griseus (Gmel.).
Dark-bodied Shearwater.

Procellaria grisea Gmel. S. N. I. ii. 1788, 564.
Puffinus griseus Finsch, J. f. O. 1874, 209.

[B —, C 603, R 715, C 838.]

Geog. Dist.— South Pacific, north on the American coast, casually to San Francisco, California.

96. Puffinus tenuirostris (Temm.).
Slender-billed Shearwater.

Procellaria tenuirostris Temm. Pl. Col. 1828, 587.
Puffinus tenuirostris Temm. & Schleg. Faun. Jap. Aves, 1849, 131, pl. 86.

[B —, C 604, R 716, C 839.]

Geog. Dist.—Both coasts of the North Pacific, from Japan and Kotzebue Sound south to Australia and New Zealand; on the American coast to British Columbia.

Subgenus **PRIOFINUS** Hombron & Jacquinot.

Priofinus Hombr. & Jacq. Compt. Rend. XVIII. 1844, 355. Type, *Procellaria cinerea* Gmel.

[97.] Puffinus cinereus (Gmel.).
Black-tailed Shearwater.

Procellaria cinerea Gmel. S. N. I. ii. 1788, 563.
Puffinus cinereus Lawr. in Baird's B. N. Am. 1858, 835.

[B 651, C 595, R 707, C 830.]

Geog. Dist.— South Pacific; accidental off the coast of California.

GENUS **ÆSTRELATA** BONAPARTE.

Æstrelata BONAP. Consp. II. 1856, 188.   Type, *Procellaria hasitata* KUHL.

[98.] **Æstrelata hasitata** (KUHL).
　　Black-capped Petrel.

Procellaria hasitata KUHL, Mon. Proc. Beitr. Zool. 1 Abt. 1820, 142.
Æstrelata hæsitata COUES, Pr. Ac. Nat. Sci. Phila. 1866, 139.

[B 638, C 585, R 717, C 819.]

GEOG. DIST.— Warmer parts of the Atlantic Ocean, straying to Florida, Virginia, New York (Ulster County, Oneida Lake and Long Island), Vermont and Ontario. Also England and France.

[99.] **Æstrelata scalaris** BREWST.
　　Scaled Petrel.

Æstrelata scalaris BREWST. Auk, III. July, 1886, 300.

[B—, C—, R—, C—.]

GEOG. DIST.— Unknown, the single specimen obtained having been taken in Livingston Co., N. Y., in April, 1880.

100. **Æstrelata fisheri** RIDGW.
　　Fisher's Petrel.

Æstrelata fisheri RIDGW. Pr. U. S. Nat. Mus. V. June 26, 1883, 656.

[B—, C—, R—, C—.]

GEOG. DIST.— The only known specimen was taken at Kadiak, Alaska.

GENUS **BULWERIA** BONAPARTE.

Bulweria BONAP. Cat. Met. Ucc. Eur. 1842, 81.   Type, *Procellaria bulweri* JARD. & SELBY.

ORDER TUBINARES.

[101.] **Bulweria bulweri** (JARD. & SELBY).
    Bulwer's Petrel.

Procellaria bulweri JARD. & SELBY, Illustr. Orn. ——, pl. 65.
Bulweria bulweri BOUCARD, Cat. Av. 1876, 69.

[B—, C—, R 718, C 820.]

GEOG. DIST.— Eastern Atlantic, including coasts of Europe and Africa. Accidental in Greenland. Also various parts of the Pacific Ocean.

GENUS **DAPTION** STEPHENS.

Daption STEPH. Gen. Zool. XIII. 1825, 239. Type, *Procellaria capensis* LINN.

[102.] **Daption capensis** (LINN.).
    Pintado Petrel.

Procellaria capensis LINN. S. N. ed. 10, I. 1758, 132.
Daption capensis STEPH. Gen. Zool. XIII. pt. i. 1825, 241.

[B 639, C 584, R 719, C 818.]

GEOG. DIST.— Oceans of the southern hemisphere, north to about latitude 25°. Accidental on the coasts of California and England.

GENUS **HALOCYPTENA** COUES.

Halocyptena COUES, Pr. Ac. Nat. Sci. Phila. March, 1864, 78. Type, *H. microsoma* COUES.

103. **Halocyptena microsoma** COUES.
    Least Petrel.

Halocyptena microsoma COUES, Pr. Ac. Nat. Sci. Phila. 1864, 79.

[B—, C 586, R 720, C 821.]

GEOG. DIST.— Coast of Lower California and south to Panama.

Genus **PROCELLARIA** Linnæus.

Procellaria Linn. S. N. ed. 10, I. 1758, 131. Type, by elimination, *P. pelagica* Linn.

104. **Procellaria pelagica** Linn.
Stormy Petrel.

Procellaria pelagica Linn. S. N. ed. 10, I. 1758, 131.

[B 645, C 587, R 721, C 822.]

Geog. Dist.— Atlantic Ocean, south on the American side to the Newfoundland Banks. West coast of Africa and coast of Europe.

Genus **OCEANODROMA** Reichenbach.

Oceanodroma Reich. Syst. Av. 1852, p. iv. Type, *Procellaria furcata* Gmel.

105. **Oceanodroma furcata** (Gmel.).
Forked-tailed Petrel.

Procellaria furcata Gmel. S. N. I. ii. 1788, 561.
Oceanodroma furcata Reich. Syst. Av. 1852, p. iv.

[B 640, C 591, R 726, C 826.]

Geog. Dist.— North Pacific, south on the American coast, in winter, to Humboldt Bay, California. Breeds on the Aleutian Islands and on Copper Island.

106. **Oceanodroma leucorhoa** (Vieill.).
Leach's Petrel.

Procellaria leucorhoa Vieill. Nouv. Dict. d'Hist. Nat. XXV. 1817, 422.
Oceanodroma leucorhoa Stejn. Orn. Expl. Kamtsch. 1885, 97.

[B 642, C 588, R 723, C 823.]

Geog. Dist.— North Atlantic and North Pacific Oceans; south on the coast of the United States to Virginia and California; breeds from Maine and the Hebrides northward on the coasts of the Atlantic; also on the Aleutian Islands and on Copper Island, Bering Sea.

ORDER TUBINARES.

106.1. Oceanodroma macrodactyla (BRYANT).
  Guadalupe Petrel.

  Oceanodroma leucorhoa macrodactyla BRYANT, Bull. Cal. Ac. Sci. II. No. 8, July 23, 1887, 450.
  Oceanodroma macrodactyla A. O. U. COMM. Suppl. Check-List N. A. Birds, 1889, 5.

  [B—, C—, R—, C—.]

  GEOG. DIST.—Guadalupe Island, Lower California.

107. Oceanodroma melania (BONAP.).
  Black Petrel.

  Procellaria melania BONAP. Compt. Rend. XXVIII. 1854, 662.
  Oceanodroma melania STEJN. Orn. Expl. Kamtsch. 1885, 371.

  [B—, C 589, R 724, C 824.]

  GEOG. DIST.—South Pacific, northward to southern California.

108. Oceanodroma homochroa (COUES).
  Ashy Petrel.

  Cymochorea homochroa COUES, Pr. Ac. Nat. Sci. Phila. 1864, 77.
  Oceanodroma homochroa RIDGW. Pr. U. S. Nat. Mus. VIII. 1885, 356.

  [B 643, C 590, R 725, C 825.]

  GEOG. DIST.—Coast of California. Breeds on the Santa Barbara and Farallone Islands.

SUBFAMILY **OCEANITINÆ**.

GENUS **OCEANITES** KEYSERLING & BLASIUS.

Oceanites KEYS. & BLAS. Wirb. Eur. I. 1840, xciii, 131, 238. Type, *Procellaria oceanica* KUHL.

109. Oceanites oceanicus (KUHL).
  Wilson's Petrel.

  Procellaria oceanica KUHL, Beitr. Zool. Mon. Proc. 1820, 136, pl. 10, fig. 1.
  Oceanites oceanica LICHT. Nomencl. Mus. Berol. 1854, 99.

[B 644, C 593, R 722, C 828.]

GEOG. DIST.— North and South Atlantic and Southern Oceans, breeding on Kerguelen Island in February. Abundant off the eastern coast of the United States during the entire summer.

GENUS **CYMODROMA** RIDGWAY.

Cymodroma RIDGW. Water B. N. Am. II. 1884, 418. Type, *Procellaria grallaria* VIEILL.

[110.] **Cymodroma grallaria** (VIEILL.).
    White-bellied Petrel.

Procellaria grallaria VIEILL. Nouv. Dict. d'Hist. Nat. XXVI. 1817, 418.
Cymodroma grallaria RIDGW. Water B. N. Am. II. 1884, 419.

[B 646, C 594, R 728, C 829.]

GEOG. DIST.— Tropical oceans generally; accidental on the coast of Florida.

GENUS **PELAGODROMA** REICHENBACH.

Pelagodroma REICH. Syst. Av. 1852, p. iv. Type, *Procellaria marina* LATH.

[111.] **Pelagodroma marina** (LATH.).
    White-faced Petrel.

Procellaria marina LATH. Ind. Orn. II. ii. 1790, 826.
Pelagodroma marina REICH. Syst. Av. 1852, p. iv.

[B —, C —, R —, C —.]

GEOG. DIST.— South Atlantic, and Southern Seas. Accidental off the coast of Massachusetts.

Order STEGANOPODES. Totipalmate Swimmers.

Family **PHAËTHONTIDÆ**. Tropic Birds.

Genus **PHAËTHON** Linnæus.

Phaëthon Linn. S. N. ed. 10, I. 1758, 134. Type, *P. æthereus* Linn.

112. Phaëthon flavirostris Brandt.
Yellow-billed Tropic Bird.

Phaëthon flavirostris Brandt, Bull. Ac. St. Pétersb. II. 1837, 349.

[B 629, C 538, R 654, C 763.]

Geog. Dist.— West Indies and Atlantic coast of Central America, north to Florida and Bermuda; accidental in western New York. South Pacific and Indian Oceans.

113. Phaëthon æthereus Linn.
Red-billed Tropic Bird.

Phaëthon æthereus Linn. S. N. ed. 10, I. 1758, 134.

[B —, C —, R 655, C 762.]

Geog. Dist.— Coasts of tropical America, north on the Pacific coast to Cape Colnett, Lower California; accidental on the Newfoundland Banks. Breeds on San Pedro Martir and other islands in the Gulf of California.

Family **SULIDÆ**. Gannets.

Genus **SULA** Brisson.

Subgenus **SULA**.

Sula Briss. Orn. VI. 1760, 495. Type, by elimination, *Pelecanus sula* Linn.

[114.] **Sula cyanops** Sund.
Blue-faced Booby.

Dysporus cyanops Sund. Phys. Tidskr. Lund, 1837, pt. 5.
Sula cyanops Sund. Isis, 1842, 858.

[B —, C —, R 651, C —.]

Geog. Dist.— South Atlantic, South Pacific, and Indian Oceans; West Indies, and northward to southern Florida.

114.1. **Sula gossi** Goss.
Blue-footed Booby.

Sula gossi (Ridgw. MS.) Goss, Auk, V. July, 1888, 241.

[B —, C —, R —, C —.]

Geog. Dist.— Islands in the Gulf of California, and south to the Galapagos.

115. **Sula sula** (Linn.).
Booby.

Pelecanus sula Linn. Syst. Nat. ed. 12, I. 1766, 218.
Sula sula Ridgw. Pr. U. S. Nat. Mus. VIII, 1885, 356.

[B 618, C 525, R 652, C 747.]

Geog. Dist.— Atlantic coasts of tropical and subtropical America, north to Georgia. Also, western Pacific and Indian Oceans.

115.1. **Sula brewsteri** Goss.
Brewster's Booby.

Sula brewsteri Goss, Auk, V. July, 1888, 242.

[B —, C —, R —, C —.]

Geog. Dist.— Coasts and islands of the eastern South Pacific Ocean, north to Lower California; breeding as far north as Georges Island at the head of the Gulf of California.

[116.] **Sula piscator** (Linn.).
Red-footed Booby.

Pelecanus piscator Linn. S. N. ed. 10, I. 1758, 134.
Sula piscator Gray, Gen. Bds. III. 1845, 666.

[B —, C —, R 653, C —.]

Geog. Dist.—Coasts and islands of tropical and subtropical seas, north to western Mexico and Florida.

Subgenus **DYSPORUS** Illiger.

Dysporus Illig. Prodr. 1811, 279.   Type, by elimination, *Pelecanus bassanus* Linn.

117. Sula bassana (Linn.).
Gannet.

Pelecanus bassanus Linn. S. N. ed. 10, I. 1758, 133.
Sula bassana Boie, Isis, 1822, p. 563.

[B 617, C 524, R 650, C 746.]

Geog. Dist.—Coasts of the North Atlantic, south in winter to the Gulf of Mexico and Africa; breeds from Nova Scotia and the British Islands northward.

Family **ANHINGIDÆ**.   Darters.

Genus **ANHINGA** Brisson.

Anhinga Brisson, Orn. VI. 1760, 476.   Type, *Anhinga* Marcgr. = *Plotus anhinga* Linn.

118. Anhinga anhinga (Linn.).
Anhinga.

Plotus anhinga Linn. S. N. ed. 12, I. 1766, 218.
Anhinga anhinga Stejn. Stand. Nat. Hist. IV. 1885, 193.

[B 628, C 536, R 649, C 760.]

Geog. Dist.—Tropical and subtropical America, north in the United States to the Carolinas, the mouth of the Ohio River, and southern Kansas.

FAMILY **PHALACROCORACIDÆ**. CORMORANTS.

GENUS **PHALACROCORAX** BRISSON.

SUBGENUS **PHALACROCORAX**.

Phalacrocorax BRISS. Orn. VI. 1760, 511. Type, *Pelecanus carbo* LINN.

119. **Phalacrocorax carbo** (LINN.).
Cormorant.

Pelecanus carbo LINN. S. N. ed. 10, I. 1758, 133.
Phalacrocorax carbo LEACH, Syst. Cat. Mam. and Bds. Brit. Mus. 1816, 34.

[B 620, C 528, R 642, C 750.]

GEOG. DIST.— Coasts of the North Atlantic, south in winter on the coast of the United States, casually, to the Carolinas; breeding (formerly) from Massachusetts northward.

120. **Phalacrocorax dilophus** (SWAIN.).
Double-crested Cormorant.

Pelecanus (Carbo) dilophus SWAIN. in Sw. & RICH. F. B. A. II. 1831, 473.
Phalacrocorax dilophus NUTT. Man. II. 1834, 483.

[B 623, C 530, R 643, C 751.]

GEOG. DIST.— Eastern North America, breeding from the Bay of Fundy, the Great Lakes, Minnesota and Dakota northward; south in winter to the Southern States.

120 *a*. **Phalacrocorax dilophus floridanus** (AUD.).
Florida Cormorant.

Phalacrocorax floridanus AUD. Orn. Biog. III. 1835, 387.
Phalacrocorax dilophus floridanus RIDGW. Pr. U. S. Nat. Mus. III. Aug. 24, 1880, 205.

ORDER STEGANOPODES. 43

[B 624, C 530*a*, R 643*a*, C 753.]

GEOG. DIST.— South Atlantic and Gulf States, northward in the Mississippi Valley to southern Illinois.

120 *b*. **Phalacrocorax dilophus cincinatus** (BRANDT).
White-crested Cormorant.

Carbo cincinatus BRANDT, Bull. Sc. Ac. St. Pétersb. III. 1838, 55.
Phalacrocorax dilophus cincinnatus RIDGW. Pr. U. S. Nat. Mus. III. Aug. 24, 1880, 205.

[B 622, C 529, R 643*b*, C 752.]

GEOG. DIST.— West coast of North America, south in winter to California.

120 *c*. **Phalacrocorax dilophus albociliatus** RIDGW.
Farallone Cormorant.

Phalacrocorax dilophus albociliatus RIDGW. Proc. Biol. Soc. Wash. II. Apr. 10, 1884, 94.

[B —, C —, R —, C —.]

GEOG. DIST.— California, south to Cape St. Lucas and the Revillagigedo Islands.

121. **Phalacrocorax mexicanus** (BRANDT).
Mexican Cormorant.

Carbo mexicanus BRANDT, Bull. Sc. Ac. St. Pétersb. III. 1838, 55.
Phalacrocorax mexicanus SCL. & SALV. Nom. Neotr. 1873, 124.

[B 625, C 531, R 644, C 754.]

GEOG. DIST.— West Indies and Central America to southern United States; north in the interior to Kansas and southern Illinois.

SUBGENUS **COMPSOHALIEUS** RIDGWAY.

Compsohalieus RIDGW. Water B. N. Am. II. 1884, 145. Type, *Carbo penicillatus* BRANDT.

122. Phalacrocorax penicillatus (BRANDT).
Brandt's Cormorant.

Carbo penicillatus BRANDT, Bull. Sc. Ac. St. Pétersb. III. 1838, 55.
Phalacrocorax penicillatus HEERM. Pr. Ac. Nat. Sci. Phila. VII. 1854, 178.

[B 626, C 532, R 645, C 755.]

GEOG. DIST.— Pacific coast of North America, from Cape St. Lucas to Washington.

SUBGENUS **URILE** BONAPARTE.

Urile BONAP. Consp. II. 1855, 175. Type, *Pelecanus urile* GMEL.

123. Phalacrocorax pelagicus PALL.
Pelagic Cormorant.

Phalacrocorax pelagicus PALL. Zoog. Rosso-As. II. 1826, 303.

[B —, C —, R —, C —.]

GEOG. DIST.— Aleutian and Kuril Islands, and Kamchatka, south to Japan.

123 a. Phalacrocorax pelagicus robustus RIDGW.
Violet-green Cormorant.

Phalacrocorax pelagicus robustus RIDGW. Water B. N. Am. II. 1884, 160.

[B 627, C 535, R 646, C 758.]

GEOG. DIST.— Coast of Alaska, from Norton Sound south to Washington.

123 b. Phalacrocorax pelagicus resplendens (AUD.).
Baird's Cormorant.

Phalacrocorax resplendens AUD. Orn. Biog. V. 1839, 148.
Phalacrocorax pelagicus resplendens RIDGW. Water B. N. Am. I. 1884, 160.

ORDER STEGANOPODES.   45

[B —, C —, R 646a, C 759.]

GEOG. DIST.—Pacific coast of North America, from Washington south to Cape St. Lucas and Mazatlan, Mexico.

124. Phalacrocorax urile (GMEL.).
Red-faced Cormorant.

Pelecanus urile GMEL. S. N. I. ii. 1788, 575.
Phalacrocorax urile RIDGW. Water B. N. Am. II. 1884, 162.

[B —, C 534, R 647, C 757.]

GEOG. DIST.— Pribilof, Aleutian and Kuril Islands, and coast of Kamchatka. South in winter to northern Japan.

FAMILY **PELECANIDÆ**.   PELICANS.

GENUS **PELECANUS** LINNÆUS.

Pelecanus LINN. S. N. ed. 10, I. 1758, 132. Type, by elimination, *P. onocrotalus* LINN.

SUBGENUS **CYRTOPELICANUS** REICHENBACH.

Cyrtopelicanus REICH. Syst. Av. 1852, p. vii. Type, *Pelecanus erythrorhynchos* GMEL.

125. Pelecanus erythrorhynchos GMEL.
American White Pelican.

Pelecanus erythrorhynchos GMEL. S. N. I. ii. 1788, 571.

[B 615, C 526, R 640, C 748.]

GEOG. DIST.— Temperate North America, north in the interior to about Lat. 61°, south in winter to western Mexico and Guatemala; now rare or accidental in the northeastern States; abundant in the interior and along the Gulf coast; common on the coast of California.

Subgenus **LEPTOPELICANUS** Reichenbach.

Leptopelicanus Reich. Syst. Av. 1852, p. vii. Type, *Pelecanus fuscus* Linn.

126. **Pelecanus fuscus** Linn.
Brown Pelican.

Pelecanus fuscus Linn. S. N. ed. 12, I. 1766, 215.

[B 616, C 527, R 641, C 749.]

Geog. Dist.— Atlantic coast of tropical and subtropical America, north on the Atlantic coast to North Carolina; accidental in Illinois.

127. **Pelecanus californicus** Ridgw.
California Brown Pelican.

Pelecanus (fuscus?) californicus Ridgw. Water B. N. Am. II. 1884, 143.

P[elecanus] californicus Ridgw. l. c.

[B —, C —, R —, C —.]

Geog. Dist.— Pacific coast, from Burrard Inlet, British Columbia, to the Galapagos.

Family **FREGATIDÆ**. Man-o'-War Birds.

Genus **FREGATA** Brisson.

Fregata Briss. Orn. VI. 1760, 506. Type, *Pelecanus aquilus* Linn.

128. **Fregata aquila** Linn.
Man-o'-War Bird.

Pelecanus aquilus Linn. S. N. ed. 10, I. 1758, 133.
Fregata aquila Reich. Syst. Av. 1852, p. vi.

[B 619, C 537, R 639, C 761.]

Geog. Dist.—Tropical and subtropical coasts generally; in America, north to Florida and Texas, and casually to Nova Scotia, Ohio, Wisconsin, Kansas, and Humboldt Bay, California.

Order ANSERES. Lamellirostral Swimmers.

Family **ANATIDÆ**. Ducks, Geese, and Swans.

Subfamily **MERGINÆ**. Mergansers.

Genus **MERGANSER** Brisson.

Merganser Briss. Orn. VI. 1760, 230. Type, *Mergus merganser* Linn.

129. **Merganser americanus** (Cass.).
American Merganser.

Mergus americanus Cassin, Pr. Ac. Nat. Sci. Phila. VI. 1853, 187.
Merganser americanus Stejn. Orn. Expl. Kamtsch. 1885, 177.

[B—, C—, R—, C—.]

Geog. Dist.—North America generally, breeding south in the United States to Pennsylvania and the mountains of Colorado and California. Bermuda.

130. **Merganser serrator** (Linn.).
Red-breasted Merganser.

Mergus serrator Linn. S. N. ed. 10, I. 1758, 129.
Merganser serrator Schäffer, Mus. Orn. 1789, 66.

[B 612, C 522, R 637, C 744.]

Geog. Dist.—Northern portions of northern hemisphere; south, in winter, throughout the United States.

Genus **LOPHODYTES** Reichenbach.

Lophodytes Reichenbach, Syst. Av. 1852, p. ix. Type, *Mergus cucullatus* Linn.

131. Lophodytes cucullatus (LINN.).
Hooded Merganser.

Mergus cucullatus LINN. S. N. ed. 10, I. 1758, 129.
Lophodytes cucullatus REICHENBACH, Syst. Av. 1852, p. ix.

[B 613, C 523, R 638, C 745.]

GEOG. DIST.— North America generally, south to Mexico and Cuba, breeding nearly throughout its range. Casual in Europe.

SUBFAMILY **ANATINÆ**. RIVER DUCKS.

GENUS **ANAS** LINNÆUS.

Anas LINN. S. N. ed. 10, I, 1758, 122. Type, *A. boschas* LINN.

132. Anas boschas LINN.
Mallard.

Anas boschas LINN. S. N. ed. 10, I, 1758, 127.

[B 576, C 488, R 601, C 707.]

GEOG. DIST.— Northern parts of northern hemisphere; in America south to Panama and Cuba, breeding southward to the southern United States; less common in the East.

133. Anas obscura GMEL.
Black Duck.

Anas obscura GMEL. S. N. I. 1788, 541.

[B 577, C 489, R 602, C 708.]

GEOG. DIST.— Eastern North America, west to the Mississippi Valley, north to Labrador, breeding southward to the northern parts of the United States.

134. Anas fulvigula RIDGW.
Florida Duck.

Anas obscura var. *fulvigula* RIDGW. Am. Nat. VIII. Feb. 1874, 111.
Anas fulvigula RIDGW. Pr. U. S. Nat. Mus. III. Aug. 24, 1880, 203.

[B —, C 489a, R 603, C 709.]

GEOG. DIST. — Florida.

134 a. Anas fulvigula maculosa (SENN.).
Mottled Duck.

Anas maculosa SENNETT, Auk, VI, July, 1889, 263.

[B 577, *part*, C 489, *part*, R 602, *part*, C 708, *part*.]

GEOG. DIST. — Eastern Texas and north to Kansas.

SUBGENUS **CHAULELASMUS** BONAPARTE.

Chaulelasmus BONAP. Comp. List, 1838, 56. Type, *Anas strepera* LINN.

135. Anas strepera LINN.
Gadwall.

Anas strepera LINN. S. N. ed. 10, I. 1758, 125.

[B 584, C 491, R 604, C 711.]

GEOG. DIST.— Nearly cosmopolitan. In North America breeds chiefly within the United States.

SUBGENUS **MARECA** STEPHENS.

Mareca STEPHENS, Gen. Zool. XII. pt. ii. 1824, 130. Type, *Anas penelope* LINN.

136. Anas penelope LINN.
Widgeon.

Anas penelope LINN. S. N. ed. 10, I. 1758, 126.

[B 586, C 492, R 606, C 712.]

GEOG. DIST.— Northern parts of the Old World. In North America breeds in the Aleutian Islands, and occurs frequently in the eastern United States, and occasionally in California.

137. Anas americana GMEL.
Baldpate.

Anas americana GMELIN, S. N. I. 1788, 526.

[B 585, C 493, R 607, C 713.]

GEOG. DIST.— North America, from the Arctic Ocean south, in winter, to Guatemala and Cuba. Breeds chiefly north of United States.

SUBGENUS **NETTION** KAUP.

Nettion KAUP, Sk. Ent. Europ. Thierw. 1829, 95.   Type, *Anas crecca* LINN.

[138.] **Anas crecca** LINN.
European Teal.

Anas crecca LINN. S. N. ed. 10, I. 1758, 126.

[B 580, C 494, R 611, C 714.]

GEOG. DIST.— Northern parts of the Old World. Occasional in eastern North America, the Aleutian Islands, and California.

139. **Anas carolinensis** GMEL.
Green-winged Teal.

Anas carolinensis GMEL. S. N. I. 1788, 533.

[B 579, C 495, R 612, C 715.]

GEOG. DIST.— North America, breeding chiefly north of the United States, and migrating south to Honduras and Cuba.

SUBGENUS **QUERQUEDULA** STEPHENS.

Querquedula STEPHENS, Gen. Zool. XII. pt. ii. 1824, 142. Type, *Anas querquedula* LINN.

140. **Anas discors** LINN.
Blue-winged Teal.

Anas discors LINN. S. N. ed. 12, I. 1766, 205.

[B 581, C 496, R 609, C 716.]

GEOG. DIST.—North America in general, but chiefly eastward; north to Alaska, and south to the West Indies, Lower California, and northern South America. Casual in California. Breeds from Kansas and southern Illinois northward.

ORDER ANSERES.

141. Anas cyanoptera VIEILL.
   Cinnamon Teal.

Anas cyanoptera VIEILLOT, Nouv. Dict. d'Hist. Nat. V. 1816, 104.

[B 582, C 497, R 610, C 717.]

GEOG. DIST.—Western America from British Columbia south to Chili, Patagonia, and Falkland Islands; east in North America to the Rocky Mountains and southern Texas; casual in the Mississippi Valley and Florida.

GENUS **SPATULA** BOIE.

Spatula BOIE, Isis, 1822, 564.   Type, *Anas clypeata* LINN.

142. Spatula clypeata (LINN.).
   Shoveller.

Anas clypeata LINN. S. N. ed. 10, I. 1758, 124.
Spatula clypeata BOIE, Isis, 1822, 564.

[B 583, C 498, R 608, C 718.]

GEOG. DIST.—Northern hemisphere. In North America breeding from Alaska to Texas; not abundant on the Atlantic coast north of the Carolinas.

GENUS **DAFILA** STEPHENS.

Dafila STEPHENS, Gen. Zool. XII. pt. ii. 1824, 126.

143. Dafila acuta (LINN.).
   Pintail.

Anas acuta LINN. S. N. ed. 10, I. 1758, 126.
Dafila acuta BONAP. Comp. List, 1838, 56.

[B 578, C 490, R 605, C 710.]

GEOG. DIST.—Northern hemisphere. In North America breeds from the northern parts of the United States northward, and migrates south to Panama and Cuba.

Genus **AIX** Boie.

Aix Boie, Isis, 1828, 329.   Type, *Anas sponsa* Linn.

144. Aix sponsa (Linn.).
    Wood Duck.

Anas sponsa Linn. S. N. ed. 10, I. 1758, 128.
Aix sponsa Bonap. Comp. List, 1838, 57.

[B 587, C 499, R 613, C 719.]

Geog. Dist.— Temperate North America, breeding throughout its range.   Cuba.   Accidental in Europe.

Subfamily **FULIGULINÆ**.   Sea Ducks.

Genus **NETTA** Kaup.

Netta Kaup, Sk. Ent. Europ. Thierw. 1829, 102.   Type, *Anas rufina* Pall.

[145.] Netta rufina (Pall.).
    Rufous-crested Duck.

Anas rufina Pall. It. II. App. 1773, 713.
Netta rufina Kaup, Sk. Ent. Europ. Thierw. 1829, 102.

[B —, C —, R —, C 886.]

Geog. Dist.— Eastern hemisphere; accidental in eastern United States.

Genus **AYTHYA** Boie.

Aythya Boie, Isis, 1822, 564.   Type, by elimination, *Anas ferina* Linn.

146. Aythya americana (Eyt.).
    Redhead.

Fuligula americana Eyton, Monogr. Anat. 1838, 155.
Aythya americana Baird, B. N. Am. 1858, 793.

[B 591, C 503, R 618, C 723.]

GEOG. DIST.— North America, breeding from California, southern Michigan, and Maine northward.

147. **Aythya vallisneria** (WILS.).
Canvas-back.

Anas vallisneria WILSON, Am. Orn. VIII. 1814, 103.
Aythya vallisneria BOIE, Isis, 1826, 980.

[B 592, C 504, R 617, C 724.]

GEOG. DIST.— Nearly all of North America, breeding from the northwestern States northward to Alaska.

SUBGENUS **FULIGULA** STEPHENS.

Fuligula STEPHENS, Gen. Zool. XII. pt. ii. 1824, 187. Type, by elimination, *Anas fuligula* LINN.

148. **Aythya marila nearctica** STEJN.
American Scaup Duck.

Aythya marila nearctica STEJN. Orn. Expl. Kamtsch. 1885, 161.

[B 588, C 500, R 614, C 720.]

GEOG. DIST.— North America, breeding far north. South in winter to Guatemala.

149. **Aythya affinis** (EYT.).
Lesser Scaup Duck.

Fuligula affinis EYT. Mon. Anat. 1838, 157.
Aythya affinis STEJN. Orn. Expl. Kamtsch. 1885, 161.

[B 589, C 501, R 615, C 721.]

GEOG. DIST.— North America in general, breeding chiefly north of the United States, migrating south to Guatemala and the West Indies.

150. **Aythya collaris** (DONOV.).
Ring-necked Duck.

Anas collaris DONOV. Br. Birds, VI. 1809, pl. 147.
Aythya collaris RIDGW. Pr. U. S. Nat. Mus. VIII. 1885, 356.

[B 590, C 502, R 616, C 722.]

GEOG. DIST.— North America, breeding far north and migrating south to Guatemala and the West Indies.

GENUS **GLAUCIONETTA** STEJNEGER.

Glaucionetta STEJN. Pr. U. S. Nat. Mus. VIII. 1885, 409. Type, *Anas clangula* LINN.

151. Glaucionetta clangula americana (BONAP.).
American Golden-eye.

Clangula americana BONAP. Comp. List, 1838, 58.
Glaucionetta clangula americana STEJN. Pr. U. S. Nat. Mus. VIII. 1885, 409.

GEOG. DIST.— North America, breeding from Maine and the British Provinces northward; in winter, south to Cuba and Mexico.

152. Glaucionetta islandica (GMEL.).
Barrow's Golden-eye.

Anas islandica GMEL. S. N. I. 1788, 541.
Glaucionetta islandica STEJN. Pr. U. S. Nat. Mus. VIII. 1885, 409.

[B 594, C 506, R 619, C 726.]

GEOG. DIST.— Northern North America, south in winter to New York, Illinois, and Utah; breeding from the Gulf of St. Lawrence northward, and south in the Rocky Mountains to Colorado; Greenland; Iceland. Accidental in Europe.

GENUS **CHARITONETTA** STEJNEGER.

Charitonetta STEJN. Orn. Expl. Kamtsch. 1885, 163. Type, *Anas albeola* LINN.

153. Charitonetta albeola (LINN.).
Buffle-head.

Anas albeola LINN. Syst. Nat. ed. 10, I. 1758, 124.
Charitonetta albeola STEJN. Orn. Expl. Kamtsch. 1885, 166.

ORDER ANSERES. 55

[B 595, C 507, R 621, C 727.]

GEOG. DIST.— North America; south in winter to Cuba and Mexico. Breeds from Maine and Montana northward, through the Fur Countries and Alaska.

GENUS **CLANGULA** LEACH.

Clangula LEACH, in Ross's Voy. Disc. 1819, App. p. xlviii. Type, *Anas glacialis* LINN.

154. **Clangula hyemalis** (LINN.).
Old-squaw.

Anas hyemalis LINN. S. N. ed. 10, I. 1758, 126.
Clangula hiemalis BREHM, Handb. Vög. Deutschl. 1831, 933.

[B 597, C 508, R 623, C 728.]

GEOG. DIST.— Northern hemisphere; in North America south to the Potomac and the Ohio (more rarely to Florida and Texas) and California; breeds far northward.

GENUS **HISTRIONICUS** LESSON.

Histrionicus LESSON, Man. d'Orn. II. 1828, 415. Type, *Anas histrionica* LINN.

155. **Histrionicus histrionicus** (LINN.).
Harlequin Duck.

Anas histrionica LINN. S. N. ed. 10, I. 1758, 127.
Histrionicus histrionicus BOUCARD, Cat. Av. 1876, 60.

[B 596, C 510, R 622, C 730.]

GEOG. DIST.— Northern North America, breeding from Newfoundland, the northern Rocky Mountains, and the Sierra Nevada (lat. 38°), northward; south in winter to the Middle States and California; Eastern Asia; Iceland.

Genus CAMPTOLAIMUS Gray.

Camptolaimus Gray, List Gen. 1841, 95. Type, *Anas labradoria* Gmel.

156. Camptolaimus labradorius (Gmel.).
Labrador Duck.

Anas labradoria Gmel. S. N. I. 1788, 537.
Camptolaimus labradorus Gray, List Gen. 1841, 95.

[B 600, C 510, R 624, C 730.]

Geog. Dist.— Formerly Northern Atlantic coast, from New Jersey (in winter) northward, breeding from Labrador northward. Now extinct.

Genus ENICONETTA Gray.

Eniconetta Gray, List Gen. 1840, 75. Type, *Anas stelleri* Pall.

157. Eniconetta stelleri (Pall.).
Steller's Duck.

Anas stelleri Pall. Spicil. Zool. VI. 1769, 35.
Eniconetta stelleri Gray, List Gen. 1840, 75.

[B 598, C 511, R 625, C 731.]

Geog. Dist.— Arctic and subarctic coasts of the northern hemisphere. Aleutian Islands, east to Unalaska and Kadiak; Kenai Peninsula.

Genus ARCTONETTA Gray.

Arctonetta Gray, P. Z. S. 1855 (Feb. 1856), 212. Type, *Fuligula fischeri* Brandt.

158. Arctonetta fischeri (Brandt).
Spectacled Eider.

Fuligula fischeri Brandt, Mém. Acad. St. Pétersb. VI. 1849, 6, 10.
Arctonetta fischeri Blakiston, Ibis, 1863, 150.

ORDER ANSERES. 57

[B 599, C 512, R 626, C 732.]

GEOG. DIST.— Alaskan coast of Bering Sea and north to Point Barrow.

GENUS **SOMATERIA** LEACH.

SUBGENUS **SOMATERIA**.

Somateria LEACH, in Ross's Voy. Disc. 1819, App. p. xlviii. Type, *Anas mollissima* LINN.

159. **Somateria mollissima borealis** A. E. BREHM.
Northern Eider.

Somateria mollissima borealis A. E. BREHM, Verz. Samml. Eur. Vög. 1866, 14.

[B 606, *part*, C 513, *part*, R 627, C 733.]

GEOG. DIST.— Northeastern North America, including Greenland; south, in winter, to coast of Massachusetts.

160. **Somateria dresseri** SHARPE.
American Eider.

Somateria dresseri SHARPE, Ann. Mag. Nat. Hist. July, 1871, 51.

[B 606, *part*, C 513, *part*, R 627a, C 734.]

GEOG. DIST.— Atlantic coast of North America, from Maine to Labrador; south in winter to the Delaware and west to the Great Lakes.

161. **Somateria v-nigra** GRAY.
Pacific Eider.

Somateria v-nigra GRAY, P. Z. S. 1855 (Feb. 1856), 212, pl. cvii.

[B 607, C 514, R 628, C 735.]

GEOG. DIST.— Coasts of the North Pacific; in the interior to the Great Slave Lake district; eastern Siberia.

SUBGENUS **ERIONETTA** COUES.

Erionetta COUES, Key N. A. Birds, ed. 2, 1884, 709. Type, *Anas spectabilis* LINN.

162. **Somateria spectabilis** (LINN.).
King Eider.

Anas spectabilis LINN. S. N. ed. 10, I. 1758, 123.
Somateria spectabilis LEACH, in Ross's Voy. Disc. 1819, App. p. xlviii.

[B 608, C 515, R 629, C 736.]

GEOG. DIST.— Northern parts of northern hemisphere, breeding in the Arctic regions; in North America south casually in winter to Georgia and the Great Lakes.

GENUS **OIDEMIA** FLEMING.

SUBGENUS **OIDEMIA**.

Oidemia FLEMING, Philos. Zool. II. 1822, 260. Type, by elimination, *Anas nigra* LINN.

163. **Oidemia americana** Sw. & RICH.
American Scoter.

Oidemia americana Sw. & RICH. Faun. Bor. Amer. II. 1831, 450.

[B 604, C 516, R 630, C 737.]

GEOG. DIST.— Coasts and larger inland waters of northern North America; breeds in Labrador and the northern interior; south in winter to New Jersey, the Great Lakes, Colorado, and California.

SUBGENUS **MELANITTA** BOIE.

Melanitta BOIE, Isis, 1822, 564. Type, by elimination, *Anas fusca* LINN.

[164.] **Oidemia fusca** (LINN.).
Velvet Scoter.

Anas fusca LINN. S. N. ed. 10, I. 1758, 123.
Oidemia fusca STEPHENS, Gen. Zool. XII. pt. ii. 1824, 216.

[B —, C —, R 631, C —.]

GEOG. DIST.— Northern Old World; accidental (?) in Greenland.

165. **Oidemia deglandi** BONAP.
    White-winged Scoter.

Oidemia deglandi BONAP. Rev. Crit. de l'Orn. Europ. de Dr. Degl., 1850, 108.

[B 601, C 517, R 632, C 738.]

GEOG. DIST.— Northern North America, breeding in Labrador and the Fur Countries; south in winter to Chesapeake Bay, Southern Illinois, and San Quentin Bay, Lower California.

SUBGENUS **PELIONETTA** KAUP.

Pelionetta KAUP, Sk. Ent. Eur. Thierw. 1829, 107. Type, *Anas perspicillata* LINN.

166. **Oidemia perspicillata** (LINN.).
    Surf Scoter.

Anas perspicillata LINN. S. N. ed. 10, I. 1758, 125.
Oidemia perspicillata STEPHENS, Gen. Zool. XII. pt. ii. 1824, 219.

[B 602, 603, C 518, 518*a*, R 633, C 739, 740.]

GEOG. DIST.— Coasts and larger inland waters of northern North America; in winter south to Florida, the Ohio River, and San Quentin' Bay, Lower California. Accidental in Europe.

GENUS **ERISMATURA** BONAPARTE.

Erismatura BONAP. Saggio Distr. Meth. 1832, 143. Type, *Anas rubidus* WILS.

167. **Erismatura rubida** (WILS.).
    Ruddy Duck.

Anas rubidus WILSON, Am. Orn. VIII. 1814, 128.
Erismatura rubida BONAP. Comp. List, 1838, 59.

[B 609, C 519, R 634, C 741.]

GEOG. DIST.— North America in general, south to the West Indies and through Central America to Colombia; breeds throughout much of its North American range and south to Guatemala.

GENUS **NOMONYX** RIDGWAY.

Nomonyx RIDGW. Pr. U. S. Nat. Mus. III. 1880, 15. Type, *Anas dominica* LINN.

[168.] **Nomonyx dominicus** (LINN.).
   Masked Duck.

Anas dominica LINN. S. N. ed. 12, 1766, 201.
Nomonyx dominicus RIDGW. Pr. U. S. Nat. Mus. III. 1880, 15.

[B 610, C 520, R 635, C 742.]

GEOG. DIST.— Tropical America in general, including West Indies, north on the Gulf coast to the Lower Rio Grande; accidental in eastern North America (Wisconsin; Lake Champlain; Massachusetts).

SUBFAMILY **ANSERINÆ.** GEESE.

GENUS **CHEN** BOIE.

Chen BOIE, Isis, 1822, 563. Type, *Anser hyperboreus* PALL.

169. **Chen hyperborea** (PALL.).
   Lesser Snow Goose.

Anser hyperboreus PALL. Spicil. Zool. VI. 1769, 25.
Chen hyperborea BOIE, Isis, 1822, 563.

[B —, C 480*a*, R 591*a*, C 696.]

GEOG. DIST.— Pacific coast to the Mississippi Valley, breeding in Alaska; south in winter to southern Illinois and southern California; casually to New England. Northeastern Asia.

169 *a*. **Chen hyperborea nivalis** (FORST.).
   Greater Snow Goose.

Anas nivalis FORSTER, Philos. Trans. LXII. 1772, 413.
Chen hyperboreus nivalis RIDGW. Pr. Biol. Soc. Wash. II. 1884, 107.

[B 563, C 480, R 591, C 695.]

GEOG. DIST.— North America, breeding far north (east of Mackenzie basin) and migrating south in winter, chiefly along the Atlantic coast, reaching Cuba.

169.1. Chen cærulescens (LINN.).
Blue Goose.

Anas cærulescens LINN. S. N. ed. 10, I. 1758, 124.
Chen cærulescens GUNDL. in POEY's Repert. Fis.-nat. Isla Cuba, I, 1865-66, 387.

[B 564, C 479, R 590, C 694.]

GEOG. DIST.— Interior of North America, breeding on eastern shores of Hudson Bay and migrating south, in winter, through Mississippi Valley to Gulf coast; occasional on Atlantic coast.

170. Chen rossii (CASSIN).
Ross's Snow Goose.

Anser rossii "BAIRD MSS.," CASS. Pr. Ac. Nat. Sci. Phila. 1861, 73.
Chen rossii RIDGW. Pr. U. S. Nat. Mus. III. Aug. 24, 1880, 203.

[B —, C 481, R 592, C 697.]

GEOG. DIST.— Arctic America in summer, Pacific coast to southern California and east to Montana in winter.

GENUS **ANSER** BRISSON.

Anser BRISSON, Orn. VI. 1760, 261.   Type, *Anas anser* LINN.

[171.] Anser albifrons (GMEL.).
White-fronted Goose.

Anas albifrons GMEL. S. N. I. 1788, 509.
Anser albifrons BECHST. Gem. Naturg. Deutschl. IV. 1809, 898.

[B —, C —, R 593, C 692.]

GEOG. DIST.— Northern parts of eastern hemisphere.   Eastern Greenland?

171 *a*. Anser albifrons gambeli (HARTL.).
American White-fronted Goose.

Anser gambeli HARTLAUB, Rev. Mag. Zool. 1852, 7.
Anser albifrons var. *gambeli* COUES, Key, 1872, 282.

[B 565, 566, C 478, R 593a, C 693.]

GEOG. DIST.— North America (rare on the Atlantic coast), breeding far northward; in winter south to Cape St. Lucas, Mexico, and Cuba.

GENUS **BRANTA** SCOPOLI.

Branta SCOPOLI, Ann. I. Hist. Nat. 1769, 67. Type, *Anas bernicla* LINN.

172. Branta canadensis (LINN.).
Canada Goose.

Anas canadensis LINN. S. N. ed. 10, I. 1758, 123.
Branta canadensis BANNISTER, Pr. Ac. Nat. Sci. Phila. 1870, 131.

[B 567, C 485, R 594, C 702.]

GEOG. DIST.—Temperate North America, breeding in the northern United States and British Provinces; south in winter to Mexico.

172 a. Branta canadensis hutchinsii (RICH.).
Hutchins's Goose.

Anser hutchinsii RICH. in Sw. & RICH. Faun. Bor. Am. II. 1831, 470.
Branta canadensis var. *hutchinsii* COUES, Key, 1872, 284.

[B 569, C 485b, R 594a, C 704.]

GEOG. DIST.— North America, breeding in the Arctic regions, and migrating south in winter, chiefly through the western United States and Mississippi Valley; northeastern Asia.

172 b. Branta canadensis occidentalis (BAIRD).
White-cheeked Goose.

Bernicla occidentalis BAIRD, B. N. Am. 1858, 766.
Branta canadensis occidentalis RIDGW. Pr. U. S. Nat. Mus. VIII. 1885, 355.

[B 567a, C —, R 594c, C —.]

GEOG. DIST.— Pacific coast region, from Sitka south, in winter, to California.

172 c. **Branta canadensis minima** RIDGW.
　　Cackling Goose.

　　Branta minima RIDGW. Pr. U. S. Nat. Mus. VIII. No. 2, April 20, 1885, 23.
　　Branta canadensis minima RIDGW. Pr. U. S. Nat. Mus. VIII. 1885, 355.

　　　　[B 568, C 485*a*, R 594*b*, C 703.]

GEOG. DIST.— Coast of Alaska, chiefly about Norton Sound and Lower Yukon, migrating southward into the western United States, east to Wisconsin.

173. **Branta bernicla** (LINN.).
　　Brant.

　　Anas bernicla LINN. S. N. ed. 10, I. 1758, 124.
　　Branta bernicla SCOPOLI, Ann. I. Hist. Nat. 1769, 67.

　　　　[B 570, C 484, R 595, C 700.]

GEOG. DIST.— Northern parts of the northern hemisphere; in North America chiefly on the Atlantic coast; rare in the interior, or away from salt water.

174. **Branta nigricans** (LAWR.).
　　Black Brant.

　　Anser nigricans LAWRENCE, Ann. Lyc. N. Y. IV. 1846, 171.
　　Branta nigricans BANNISTER, Pr. Ac. Nat. Sci. Phila. 1870, 131.

　　　　[B 571, C —, R 596, C 701.]

GEOG. DIST.— Arctic and western North America, south in winter to Lower California; casual in the Atlantic States.

[175.] **Branta leucopsis** (BECHST.).
　　Barnacle Goose.

　　Anas leucopsis BECHSTEIN, Orn. Taschb. Deutschl. 1803, 424.
　　Branta leucopsis BANNISTER, Pr. Ac. Nat. Sci. Phila. 1870, 131.

　　　　[B 572, C 483, R 597, C 699.]

GEOG. DIST.— Northern parts of the Old World; casual in eastern North America.

Genus PHILACTE Bannister.

Philacte Bannister, Pr. Ac. Nat. Sci. Phila. 1870, 131. Type, *Anas canagica* Sevast.

176. Philacte canagica (Sevast.).
Emperor Goose.

Anas canagica Sevastianoff, N. Act. Petrop. XIII. 1800, 346.
Philacte canagica Bannister, Pr. Ac. Nat. Sci. Phila. 1870, 131.

[B 573, C 482, R 598, C 698.]

Geog. Dist.— Coast and islands of Alaska north of the Peninsula; chiefly about Norton Sound and valley of the Lower Yukon; Commander Islands, Kamchatka; casually southward to Humboldt Bay, California.

Genus DENDROCYGNA Swainson.

Dendrocygna Swainson, Classif. Birds, II. 1837, 365. Type, *Anas arcuata* Cuv.

177. Dendrocygna autumnalis (Linn.).
Black-bellied Tree-duck.

Anas autumnalis Linn. S. N. ed. 10, I. 1758, 127.
Dendrocygna autumnalis Eyton, Monogr. Anat. 1838, 109.

[B 574, C 487, R 599, C 706.]

Geog. Dist.— Southwestern border of the United States and southward (Mexico, West Indies, etc.).

178. Dendrocygna fulva (Gmel.).
Fulvous Tree-duck.

Anas fulva Gmel. S. N. I. 1788, 530.
Dendrocygna fulva Burmeister, Reise durch die La Plata Staaten, 1856, 515.

[B 575, C 486, R 600, C 705.]

GEOG. DIST.— Southern border of the United States (Louisiana, Texas, Nevada, California), south to Mexico, reappearing in southern Brazil and Argentine Republic. Casual in North Carolina and Missouri.

SUBFAMILY **CYGNINÆ**. SWANS.

GENUS **OLOR** WAGLER.

Olor WAGLER, Isis, 1832, 1234. Type, *Anas cygnus* LINN.

[179.] **Olor cygnus** (LINN.).
Whooping Swan.

Anas cygnus LINN. S. N. ed. 10, I. 1758, 122.
Olor cygnus BONAPARTE, Catal. Parzudaki, 1856, 15.

[B —, C —, R 586, C 690.]

GEOG. DIST.— Europe and Asia; occasional in southern Greenland.

180. **Olor columbianus** (ORD).
Whistling Swan.

Anas columbianus ORD, in GUTHRIE'S Geogr. 2d Am. ed. 1815, 319.
Olor columbianus STEJN. Pr. U. S. Nat. Mus. V. 1882, 210.

[B 561 *bis*, C 477, R 588, C 689.]

GEOG. DIST.— The whole of North America, breeding far north. Commander Islands, Kamchatka; accidental in Scotland.

181. **Olor buccinator** (RICH.).
Trumpeter Swan.

Cygnus buccinator RICH. in Sw. & RICH. Fauna Bor. Am. II. 1831, 464.
Olor buccinator WAGLER, Isis, 1832, 1234.

[B 562, C 476, R 589, C 688.]

GEOG. DIST.— Chiefly the interior of North America, from the Gulf coast to the Fur Countries, breeding from Iowa and the Dakotas northward; west to the Pacific coast; rare or casual on the Atlantic.

Order ODONTOGLOSSÆ. Lamellirostral Grallatores.

Family **PHŒNICOPTERIDÆ**. Flamingoes.

Genus **PHŒNICOPTERUS** Linn.

Phœnicopterus Linn. S. N. ed. 10, I. 1758, 139. Type, *P. ruber* Linn.

182. **Phœnicopterus ruber** Linn.
   American Flamingo.

Phœnicopterus ruber Linn. S. N. ed. 10, I. 1758, 139.

[B 502, C 475, R 585, C 687.]

Geog. Dist.— Atlantic coasts of subtropical and tropical America; southern Florida. Galapagos.

Order HERODIONES. Herons, Storks, Ibises, etc.

Suborder IBIDES. Spoonbills and Ibises.

Family **PLATALEIDÆ**. Spoonbills.

Genus **AJAJA** Reich.

Ajaja Reich. Handb. 1852, p. xvi. Type, *Platalea ajaja* Linn.

ORDER HERODIONES.

183. Ajaja ajaja (LINN.).
Roseate Spoonbill.
Platalea ajaja LINN. S. N. ed. 10, I. 1758, 140.
Ajaja ajaja BOUCARD, Cat. Av. 1876, 54.

[B 501, C 488, R 505, C 653.]

GEOG. DIST.— Southern Atlantic and Gulf States southward to the Falkland Islands and Patagonia. Formerly north to southern Illinois.

FAMILY **IBIDIDÆ**. IBISES.

GENUS **GUARA** REICHENBACH.

Guara REICH. Syst. Av. 1852, p. xiv. Type, *Tantalus ruber* LINN.

184. Guara alba (LINN.).
White Ibis.
Scolopax alba LINN. S. N. ed. 10, I. 1758, 145.
Guara alba STEJN. Stand. Nat. Hist. IV. 1885, 9.

[B 499, C 446, R 501, C 651.]

GEOG. DIST.— South Atlantic and Gulf States southward to the West Indies and northern South America; north to North Carolina, southern Illinois, Great Salt Lake, and Lower California; casually to Long Island, Connecticut, and South Dakota.

[185.] Guara rubra (LINN.).
Scarlet Ibis.
Tantalus ruber LINN. S. N. ed. 12, I. 1766, 241.
Guara rubra REICH. Syst. Av. 1852, p. xiv.

[B 498, C 447, R 502, C 652.]

GEOG. DIST.— Florida, Louisiana, and Texas, southward to the West Indies and northern South America. No record of its recent occurrence in the United States.

GENUS **PLEGADIS** KAUP.

Plegadis KAUP, Skizz. Entw. Gesch. Eur. Thierw. 1829, 82. Type, *Tantalus falcinellus* LINN. = *Tringa autumnalis* HASSELQ.

186. **Plegadis autumnalis** (HASSELQ.).
Glossy Ibis.

Tringa autumnalis HASSELQUIST, Reise nach Paläst. Deutsche Ausg. 1762, 306.
Plegadis autumnalis STEJN. Stand. Nat. Hist. IV. 1885, 160.

[B 500, C 445, R 503, C 649.]

GEOG. DIST.— Warmer parts of eastern hemisphere, West Indies and southern portions of eastern United States, wandering northward to New England and Illinois. In America only locally abundant and of irregular distribution.

187. **Plegadis guarauna** (LINN.).
White-faced Glossy Ibis.

Scolopax guarauna LINN. S. N. ed. 12, I. 1766, 242.
Plegadis guarauna RIDGW. Pr. U. S. Nat. Mus. I. Oct. 2, 1878, 163.

[B —, C 445 *bis*, 445 *ter*, R 504, C 650.]

GEOG. DIST.— Western United States, from Texas to California, Oregon, and casually to southern British Columbia, Kansas and Florida (breeding); southward through the West Indies and Mexico to South America.

SUBORDER CICONIÆ. STORKS, ETC.

FAMILY **CICONIIDÆ**. STORKS AND WOOD IBISES.

SUBFAMILY **TANTALINÆ**. WOOD IBISES.

GENUS **TANTALUS** LINNÆUS.

Tantalus LINN. S. N. ed. 10, I. 1758, 140. Type, *T. loculator* LINN.

ORDER HERODIONES.

188. **Tantalus loculator** LINN.
Wood Ibis.

Tantalus loculator LINN. S. N. ed. 10, I. 1758, 140.

[B 497, C 444, R 500, C 648.]

GEOG. DIST.—Southern United States, from the Ohio Valley, Colorado, Utah, southeastern California, etc., south to Argentine Republic; casually northward to Pennsylvania and New York.

SUBFAMILY **CICONIINÆ**. STORKS.

GENUS **MYCTERIA** LINNÆUS.

Mycteria LINN. S. N. ed. 10, I. 1758, 140. Type, *M. americana* LINN.

[189.] **Mycteria americana** LINN.
Jabiru.

Mycteria americana LINN. S. N. ed. 10, I. 1758, 140.

[B—, C 448 *bis*, R 499, C 654.]

GEOG. DIST.—Tropical America, north casually to southern Texas.

SUBORDER **HERODII**. HERONS, EGRETS, BITTERNS, ETC.

FAMILY **ARDEIDÆ**. HERONS, BITTERNS, ETC.

SUBFAMILY **BOTAURINÆ**. BITTERNS.

GENUS **BOTAURUS** HERMANN.

Botaurus HERMANN, Tabl. Affin. Anim. 1783, 135. Type, *Ardea stellaris* LINN.

190. **Botaurus lentiginosus** (Montag.).
American Bittern.

Ardea lentiginosa Montag. Orn. Dict. Suppl. 1813, —.
Botaurus lentiginosus Steph. Gen. Zool. XI. ii. 1819, 592.

[B 492, C 460, R 497, C 666.]

Geog. Dist.— Temperate North America, south to Guatemala, Cuba, Jamaica, and Bermuda; occasional in British Islands.

Genus **ARDETTA** Gray.

Ardetta Gray, List Gen. B. App. 1842, 13. Type, *Ardea minuta* Linn.

191. **Ardetta exilis** (Gmel.).
Least Bittern.

Ardea exilis Gmel. S. N. I. ii. 1788, 645.
Ardetta exilis Gundl. J. f. O. 1856, 345.

[B 491, C 461, R 498, C 667.]

Geog. Dist.— Temperate North America, north to the British Provinces and south to the West Indies and Brazil. Less common west of the Rocky Mountains; on the Pacific coast north to northern California.

191.1. **Ardetta neoxena** Cory.
Cory's Least Bittern.

Ardetta neoxena Cory, Auk, III. April, 1886, 262.

[B —, C —, R —, C —.]

Geog. Dist.—Southern Florida (Caloosahatchie River, near Lake Okeechobee); Ontario; Michigan.

Subfamily **ARDEINÆ**. Herons and Egrets.

Genus **ARDEA** Linn.

Subgenus **ARDEA**.

Ardea Linn. S. N. ed. 10, I. 1758, 141. Type, by elimination, *A. cinerea* Linn.

192. **Ardea occidentalis** AUD.
　　Great White Heron.
　Ardea occidentalis AUD. Orn. Biog. III. 1835, 542.
$$[\text{B 489, C 451, R 486, C 656, }part.]$$
GEOG. DIST.— Florida; Cuba; Jamaica.

193. **Ardea wardi** RIDGW.
　　Ward's Heron.
　Ardea wardi RIDGW. Bull. Nutt. Orn. Club, VII. Jan. 1882, 5.
$$[\text{B —, C —, R —, C —.}]$$
GEOG. DIST.— Florida.

194. **Ardea herodias** LINN.
　　Great Blue Heron.
　Ardea herodias LINN. S. N. ed. 10, I. 1758, 143.
$$[\text{B 487, C 449, R 487, C 655.}]$$
GEOG. DIST.— North America, from the Arctic regions southward to the West Indies and northern South America. Bermudas; Galapagos.

[195.] **Ardea cinerea** LINN.
　　European Blue Heron.
　Ardea cinerea LINN. S. N. ed. 10, I. 1758, 143.
$$[\text{B —, C —, R 488, C 657.}]$$
GEOG. DIST.— Most of the eastern hemisphere; accidental in southern Greenland.

SUBGENUS **HERODIAS** BOIE.

　Herodias BOIE, Isis, 1822, 559. Type, by elimination, *Ardea egretta* GMEL.

196. **Ardea egretta** GMEL.
　　American Egret.
　Ardea egretta GMEL. S. N. I. ii. 1788, 629.

[B 486, 486*, C 452, R 489, C 658.]

GEOG. DIST.— Temperate and tropical America, from New Jersey, Minnesota, and Oregon south to Patagonia; casually on the Atlantic coast to Nova Scotia.

SUBGENUS **GARZETTA** KAUP.

Garzetta KAUP, Skizz. Entw. Gesch. Eur. Thierw. 1829, 76. Type, *Ardea garzetta* LINN.

197. **Ardea candidissima** GMEL.
Snowy Heron.

Ardea candidissima GMEL. S. N. I. ii. 1788, 633.

[B 485, C 453, R 490, C 659.]

GEOG. DIST.— Temperate and tropical America, from Long Island and Oregon south to Argentine Republic and Chili; casually to Nova Scotia and southern British Columbia.

SUBGENUS **DICHROMANASSA** RIDGWAY.

Dichromanassa RIDGW. Bull. U. S. Geol. & Geog. Surv. Terr. IV. Feb. 5, 1878, 246. Type, *Ardea rufa* BODD.

198. **Ardea rufescens** GMEL.
Reddish Egret.

Ardea rufescens GMEL. S. N. I. ii. 1788, 628.

[B 483, 482, C 455, R 491, C 661.]

GEOG. DIST.— Gulf States, north to southern Illinois; Lower California and Mexico (both coasts), south to Guatemala; Jamaica, and Cuba.

SUBGENUS **HYDRANASSA** BAIRD.

Hydranassa BAIRD, B. N. Am. 1858, 660 (in text). Type, *Ardea ludoviciana* WILS. = *Egretta ruficollis* GOSSE.

199. **Ardea tricolor ruficollis** (GOSSE).
Louisiana Heron.

Egretta ruficollis GOSSE, B. Jamaica, 1847, 338.
Ardea tricolor ruficollis RIDGW. Pr. U. S. Nat. Mus. VIII. 1885, 355.

[B 484, C 454, R 492, C 660.]

GEOG. DIST.— Gulf States, Mexico (both coasts), Central America, and West Indies; casually northward to New Jersey and Indiana.

SUBGENUS **FLORIDA** BAIRD.

Florida BAIRD, B. N. Am. 1858, 671.   Type, *Ardea cærulea* LINN.

200. **Ardea cærulea** LINN.
Little Blue Heron.

Ardea cærulea LINN. S. N. ed. 10, I. 1758, 143.

[B 490, C 456, R 493, C 662.]

GEOG. DIST.— Eastern United States, from New Jersey, Illinois, and Kansas, southward through Central America and the West Indies to Guiana and Colombia; casually north on the Atlantic coast to Massachusetts and Maine.

SUBGENUS **BUTORIDES** BLYTH.

Butorides BLYTH, Cat. B. Mus. As. Soc. 1849, 281.   Type, *Ardea javanica* HORSF.

201. **Ardea virescens** LINN.
Green Heron.

Ardea virescens LINN. S. N. ed. 10, I. 1758, 144.

[B 493, C 457, R 494, C 663.]

GEOG. DIST.— Temperate North America, from Ontario and Oregon, southward to Colombia, Venezuela, and the West Indies. Bermuda.

201 a. **Ardea virescens frazari** BREWST.
Frazar's Green Heron.

Ardea virescens frazari BREWST. Auk, V. Jan. 1888, 83.

[B —, C —, R —, C —.]

GEOG. DIST.— Lower California (vicinity of La Paz).

Genus **NYCTICORAX** Stephens.

Subgenus **NYCTICORAX**.

Nycticorax Steph. Gen. Zool. XI. ii. 1819, 608. Type, *Ardea nycticorax* Linn.

202. Nycticorax nycticorax nævius (Bodd.).
Black-crowned Night Heron.

Ardea nævia Bodd. Tabl. Pl. Enl. 1783, 56.
Nycticorax nycticorax nævius Zeledon, Pr. U. S. Nat. Mus. VIII. 1885, 113.

[B 495, C 458, R 495, C 664.]

Geog. Dist.— America, from Ontario and Manitoba southward to the Falkland Islands, including part of the West Indies.

Subgenus **NYCTANASSA** Stejneger.

Nyctanassa Stejn. Proc. U. S. Nat. Mus. X. 1887, 295. Type, *Ardea violacea* Linn.

203. Nycticorax violaceus (Linn.).
Yellow-crowned Night Heron.

Ardea violacea Linn. S. N. ed. 10, I. 1758, 143.
Nycticorax violacea Vigors, Zool. Journ. III. 1827, 446.

[B 496, C 459, R 496, C 665.]

Geog. Dist.— Tropical and warm temperate North America, from the Carolinas, the lower Ohio Valley and Lower California, south to Brazil; casually north to Massachusetts and Colorado.

Order PALUDICOLÆ. Cranes, Rails, etc.

Suborder GRUES. Cranes.

Family GRUIDÆ. Cranes.

Genus GRUS Pallas.

Grus Pall. Misc. Zool. 1766, 66. Type, *Ardea grus* Linn.

204. Grus americana (Linn.).
    Whooping Crane.

Ardea americana Linn. S. N. ed. 10, I. 1758, 142.
Grus americana Vieill. Nouv. Dict. d'Hist. Nat. XIII. 1817, 557.

[B 478, C 462, R 582, C 668.]

Geog. Dist.— Interior of North America, from the Fur Countries to Florida, Texas, and Mexico, and from Ohio to Colorado. Formerly on the Atlantic coast, at least casually, to New England.

205. Grus canadensis (Linn.).
    Little Brown Crane.

Ardea canadensis Linn. S. N. ed. 10, I. 1758, 141.
Grus canadensis Temm. Man. I. 1820, p. c.

[B 480, C 463, R 584, C 669.]

Geog. Dist.— Arctic and subarctic America, breeding from the Fur Countries and Alaska to the Arctic coast, migrating south in winter into the western United States.

206. Grus mexicana (Müll.).
    Sandhill Crane.

Ardea (grus) mexicana Müll. S. N. Suppl. 1776, 110.
Grus mexicana Vieill. Nouv. Dict. d'Hist. Nat. XIII. 1817, 561.

[B 479, C —, R 583, C 670.]

GEOG. DIST.— Southern half of North America; now rare near the Atlantic coast, except in Georgia and Florida.

SUBORDER RALLI. RAILS, GALLINULES, COOTS, ETC.

FAMILY **ARAMIDÆ**. COURLANS.

GENUS **ARAMUS** VIEILLOT.

Aramus VIEILL. Analyse, 1816, 58.   Type, *Ardea scolopacea* GMEL.

207. Aramus giganteus (BONAP.).
Limpkin.

Rallus giganteus BONAP. Jour. Ac. Nat. Sci. Phila. V. 1825, 31.
Aramus giganteus BAIRD, B. N. Am. 1858, 657.

[B 481, C 464, R 581, C 671.]

GEOG. DIST.— Florida, Greater Antilles, and both coasts of Central America.

FAMILY **RALLIDÆ**.   RAILS, GALLINULES, AND COOTS.

SUBFAMILY **RALLINÆ**. RAILS.

GENUS **RALLUS** LINNÆUS.

Rallus LINN. S. N. ed. 10, I. 1758, 153.   Type, *R. aquaticus* LINN.

208. Rallus elegans AUD.
King Rail.

Rallus elegans AUD. Orn. Biog. III. 1835, 27, pl. 203.

ORDER PALUDICOLÆ. 77

[B 552, C 466, R 569, C 676.]

GEOG. DIST.— Fresh-water marshes of the eastern United States, north to the Middle States, northern Illinois, Wisconsin, and Kansas, casually to Massachusetts, Maine, and Ontario.

209. Rallus beldingi RIDGW.
Belding's Rail.

Rallus beldingi RIDGW. Pr. U. S. Nat. Mus. V. 1882, 345.

[B —, C —, R —, C —.]

GEOG. DIST.— Lower California (Espiritu Santo Island and vicinity of La Paz).

210. Rallus obsoletus RIDGW.
California Clapper Rail.

Rallus elegans var. *obsoletus* RIDGW. Am. Nat. VIII. 1871, 111.
Rallus obsoletus RIDGW. Bull. Nutt. Orn. Club, V. July, 1880, 139.

[B —, C 466a, R 570, C 674.]

GEOG. DIST.— Salt marshes of the Pacific coast, from Washington (?) to Lower California.

211. Rallus crepitans GMEL.
Clapper Rail.

Rallus crepitans GMEL. S. N. I. ii. 1788, 713.

[B 553, C 465, R 571, C 673.]

GEOG. DIST.— Salt marshes of the Atlantic and Gulf coasts of the United States, breeding from southern Connecticut southward; resident from the Potomac southward, occasionally wintering further north. Casual north to Massachusetts.

211 a. Rallus crepitans saturatus RIDGW.
Louisiana Clapper Rail.

Rallus longirostris saturatus RIDGW. Bull. Nutt. Orn. Club, V. July, 1880, 140.
Rallus crepitans saturatus SENNETT, Auk, VI. April, 1889, pp. 164, 166.

[B—, C—, R 571a, C 675.]

GEOG. DIST.— Coast of Louisiana.

211.1. **Rallus scottii** (SENN.).
Florida Clapper Rail.

Rallus longirostris scottii SENN. Auk, V. July, 1888, 305.
Rallus scottii SENNETT, Auk, VI. April, 1889, pp. 165, 166.

[B—, C—, R—, C—.]

GEOG. DIST.— Western Florida (salt marshes).

[211.2.]. **Rallus longirostris caribæus** RIDGW.
Caribbean Clapper Rail.

Rallus longirostris caribæus RIDGW. Bull. Nutt. Orn. Club, V. July, 1880, 140.

[B—, C—, R—, C—.]

GEOG. DIST.— West Indies and Gulf coast of Mexico, north to Texas (Corpus Christi and Galveston).

212. **Rallus virginianus** LINN.
Virginia Rail.

Rallus virginianus LINN. S. N. ed. 12, I. 1766, 263.

[B 554, C 467, R 572, C 677.]

GEOG. DIST.— North America, from the British Provinces south to Guatemala and Cuba.

GENUS **PORZANA** VIEILLOT.

SUBGENUS **PORZANA**.

Porzana VIEILL. Analyse, 1816, 61. Type, *Rallus porzana* LINN.

[213.] **Porzana porzana** (LINN.).
Spotted Crake.

Rallus porzana LINN. S. N. ed. 12, I. 1766, 262.
Porzana porzana BOUCARD, Cat. Av. 1876, 7.

[B—, C—, R 573, C 678.]

GEOG. DIST.— Northern parts of the Old World; occasional in Greenland.

214. **Porzana carolina** (LINN.).
Sora.

Rallus carolinus LINN. S. N. ed. 10, I. 1758, 153.
Porzana carolina BAIRD, Lit. Rec. & Jour. Linn. Assoc. Penn. Coll. Oct. 1845, 255.

[B 555, C 648, R 574, C 679.]

GEOG. DIST.— Temperate North America, breeding chiefly northward, but less commonly on the Pacific coast. Casually north to South Greenland. South to the West Indies and northern South America.

SUBGENUS **COTURNICOPS** BONAPARTE.

Coturnicops BONAP. Compt. Rend. XLIII. 1856, 599. Type, *Fulica noveboracensis* GMEL.

215. **Porzana noveboracensis** (GMEL.).
Yellow Rail.

Fulica noveboracensis GMEL. S. N. I. ii. 1788, 701.
Porzana noveboracensis BAIRD, Lit. Rec. & Jour. Linn. Assoc. Penn. Coll. Oct. 1845, 255.

[B 557, C 469, R 575, C 680.]

GEOG. DIST.— Chiefly eastern North America, north to Nova Scotia, Hudson Bay, etc., less commonly west to Nevada and California. No extralimital records except for Cuba and Bermuda.

SUBGENUS **CRECISCUS** CABANIS.

Creciscus CAB. J. f. O. 1856, 428. Type, *Rallus jamaicensis* LINN.

216. **Porzana jamaicensis** (GMEL.).
Black Rail.

Rallus jamaicensis GMEL. S. N. I. ii. 1788, 718.
Porzana jamaicensis BAIRD, Lit. Rec. & Jour. Linn. Assoc. Penn. Coll. Oct. 1845, 257.

[B 556, C 470, R 576, C 681.]

GEOG. DIST.— Temperate North America, north to Massachusetts, northern Illinois, and Oregon; south to West Indies and Guatemala.

216.1. **Porzana coturniculus** (RIDGW.).
Farallone Rail.

Porzana jamaicensis var. *coturniculus* "BAIRD, MS." RIDGW. Am. Nat. VIII. Feb. 1874, 111.
Porzana coturniculus RIDGW. Proc. U. S. Nat. Mus. XIII. 1890, 311.

[B —, C 470a, R 576a, C 682.]

GEOG. DIST.— Known only from the type specimen, from Farallone Islands, California.

GENUS **CREX** BECHSTEIN.

Crex BECHST. Orn. Taschb. Deutschl. 1802, 336. Type, *Rallus crex* LINN.

[217.] **Crex crex** (LINN.).
Corn Crake.

Rallus crex LINN. S. N. ed. 10, I. 1758, 153.
Crex crex SHARPE, LAYARD'S Bds. S. Africa, 1884, 611.

[B 558, C 471, R 577, C 683.]

GEOG. DIST.— Europe and northern Asia; casual in Greenland, Bermuda, and eastern North America.

SUBFAMILY **GALLINULINÆ**. GALLINULES.

GENUS **IONORNIS** REICHENBACH.

Ionornis REICH. Syst. Av. 1852, p. xxi. Type, *Fulica martinica* LINN.

218. **Ionornis martinica** (LINN.).
Purple Gallinule.

Fulica martinica LINN. S. N. ed. 12, I. 1766, 259.
Ionornis martinica REICH. Syst. Av. 1852, p. xxi.

ORDER PALUDICOLÆ.

[B 561, C 473, R 578, C 685.]

Geog. Dist.— South Atlantic and Gulf States, casually northward to Maine, New York, Wisconsin, etc.; south throughout the West Indies, Mexico, Central America and northern South America to Brazil.

Genus **GALLINULA** Brisson.

Gallinula Briss. Orn. VI. 1760, 2. Type, *Fulica chloropus* Linn.

219. Gallinula galeata (Licht.).
Florida Gallinule.

Crex galeata Licht. Verz. Doubl. 1823, 80.
Gallinula galeata Bonap. Am. Orn. IV. 1832, 128.

[B 560, C 472, R 579, C 685.]

Geog. Dist.— Temperate and tropical America, from Canada to Brazil and Chili.

Subfamily **FULICINÆ**. Coots.

Genus **FULICA** Linnæus.

Fulica Linn. S. N. ed. 10, I. 1758, 152. Type, *F. atra* Linn.

[220.] Fulica atra Linn.
European Coot.

Fulica atra Linn. S. N. ed. 10, I. 1758, 152.

[B —, C —, R —, C 885.]

Geog. Dist.— Northern parts of the eastern hemisphere in general; accidental in Greenland.

221. Fulica americana Gmel.
American Coot.

Fulica americana Gmel. S. N. I. ii. 1788, 704.

[B 559, C 474, R 580, C 686.]

Geog. Dist.— North America, from Greenland and Alaska southward to the West Indies and Veragua.

Order LIMICOLÆ. Shore Birds.

Family **PHALAROPODIDÆ**. Phalaropes.

Genus **CRYMOPHILUS** Vieillot.

Crymophilus Vieill. Anal. 1816, 62. Type, *Tringa fulicaria* Linn.

222. Crymophilus fulicarius (Linn.).
Red Phalarope.
Tringa fulicaria Linn. S. N. ed. 10, I. 1758, 148.
Crymophilus fulicarius Stejn. Auk, II. 1885, 183.

[B 521, C 411, R 563, C 604.]

Geog. Dist.— Northern parts of northern hemisphere, breeding in the Arctic regions and migrating south in winter; in the United States south to the Middle States, Ohio Valley, and Cape St. Lucas; chiefly maritime.

Genus **PHALAROPUS** Brisson.

Subgenus **PHALAROPUS**.

Phalaropus Briss. Orn. VI. 1760, 12. Type, by elimination, *Tringa lobata* Linn.

223. Phalaropus lobatus (Linn.).
Northern Phalarope.
Tringa lobata Linn. S. N. ed. 10, I. 1758, 148, 824.
Phalaropus lobatus Salvad. Ucc. d'Italia, II. 1872, 210 (nec Latham qui *Crymophilus fulicarius*, nec Wilson qui *Ph. tricolor*).

[B 520, C 410, R 564, C 603.]

Geog. Dist. — Northern portions of northern hemisphere, breeding in arctic latitudes; south in winter to the tropics.

ORDER LIMICOLÆ.

SUBGENUS **STEGANOPUS** VIEILLOT.

Steganopus VIEILL. Nouv. Dict. d'Hist. Nat. XXXII. 1819, 136.
Type, *S. tricolor* VIEILL.

224. Phalaropus tricolor (VIEILL.).
Wilson's Phalarope.

Steganopus tricolor VIEILL. Nouv. Dict. d'Hist. Nat. XXXII. 1819, 136.
Phalaropus tricolor STEJN. Auk, II. 1885, 183.

[B 519, C 409, R 565, C 602.]

GEOG. DIST.— Temperate North America, chiefly the interior, breeding from northern Illinois and Utah northward to the Saskatchewan region; south in winter to Brazil and Patagonia.

FAMILY **RECURVIROSTRIDÆ.** AVOCETS AND STILTS.

GENUS **RECURVIROSTRA** LINNÆUS.

Recurvirostra LINN. S. N. ed. 10, I. 1758, 151. Type, *R. avosetta* LINN.

225. Recurvirostra americana GMEL.
American Avocet.

Recurvirostra americana GMEL. S. N. I. ii. 1788, 693.

[B 517, C 407, R 566, C 600.]

GEOG. DIST.— Temperate North America, north to the Saskatchewan and Great Slave Lake; in winter, south to Guatemala and the West Indies. Rare in the eastern United States.

GENUS **HIMANTOPUS** BRISSON.

Himantopus BRISS. Orn. VI. 1760, 33. Type, *Charadrius himantopus* LINN.

226. Himantopus mexicanus (Müll.).
   Black-necked Stilt.

Charadrius mexicanus Müll. S. N. Suppl. 1776, 117.
Himantopus mexicanus Ord, Wils. Orn. VII. 1824, 52.

[B 518, C 408, R 567, C 601.]

Geog. Dist.— Temperate North America, from the northern United States southward to the West Indies, northern Brazil, and Peru. Rare in eastern United States, except in Florida.

Family **SCOLOPACIDÆ**. Snipes, Sandpipers, etc.

Genus **SCOLOPAX** Linnæus.

Scolopax Linn. S. N. ed. 10, I. 1758, 145. Type, *S. rusticola* Linn.

[227.] **Scolopax rusticola** Linn.
   European Woodcock.

Scolopax rusticola Linn. S. N. ed. 10, I. 1758, 146.

[B —, C 413, R 524, C 606.]

Geog. Dist.— Northern parts of the Old World; occasional in eastern North America.

Genus **PHILOHELA** Gray.

Philohela Gray, List Gen. B. 1841, 90. Type, *Scolopax minor* Gm.

228. Philohela minor (Gmel.).
   American Woodcock.

Scolopax minor Gmel. S. N. I. ii. 1788, 661.
Philohela minor Gray, List Gen. B. 1841, 90.

[B 522, C 412, R 525, C 605.]

Geog. Dist.— Eastern North America, north to the British Provinces, west to Dakota, Kansas, etc.; breeding throughout its range. No extralimital record except Bermuda.

Genus GALLINAGO Leach.

Gallinago Leach, Syst. Cat. Brit. Mam. & Birds, 1816, 31.
Type, *Scolopax major* Linn.

[229.] Gallinago gallinago (Linn.).
European Snipe.

Scolopax gallinago Linn. S. N. ed. 10, I. 1758, 147.
Gallinago gallinago Licht. Nom. Mus. Berol. 1854, 93.

[B—, C—, R 526, C 607.]

Geog. Dist.— Northern parts of the Old World; frequent in Greenland, accidental in Bermuda.

230. Gallinago delicata (Ord).
Wilson's Snipe.

Scolopax delicata Ord, Wils. Orn. IX. 1825, p. ccxviii.
Gallinago delicata A. O. U. Check-List, 1886, 148.

[B 523, C 414, R 526a, C 608.]

Geog. Dist.— North and Middle America, breeding from the northern United States northward; south in winter to the West Indies and northern South America.

Genus MACRORHAMPHUS Leach.

Macrorhamphus Leach, Syst. Cat. Brit. Mam. & B. 1816, 31.
Type, *Scolopax grisea* Gmel.

231. Macrorhamphus griseus (Gmel.).
Dowitcher.

Scolopax grisea Gmel. S. N. I. ii. 1788, 658.
Macrorhamphus griseus Leach, Syst. Cat. Brit. Mam. & B. 1816, 31.

[B 524, C 415, R 527, C 609.]

Geog. Dist.— Eastern North America, breeding far north; south in winter to the West Indies and Brazil. Casual (?) in Alaska (Nushagak River), Bermuda, Great Britain, and Europe.

232. **Macrorhamphus scolopaceus** (Say).
    Long-billed Dowitcher.

Limosa scolopacea Say, Long's Exp. II. 1823, 170.
Macrorhamphus scolopaceus Lawr. Ann. Lyc. N. Y. V. 1852, 4, pl. 1.

    [B 525, C 415a, R 527a, C 610.]

Geog. Dist.— Western North America, breeding in Alaska to the Arctic coast, migrating south in winter through the western United States (including Mississippi Valley) to Mexico, and, less commonly, along Atlantic coast.

Genus **MICROPALAMA** Baird.

Micropalama Baird, B. N. Am. 1858, 726. Type, *Tringa himantopus* Bonap.

233. **Micropalama himantopus** (Bonap.).
    Stilt Sandpiper.

Tringa himantopus Bonap. Ann. Lyc. N. Y. II. 1826, 157.
Micropalama himantopus Baird, B. N. Am. 1858, 726.

    [B 536, C 416, R 528, C 611.]

Geog. Dist.— Eastern North America, breeding north of the United States, and migrating in winter to Bermuda, West Indies and Central and South America.

Genus **TRINGA** Linnæus.

Subgenus **TRINGA**.

Tringa Linn. S. N. ed. 10, I. 1758, 148. Type, by elimination, *T. canutus* Linn.

234. **Tringa canutus** Linn.
    Knot.

Tringa canutus Linn. S. N. ed. 10, I. 1758, 149.

    [B 526, C 426, R 529, C 626.]

Geog. Dist.— Nearly cosmopolitan. Breeds in high northern latitudes, but visits the southern hemisphere during its migrations.

SUBGENUS **ARQUATELLA** BAIRD.

Arquatella BAIRD, B. N. Am. 1858, 714, 717.   Type, *Tringa maritima* BRÜNN.

235. **Tringa maritima** BRÜNN.
Purple Sandpiper.
Tringa maritima BRÜNN. Orn. Bor. 1764, 54.

[B 528, C 423, R 530, C 620.]

GEOG. DIST.— Northern portions of the northern hemisphere; in North America chiefly the northeastern portions, breeding in the high north, migrating in winter to the Eastern and Middle States (casually to Florida), the Great Lakes, and the shores of the larger streams in the upper Mississippi Valley.

236. **Tringa couesi** (RIDGW.).
Aleutian Sandpiper.
Arquatella couesi RIDGW. Bull. Nutt. Orn. Club, V. July, 1880, 160.
Tringa couesi HARTLAUB, Journ. f. Orn. 1883, 280.

[B —, C —, R 531, C 621.]

GEOG. DIST. — Aleutian Islands and coast of Alaska, north to Kowak River, west to Commander Islands, Kamchatka.

237. **Tringa ptilocnemis** COUES.
Pribilof Sandpiper.
Tringa ptilocnemis COUES, ELLIOTT's Rep. Seal Isl. Alaska, 1873 (not paged).

[B —, C 426 *bis*, R 532, C 622.]

GEOG. DIST.— Breeding in the Pribilof Islands, Alaska, and migrating to coast of adjacent mainland south of Norton Sound.

SUBGENUS **ACTODROMAS** KAUP.

Actodromas KAUP, SKIZZ. Entw.-Gesch. Eur. Thierw. 1829, 37. Type, *Tringa minuta* LEISL.

238. **Tringa acuminata** (Horsf.).
Sharp-tailed Sandpiper.

Totanus acuminatus Horsf. Linn. Trans. XIII. 1821, 192.
Tringa acuminata Swinh. P. Z. S. 1863, 316.

[B —, C —, R 533, C 619.]

Geog. Dist.— Eastern Asia, and coast of Alaska, migrating south to Java and Australia.

239. **Tringa maculata** Vieill.
Pectoral Sandpiper.

Tringa maculata Vieill. Nouv. Dict. d'Hist. Nat. XXXIV. 1819, 465.

[B 531, C 420, R 534, C 616.]

Geog. Dist.— The whole of North America, the West Indies, and the greater part of South America. Breeds in the Arctic regions. Of frequent occurrence in Europe.

240. **Tringa fuscicollis** Vieill.
White-rumped Sandpiper.

Tringa fuscicollis Vieill. Nouv. Dict. d'Hist. Nat. XXXIV. 1819, 461.

[B 533, C 421, R 536, C 617.]

Geog. Dist.— Eastern North America, breeding in the high north. In winter, the West Indies, Central and South America, south to the Falkland Islands. Occasional in Europe.

241. **Tringa bairdii** (Coues).
Baird's Sandpiper.

Actodromas bairdii Coues, Pr. Ac. Nat. Sci. Phila. 1861, 194.
Tringa bairdii Scl. P. Z. S. 1867, 332.

[B —, C 419, R 537, C 615.]

Geog. Dist.— Nearly the whole of North and South America, but chiefly the interior of North and the western portions of South America, south to Chili and Patagonia. Breeds in Alaska and on the Barren Grounds. Rare along the Atlantic coast, and not yet recorded from the Pacific coast of the United States.

ORDER LIMICOLÆ.

242. Tringa minutilla VIEILL.
Least Sandpiper.

Tringa minutilla VIEILL. Nouv. Dict. d'Hist. Nat. XXXIV. 1819, 452.

[B 532, C 418, R 538, C 614.]

GEOG. DIST.— The whole of North and South America, breeding north of the United States. Accidental in Europe.

[242.1.] Tringa damacensis (HORSF.).
Long-toed Stint.

Totanus damacensis HORSF. Trans. Linn. Soc. XIII. 1821, 129.
Tringa damacensis SWINH. Ibis, Oct. 1863, 413.

[B—, C—, R—, C—.]

GEOG. DIST.— Asia, breeding toward Arctic coast; accidental in Alaska (Otter Island, Bering Sea).

SUBGENUS **PELIDNA** CUVIER.

Pelidna CUV. Règne An. 1817, 490.   Type, *Tringa alpina* LINN.

[243.] Tringa alpina LINN.
Dunlin.

Tringa alpina LINN. S. N. ed. 10, I. 1758, 149.

[B —, C —, R 539, C 623.]

GEOG. DIST.— Northern parts of the Old World; accidental in eastern North America (west side of Hudson Bay and Long Island).

243a. Tringa alpina pacifica (COUES).
Red-backed Sandpiper.

Pelidna pacifica COUES, Pr. Ac. Nat. Sci. Phila. 1861, 189.
Tringa alpina pacifica A. O. U. Check-List, 1886, 152.

[B 530, C 424, R 539a, C 624.]

GEOG. DIST.— North America in general, breeding far north. Eastern Asia.

Subgenus **ANCYLOCHEILUS** Kaup.

Ancylocheilus Kaup, Skizz. Entw.-Gesch. Eur. Thierw. 1829, 50.
Type, *Tringa subarquata* Temm. = *T. ferruginea* Brünn.

244. Tringa ferruginea Brünn.
Curlew Sandpiper.

Tringa ferruginea Brünn. Orn. Bor. 1764, 53.

[B 529, C 425, R 540, C 625.]

Geog. Dist.— Old World in general; occasional in eastern North America and Alaska.

Genus **EURYNORHYNCHUS** Nilsson.

Eurynorhynchus Nilss. Orn. Suec. II. 1821, 29. Type, *Platalea pygmæa* Linn.

[245.] Eurynorhynchus pygmæus (Linn.).
Spoon-bill Sandpiper.

Platalea pygmæa Linn. S. N. ed. 10, I. 1758, 140.
Eurynorhynchus pygmæus Pearson, Jour. As. Soc. Beng. V. 1836, 127.

[B—, C—, R 542*, C 884.]

Geog. Dist.— Asia; in summer along the Arctic coast, in winter southern and southeastern Asia. Accidental on the coast of Alaska (Choris Peninsula).

Genus **EREUNETES** Illiger.

Ereunetes Illig. Prodr. 1811, 262. Type, *E. petrificatus* Illig.
= *Tringa pusilla* Linn.

246. Ereunetes pusillus (Linn.).
Semipalmated Sandpiper.

Tringa pusilla Linn. S. N. ed. 12, I. 1766, 252.
Ereunetes pusillus Cass. Pr. Ac. Nat. Sci. Phila. 1860, 195.

ORDER LIMICOLÆ.   91

[B 535, C 417, R 541, C 612.]

GEOG. DIST.— Eastern North America, breeding north of the United States; south in winter to the West Indies and South America.

247. **Ereunetes occidentalis** LAWR.
Western Sandpiper.

Ereunetes occidentalis LAWR. Pr. Ac. Nat. Sci. Phila. 1864, 107.

[B —, C 417a, R 541a, C 613.]

GEOG. DIST.— Chiefly western United States, frequent eastward to the Atlantic coast; breeding far north and migrating in winter to Central and South America.

GENUS **CALIDRIS** CUVIER.

Calidris CUV. Leç. Anat. Comp. I. 1799–1800, tabl. ii. Type, *Tringa arenaria* LINN.

248. **Calidris arenaria** (LINN.).
Sanderling.

Tringa arenaria LINN. S. N. ed. 12, I. 1766, 251.
Calidris arenaria LEACH, Syst. Cat. Brit. Mam. & B. 1816, 28.

[B 534, C 427, R 542, C 627.]

GEOG. DIST.— Nearly cosmopolitan, breeding in the arctic and subarctic regions, migrating, in America, south to Chili and Patagonia.

GENUS **LIMOSA** BRISSON.

Limosa BRISS. Orn. V. 1760, 261. Type, *Scolopax limosa* LINN.

249. **Limosa fedoa** (LINN.).
Marbled Godwit.

Scolopax fedoa LINN. S. N. ed. 10, I. 1758, 146.
Limosa fedoa SABINE, FRANKLIN'S Journ. Polar Sea, 1823, 689.

[B 547, C 428, R 543, C 628.]

GEOG. DIST.— North America; breeding in the interior (from Iowa and Nebraska, northward to Manitoba and the Saskatchewan), migrating in winter to Guatemala, Yucatan, etc., and Cuba.

250. Limosa lapponica baueri (NAUM.).
Pacific Godwit.

Limosa baueri NAUMANN, Vög. Deutschl. VIII. 1834, 429.
Limosa lapponica baueri STEJN. Orn. Expl. Kamtsch. 1885, 122.

[B —, C 430, R 544, C 631.]

GEOG. DIST.— Shores and islands of the Pacific Ocean, from New Zealand and Australia to Kamchatka and Alaska. On the American coast recorded south of Alaska only from La Paz, Lower California.

251. Limosa hæmastica (LINN.).
Hudsonian Godwit.

Scolopax hæmastica LINN. S. N. ed. 10, I. 1758, 147.
Limosa hæmastica COUES, Birds Northwest, 1874, 760.

[B 548, C 429, R 545, C 629.]

GEOG. DIST.— Eastern North America and the whole of Middle and South America. Breeds only in the high north.

[252.] Limosa limosa (LINN.).
Black-tailed Godwit.

Scolopax limosa LINN. S. N. ed. 10, I. 1758, 147.
Limosa limosa RIDGW. Pr. U. S. Nat. Mus. VIII. 1885, 356.

[B —, C —, R 546, C 630.]

GEOG. DIST.— Northern parts of the Old World; accidental in Greenland.

GENUS **TOTANUS** BECHSTEIN.

Totanus BECH. Orn. Tasch. Deutschl. 1803, 282. Type, *Scolopax totanus* LINN.

SUBGENUS **GLOTTIS** KOCH.

Glottis KOCH, Baier. Zool. 1816, 304. Type, *Totanus glottis* BECHST. = *Scolopax nebularius* GUNNER.

[253.] **Totanus nebularius** (GUNN.).
Green-shank.

Scolopax nebularius GUNNER. in LEEM, Lapp. Beskr. 1767, 251.
Totanus nebularius STEJN. Pr. U. S. Nat. Mus. V. 1882, 37.

[B 538, C 434, R 547, C 635.]

GEOG. DIST.— Eastern hemisphere; accidental in Florida.

254. **Totanus melanoleucus** (GMEL.).
Greater Yellow-legs.

Scolopax melanoleuca GMEL. S. N. I. ii. 1788, 659.
Totanus melanoleucus VIEILL. Nouv. Dict. d'Hist. Nat. VI. 1816, 398.

[B 539, C 432, R 548, C 633.]

GEOG. DIST.— America in general, breeding from Iowa and northern Illinois, etc., northward, and migrating south to Chili and Argentine Republic.

255. **Totanus flavipes** (GMEL.).
Yellow-legs.

Scolopax flavipes GMEL. S. N. I. ii. 1788, 659.
Totanus flavipes VIEILL. Nouv. Dict. d'Hist. Nat. VI. 1816, 410.

[B 540, C 433, R 549, C 634.]

GEOG. DIST.— America in general, breeding in the cold temperate and subarctic districts, and migrating south in winter to southern South America. Less common in western than in eastern North America.

SUBGENUS **HELODROMAS** KAUP.

Helodromas KAUP, Skizz. Entw.-Gesch. Eur. Thierw. 1829, 144. Type, *Tringa ochropus* LINN.

256. **Totanus solitarius** (Wils.).
Solitary Sandpiper.

Tringa solitaria Wils. Am. Orn. VII. 1813, 53, pl. 58, fig. 3.
Totanus solitarius Bonap. Journ. Ac. Nat. Sci. Phila. V. 1825, 86.

[B 541, C 435, R 550, C 637.]

Geog. Dist.— North America, breeding occasionally in the northern United States, more commonly northward, and migrating southward as far as the Argentine Republic and Peru.

256 a. **Totanus solitarius cinnamomeus** Brewster.
Western Solitary Sandpiper.

Totanus solitarius cinnamomeus Brewster, Auk, VII. Oct. 1890, 377.

[B 541, *part*, C 435, *part*, R 550, *part*, C 637, *part*.]

Geog. Dist.— Pacific coast region, eastward to the Plains.

[257.] **Totanus ochropus** (Linn.).
Green Sandpiper.

Tringa ocrophus (err. typ.) Linn. S. N. ed. 10, I. 1758, 149.
Totanus ochropus Temm. Man. 1815, 420.

[B —, C —, R 551, C 636.]

Geog. Dist.— Northern parts of the Old World. Accidental in Nova Scotia.

Genus **SYMPHEMIA** Rafinesque.

Symphemia Rafinesque, Jour. de Phys. LXXXVIII. 1819, 418.
Type, *Scolopax semipalmata* Gmel.

258. **Symphemia semipalmata** (Gmel.).
Willet.

Scolopax semipalmata Gmel. S. N. I. ii. 1788, 659.
Symphemia semipalmata Hartl. Rev. Zool. 1845, 342.

[B 537, C 431, R 552, C 632.]

Geog. Dist.— Eastern temperate North America, south to the West Indies and Brazil. Breeds from Florida to New Jersey and locally and rarely to Maine. Accidental in Bermuda and Europe.

ORDER LIMICOLÆ.

258 a. **Symphemia semipalmata inornata** BREWST.
   Western Willet.

Symphemia semipalmata inornata BREWST. Auk, IV. April, 1887, 145.

[B 537, *part,* R 431, *part,* R 552, *part,* C 632, *part.*]

GEOG. DIST.— Western North America, east to Mississippi Valley and Gulf States; in winter, south to Mexico, and, during migrations, sparingly along coast of southern Atlantic States. Breeds from coast of Texas to Manitoba.

GENUS **HETERACTITIS** STEJNEGER.

Heteractitis STEJN. Auk, I. July, 1884, 236. Type, *Scolopax incanus* GMEL.

259. **Heteractitis incanus** (GMEL.).
   Wandering Tatler.

Scolopax incanus GMEL. S. N. I. ii. 1788, 658.
Heteractitis incanus STEJN. Auk, I. July, 1884, 236.

[B 542, C 440, R 553, C 642.]

GEOG. DIST.— Pacific coast of America, from Norton Sound, Alaska, to the Galapagos, and west to Kamchatka and Hawaiian Islands; also the more eastern island groups of Polynesia.

GENUS **PAVONCELLA** LEACH.

Pavoncella LEACH, Syst. Cat. Brit. Mam. & B. 1816, 29. Type, *Tringa pugnax* LINN.

[260.] **Pavoncella pugnax** (LINN.).
   Ruff.

Tringa pugnax LINN. S. N. ed. 10, I. 1758, 148.
Pavoncella pugnax LEACH, Syst. Cat. Brit. Mam. & B. 1816, 29.

[B 544, C 437, R 554, C 639.]

GEOG. DIST.— Northern parts of the Old World, straying occasionally to eastern North America.

Genus **BARTRAMIA** Lesson.

Bartramia Less. Traité, 1831, 553. Type, *B. laticauda* Less.
= *Tringa longicauda* Bechst.

261. **Bartramia longicauda** (Bechst.).
Bartramian Sandpiper.

Tringa longicauda Bechst. Uebers. Lath. Ind. Orn. II. 1812, 453.
Bartramius longicaudus Bonap. Rev. et Mag. Zool. XX. 1857, 59.

[B 545, C 438, R 555, C 640.]

Geog. Dist.— North America, mainly east of the Rocky Mountains, north to Nova Scotia and Alaska, breeding throughout most of its North American range; migrating in winter southward, as far as Brazil and Peru. Occasional in Europe.

Genus **TRYNGITES** Cabanis.

Tryngites Cab. Jour. für Orn. 1856, 418. Type, *Tringa rufescens* Vieill. = *T. subruficollis* Vieill.

262. **Tryngites subruficollis** (Vieill.).
Buff-breasted Sandpiper.

Tringa subruficollis Vieill. Nouv. Dict. d'Hist. Nat. XXXIV. 1819, 465.
Tryngites subruficollis Ridgw. Pr. U. S. Nat. Mus. VIII. 1885, 356.

[B 546, C 439, R 556, C 641.]

Geog. Dist.— North America, especially in the interior; breeds in the Yukon district and the interior of British America, northward to the Arctic coast; South America in winter as far as Uruguay and Peru. Of frequent occurrence in Europe.

Genus **ACTITIS** Illiger.

Actitis Illig. Prodr. 1811, 262. Type, *Tringa hypoleucos* Linn.

ORDER LIMICOLÆ.

263. Actitis macularia (LINN.).
   Spotted Sandpiper.

Tringa macularia LINN. S. N. ed. 12, I. 1766, 249.
Actitis macularia NAUMANN, Vög. Deutschl. VIII. 1836, 34.

[B 543, C 436, R 557, C 638.]

GEOG. DIST.— North and South America, from Alaska south to southern Brazil. Breeds throughout temperate North America, less commonly on the Pacific coast. Occasional in Europe.

GENUS **NUMENIUS** BRISSON.

Numenius BRISS. Orn. VI. 1760, 311. Type, *Scolopax arquata* LINN.

264. Numenius longirostris WILS.
   Long-billed Curlew.

Numenius longirostris WILS. Am. Orn. VIII. 1814, 24, pl. 64, fig. 4.

[B 549, C 441, R 558, C 643.]

GEOG. DIST.— Temperate North America, migrating south to Guatemala, Cuba, and Jamaica. Breeds in the South Atlantic States, and in the interior through most of its North American range.

265. Numenius hudsonicus LATH.
   Hudsonian Curlew.

Numenius hudsonicus LATH. Ind. Orn. II. 1790, 712.

[B 550, C 442, R 559, C 645.]

GEOG. DIST.— All of North and South America, including the West Indies; breeds in the high north, and winters chiefly south of the United States.

266. Numenius borealis (FORST.).
   Eskimo Curlew.

Scolopax borealis FORST. Phil. Trans. LXII. 1772, 411, 431.
Numenius borealis LATH. Ind. Orn. II. 1790, 712.

[B 551, C 443, R 560, C 646.]

GEOG. DIST.— Eastern North America, breeding in the Arctic regions, and migrating south throughout South America.

[267.] **Numenius phæopus** (LINN.).
   Whimbrel.

Scolopax phæopus LINN. S. N. ed. 10, I. 1758, 146.
Numenius phæopus LATH. Gen. Syn. Suppl. I. 1787, 291.

[B —, C —, R 561, C 644.]

GEOG. DIST.— Northern parts of the Old World; occasional in Greenland.

[268.] **Numenius tahitiensis** (GMEL.).
   Bristle-thighed Curlew.

Scolopax tahitiensis GMEL. S. N. I. ii. 1788, 656.
Numenius tahitiensis RIDGW. Pr. U. S. Nat. Mus. III. Aug. 24, 1880, 201.

[B —, C 442 *bis*, R 562, C 647.]

GEOG. DIST.— Islands of the Pacific Ocean. Occasional on the coast of Alaska and Lower California.

FAMILY **CHARADRIIDÆ**. PLOVERS.

GENUS **VANELLUS** BRISSON.

Vanellus BRISS. Orn. V. 1760, 94.   Type, *Tringa vanellus* LINN.

[269.] **Vanellus vanellus** (LINN.).
   Lapwing.

Tringa vanellus LINN. S. N. ed. 10, I. 1758, 148.
Vanellus vanellus LICHT. Nom. Mus. Berol. 1854, 95.

[B —, C —, R 512, C 593.]

GEOG. DIST.— Northern parts of eastern hemisphere. In North America, occasional in Greenland, the islands in Norton Sound, Alaska, and on Long Island.

ORDER LIMICOLÆ. 99

GENUS **CHARADRIUS** LINNÆUS.

SUBGENUS **SQUATAROLA** CUVIER.

Squatarola CUV. Règ. An. I. 1817, 467. Type, *Tringa squatarola* LINN.

270. **Charadrius squatarola** (LINN.).
Black-bellied Plover.
Tringa squatarola LINN. S. N. ed. 10, I. 1758, 149.
Charadrius squatarola NAUM. Vög. Deutschl. VII. 1834, 250.

[B 510, C 395, R 513, C 580.]

GEOG. DIST.— Nearly cosmopolitan, but chiefly in the northern hemisphere, breeding far north, and migrating south in winter; in America, to the West Indies, Brazil, and Colombia.

SUBGENUS **CHARADRIUS** LINNÆUS.

Charadrius LINN. S. N. ed. 10, I. 1758, 150. Type, *C. apricarius* LINN.

[271.] **Charadrius apricarius** LINN.
Golden Plover.
Charadrius apricarius LINN. S. N. ed. 10, I. 1758, 150.

[B —, C —, R 514, C 583.]

GEOG. DIST.— Europe, south to Africa in winter; eastern Greenland.

272. **Charadrius dominicus** MÜLL.
American Golden Plover.
Charadrius dominicus MÜLL. S. N. Suppl. 1776, 116.

[B 503, C 396, R 515, C 581.]

GEOG. DIST.— Arctic America except coast of Bering Sea, migrating southward throughout North and South America to Patagonia.

272 a. **Charadrius dominicus fulvus** (GMEL.).
   Pacific Golden Plover.

Charadrius fulvus GMEL. S. N. I. ii. 1788, 687.
Charadrius dominicus fulvus RIDGW. Pr. U. S. Nat. Mus. III. 1880, 198.

[B—, C—, R 515a, C 582.]

GEOG. DIST.— Breeding from northern Asia to the Pribilof Islands and coast of Alaska, south in winter through China and India to Australia and Polynesia.

GENUS **ÆGIALITIS** BOIE.

SUBGENUS **OXYECHUS** REICHENBACH.

Oxyechus REICH. Syst. Av. 1853, p. xviii. Type, *Charadrius vociferus* LINN.

273. **Ægialitis vocifera** (LINN.).
   Killdeer.

Charadrius vociferus LINN. S. N. ed. 10, I. 1758, 150.
Ægialites vociferus BONAP. Geog. & Comp. List, 1838, 45.

[B 504, C 397, R 516, C 584.]

GEOG. DIST.— Temperate North America, breeding north to Newfoundland and Manitoba, migrating to the West Indies, and Central and northern South America. Bermuda.

SUBGENUS **ÆGIALITIS** BOIE.

Ægialitis BOIE, Isis, 1822, 558. Type, by elimination, *Charadrius hiaticula* LINN.

274. **Ægialitis semipalmata** BONAP.
   Semipalmated Plover.

Charadrius semipalmatus BONAP. Journ. Acad. Nat. Sci. Phila. V. 1825, 98.
Ægialites semipalmatus BONAP. Geog. & Comp. List, 1838, 45.

[B 507, C 399, R 517, C 586.]

GEOG. DIST.— Arctic and subarctic America, migrating south throughout tropical America, as far as Brazil, Peru, and the Galapagos.

275. Ægialitis hiaticula (LINN.).
Ring Plover.

Charadrius hiaticula LINN. S. N. ed. 10, I. 1758, 150.
Ægialitis hiaticula BOIE, Isis, 1822, 558.

[B —, C —, R 518, C 589.]

GEOG. DIST.— Northern parts of the Old World and portions of Arctic America, breeding on the west shore of Cumberland Gulf.

[276.] Ægialitis dubia (SCOP.).
Little Ring Plover.

Charadrius dubius SCOPOLI, Delic. F. et Fl. Insubr. II. 1786, 93.
Ægialites dubius SWINH. P. Z. S. 1871, 404.

[B —, C 400 *bis*, R 519, C 590.]

GEOG. DIST.— Most of the eastern hemisphere, breeding northward. Accidental on the coast of California and in Alaska.

277. Ægialitis meloda (ORD).
Piping Plover.

Charadrius melodus ORD, ed. WILS. VII. 1824, 71.
Ægialites melodus BONAP. Geog. & Comp. List, 1838, 45.

[B 508, C 400, R 520, C 587.]

GEOG. DIST.— Eastern North America, breeding from the coast of Virginia northward to Newfoundland; in winter, West Indies.

277 a. Ægialitis meloda circumcincta RIDGW.
Belted Piping Plover.

Ægialitis melodus var. *circumcinctus* RIDGW. Am. Nat. VIII. Feb. 1874, 109.

[B —, C 400*a*, R 520*a*, C 588.]

GEOG. DIST.— Mississippi Valley, breeding from northern Illinois north to Lake Winnipeg; more or less frequent eastward to the Atlantic coast.

278. Ægialitis nivosa Cass.
Snowy Plover.

Ægialitis nivosa Cass. in Baird, B. N. Am. 1858, 696.

[B 509, C 401, R 521, C 591.]

Geog. Dist.— Western United States, from California east to Kansas and western Gulf States; in winter, both coasts of Central America, and western South America to Chili. Western Cuba.

[279.] Ægialitis mongola (Pall.).
Mongolian Plover.

Charadrius mongolus Pall. Reise Russ. Reich. III. 1776, 700.
Ægialites mongolus Swinh. P. Z. S. 1870, 140.

[B —, C —, R —, C —.]

Geog. Dist.— Northern Asia, south in winter to India, Malay Archipelago, Philippines, and Australia. Choris Peninsula, Alaska; accidental.

Subgenus OCHTHODROMUS Reichenbach.

Ochthodromus Reich. Syst. Av. 1852, p. xviii. Type, *Charadrius wilsonius* Ord.

280. Ægialitis wilsonia (Ord).
Wilson's Plover.

Charadrius wilsonia Ord, Wils. Orn. IX. 1814, 77, pl. 73, fig. 5.
Ægialites wilsonius Bonap. Geog. & Comp. List, 1838, 45.

[B 506, C 398, R 522, C 585.]

Geog. Dist.— Coasts of North and South America, from Long Island and Lower California southward to Brazil and Peru, including the West Indies. Casual north to Nova Scotia.

Subgenus PODASOCYS Coues.

Podasocys Coues, Pr. Ac. Nat. Sci. Phila. 1866, 96. Type, *Charadrius montanus* Towns.

281. **Ægialitis montana** (TOWNS.).
   Mountain Plover.

   Charadrius montanus TOWNS. Jour. Ac. Nat. Sci. Phila. VII. 1837, 192.
   Ægialitis montanus CASS. in BAIRD, B. N. Am. 1858, 693.
   [B 505, C 402, R 523, C 592.]

   GEOG. DIST.—Chiefly the Plains, from central Kansas to the Rocky Mountains, north to the British boundary, breeding from Kansas northward; westward, especially in winter, to central and southern California, and south to Lower California and San Luis Potosi, Mexico. Accidental in Florida.

FAMILY **APHRIZIDÆ**. SURF BIRDS AND TURNSTONES.

SUBFAMILY **APHRIZINÆ**. SURF BIRDS.

GENUS **APHRIZA** AUDUBON.

Aphriza AUD. Orn. Biog. V. 1839, 249. Type, *A. townsendi* AUD. = *Tringa virgata* GMEL.

282. **Aphriza virgata** (GMEL.).
   Surf Bird.

   Tringa virgata GMEL. S. N. I. ii. 1788, 674.
   Aphriza virgata GRAY, Gen. B. III. 1847, pl. cxlvii.
   [B 511, C 403, R 511, C 594.]

   GEOG. DIST.— Pacific coast of America, from Alaska to Chili.

SUBFAMILY **ARENARIINÆ**. TURNSTONES.

GENUS **ARENARIA** BRISSON.

Arenaria BRISS. Orn. V. 1760, 132. Type, *Tringa interpres* LINN.

283. **Arenaria interpres** (LINN.).
   Turnstone.

   Tringa interpres LINN. S. N. ed. 10, I. 1758, 148.
   Arenaria interpres VIEILL. Nouv. Dict. d'Hist. Nat. XXIV, 1819, 345.

[B 515, C 406, R 509, C 598.]

GEOG. DIST.— Nearly cosmopolitan. In America from Greenland and Alaska to the Straits of Magellan; more or less common in the interior of North America, on the shores of the Great Lakes and the larger rivers. Breeds in high northern latitudes.

284. Arenaria melanocephala (VIG.).
Black Turnstone.

Strepsilas melanocephalus VIG. Zool. Jour. IV. Jan. 1829, 356.
Arenaria melanocephala STEJN. Auk, I. July, 1884, 229.

[B 516, C 406a, R 510, C 599.]

GEOG. DIST.— Pacific coast of North America, from Point Barrow, Alaska, to Santa Margarita Island, Lower California; breeding from Alaska south to British Columbia. Accidental in India.

FAMILY HÆMATOPODIDÆ. OYSTER-CATCHERS.

GENUS HÆMATOPUS LINNÆUS.

Hæmatopus LINN. S. N. ed. 10, I. 1758, 152. Type, *H. ostralegus* LINN.

[285.] Hæmatopus ostralegus LINN.
Oyster-catcher.

Hæmatopus ostralegus LINN. S. N. ed. 10, I. 1758, 152.

[B —, C —, R 506, C 595.]

GEOG. DIST.— Sea-coasts of Europe and part of Asia and Africa; occasional in Greenland.

286. Hæmatopus palliatus TEMM.
American Oyster-catcher.

Hæmatopus palliatus TEMM. Man. II. 1820, 532.

[B 512, C 404, R 507, C 596.]

GEOG. DIST.— Sea-coasts of temperate and tropical America, from New Jersey and western Mexico to Patagonia; occasional or accidental on the Atlantic coast north to Massachusetts and Grand Menan.

286.1. Hæmatopus frazari BREWST.
Frazar's Oyster-catcher.

Hæmatopus frazari BREWST. Auk, V. Jan. 1888, 84.

[B —, C —, R —, C —.]

GEOG. DIST.— Lower California (both coasts), north to Los Coronados Islands.

287. Hæmatopus bachmani AUD.
Black Oyster-catcher.

Hæmatopus bachmani AUD. Orn. Biog. V. 1839, 245, pl. 427.

[B 513, C 405, R 508, C 597.]

GEOG. DIST.— Pacific coast of North America, from the Aleutian Islands to La Paz, Lower California.

FAMILY **JACANIDÆ**. JACANAS.

GENUS **JACANA** BRISSON.

Jacana BRISS. Orn. V. 1760, 121. Type, by elimination, *Fulica spinosa* LINN.

[288.] Jacana spinosa (LINN.).
Mexican Jacana.

Fulica spinosa LINN. S. N. ed. 10, I. 1758, 152.
Jacana spinosa ELLIOT, Auk, V. July, 1888, 297.

[B —, C —, R 568, C 672.]

GEOG. DIST.— Lower Rio Grande Valley, Texas, south to Panama. Cuba; Haiti.

Order GALLINÆ. Gallinaceous Birds.

Suborder PHASIANI. Pheasants, Grouse, Partridges, Quails, etc.

Family **TETRAONIDÆ**. Grouse, Partridges, etc.

Subfamily **PERDICINÆ**. Partridges.

Genus **COLINUS** Lesson.

Colinus Less. Man. d'Orn. II. 1828, 190. Type, *Tetrao virginianus* Linn.

289. Colinus virginianus (Linn.).
Bob-white.

Tetrao virginianus Linn. S. N. ed. 10, I. 1758, 161.
Colinus virginianus Stejn. Auk, II. Jan. 1885, 45.

[B 471, C 389, R 480, C 571.]

Geog. Dist.— Eastern United States and southern Ontario, from southern Maine to the South Atlantic and Gulf States; west to central South Dakota, Nebraska, Kansas, Oklahoma and eastern Texas. Of late years has gradually extended its range westward along lines of railroad and settlements; also, introduced at various points in Colorado, New Mexico, Utah, Idaho, California, Oregon, and Washington. Breeds throughout its range.

289 *a*. Colinus virginianus floridanus (Coues).
Florida Bob-white.

Ortyx virginianus var. *floridanus* Coues, Key, 1872, 237.
Colinus virginianus floridanus Stejn. Auk, II. Jan. 1885, 45.

ORDER GALLINÆ.

[B—, C 389*a*, R 480*a*, C 572.]

GEOG. DIST.— Florida.

289 *b*. Colinus virginianus texanus (LAWR.).
Texan Bob-white.

Ortyx texanus LAWR. Ann. Lyc. N. Y. VI. April, 1853, 1.
Colinus virginianus texanus STEJN. Auk, II. Jan. 1885, 45.

[B 472, C 389*b*, R 480*b*, C 573.]

GEOG. DIST.— Southern and western Texas, south to central Tamaulipas and southern Nuevo Leon, Mexico. Western Mexico, near Guadalajara.

291. Colinus ridgwayi BREWST.
Masked Bob-white.

Colinus ridgwayi BREWST. Auk, II. April, 1885, 199.

[B—, C—, R—, C—.]

GEOG. DIST.— Sonora to southern Arizona.

GENUS **OREORTYX** BAIRD.

Oreortyx BAIRD, B. N. Am. 1858, 642. Type, *Ortyx picta* DOUGL.

292. Oreortyx pictus (DOUGL.).
Mountain Partridge.

Ortyx picta DOUGL. Trans. Linn. Soc. XVI. 1829, 143.
Oreortyx pictus BAIRD, B. N. Am. 1858, 642.

[B 473, C 390, R 481, C 574.]

GEOG. DIST. — Pacific coast region, from San Francisco Bay north to Washington. Introduced on Vancouver Island.

292 *a*. Oreortyx pictus plumiferus (GOULD).
Plumed Partridge.

Ortyx plumifera GOULD, P. Z. S. 1837, 42.
Oreortyx pictus var. *plumiferus* RIDGW. in Hist. N. Am. B. III. 1874, 476.

[B—, C—, R 481*a*, C—.]

GEOG. DIST.— Sierra Nevada (both slopes), east to Panamint Mountains, and to Mount Magruder, Nevada; south in the coast ranges from San Francisco Bay to Lower California (Campos).

292 *b*. **Oreortyx pictus confinis** ANTHONY.
San Pedro Partridge.

Oreortyx picta confinis ANTHONY, Proc. Cal. Ac. Sci. 2d. ser. II. Oct. 11, 1889, 74.

[B—, C—, R—, C—.]

GEOG. DIST.— San Pedro Mountains, Lower California.

GENUS **CALLIPEPLA** WAGLER.

SUBGENUS **CALLIPEPLA**.

Callipepla WAGLER, Isis, 1832, 277. Type, *C. strenua* WAGL. = *Ortyx squamatus* VIG.

293. **Callipepla squamata** (VIG.).
Scaled Partridge.

Ortyx squamatus VIG. Zool. Jour. V. 1830, 275.
Callipepla squamata GRAY, List Gen. B. ed. 1, 1840, 61.

[B 476, C 393, R 484, C 577.]

GEOG. DIST.— Tablelands of Mexico, from the valley of Mexico, north to central and western Texas, Santa Fé, New Mexico, and southern Arizona.

293 *a*. **Callipepla squamata castanogastris** BREWST.
Chestnut-bellied Scaled Partridge.

Callipepla squamata castanogastris BREWST. Bull. Nutt. Orn. Club, VIII. Jan. 1883, 34.

[B—, C—, R—, C—.]

GEOG. DIST.— Northeastern Mexico and Lower Rio Grande Valley in Texas.

SUBGENUS **LOPHORTYX** BONAPARTE.

Lophortyx BONAP. Geog. & Comp. List, 1838, 42. Type, *Tetrao californicus* SHAW.

294. Callipepla californica (SHAW).
California Partridge.

Tetrao californicus SHAW, Nat. Misc. IX. 1797 (?), pl. cccxlv.
Callipepla californica GOULD, Mon. Odont. "pt. i. 1844," pl. xvi.

[B 474, C 391, R 482, C 575.]

GEOG. DIST.— Coast region of California, south to Monterey. Introduced in Oregon, Washington, and British Columbia.

294 a. Callipepla californica vallicola RIDGWAY.
Valley Partridge.

Callipepla californica vallicola RIDGW. Pr. U. S. Nat. Mus. VIII. 1885, 355.

[B—, C—, R—, C—.]

GEOG. DIST.— Interior valleys of California and foothills of the Sierra Nevada, east to the Panamint Mountains, south to Cape St. Lucas.

295. Callipepla gambelii (GAMBEL).
Gambel's Partridge.

Lophortyx gambelii "NUTTALL," GAMB. Pr. Ac. Nat. Sci. Phila. 1843, 260.
Callipepla gambeli GAMBEL, Journ. Ac. Nat. Sci. Phila. n. s. I, 1849, 219.

[B 475, C 392, R 483, C 576.]

GEOG. DIST.— Western Texas, New Mexico, Arizona, southern Utah, southern Nevada, southern California in the Colorado Valley, and southward into northwestern Mexico.

GENUS **CYRTONYX** GOULD.

Cyrtonyx GOULD, Mon. Odont. "pt. i, 1844, pl. vii." Type, *Ortyx massena* LESS. = *O. montezumæ* VIG.

296. **Cyrtonyx montezumæ** (VIG.).
   Massena Partridge.

Ortyx montezumæ VIGORS, Zool. Journ. V. 1830, 275.
Cyrtonyx montezumæ STEJN. Auk, II. Jan. 1885, 46.

[B 477, C 394, R 485, C 578.]

GEOG. DIST.— Tablelands of Mexico, from the city of Mexico north to western Texas, New Mexico, and Arizona.

SUBFAMILY **TETRAONINÆ**. GROUSE.

GENUS **DENDRAGAPUS** ELLIOT.

SUBGENUS **DENDRAGAPUS**.

Dendragapus ELLIOT, Pr. Ac. Nat. Sci. Phila. 1864, 23. Type, *Tetrao obscurus* SAY.

297. **Dendragapus obscurus** (SAY).
   Dusky Grouse.

Tetrao obscurus SAY, LONG'S Exp. II. 1823, 14.
Dendragapus obscurus ELLIOT, Pr. Ac. Nat. Sci. Phila. 1864, 23.

[B 459, C 381, R 471, C 557.]

GEOG. DIST.— Rocky Mountains, from central Montana and southeastern Idaho to New Mexico and Arizona, eastward to the Black Hills, South Dakota, and westward to East Humboldt Mountains, Nevada.

297 *a*. **Dendragapus obscurus fuliginosus** RIDGW.
   Sooty Grouse.

Canace obscura var. *fuliginosa* RIDGW. Bull. Essex Inst. V. Dec. 1873, 199.
Dendragapus obscurus fuliginosus RIDGW. Pr. U. S. Nat. Mus. VIII. 1885, 355.

[B —, C 381*b*, R 471*a*, C 559.]

GEOG. DIST.— Northwest coast mountains, from California to Sitka, east to Nevada, western Idaho, and portions of British Columbia.

297 *b*. **Dendragapus obscurus richardsonii** (Dougl.).
   Richardson's Grouse.

Tetrao richardsonii "Sab. MS." Dougl. Linn. Trans. XVI. iii.
 1829, 141.
Dendragapus obscurus richardsoni Ridgw. Pr. U. S. Nat. Mus.
 VIII. 1885, 355.
   [B—, C 381*a*, R 471*b*, C 558.]

Geog. Dist.— Rocky Mountains, especially on the eastern slopes, from central Montana, northern Wyoming, and southeastern Idaho into British America to Liard River.

Subgenus **CANACHITES** Stejneger.

Canachites Stejn. Pr. U. S. Nat. Mus. VIII. 1885, 410. Type.
Tetrao canadensis Linn.

298. **Dendragapus canadensis** (Linn.).
   Canada Grouse.

Tetrao canadensis Linn. S. N. ed. 10, I. 1758, 159.
Dendragapus canadensis Turner, Pr. U. S. Nat. Mus. VIII.
 1885, 245.
   [B 460, C 380, R 472, C 555.]

Geog. Dist.— British America, east of the Rocky Mountains, and west in Alaska to the Pacific coast at Kadiak and St. Michaels, southeastward to northern Minnesota, northern Michigan, northern New York, and northern New England.

299. **Dendragapus franklinii** (Dougl.).
   Franklin's Grouse.

Tetrao franklinii Dougl. Trans. Linn. Soc. XVI. iii. 1829, 139.
Dendragapus franklinii Ridgw. Pr. U. S. Nat. Mus. VIII. 1885,
 355.
   [B 461, C 380*a*, R 472*a*, C 556.]

Geog. Dist.— Northern Rocky Mountains, from northwestern Montana to the coast ranges of Oregon and Washington, and northward in British America, reaching the Pacific coast of southern Alaska (lat. 60° N.).

Genus **BONASA** Stephens.

Bonasa Steph. Gen. Zool. XI. 1819, 298. Type, *Tetrao umbellus* Linn.

300. **Bonasa umbellus** (Linn.).
Ruffed Grouse.

Tetrao umbellus Linn. S. N. ed. 12, I. 1766, 275.
Bonasa umbellus Steph. Gen. Zool. XI. 1819, 300.

[B 465, C 385, R 473, C 565.]

Geog. Dist.— Eastern United States and southern Canada, west to Minnesota, south in the mountains to northern Georgia, Mississippi, and Arkansas.

300 a. **Bonasa umbellus togata** (Linn.).
Canadian Ruffed Grouse.

Tetrao togatus Linn. S. N. ed. 12, 1766, 275.
Bonasa umbellus togata Ridgw. Pr. U. S. Nat. Mus. VIII. 1885, 355.

[B —, C —, R —, C —.]

Geog. Dist.— The spruce forests of northern New England, northern New York, and the British Provinces, west to Oregon, Washington, and British Columbia, north to James Bay.

300 b. **Bonasa umbellus umbelloides** (Dougl.).
Gray Ruffed Grouse.

Tetrao umbelloides Dougl. Trans. Linn. Soc. XVI. iii. 1829, 148.
Bonasa umbellus var. *umbelloides* Baird, B. N. Am. 1858, 925.

[B 465*, C 385*a*, R 473*a*, C 566.]

Geog. Dist.— Rocky Mountain region of the United States and British America, north to Alaska, east to Manitoba.

300 c. **Bonasa umbellus sabini** (Dougl.).
Oregon Ruffed Grouse.

Tetrao sabini Dougl. Trans. Linn. Soc. XVI. iii. 1829, 137.
Bonasa umbellus var. *sabinei* Coues, Key, 1872, 235.

ORDER GALLINÆ.

[B 466, C 385*b*, R 473*b*, C 567.]

GEOG. DIST.— Coast ranges of northern California, Oregon, Washington, and British Columbia.

GENUS **LAGOPUS** BRISSON.

Lagopus BRISS. Ornith. I. 1760, 181. Type, *Tetrao lagopus* LINN.

301. **Lagopus lagopus** (LINN.).
Willow Ptarmigan.

Tetrao lagopus LINN. S. N. ed. 10, I. 1758, 159.
Lagopus lagopus STEJN. Pr. U. S. Nat. Mus. VIII. 1885, 20.

[B 467, 470, C 386, R 474, C 568.]

GEOG. DIST.— Arctic regions; in America south to Sitka and the British Provinces. Breeding range restricted to the arctic and subarctic regions, mainly north of 55° N. lat. Accidental in New England (Bangor, Me., and Essex Co., Mass.).

301*a*. **Lagopus lagopus alleni** STEJN.
Allen's Ptarmigan.

Lagopus alba alleni STEJN. Auk, I. Oct. 1884, 369.
Lagopus lagopus alleni STEJN. Pr. U. S. Nat. Mus. VIII. 1885, 20.

[B —, C —, R —, C —.]

GEOG. DIST.— Newfoundland.

302. **Lagopus rupestris** (GMEL.).
Rock Ptarmigan.

Tetrao rupestris GMEL. S. N. I. ii. 1788, 751.
Lagopus rupestris LEACH, Zool. Misc. II. 1817, 290.

[B 468, C 387, R 475, C 569.]

GEOG. DIST.— Arctic America (except the northern extremity), from Alaska to Labrador and the Gulf of St. Lawrence; portions of Greenland; Aleutian Islands.

302 *a*. **Lagopus rupestris reinhardi** (BREHM).
    Reinhardt's Ptarmigan.

Tetrao reinhardi BREHM, Lehrb. Eur. Vög. 1823, 440.
Lagopus rupestris reinhardti BLASIUS, List Eur. B. 1862, 16.

[B —, C —, R —, C —.]

GEOG. DIST.— Greenland, western shores of Cumberland Gulf, and northern extremity of Labrador.

302 *b*. **Lagopus rupestris nelsoni** STEJN.
    Nelson's Ptarmigan.

Lagopus rupestris nelsoni STEJN. Auk, I. July, 1884, 226.

[B —, C —, R —, C —.]

GEOG. DIST.— Unalaska, and some adjacent Aleutian Islands.

302 *c*. **Lagopus rupestris atkhensis** (TURNER).
    Turner's Ptarmigan.

Lagopus mutus atkhensis TURNER, Pr. U. S. Nat. Mus. V. July 29, 1882, 227, 230.
Lagopus rupestris atkhensis NELSON, Cruise Corwin, 1883, 56 e + 82.

[B —, C —, R —, C —.]

GEOG. DIST.— Atka, one of the Aleutian Islands.

303. **Lagopus welchi** BREWST.
    Welch's Ptarmigan.

Lagopus welchi BREWST. Auk, II. April, 1885, 194.

[B —, C —, R —, C —.]

GEOG. DIST.— Newfoundland.

304. **Lagopus leucurus** SWAINS. & RICH.
    White-tailed Ptarmigan.

Lagopus leucurus SWAINS. & RICH. Fauna Bor. Amer. II. 1831, pl. 63.

[B 469, C 388, R 476, C 570.]

GEOG. DIST.— Alpine summits of the mountains of western North America, from New Mexico to Liard River, British America, west on the highest ranges of Oregon, Washington, and British Columbia.

GENUS **TYMPANUCHUS** GLOGER.

Tympanuchus GLOGER, Gemeinnutzig. Hand. und Hilfsbuch Naturg. 1842, 396. Type, *Tetrao cupido* LINN.

305. Tympanuchus americanus (REICH.).
Prairie Hen.

Cupidonia americanus REICH. Syst Av. 1852, p. xxix; based on Vollst. Naturg. Hühnen. pl. 217, figs. 1896-1898.
Tympanuchus americanus RIDGW. Auk, Jan. III. 1886, 133.

[B 464, C 384, R 477, C 563.]

GEOG. DIST.— Prairies of the Mississippi Valley; south to Louisiana and Texas, east to Kentucky, Indiana, Ohio, Michigan, and Ontario; west through eastern portions of North Dakota, South Dakota, Nebraska, Kansas, and the Indian Territory; north to Manitoba; general tendency to extension of range westward and contraction eastward; migration north and south in Minnesota, Iowa, and Missouri.

305 *a*. Tympanuchus americanus attwateri (BENDIRE).
Attwater's Prairie Hen.

Tympanuchus attwateri BENDIRE, Forest and Stream, XL. No. 20, May 18, 1893, 425.
Tympanuchus americanus attwateri A. O. U. Check-List, 6th Suppl. Auk, XI. April, 1894, 130.

[B 464, *part*, C 384, *part*, R 477, *part*, C 563, *part*.]

GEOG. DIST.— Coast region of Louisiana and Texas.

306. Tympanuchus cupido (LINN.).
Heath Hen.

Tetrao cupido LINN. S. N. ed. 10, I. 1758, 160.
Tympanuchus cupido RIDGW. Pr. U. S. Nat. Mus. VIII. 1885, 355.

[B 464, *part*, C 384, *part*, R 477, *part*, C 563 *part*.]

GEOG. DIST.— Island of Martha's Vineyard, Mass. (Formerly southern New England and parts of the Middle States.)

307. Tympanuchus pallidicinctus RIDGW.
Lesser Prairie Hen.

Cupidonia cupido var. *pallidicincta* RIDGW. Bull. Essex Inst. V. Dec. 1873, 199.
Tympanuchus pallidicinctus RIDGW. Pr. U. S. Nat. Mus. VIII. 1885, 355.

[B—, C 384*a*, R 477*a*, C 564.]

GEOG. DIST.— Eastern edge of the Great Plains from western and probably southern Texas northward through Indian Territory to Kansas.

GENUS **PEDIOCÆTES** BAIRD.

Pediocætes BAIRD, B. N. Am. 1858, 625. Type, *Tetrao phasianellus* LINN.

308. Pediocætes phasianellus (LINN.).
Sharp-tailed Grouse.

Tetrao phasianellus LINN. S. N. ed. 10, I. 1758, 160.
Pediocætes phasianellus ELLIOT, Pr. Ac. Nat. Sci. Phila. 1862, 403 (nec BAIRD, 1858, qui subsp. *columbianus*).

[B—, C 383, R 478, C 561.]

GEOG. DIST.— Interior of British America, from Lake Superior and Hudson Bay to Fort Simpson.

308 *a*. Pediocætes phasianellus columbianus (ORD).
Columbian Sharp-tailed Grouse.

Phasianus columbianus ORD, GUTHRIE'S Geog. 2d Am. ed. II. 1815, 317.
Pediæcetes phasianellus var. *columbianus* COUES, Key, 1872, 234.

[B 463, C 383*a*, R 478*a*, C 562.]

GEOG. DIST.— Plains of the northwestern United States and British Columbia to central portions of Alaska; northward chiefly west of the main Rocky Mountains; eastward in Montana and Wyoming; southward to Utah, northern Nevada, and northeastern California.

308 *b*. **Pediocætes phasianellus campestris** Ridgw.
   Prairie Sharp-tailed Grouse.

Pediæcetes phasianellus campestris Ridgw. Proc. Biol. Soc. Wash. II. April 10, 1884, 93.

[B —, C —, R —, C —.]

Geog. Dist.— Plains and prairies of the United States east of the Rocky Mountains; north to Manitoba; east to Wisconsin and Illinois; south to New Mexico.

Genus **CENTROCERCUS** Swainson.

Centrocercus Swains. in Sw. & Rich. Fauna Bor. Am. II. 1831, 358, 496.   Type, *Tetrao urophasianus* Bonap.

309. **Centrocercus urophasianus** (Bonap.).
   Sage Grouse.

Tetrao urophasianus Bonap. Zool. Journ. III. 1827, 213.
Centrocercus urophasianus Swains. in Sw. & Rich. Fauna Bor. Am. II. 1831, 497, pl. 58.

[B 462, C 382, R 479, C 560.]

Geog. Dist.— Sage regions of the Rocky Mountain plateau and westward, chiefly within the United States, but north to Assiniboia and the dry interior of British Columbia; east to North Dakota, South Dakota, Nebraska, and Colorado; south to northern New Mexico, Utah, and Nevada; west in California, Oregon and Washington to the Sierra Nevada and Cascade Range.

Family **PHASIANIDÆ**.   Pheasants, etc.

Subfamily **MELEAGRINÆ**.   Turkeys.

Genus **MELEAGRIS** Linnæus.

Meleagris Linn. S. N. ed. 10, I. 1758, 156.   Type, *M. gallopavo* Linn.

310. **Meleagris gallopavo** LINN.
Wild Turkey.

Meleagris gallopavo LINN. S. N. ed. 10, I. 1758, 156.

[B 457, C 379*a*, R 470*a*, C 554.]

GEOG. DIST.— United States, from Chesapeake Bay to the Gulf coast, and west to the Plains, along wooded river valleys; formerly north to southern Maine, southern Ontario, and up the Missouri River to North Dakota.

310 *a*. **Meleagris gallopavo mexicana** (GOULD).
Mexican Turkey.

Meleagris mexicana GOULD, P. Z. S. 1856, 61.
Meleagris gallopavo var. *mexicana* BAIRD, Hist. N. Am. B. III. 1874, 410.

[B 458, C 379, R 470, C 553.]

GEOG. DIST.— Southwestern United States, from western Texas to Arizona; south over the tablelands of Mexico.

310 *b*. **Meleagris gallopavo osceola** SCOTT.
Florida Wild Turkey.

Meleagris gallopavo osceola SCOTT, Auk, VII. Oct. 1890, 376.

[B 457, *part*, C 379*a*, *part*, R 470*a*, *part*, C 554, *part*.]

GEOG. DIST.— Southern Florida.

310 *c*. **Meleagris gallopavo ellioti** SENNETT.
Rio Grande Turkey.

Meleagris gallopavo ellioti SENNETT, Auk, IX. April, 1892, 167, pl. iii.

[B 458, *part*, C 379, *part*, R 470, *part*, C 553, *part*.]

GEOG. DIST.— Lowlands of southern Texas and northeastern Mexico.

SUBORDER **PENELOPES.** CURASSOWS AND GUANS.

FAMILY **CRACIDÆ.** CURASSOWS AND GUANS.

SUBFAMILY **PENELOPINÆ.** GUANS.

GENUS **ORTALIS** MERREM.

Ortalis MERR. Av. Rar. Icones et Desc. II. 1786, 40. Type, *Phasianus motmot* LINN.

311. **Ortalis vetula maccalli** BAIRD.
   Chachalaca.
Ortalida maccalli BAIRD, B. N. Am. 1858, 611.
Ortalida vetula var. *maccalli* BAIRD, Hist. N. Am. B. III. 1874, 398.
[B 456, C 378, R 469, C 552.]
   GEOG. DIST.— Valley of the Lower Rio Grande, and southward in Mexico to Vera Cruz.

ORDER COLUMBÆ. PIGEONS.

FAMILY **COLUMBIDÆ.** PIGEONS.

GENUS **COLUMBA** LINNÆUS.

Columba LINN. S. N. ed. 10, I. 1758, 162. Type, by elimination, *C. œnas* LINN.

312. **Columba fasciata** SAY.
   Band-tailed Pigeon.
Columba fasciata SAY, LONG'S Exp. II. 1823, 10.

[B 445, C 367, R 456, C 539.]

GEOG. DIST.— Western United States, from the Rocky Mountains to the Pacific; north to Washington and British Columbia; south to Mexico and the highlands of Guatemala; distribution irregular, chiefly in wooded mountain regions.

312 a. Columba fasciata vioscæ BREWST.
Viosca's Pigeon.

Columba fasciata vioscæ BREWST. Auk, V. Jan. 1888, 86.

[B —, C —, R —, C —.]

GEOG. DIST.— Lower California.

313. Columba flavirostris WAGL.
Red-billed Pigeon.

Columba flavirostris WAGL. Isis, 1831, 519.

[B 446, C 368, R 457, C 540.]

GEOG. DIST.— Southern border of the United States, from Arizona and the Rio Grande Valley south to Costa Rica, breeding throughout its United States range.

314. Columba leucocephala LINN.
White-crowned Pigeon.

Columba leucocephala LINN. S. N. ed. 10, I. 1758, 164.

[B 447, C 369, R 458, C 541.]

GEOG. DIST.— Southern Keys of Florida, the Bahamas, the Greater Antilles and some of the Lesser Antilles, and the coast of Honduras.

GENUS **ECTOPISTES** SWAINSON.

Ectopistes SWAINS. Zool. Journ. III. 1827, 362. Type, *Columba migratoria* LINN.

315. Ectopistes migratorius (LINN.).
Passenger Pigeon.

Columba migratoria LINN. S. N. ed. 12, I. 1766, 285 ($\male$).
Ectopistes migratoria SWAINS. Zool. Journ. III. 1827, 362.

ORDER COLUMBÆ.

[B 448, C 370, R 459, C 543.]

GEOG. DIST.— Eastern North America, from Hudson Bay southward, and west to the Great Plains, straggling thence to Nevada and Washington. Breeding range now mainly restricted to portions of the Canadas and the northern border of the United States, as far west as Manitoba and the Dakotas.

GENUS **ZENAIDURA** BONAPARTE.

Zenaidura BONAP. Consp. Av. II. Dec. 1854, 84. Type, *Columba carolinensis* LINN. = *C. macroura* LINN.

316. **Zenaidura macroura** (LINN.).
Mourning Dove.

Columba macroura LINN. S. N. ed. 10, 1758, 164 (part).
Zenaidura macroura RIDGW. Pr. U. S. Nat. Mus. VIII. 1885, 355.

[B 451, C 371, R 460, C 544.]

GEOG. DIST.— Temperate North America; from southern Maine, southern Canada, and British Columbia, south to Panama and the West Indies, breeding throughout its North American range.

GENUS **ZENAIDA** BONAPARTE.

Zenaida BONAP. Geog. & Comp. List, 1838, 41. Type, *Columba zenaida* BONAP.

317. **Zenaida zenaida** (BONAP.).
Zenaida Dove.

Columba zenaida BONAP. Jour. Ac. Nat. Sci. Phila. V. 1825, 30.
Zenaida zenaida RIDGW. Pr. U. S. Nat. Mus. VIII. 1885, 355.

[B 449, C 372, R 462, C 545.]

GEOG. DIST.— Florida Keys, Bahamas, Cuba, Jamaica, Porto Rico, Santa Cruz, Sombrero, and coast of Yucatan.

GENUS **LEPTOTILA** SWAINSON.

Leptotila SWAINS. Class. Bds. II. 1837, 349. Type, *P*[*eristera*]. *rufaxilla* Selby, Nat. Libr. V. pl. 24.

318. Leptotila fulviventris brachyptera (SALVADORI).
   White-fronted Dove.
   Leptoptila brachyptera SALVADORI, Cat. Bds. Brit. Mus. XXI. 1893, p. 545.
   Leptotila fulviventris brachyptera A. O. U. Check-List, 7th Suppl. Auk, XII, April, 1895, 167.
   [B—, C—, R 463, C 542.]
   GEOG. DIST.— Valley of the Lower Rio Grande in Texas, and southward to Nicaragua.

GENUS **MELOPELIA** BONAPARTE.

Melopelia BONAP. Consp. Av. II. Dec. 1854, 81. Type, *Columba leucoptera* LINN.

319. Melopelia leucoptera (LINN.).
   White-winged Dove.
   Columba leucoptera LINN. S. N. ed. 10, I. 1758, 164.
   Melopelia leucoptera BONAP. Consp. Av. II. Dec. 1854, 81.
   [B 450, C 373, R 464, C 546.]
   GEOG. DIST.— Southern border of the United States, from Florida, Texas, New Mexico, Arizona, and Lower California, southward to Costa Rica and the West Indies; Cuba; Jamaica; straggles northward to Colorado. Breeding range, in the United States, southern Texas, New Mexico, and Arizona.

GENUS **COLUMBIGALLINA** BOIE.

Columbigallina BOIE, Isis, 1826, 977. Type, *Columba passerina* LINN.

320. Columbigallina passerina terrestris CHAPM.
   Ground Dove.
   Columba passerina LINN. Syst. Nat. ed. 10, I. 1758, 165.
   Columbigallina passerina terrestris CHAPMAN, Bull Am. Mus. Nat. Hist., IV, 1892, 292.
   [B 453, C 374, R 465, C 547.]
   GEOG. DIST.— South Atlantic and Gulf States; West Indies and northern South America. Breeding, in the United States, from South Carolina to Louisiana, chiefly coastwise.

ORDER COLUMBÆ.   123

320 *a*. **Columbigallina passerina pallescens** (BAIRD).
   Mexican Ground Dove.

   Chamæpelia passerina ? var. *pallescens* BAIRD, Proc. Acad. Nat. Sci. Phila. 1859, 305.
   Columbigallina passerina pallescens FERRARI-PEREZ, Pr. U. S. Nat. Mus. IX, 1886, 175.

   [B 453, *part*, C 374, *part*, R 465, *part*, C 547, *part*.]

   GEOG. DIST.— Mexico, and contiguous territory of United States from Texas to Lower California; south on both Mexican coasts to Central America.

   GENUS **SCARDAFELLA** BONAPARTE.

   Scardafella BONAP. Consp. Av. II. Dec. 1854, 85. Type, *Columba squamosa* TEMM.

321. **Scardafella inca** (LESS.).
   Inca Dove.

   Chamæpelia inca LESSON, Descr. Mam. et Ois. 1847, 211.
   Scardafella inca BONAP. Consp. Av. II. Dec. 1854, 85.

   [B 452, C 375, R 466, C 549.]

   GEOG. DIST.— Rio Grande Valley, southern Arizona, and Lower California, south to Nicaragua.

   GENUS **GEOTRYGON** GOSSE.

   Geotrygon GOSSE, B. Jam. 1847, 316, foot-note. Type, *G. sylvatica* GOSSE = *Columba cristata* TEMM.

[322.] **Geotrygon martinica** (LINN.).
   Key West Quail-Dove.

   Columba martinica LINN. S. N. ed. 12, I. 1766, 283.
   Geotrygon martinica BONAP. Consp. Av. II. Dec. 1854, 74.

   [B 454, C 376, R 467, C 550.]

   GEOG. DIST.— Key West, and some of the other Florida Keys; Bahamas; Cuba; Hayti.

[322.1.] **Geotrygon montana** (LINN.).
   Ruddy Quail-Dove.
Columba montana LINN. S. N. ed. 10, I. 1758, 163.
Geotrygon montana BONAP. Consp. II, Dec. 1854, 72.

[B —, C —, R —, C —.]

GEOG. DIST.—Tropical America in general, including West Indies; north to Cuba and eastern Mexico; accidental at Key West, Florida.

GENUS **STARNŒNAS** BONAPARTE.

Starnœnas BONAP. Geog. & Comp. List, 1838, 41. Type, *Columba cyanocephala* LINN.

[323.] **Starnœnas cyanocephala** (LINN.).
   Blue-headed Quail-dove.
Columba cyanocephala LINN. S. N. ed. 10, I. 1758, 163.
Starnœnas cyanocephala BONAP. Geog. & Comp. List, 1838, 41.

[B 455, C 377, R 468, C 551.]

GEOG. DIST.— Florida Keys and Cuba.

ORDER RAPTORES. BIRDS OF PREY.

SUBORDER SARCORHAMPHI. AMERICAN VULTURES.

FAMILY **CATHARTIDÆ**. AMERICAN VULTURES.

GENUS **PSEUDOGRYPHUS** RIDGWAY.

Pseudogryphus RIDGW. Hist. N. Am. B. III. Jan. 1874, 337, 338. Type, *Vultur californianus* SHAW.

324. Pseudogryphus californianus (SHAW).
California Vulture.

Vultur californianus SHAW, Nat. Misc. IX. 1797, pl. ccci.
Pseudogryphus californianus RIDGW. Hist. N. Am. B. III. 1874, 338.

[B 2, C 364, R 453, C 536.]

GEOG. DIST.— Coast ranges of southern California from Monterey Bay southward into Lower California; formerly north to Frazer River.

GENUS **CATHARTES** ILLIGER.

Cathartes ILLIG. Prodr. 1811, 236. Type, by elimination, *Vultur aura* LINN.

325. Cathartes aura (LINN.).
Turkey Vulture.

Vultur aura LINN. S. N. ed. 10, I. 1758, 86.
Cathartes aura SPIX, Aves Bras. I. 1825, 2.

[B 1, C 365, R 454, C 537.]

GEOG. DIST.— Temperate North America, from New Jersey, Ohio Valley, Saskatchewan region, and British Columbia southward to Patagonia and the Falkland Islands. Casual in New England.

GENUS **CATHARISTA** VIEILLOT.

Catharista VIEILL. Analyse, 1816, 21. Type, by elimination, *Vultur atratus* BARTR.

326. Catharista atrata (BARTR.).
Black Vulture.

Vultur atratus BARTR. Trav. Car. 1792, 285.
Catharista atrata GRAY, Handl. I. 1869, 3.

[B 3, C 366, R 455, C 538.]

GEOG. DIST.— South Atlantic and Gulf States, north regularly to North Carolina and the lower Ohio Valley, west to the Great Plains, and south through Mexico and Central America, the West Indies, and most of South America. Straggling north to New York, New England, and South Dakota. Breeds in the United States from North Carolina coastwise to Texas, and in the interior to Indiana, Illinois, and Kansas.

Suborder FALCONES. Vultures, Falcons, Hawks, Buzzards, Eagles, Kites, Harriers, etc.

FAMILY **FALCONIDÆ**. VULTURES, FALCONS, HAWKS, EAGLES, ETC.

SUBFAMILY **ACCIPITRINÆ**. KITES, BUZZARDS, HAWKS, GOSHAWKS, EAGLES, ETC.

GENUS **ELANOIDES** VIEILLOT.

Elanoides VIEILL. Nouv. Dict. d'Hist. Nat. XXIV. 1818, 101.
Type, *Falco furcatus* = *F. forficatus* LINN.

327. Elanoides forficatus (LINN.).
    Swallow-tailed Kite.

Falco forficatus LINN. S. N. ed. 10, I. 1758, 89.
Elanoides forficatus COUES, Pr. Ac. Nat. Sci. Phila. 1875, 345.

[B 34, C 337, R 426, C 493.]

GEOG. DIST.— United States, especially in the interior, from the Carolinas and Minnesota southward, throughout Central and South America; westward to the Great Plains. Casual eastward to southern New England, and northward to Manitoba and Assiniboia. Breeding range irregularly coincident with general distribution in the United States. Accidental in England.

GENUS **ELANUS** SAVIGNY.

Elanus SAVIG. Descr. de l'Égypte, 1809, 97. Type, *E. cæsius* = *Falco melanopterus* DAUD.

328. Elanus leucurus (VIEILL.).
    White-tailed Kite.

Milvus leucurus VIEILL. Nouv. Dict. d'Hist. Nat. XX. 1818, 563 (errore 556).
Elanus leucurus BONAP. Geog. & Comp. List, 1838, 4.

[B 35, C 336, R 427, C 492.]

GEOG. DIST.— Southern United States, from South Carolina and southern Illinois to Texas and California, southward to Chili and Argentine Republic; casual in Michigan. Breeds irregularly throughout its general distribution in the United States.

GENUS **ICTINIA** VIEILLOT.

Ictinia VIEILL. Analyse, 1816, 24. Type, *Falco mississippiensis* WILS.

329. Ictinia mississippiensis (WILS.).
   Mississippi Kite.

Falco mississippiensis WILS. Am. Orn. III. 1811, 80, pl. 25, fig. 1.
Ictinia mississippiensis GRAY, Gen. B. I. 1845, 26.

[B 36, C 335, R 428, C 491.]

GEOG. DIST.— Southern United States, east of the Rocky Mountains; southward regularly from South Carolina on the coast, and casually from Pennsylvania, Wisconsin and Iowa in the interior, to Guatemala.

GENUS **ROSTRHAMUS** LESSON.

Rostrhamus LESS. Traité, 1831, 55. Type, *Falco hamatus* ILLIG.

330. Rostrhamus sociabilis (VIEILL.).
   Everglade Kite.

Herpetotheres sociabilis VIEILL. Nouv. Dict. d'Hist. Nat. XVIII. 1817, 318.
Rostrhamus sociabilis D'ORB. Voy. Ois. II. 1847, 73.

[B 37, C 334, R 429, C 490.]

GEOG. DIST.— Florida, Cuba, eastern Mexico, Central America, and eastern South America, to the Argentine Republic.

GENUS **CIRCUS** LACÉPÈDE.

Circus LACÉP. Mem. de l'Inst. III. 1801, 506. Type, *Falco cyaneus* LINN.

331. Circus hudsonius (Linn.).
   Marsh Hawk.

Falco hudsonius Linn. S. N. ed. 12, I. 1766, 128.
Circus hudsonius Vieill. Ois. Am. Sept. I. 1807, pl. 9.

[B 38, C 333, R 430, C 489.]

Geog. Dist.— North America in general; south to Panama and Cuba. Breeds throughout its North American range.

Genus ACCIPITER Brisson.

Subgenus ACCIPITER.

Accipiter Briss. Orn. I. 1760, 310. Type, by elimination, *Falco nisus* Linn.

332. Accipiter velox (Wils.).
   Sharp-shinned Hawk.

Falco velox Wils. Am. Orn. V. 1812, 116, pl. 45, fig. 1.
Accipiter velox Vigors, Zool. Journ. I. 1824, 338.

[B 17, C 338, R 432, C 494.]

Geog. Dist.— North America in general; south to Panama. Breeds throughout its North American range.

333. Accipiter cooperii (Bonap.).
   Cooper's Hawk.

Falco cooperii Bonap. Am. Orn. II. 1828, 1, pl. x. fig. 1.
Accipiter cooperi Gray, List B. Brit. Mus. Accipitres, 1844, 38.

[B 15, 16, C 339, R 431, C 495.]

Geog. Dist.— North America, from southern British America south to southern Mexico. Breeds throughout its range.

Subgenus ASTUR Lacépède.

Astur Lacép. Mem. de l'Inst. III. 1801, 505. Type, *Falco palumbarius* Linn.

334. Accipiter atricapillus (WILS.).
American Goshawk.

Falco atricapillus WILS. Am. Orn. VI. 1812, 80, pl. 52, fig. 3.
Accipiter atricapillus SEEBOHM, Brit. Birds, I. 1883, iv.

[B 14, C 340, R 433, C 496.]

GEOG. DIST.—Northern and eastern North America, south in winter to the Middle States and southern Rocky Mountain region; casually west to Oregon. Accidental in England. Breeding range restricted to the Canadian Fauna of the United States and northward.

334 a. Accipiter atricapillus striatulus RIDGW.
Western Goshawk.

Astur atricapillus var. *striatulus* RIDGW. in Hist. N. Am. B. III. 1874, 240.
Accipiter atricapillus striatulus RIDGW. Pr. U. S. Nat. Mus. VIII. 1885, 355.

[B—, C—, R 433 a, C 497.]

GEOG. DIST.— Western North America; north to Sitka, Alaska; south to California; east to Idaho. Breeds in the Sierra Nevada south to Lat. 38°.

GENUS **PARABUTEO** RIDGWAY.

Parabuteo RIDGW. in Hist. N. Am. B. III. Jan. 1874, 250. Type, *Falco harrisi* AUD.

335. Parabuteo unicinctus harrisi (AUD.).
Harris's Hawk.

Falco harrisi AUD. B. Am. V. 1839, 30, pl. 392.
Parabuteo unicinctus var. *harrisi* RIDGW. in Hist. N. Am. B. III. Jan. 1874, 250.

[B 46, C 348, R 434, C 512.]

GEOG. DIST.— Mississippi, Louisiana, Texas, southern New Mexico, southern Arizona, and Lower California; southward to Panama. Breeds from southern Texas westward to California, and southward.

GENUS **BUTEO** CUVIER.

Buteo CUV. Leç. Anat. Comp. I. tabl. ii. Ois. 1779–1800. Type, *Falco buteo* LINN.

[336.] **Buteo buteo** (LINN.).
European Buzzard.

Falco buteo LINN. S. N. ed. 10, I. 1758, 90.
Buteo buteo LICHT. Nomencl. Mus. Berol. 1854, 3.

[B —, C —, R 435, C —.]

GEOG. DIST.— Europe and Western Asia. Accidental in North America (Michigan?).

337. **Buteo borealis** (GMEL.).
Red-tailed Hawk.

Falco borealis GMEL. S. N. I. ii. 1788, 266.
Buteo borealis VIEILL. Nouv. Dict. d'Hist. Nat. IV. 1816, 478.

[B 23, C 351, R 436, C 516.]

GEOG. DIST.— Eastern North America, west to the Great Plains, north to about Lat. 60°, south to eastern Mexico. Breeds throughout its range, except possibly the extreme southern portion.

337 *a*. **Buteo borealis kriderii** HOOPES.
Krider's Hawk.

Buteo borealis var. *kriderii* HOOPES, Pr. Ac. Nat. Sci. Phila. 1873, 238, pl. 5.

[B —, C 351*c*, R 436*a*, C 519.]

GEOG. DIST.— Plains of the United States, from Wyoming and the Dakotas to Minnesota, and south to Texas; casual in Iowa and Illinois.

337 *b*. **Buteo borealis calurus** (CASS.).
Western Red-tail.

Buteo calurus CASS. Pr. Ac. Nat. Sci. Phila. VII. 1855, 281.
Buteo borealis var. *calurus* RIDGW. Bull. Essex Inst. V. Nov. 1873, 186.

[B 20, 24, C 351*a*, R 436*b*, C 517.]

GEOG. DIST.— Western North America, from the Rocky Mountains to the Pacific, south into Mexico; casual east to Illinois.

337 *c*. **Buteo borealis lucasanus** RIDGW.
Saint Lucas Red-tail.

Buteo borealis var. *lucasanus* RIDGW. in COUES'S Key, 1872, 216 (under *B. borealis*).

[B—, C 351*b*, R 436*c*, C 518.]

GEOG. DIST.— Peninsula of Lower California.

337 *d*. **Buteo borealis harlani** (AUD.).
Harlan's Hawk.

Falco harlani AUD. Orn. Biog. I. 1830, 441, pl. 86.
Buteo borealis harlani RIDGW. Auk, VII. April, 1890, p. 205.

[B 22, C 350, R 438, C 515.]

GEOG. DIST.— Gulf States and lower Mississippi Valley, north casually to Pennsylvania, Iowa, and Kansas; south to Central America.

339. **Buteo lineatus** (GMEL.).
Red-shouldered Hawk.

Falco lineatus GMEL. S. N. I. ii. 1788, 268.
Buteo lineatus VIEILL. Nouv. Dict. d'Hist. Nat. IV. 1816, 478.

[B 25, C 352, R 439, C 520.]

GEOG. DIST.— Eastern North America to Manitoba and Nova Scotia; west to Texas and the Plains; south to the Gulf States and Mexico. Breeds throughout its range.

339 *a*. **Buteo lineatus alleni** RIDGW.
Florida Red-shouldered Hawk.

Buteo lineatus alleni RIDGW. Pr. U. S. Nat. Mus. VII. Jan. 19, 1885, 514.

[B—, C—, R—, C—.]

GEOG. DIST.— South Atlantic and Gulf States, chiefly coastwise from South Carolina to Texas. Breeds throughout its range.

339 b. Buteo lineatus elegans (Cass.).
Red-bellied Hawk.

Buteo elegans Cass. Pr. Ac. Nat. Sci. Phila. 1855, 281.
Buteo lineatus var. *elegans* Ridgw. in Hist. N. Am. B. III. Jan. 1874, 257, 277.

[B 26, C 352a, R 439a, C 521.]

Geog. Dist.— Western United States, from western Texas to California and Oregon, south into Lower California, Sonora, and Chihuahua. Breeds along the Pacific coast of central Oregon, south to northern Lower California.

340. Buteo abbreviatus Cab.
Zone-tailed Hawk.

Buteo abbreviatus Cab. in Schomb. Reise Brit. Guian. III. 1848, 739.

[B—, C 353, R 440, C 522.]

Geog. Dist.— Texas, New Mexico, Arizona, and southern California, south to northern South America.

Subgenus **TACHYTRIORCHIS** Kaup.

Tachytriorchis Kaup, Class. Säug. u. Vög. 1844, 123. Type, *Falco pterocles* Temm. = *Buteo albicaudatus* Vieill.

341. Buteo albicaudatus sennetti Allen.
Sennett's White-tailed Hawk.

Buteo albicaudatus sennetti Allen, Bull. Am. Mus. Nat. Hist. V. 1893, 144.

[B—, C—, R 441, C 513.]

Geog. Dist. — Lower Rio Grande Valley, Texas, and southward into Mexico.

342. Buteo swainsoni Bonap.
Swainson's Hawk.

Buteo swainsoni Bonap. Geog. & Comp. List, 1838, 3.

ORDER RAPTORES. 133

[B 18, 19, 21, 28, C 354, R 442, C 523.]

GEOG. DIST.—Western North America, from Wisconsin, Illinois, Arkansas, and Texas to the Pacific coast; north to the arctic regions, and south to Argentine Republic. Casual east to Maine and Massachusetts. Breeds nearly throughout its North American range.

343. Buteo latissimus (WILS.).
Broad-winged Hawk.

Falco latissimus WILS. Am. Orn. VI. 1812, 92, pl. 54, fig. 1.
Buteo latissimus SHARPE, Cat. B. Brit. Mus. I. Accip. 1874, 193.

[B 27, C 355, R 443, C 524.]

GEOG. DIST.—Eastern North America, from New Brunswick and the Saskatchewan region to Texas and Mexico, and thence southward to northern South America and the West Indies. Breeds throughout its United States range.

SUBGENUS **BUTEOLA** BONAPARTE.

Buteola BONAP. Compt. Rend. XLI. 1855, 651. Type, *Buteo brachyurus* VIEILL.

344. Buteo brachyurus VIEILL.
Short-tailed Hawk.

Buteo brachyurus VIEILL. Nouv. Dict. d'Hist. Nat. IV. 1816, 477.

[B —, C —, R —, C —.]

GEOG. DIST.—Mexico, Central America, and most of South America, north to Florida, where it regularly breeds.

GENUS **URUBITINGA** LESSON.

Urubitinga LESS. Rev. Zool. 1839, 132. Type, *Falco urubitinga* GMEL.

345. Urubitinga anthracina (LICHT.).
Mexican Black Hawk.

Falco anthracinus LICHT. Preis-Verz. 1830, 3.
Urubitinga anthracina LAFR. Rev. Zool. 1848, 241.

[B—, C—, R 444, C 528.]

GEOG. DIST.—Lower Rio Grande Valley and Arizona, southward to northern South America.

GENUS **ASTURINA** VIEILLOT.

Asturina VIEILL. Analyse, 1816, 24.   Type, *Falco nitidus* GMEL.

346. Asturina plagiata SCHLEGEL.
   Mexican Goshawk.

Asturina plagiata "LICHT." SCHLEGEL, Mus. P. B. Asturinæ, 1862, 1.

[B 33, C 358, R 445, C 527.]

GEOG. DIST.—Southwestern border of the United States, southward to Panama.

GENUS **ARCHIBUTEO** BREHM.

Archibuteo BREHM, Isis, 1828, 1269.   Type, *Falco lagopus* GMEL.

[**347.**] **Archibuteo lagopus** (BRÜNN.).
   Rough-legged Hawk.

Falco lagopus BRÜNN. Orn. Bor. 1764, 4.
Archibuteo lagopus GRAY, List Gen. B. ed. 2, 1841, 3.

[B—, C—, R—, C—.]

GEOG. DIST.—Northern parts of the Old World; Alaska (?).

347a. Archibuteo lagopus sancti-johannis (GMEL.).
   American Rough-legged Hawk.

Falco sancti-johannis GMEL. S. N. I. ii. 1788, 273.
Archibuteo lagopus var. *sancti-johannis* COUES, Key, 1872, 218.

[B 30, 31, C 356, R 447, C 525.]

GEOG. DIST.—North America north of Mexico, breeding north of the United States (excepting in Alaska).

348. **Archibuteo ferrugineus** (LICHT.).
   Ferruginous Rough-Leg.

Falco ferrugineus LICHT. Abh. K. Akad. Berl. 1838, 428.
Archibuteo ferrugineus GRAY, Gen. B. fol. ed. 1849, 12.

[B 32, C 357, R 448, C 526.]

GEOG. DIST.— Western North America, from the Plains (eastern North Dakota to Texas) westward to the Pacific, and from the Saskatchewan region south into Mexico; casually east to Illinois. Breeds from Utah, Colorado, and Kansas northward to the Saskatchewan Plains.

GENUS **AQUILA** BRISSON.

Aquila BRISS. Orn. I. 1760, 419.   Type, *Falco chrysaëtos* LINN.

349. **Aquila chrysaëtos** (LINN.).
   Golden Eagle.

Falco chrysaëtos LINN. S. N. ed. 10, I. 1758, 88.
Aquila chrysaëtos DUMONT, Dict. Sci. Nat. I. 1816, 339.

[B 39, C 361, R 449, C 532.]

GEOG. DIST.— North America, south to Mexico, and northern parts of the Old World. Breeding range in the United States, practically restricted to the mountainous parts of unsettled regions.

GENUS **THRASAËTOS** GRAY.

Thrasaëtos GRAY, P. Z. S. 1837 (June, 1838), 108.   Type, *Vultur harpyia* LINN.

[350.] **Thrasaëtos harpyia** (LINN.).
   Harpy Eagle.

Vultur harpyia LINN. S. N. ed. 10, I. 1758, 86.
Thrasaëtos harpyia GRAY, P. Z. S. 1837 (June, 1838), 108.

[B —, C —, R 450, C 631.]

GEOG. DIST.— Lower Rio Grande Valley, casual; south to Paraguay.   Louisiana (?).

Genus HALIÆETUS Savigny.

Haliæetus Savigny, Descr. de l'Égypte, 1809, 35.   Type, *Falco albicilla* Linn.

[351.] Haliæetus albicilla (Linn.).
    Gray Sea Eagle.

Falco albicilla Linn. S. N. ed. 10, I. 1758, 89.
Haliæetus albicilla Leach, Syst. Cat. M. B. Br. Mus. 1816, 9.

[B 42, C —, R 452, C 533.]

Geog. Dist.— Northern Europe and Asia; Greenland.

352. Haliæetus leucocephalus (Linn.).
    Bald Eagle.

Falco leucocephalus Linn. S. N. ed. 12, I. 1766, 124.
Haliæetus leucocephalus Boie, Isis, 1822, 548.

[B 41, 43, C 362, R 451, C 534.]

Geog. Dist.— North America at large, south to Mexico, northwest through the Aleutian Islands to Kamchatka. Breeds locally throughout its range.

Subfamily FALCONINÆ. Falcons.

Genus FALCO Linnæus.

Falco Linn. S. N. ed. 10, I. 1758, 88.   Type, by elimination, *F. subbuteo* Linn.

Subgenus HIEROFALCO Cuvier.

Hierofalco Cuv. Règ. An. I. 1817, 312.   Type, *Falco candicans* Gmel. = *F. islandus* Brünn.

353. Falco islandus Brünn.
    White Gyrfalcon.

Falco islandus Brünn. Orn. Bor. 1764, 2.

ORDER RAPTORES. 137

[B 11, C 341*a*, R 412, C 501.]

GEOG. DIST.— Arctic regions, including Arctic America and Greenland, wandering south in winter to Labrador and northern Maine.

354. **Falco rusticolus** LINN.
    Gray Gyrfalcon.
Falco rusticolus LINN. S. N. ed. 10, I. 1758, 88.

[B 12, C —, R 412*a*, C 500.]

GEOG. DIST.— Arctic regions, including Iceland, southern Greenland, and Arctic America, straggling southward in winter.

354*a*. **Falco rusticolus gyrfalco** (LINN.).
    Gyrfalcon.
Falco gyrfalco LINN. S. N. ed. 10, I. 1758, 91.
Falco rusticolus gyrfalco STEJN. Auk, II. 1885, 187.

[B —, C 341, R 412*b*, C 498.]

GEOG. DIST.— Northern Europe, Greenland, and Arctic America, from northern Labrador and Hudson Bay to Alaska; rarely south in winter to New England (Massachusetts and Rhode Island).

354*b*. **Falco rusticolus obsoletus** (GMEL.).
    Black Gyrfalcon.
Falco obsoletus GMEL. S. N. I. i. 1788, 268.
Falco rusticolus obsoletus STEJN. Auk, II. 1885, 187.

[B —, C —, R 412*c*, C 499.]

GEOG. DIST.— Labrador, south in winter to Canada, Maine, and New York.

355. **Falco mexicanus** SCHLEG.
    Prairie Falcon.
Falco mexicanus SCHLEG. Abh. Geb. Zool. 1841, 15.

[B 10, C 342, R 413, C 502.]

GEOG. DIST.— United States, from the eastern border of the Plains to the Pacific, and from the Dakotas south into Mexico; casual eastward to Illinois. Breeds throughout its United States range.

SUBGENUS **RHYNCHODON** NITZSCH.

Rhynchodon NITZSCH, Pterylog. 1840, 78. Type, by elimination, *Falco peregrinus* LATH.

356. Falco peregrinus anatum (BONAP.).
Duck Hawk.

Falco anatum BONAP. Geog. & Comp. List, 1838, 4.
Falco peregrinus β. anatum BLASIUS, List B. Eur. 1862, 3.

[B 5, 6, C 343, R 414, C 503.]

GEOG. DIST.— North America at large, and south to Chili. Breeds locally throughout most of its United States range.

356 a. Falco peregrinus pealei RIDGW.
Peale's Falcon.

Falco communis var. *pealei* RIDGW. Bull. Essex Inst. V. Dec. 1873, 201.
Falco peregrinus pealei RIDGW. Pr. U. S. Nat. Mus. III. Aug. 24, 1880, 192.

[B—, C 343a, R 414a, C 504.]

GEOG. DIST.— Pacific coast region of North America, from Oregon to the Aleutian and Commander Islands, breeding throughout its range.

SUBGENUS **ÆSALON** KAUP.

Æsalon KAUP, Skizz. Entw.-Gesch. Eur. Thierw. 1829, 40. Type, *Falco æsalon* GMEL. = *F. regulus* PALL.

357. Falco columbarius LINN.
Pigeon Hawk.

Falco columbarius LINN. S. N. ed. 10, I. 1758, 90.

[B 7, C 344, R 417, C 505.]

GEOG. DIST.— The whole of North America, south to the West Indies and northern South America. Breeds chiefly north of the United States.

ORDER RAPTORES.

357 a. Falco columbarius suckleyi RIDGW.
Black Merlin.

Falco columbarius var. *suckleyi* RIDGW. Bull. Essex Inst. V. Dec. 1873, 201.

[B —, C 344*a*, R 417*a*, C 506.]

GEOG. DIST.— Northwest coast region of North America, from California to Sitka; eastward in Oregon and Washington.

358. Falco richardsonii RIDGW.
Richardson's Merlin.

Falco (Hypotriorchis) richardsonii RIDGW. Pr. Ac. Nat. Sci. Phila. Dec. 1870, 145.

[B —, C 345, R 418, C 507.]

GEOG. DIST.— Interior and western plains of North America, from the Mississippi River to the Pacific coast, and from the Saskatchewan region to Texas, Arizona, and probably into Mexico.

[358.1.] Falco regulus PALL.
Merlin.

Falco regulus PALL. Reis. Russ. Reichs. II. 1773, Anhang, 707.

[B —, C —, R —, C —.]

GEOG. DIST.— Europe, Asia, and Africa; accidental in Greenland.

SUBGENUS **RHYNCHOFALCO** RIDGWAY.

Rhynchofalco RIDGW. Pr. Boston Soc. Nat. Hist. 1873, 46. Type, *Falco femoralis* TEMM. = *F. fusco-cærulescens* VIEILL.

359. Falco fusco-cœrulescens VIEILL.
Aplomado Falcon.

Falco fusco-cærulescens VIEILL. Nouv. Dict. d'Hist. Nat. XI. 1817, 90.

[B 9, C 347, R 419, C 511.]

GEOG. DIST.— Southern Texas, New Mexico and Arizona, south to Patagonia.

Subgenus **TINNUNCULUS** VIEILLOT.

Tinnunculus VIEILL. Ois. Am. Sept. I. 1807, 39.

[359.1.] **Falco tinnunculus** LINN.
Kestrel.

Falco tinnunculus LINN. S. N. ed. 10, I. 1758, 90.

[B —, C —, R 422, C —.]

GEOG. DIST.— Europe and northern Asia; accidental in Massachusetts.

360. **Falco sparverius** LINN.
American Sparrow Hawk.

Falco sparverius LINN. S. N. ed. 10, I. 1758, 90.

[B 13, C 346, 346a, R 420, 420a, C 508, 509.]

GEOG. DIST.— North America, east of the Rocky Mountains, and from Great Slave Lake south to northern South America.

360 a. **Falco sparverius deserticolus** MEARNS.
Desert Sparrow Hawk.

Falco sparverius deserticolus MEARNS, Auk, IX. July, 1892, 263.

[B 13, *part*, C 346, *part*, R 420, *part*, C 508, *part*.]

GEOG. DIST.— Western United States, north to eastern British Columbia and western Montana, south to Mazatlan in northwestern Mexico.

360 b. **Falco sparverius peninsularis** MEARNS.
St. Lucas Sparrow Hawk.

Falco sparverius peninsularis MEARNS, Auk, IX. July, 1892, 267.

[B 13, *part*, C 346, *part*, R 420, *part*, C 508, *part*.]

GEOG. DIST.— Lower California.

[361.] **Falco dominicensis** GMEL.
Cuban Sparrow Hawk.

Falco dominicensis GMEL. Syst. Nat. I. i. 1788, 288.

[B —, C —, R 421, C 510.]

GEOG. DIST.— Cuba; casual in Florida.

GENUS **POLYBORUS** VIEILLOT.

Polyborus VIEILL. Analyse, 1816, 22.   Type, *Falco tharus* MOL.

362. Polyborus cheriway (JACQ.).
Audubon's Caracara.
Falco cheriway JACQ. Beitr. 1784, 17, tab. 4.
Polyborus cheriway CAB. in SCHOMB. Reise Brit. Guiana, III. 1848, 741.

[B 45, C 363, R 423, C 535.]

GEOG. DIST.— Florida, Texas, Arizona, and Lower California, south to Ecuador and Guiana.   Breeds throughout its United States range and southward.

363. Polyborus lutosus RIDGW.
Guadalupe Caracara.
Polyborus lutosus RIDGW. Bull. U. S. Geog. & Geol. Surv. Terr. No. 6, 2d ser. Feb. 8, 1876, 459.

[B —, C —, R 424, C —.]

GEOG. DIST.— Guadalupe Island, Lower California.

SUBFAMILY **PANDIONINÆ**.   OSPREYS.

GENUS **PANDION** SAVIGNY.

Pandion SAVIGN. Descr. de l'Égypte, Ois. 1809, 95.   Type, *Falco haliaëtus* LINN.

364. Pandion haliaëtus carolinensis (GMEL.).
American Osprey.
Falco carolinensis GMEL. S. N. I. i. 1788, 263.
Pandion haliaëtus carolinensis RIDGW. Pr. Ac. Nat. Sci. Phila. Dec. 1870, 143.

[B 44, C 360, R 425, C 530.]

GEOG. DIST.— North America, from Hudson Bay and Alaska south to the West Indies and northern South America. Breeds throughout its North American range.

Suborder STRIGES. Owls.

Family STRIGIDÆ. Barn Owls.

Genus STRIX Linnæus.

Strix LINN. S. N. ed. 10, I. 1758, 92. Type, *S. aluco* LINN. ed. 10.

365. Strix pratincola BONAP.
American Barn Owl.
Strix pratincola BONAP. Geog. & Comp. List, 1838, 7.

[B 47, C 316, R 394, C 461.]

GEOG. DIST.— United States, rarely to the northern border, and Ontario, southward through Mexico; northern limit of breeding range about Lat. 41°.

Family BUBONIDÆ. Horned Owls, etc.

Genus ASIO Brisson.

Asio BRISS. Orn. I. 1760, 28.   Type, *Strix otus* LINN.

366. Asio wilsonianus (LESS.).
American Long-eared Owl.
Otus wilsonianus LESS. Traité, 1831, 110.
Asio wilsonianus COUES, Check List, ed. 2, 1882, 81, No. 472.

[B 51, C 320, R 395, C 472.]

GEOG. DIST.— Temperate North America; south to the tablelands of Mexico. Breeds throughout its range.

367. Asio accipitrinus (PALL.).
Short-eared Owl.
Strix accipitrina PALL. Reise Russ. Reichs. I. 1771, 455.
Asio accipitrinus NEWT. YARR. Brit. B. ed. 4, I. 1872, 163.

ORDER RAPTORES. 143

[B 52, C 321, R 396, C 473.]

GEOG. DIST.— Throughout North America; nearly cosmopolitan. Breeds, somewhat irregularly and locally, from about Lat. 39° northward.

GENUS **SYRNIUM** SAVIGNY.

Syrnium SAVIGN. Descr. de l'Égypte, Ois. 1809, 298. Type, *Strix stridula* LINN.

368. **Syrnium nebulosum** (FORST.).
   Barred Owl.

Strix nebulosa FORST. Philos. Trans. XXII. 1772, 386.
Syrnium nebulosum BOIE, Isis, 1828, 315.

[B 54, C 323, R 397, C 476.]

GEOG. DIST.— Eastern United States, west to Minnesota, Nebraska, Kansas, and Texas, north to Nova Scotia and Quebec. Breeds throughout its range.

368 *a*. **Syrnium nebulosum alleni** RIDGW.
   Florida Barred Owl.

Strix nebulosa alleni RIDGW. Pr. U. S. Nat. Mus. III. March, 1880, 8.
Syrnium nebulosum alleni RIDGW. Pr. U. S. Nat. Mus. VIII. Sept. 1885, 355.

[B —, C —, R 397*a*, C 477.]

GEOG. DIST.— South Atlantic and Gulf States, chiefly coastwise, from South Carolina to Texas.

369. **Syrnium occidentale** XANTUS.
   Spotted Owl.

Syrnium occidentale XANTUS, Pr. Ac. Nat. Sci. Phila. 1859, 193.

[B —, C 324, R 398, C 478.]

GEOG. DIST.— Southern Colorado, New Mexico, Arizona, California, Lower California and Mexico.

Genus SCOTIAPTEX Swainson.

Scotiaptex Swains. Classif. B. II. 1837, 217. Type, *Strix cinerea* Gmel.

370. Scotiaptex cinerea (Gmel.).
Great Gray Owl.

Strix cinerea Gmel. S. N. I. i. 1788, 291.
Scotiaptex cinerea Swains. Classif. B. II. 1837, 217.

[B 53, C 322, R 399, C 474.]

Geog. Dist.— Arctic America, straggling southward, in winter, to southern New England, New York, New Jersey, Ohio, Illinois, Idaho and northern Montana.

[370 *a*.] **Scotiaptex cinerea lapponica** (Retz.).
Lapp Owl.

Strix lapponica Retz. Faun. Suec. 1800, 79.
Scotiaptex cinerea lapponica Ridgw. Man. N. Am. B. 1887, 260.

[B —, C —, R 399*a*, C 475.]

Geog. Dist.— Arctic portions of the Old World; accidental in Alaska (Norton Sound).

Genus NYCTALA Brehm.

Nyctala Brehm, Isis, 1828, 1271. Type, *Strix tengmalmi* Gmel.

371. Nyctala tengmalmi richardsoni (Bonap.).
Richardson's Owl.

Nyctale richardsoni Bonap. Geog. & Comp. List, 1838, 7.
Nyctale tengmalmi var. *richardsoni* Ridgw. Am. Nat. VI. May 1872, 285.

[B 55, C 327, R 400, C 482.]

Geog. Dist.— Arctic America, south in winter into the northern United States. Breeds from the Gulf of St. Lawrence and Manitoba northward.

372. **Nyctala acadica** (GMEL.).
    Saw-whet Owl.

Strix acadica GMEL. S. N. I. 1788, 296.
Nyctale acadica BONAP. Geog. & Comp. List, 1838, 7.

[B 56, 57, C 328, R 401, C 483.]

GEOG. DIST.— North America at large, breeding from the Middle States northward, and in mountainous regions of the West southward into Mexico.

GENUS **MEGASCOPS** KAUP.

Megascops KAUP, Isis, 1848, 765.   Type, *Strix asio* LINN.

373. **Megascops asio** (LINN.).
    Screech Owl.

Strix asio LINN. Syst. Nat. ed. 10, I. 1758, 92.
Megascops asio STEJN. Auk, II. April, 1885, 184.

[B 49, *part*, C 318, R 402, C 465.]

GEOG. DIST.— Temperate eastern North America, south to Georgia, and west to the Plains.   Accidental in England.

373 *a*. **Megascops asio floridanus** (RIDGW.).
    Florida Screech Owl.

Scops asio var. *floridanus* RIDGW. Bull. Essex Inst. Dec. 1873, 200.
Megascops asio floridanus STEJN. Auk, II. April, 1885, 184.

[B —, C 318*c*, R 402*a*, C 469.]

GEOG. DIST.— South Atlantic and Gulf States, from South Carolina to Louisiana, chiefly coastwise.

373 *b*. **Megascops asio trichopsis** (WAGL.).
    Texas Screech Owl.

Scops trichopsis WAGL. Isis, 1832, 276.
Megascops asio trichopsis RIDGW. Auk, XII. Oct. 1895, ——.

[B 50, C 318*b*, R 402*b*, C 468.]

GEOG. DIST.— Valley of the Lower Rio Grande in Texas, south to Guatemala.

373 *c*. **Megascops asio bendirei** (BREWST.).
California Screech Owl.

Scops asio bendirei BREWST. Bull. Nutt. Orn. Club, VII. Jan. 1882, 31.
Megascops asio bendirei STEJN. Auk, II. April, 1885, 184.

[B —, C —, R —, C —.]

GEOG. DIST.— Coast region of California.

373 *d*. **Megascops asio kennicottii** (ELLIOT).
Kennicott's Screech Owl.

Scops kennicottii ELLIOT, Pr. Ac. Nat. Sci. Phila. 1867, 99.
Megascops asio kennicottii STEJN. Auk, II. April, 1885, 184.

[B —, C 318*a*, R 402*d*, C 466.]

GEOG. DIST.— Northwest coast region, from Oregon to Sitka.

373 *e*. **Megascops asio maxwelliæ** (RIDGW.).
Rocky Mountain Screech Owl.

Scops asio var. *maxwelliæ* RIDGW. Field & Forest, June, 1877, 210, 213.
Megascops asio maxwelliæ STEJN. Auk, II. April, 1885, 184.

[B —, C —, R 402*c*, C 467.]

GEOG. DIST.— Rocky Mountains, from Colorado to Montana.

373 *f*. **Megascops asio cineraceus** RIDGW.
Mexican Screech Owl.

Megascops asio cineraceus RIDGW. Auk, XII. Oct. 1895, ——.

[B —, C —, R 403, C 470.]

GEOG. DIST.— New Mexico, Arizona, Lower California, and western Mexico.

873 *g*. **Megascops asio aikeni** BREWST.
    Aiken's Screech Owl.

Megascops asio aikeni BREWST. Auk, VIII. April, 1891, 139.

[B —, C —, R —, C —.]

GEOG. DIST.— Plains, El Paso County, Colorado, south probably to central New Mexico and northeastern Arizona.

873 *h*. **Megascops asio macfarlanei** BREWST.
    MacFarlane's Screech Owl.

Megascops asio macfarlanei BREWST. Auk, VIII. April, 1891, 140.

[B 49, *part*, C 318, *part*, R 402, *part*, C 465, *part*.]

GEOG. DIST.— East of the Cascades in Washington, interior of southern British Columbia, southward to central Oregon and eastward into Montana.

874. **Megascops flammeola** (KAUP).
    Flammulated Screech Owl.

Scops flammeola KAUP, Trans. Zool. Soc. Lond. IV. 1862, 226.
Megascops flammeolus STEJN. Auk, II. April, 1885, 184.

[B —, C 319, R 404, C 471.]

GEOG. DIST.— Highlands of Guatemala and central Mexico, north to Colorado and northern California.

874 *a*. **Megascops flammeola idahoensis** MERRIAM.
    Dwarf Screech Owl.

Megascops flammeolus idahoensis MERRIAM, North Am. Fauna, No. 5, July, 1891, 96, pl. i.

[B—, C—, R—, C—.]

GEOG. DIST.— Ketchum, Idaho. Known only from the type.

GENUS **BUBO** DUMÉRIL.

Bubo DUMÉR. Zool. Anal. 1806, 34. Type, by implication, *Strix bubo* LINN.

375. Bubo virginianus (GMEL.).
Great Horned Owl.

Strix virginiana GMEL. S. N. I. i. 1788, 287.
Bubo virginianus BONAP. Geog. & Comp. List, 1838, 6.

[B 48, C 317, R 405, C 462.]

GEOG. DIST.— Eastern North America, west to the Mississippi Valley, and from Labrador south to Costa Rica.

375 a. Bubo virginianus subarcticus (HOY).
Western Horned Owl.

Bubo subarcticus HOY, Pr. Ac. Nat. Sci. Phila. VI. 1852, 211.
Bubo virginianus β *subarcticus* RIDGW. Orn. 40th Par. 1877, 572.

[B 48, *part*, C 317a, *part*, R 405a, *part*, C 463, *part*.]

GEOG. DIST.— Western United States, from the Great Plains westward; southward to the Mexican tablelands; east, casually, to Wisconsin and Illinois; north to Manitoba and British Columbia.

375 b. Bubo virginianus arcticus (SWAINS.).
Arctic Horned Owl.

Strix (Bubo) arctica SWAINS. in Sw. & RICH. Fauna Bor. Am. II. 1831, 86, pl. 30.
Bubo virginianus var. *arcticus* CASS. Illust. B. Cal. etc. 1854, 178.

[B 48, *part*, C 317a, *part*, R 405b, C 463, *part*.]

GEOG. DIST.— Arctic America, chiefly in the interior, south, in winter, to Idaho, Montana, Wyoming, and South Dakota.

375 c. Bubo virginianus saturatus RIDGW.
Dusky Horned Owl.

Bubo virginianus saturatus RIDGW. Orn. 40th Par. 1877, 572, foot-note.

[B 48, *part*, C 317b, R 405c, C 464.]

GEOG. DIST.— Pacific coast region, from Monterey Bay, California, northward to Alaska and eastward to Hudson Bay and Labrador; southward through the mountainous regions of the West to Arizona.

ORDER RAPTORES.

Genus **NYCTEA** Stephens.

Nyctea Steph. Gen. Zool. XIII. ii. 1826, 63. Type, *Strix nyctea* Linn.

376. Nyctea nyctea (Linn.).
Snowy Owl.

Strix nyctea Linn. S. N. ed. 10, I. 1758, 93.
Nyctea nyctea Licht. Nomen. Mus. Berol. 1854, 7.

[B 61, C 325, R 466, C 479.]

Geog. Dist.— Northern portions of the northern hemisphere. In North America breeding wholly north of the United States; in winter migrating south to the Middle States, straggling to South Carolina, Texas, California, and Bermuda.

Genus **SURNIA** Duméril.

Surnia Dumér. Zool. Anal. 1806, 34. Type, *Strix ulula* Linn.

[377.] Surnia ulula (Linn.).
Hawk Owl.

Strix ulula Linn. S. N. ed. 10, I. 1758, 93.
Surnia ulula Bonap. Cat. Met. Ucc. Eur. 1842, 22.

[B—, C—, R 407*a*, C 481.]

Geog. Dist.— Arctic portions of the Old World. Casual in Alaska (St. Michaels).

377 *a*. Surnia ulula caparoch (Müll.).
American Hawk Owl.

Strix caparoch Müll. S. N. Suppl. 1776, 69.
Surnia ulula caparoch Stejn. Auk, I. Oct. 1884, 363.

[B 62, C 326, R 407, C 480.]

Geog. Dist.— Arctic America, breeding from Newfoundland northward, and migrating in winter to the northern border of the United States. Occasional in England.

Genus SPEOTYTO Gloger.

Speotyto Glog. Handb. Naturg. 1842, 226. Type, *Strix cunicularia* Mol.

378. Speotyto cunicularia hypogæa (Bonap.).
Burrowing Owl.

Strix hypogæa Bonap. Am. Orn. I. 1825, 72.
Spheotyto cunicularia var. *hypogæa* Coues Key, 1872, 208.

[B 58, 59, C 332, R 408, C 487.]

Geog. Dist.— Western United States, from the Pacific coast east throughout the Great Plains, north somewhat over the border of British America, south to Central America. Accidental in New York and Massachusetts.

378 a. Speotyto cunicularia floridana Ridgw.
Florida Burrowing Owl.

Speotyto cunicularia var. *floridana* Ridgw. Am. Sportsm. V. July 4, 1874, 216.

[B —, C —, R 408a, C 488.]

Geog. Dist.— Southern Florida; Bahamas.

Genus GLAUCIDIUM Boie.

Glaucidium Boie, Isis, 1826, 970. Type, *Strix nana* King.

379. Glaucidium gnoma Wagl.
Pygmy Owl.

Glaucidium gnoma Wagl. Isis, 1832, 275.

[B 60, C 329, R 409, C 484.]

Geog. Dist.— Western North America in mountainous regions from British Columbia to eastern slopes of the Rocky Mountains and south to the tablelands of Mexico.

379 a. **Glaucidium gnoma californicum** (Scl.).
   California Pygmy Owl.

   Glaucidium californicum Scl. P. Z. S. 1857, 4.
   Glaucidium gnoma californicum A. O. U. Check-List, 1st Suppl. 1889, 9.

   [B 60, *part*, C 329, *part*, R 409, *part*, C 484, *part*.]

   Geog. Dist.— Pacific coast region, from California to British Columbia.

379.1. **Glaucidium hoskinsii** (Brewst.).
   Hoskins's Pygmy Owl.

   Glaucidium gnoma hoskinsii Brewst. Auk, V. April, 1888, 136.
   Glaucidium hoskinsii A. O. U. Check-List, 1st Suppl. 1889, 9.

   [B —, C —, R —, C —.]

   Geog. Dist.— Lower California.

380. **Glaucidium phalænoides** (Daud.).
   Ferruginous Pygmy Owl.

   Strix phalænoides Daud. Traité d'Orn. II. 1800, 206.
   Glaucidium phalænoides Cab. J. f. O. 1869, 208.

   [B —, C 330, R 410, C 485.]

   Geog. Dist.— Southern border of the United States, from Texas to Arizona, south to southern Brazil.

Genus **MICROPALLAS** Coues.

Micropallas Coues, Auk, VI. Jan. 1889, 71. Type, *Athene whitneyi* Cooper.

381. **Micropallas whitneyi** (Cooper).
   Elf Owl.

   Athene whitneyi Cooper, Pr. Cal. Ac. Sci. 1861, 118.
   Micropallas whitneyi Sennett, Auk, VI. July, 1889, 276.

   [B —, C 331, R 411, C 486.]

   Geog. Dist.— Southern and Lower California, Arizona, New Mexico, and southern Texas, south to Puebla, Mexico.

Order PSITTACI. Parrots, Macaws, Paroquets, etc.

Family **PSITTACIDÆ**. Parrots and Paroquets.

Genus **CONURUS** Kuhl.

Conurus Kuhl, Consp. Psitt. 1820, 4. Type, *Psittacus carolinensis* Linn.

382. Conurus carolinensis (Linn.).
Carolina Paroquet.

Psittacus carolinensis Linn. S. N. ed. 10, I. 1758, 97.
Conurus carolinensis Less. Traité, 1831, 211.

[B 63, C 315, R 392, C 460.]

Geog. Dist.— Formerly Florida and the Gulf States north to Maryland, the Great Lakes, Iowa, and Nebraska, west to Colorado, the Indian Territory, and Texas, and straggling northeastward to Pennsylvania and New York. Now restricted to Florida, Arkansas, and Indian Territory, where it is only of local occurrence.

Order COCCYGES. Cuckoos, etc.

Suborder CUCULI. Cuckoos, etc.

Family CUCULIDÆ. Cuckoos, Anis, etc.

Subfamily CROTOPHAGINÆ. Anis.

Genus CROTOPHAGA Linnæus.

Crotophaga Linn. S. N. ed. 10, I. 1758, 105. Type, *C. ani* Linn.

[383.] **Crotophaga ani** Linn.
Ani.
Crotophaga ani Linn. S. N. ed. 10, I. 1758, 105.
[B 66, 67, C 288, R 389, C 425.]
Geog. Dist.— West Indies and eastern South America. Rare or casual in southern Florida and Louisiana, and accidental near Philadelphia.

384. **Crotophaga sulcirostris** Swains.
Groove-billed Ani.
Crotophaga sulcirostris Swains. Philos. Mag. I. 1827, 440.
[B—, C—, R 390, C 426.]
Geog. Dist.— Mexico, north to the southern part of the peninsula of Lower California, and valley of the Lower Rio Grande in Texas, south to Peru.

Subfamily COCCYGINÆ. American Cuckoos.

Genus GEOCOCCYX Wagler.

Geococcyx Wagler, Isis, 1831, 524. Type, *G. variegata* Wagl.
= *Saurothera californiana* Less.

385. Geococcyx californianus (LESS.).
Road-runner.

Saurothera californiana LESSON, Compl. Buff. VI. 1829, 420.
Geococcyx californianus BAIRD, B. N. Am. 1858, 73.

[B 68, C 289, R 385, C 427.]

GEOG. DIST.— Northern and central Mexico, north to head of Sacramento Valley in California, southern Utah, southeastern Colorado, southwestern Kansas, western Oklahoma, and western Texas.

GENUS COCCYZUS VIEILLOT.

Coccyzus VIEILL. Analyse, 1816, 28. Type, *Cuculus americanus* LINN.

386. Coccyzus minor (GMEL.).
Mangrove Cuckoo.

Cuculus minor GMEL. S. N. I. i. 1788, 411.
Coccyzus minor CAB. J. f. O. 1856, 104.

[B 71, C 292, R 386, C 429.]

GEOG. DIST.— Key West, Florida, Louisiana, the West Indies, and Central America to northeastern South America.

[386 a.] Coccyzus minor maynardi (RIDGW.).
Maynard's Cuckoo.

Coccyzus maynardi RIDGW. Man. N. Am. B. 1887, 274.
Coccyzus minor maynardi A. O. U. Check-List, 1st Suppl. 1889, 9.

[B 71, *part*, C 292, *part*, R 386, *part*, C 429, *part*.]

GEOG. DIST.— Bahamas and Florida Keys. Cuba?

387. Coccyzus americanus (LINN.).
Yellow-billed Cuckoo.

Cuculus americanus LINN. S. N. ed. 10, I. 1758, 111.
Coccyzus americanus BONAP. Journ. Ac. Nat. Sci. Phila. III. ii. 1824, 367.

[B 69, C 291, R 387, C 429.]

GEOG. DIST.— Eastern temperate North America, breeding from Florida north to New Brunswick, Canada, and Minnesota, west to the eastern border of the Plains, and south, in winter, to Costa Rica and the West Indies.

387 *a*. Coccyzus americanus occidentalis RIDGW.
California Cuckoo.

Coccyzus americanus occidentalis RIDGW. Man. N. Am. B. 1887, 273.

[B—, C—, R 387, *part*, C 429, *part*.]

GEOG. DIST.— Western temperate North America, from northern Lower California north to southern British Columbia, east to New Mexico and western Texas, and south over tablelands of Mexico.

388. Coccyzus erythrophthalmus (WILS.).
Black-billed Cuckoo.

Cuculus erythrophthalmus WILS. Am. Orn. IV. 1811, 16, pl. 28.
Coccyzus erythrophthalmus BONAP. Journ. Ac. Nat. Sci. Phila. III. ii. 1824, 367.

[B 70, C 290, R 388, C 428.]

GEOG. DIST.— Eastern North America, west to the Rocky Mountains, breeding north to Labrador, Manitoba, and eastern Assiniboia; south, in winter, to the West Indies and the valley of the Amazon. Accidental in the British Islands and Italy.

GENUS **CUCULUS** LINNÆUS.

Cuculus LINN. S. N. ed. 10, I. 1758, 110. Type, *C. canorus* LINN.

[388.1.] Cuculus canorus telephonus (HEINE).
Kamchatkan Cuckoo.

Cuculus telephonus HEINE, J. f. O. 1863, 352.
Cuculus canorus telephonus STEJN. Bull. 29, U. S. Nat. Mus. 1885, 224.

[B—, C—, R—, C—.]

GEOG. DIST.— An Asiatic species, occurring accidentally on the Pribilof Islands.

Suborder TROGONES. Trogons.

Family TROGONIDÆ. Trogons.

Genus TROGON Linnæus.

Trogon Linn. S. N. ed. 12, I. 1766, 167. Type, *T. viridis* Linn.

389. Trogon ambiguus Gould.
   Coppery-tailed Trogon.
Trogon ambiguus Gould, P. Z. S. 1835, 30.
   [B 65, C 284, R 384, C 422.]
Geog. Dist.— Southern and central Mexico, from Oaxaca and Guerrero, north to the valley of the Lower Rio Grande in Texas, and southern Arizona.

Suborder ALCYONES. Kingfishers.

Family ALCEDINIDÆ. Kingfishers.

Genus CERYLE Boie.

Ceryle Boie, Isis, 1828, 316. Type, *Alcedo rudis* Linn.

Subgenus STREPTOCERYLE Bonaparte.

Streptoceryle Bonap. Consp. Vol. Anisod. 1854. 10. Type, *Alcedo torquata* Linn.

390. Ceryle alcyon (Linn.).
   Belted Kingfisher.
Alcedo alcyon Linn. S. N. ed. 10, I. 1758, 115.
Ceryle alcyon Bonap. P. Z. S. for 1837 (1838), 108.

[B 117, C 286, R 382, C 423.]

GEOG. DIST.— North America, from the Arctic Ocean south to Panama and the West Indies. Breeds from the southern border of the United States northward.

[390.1.] **Ceryle torquata** (LINN.).
Ringed Kingfisher.
Alcedo torquata LINN. Syst. Nat. ed. 12, I. 1766, 180.
Ceryle torquata BOIE, Isis, 1828, 316.

[B—, C—, R—, C—.]

GEOG. DIST.— Mexico and southward to southern South America. Casual on the Lower Rio Grande, Texas.

SUBGENUS **CHLOROCERYLE** KAUP.

Chloroceryle KAUP, Fam. Eisv. 1848, 8. Type, *Alcedo superciliosa* LINN.

391. **Ceryle americana septentrionalis** SHARPE.
Texas Kingfisher.
Ceryle americana septentrionalis SHARPE, Cat. Birds Brit. Mus. XVII, 1892, 134.

[B 118, C 287, R 383, C 424.]

GEOG. DIST.— Southern Texas, south to Panama.

ORDER PICI. WOODPECKERS, WRYNECKS, ETC.

FAMILY **PICIDÆ**. WOODPECKERS.

GENUS **CAMPEPHILUS** GRAY.

Campephilus GRAY, List Gen. B. 1840, 54. Type, *Picus principalis* LINN.

392. Campephilus principalis (LINN.).
   Ivory-billed Woodpecker.

   Picus principalis LINN. S. N. ed. 10, I. 1758, 113.
   Campephilus principalis GRAY, List Gen. B. 1840, 54.

   [B 72, C 293, R 359, C 431.]

   GEOG. DIST.— Formerly South Atlantic and Gulf States, from North Carolina to Texas, north in the Mississippi Valley to Missouri, southern Illinois, and southern Indiana. Now restricted to the Gulf States and the Lower Mississippi Valley, where only locally distributed.

   GENUS **DRYOBATES** BOIE.

   Dryobates BOIE, Isis, 1826, 977. Type, *Picus pubescens* LINN.

393. Dryobates villosus (LINN.).
   Hairy Woodpecker.

   Picus villosus LINN. S. N. ed. 12, I. 1766, 175.
   Dryobates villosus CABANIS, Mus. Hein. IV. ii. June 15, 1863, 66.

   [B 74, *part*, C 298, *part*, R 360, C 438, *part*.]

   GEOG. DIST.— Northern and middle portions of the eastern United States, from the Atlantic coast to the Great Plains.

393 a. Dryobates villosus leucomelas (BODD.).
   Northern Hairy Woodpecker.

   Picus leucomelas BODDAERT, Tabl. Pl. Enl. 1783, 21.
   Dryobates villosus leucomelas RIDGW. Pr. U. S. Nat. Mus. VIII. 1885, 355.

   [B 74, *part*, C 298, *part*, R 360a, C 438, *part*.]

   GEOG. DIST.— Northern North America, south to about the northern border of the United States.

393 b. Dryobates villosus audubonii (SWAINS.).
   Southern Hairy Woodpecker.

   Picus audubonii SWAINS. in SW. & RICH. Fauna Bor. Am. II. 1831, 306.
   Dryobates villosus audubonii RIDGW. Pr. U. S. Nat. Mus. VIII. 1885, 355.

[B 74, *part*, C 298, *part*, R 360, *part*, C 438, *part*.]

GEOG. DIST.— South Atlantic and Gulf States, north to North Carolina and Tennessee, west to Louisiana and southeastern Texas.

393 c. Dryobates villosus harrisii (AUD.).
Harris's Woodpecker.

Picus harrisii AUD. Orn. Biog. V. 1839, 191.
Dryobates villosus harrisii RIDGW. Pr. U. S. Nat. Mus. VIII. 1885, 355.

[B 75, C 298a, R 360b, C 439.]

GEOG. DIST.— Pacific coast of North America, from northern California to southern Alaska.

393 d. Dryobates villosus hyloscopus (CAB.).
Cabanis's Woodpecker.

Dryobates hyloscopus CAB. & HEINE, Mus. Hein. IV. ii. 1863, 69.
[*Dryobates villosus*] *hyloscopus* BREWST. Auk, V. July, 1888, 252 (in text).

[B 75, *part*, C 298a, *part*, R 360b, *part*, C 439, *part*.]

GEOG. DIST.— Western United States, except northwest coast, and south into Mexico.

394. Dryobates pubescens (LINN.).
Downy Woodpecker.

Picus pubescens LINN. S. N. ed. 12, I. 1766, 175.
Dryobates pubescens CABANIS, Mus. Hein. IV. ii. June 15, 1863, 62.

[B 76, C 299, R 361, C 440.]

GEOG. DIST.— Northern and eastern North America, west to British Columbia and the eastern edge of the Plains; south to the Gulf of Mexico.

394 a. Dryobates pubescens gairdnerii (AUD.).
Gairdner's Woodpecker.

Picus gairdnerii AUD. Orn. Biog. V. 1839, 317.
Dryobates pubescens gairdnerii RIDGW. Pr. U. S. Nat. Mus. VIII. 1885, 355.

[B 77, *part*, C 299*a*, *part*, R 361*a*, *part*, C 441, *part*.]

GEOG. DIST.— Pacific coast of the United States, north to British Columbia (lat. 55°).

394 *b*. **Dryobates pubescens oreœcus** BATCH.
Batchelder's Woodpecker.

Dryobates pubescens oreœcus BATCH. AUK, VI. July, 1889, 253.

[B 77, *part*, C 299*a*, *part*, R 361*a*, *part*, C 441, *part*.]

GEOG. DIST.— Rocky Mountain region of the United States.

395. **Dryobates borealis** (VIEILL.).
Red-cockaded Woodpecker.

Picus borealis VIEILL. Ois. Am. Sept. II. 1807, 66.
Dryobates borealis RIDGW. Pr. U. S. Nat. Mus. VIII. 1885, 355.

[B 80, C 296, R 362, C 433.]

GEOG. DIST.— Southeastern United States, from North Carolina, Tennessee and Indian Territory, south to eastern Texas and the Gulf coast.

396. **Dryobates scalaris bairdi** (MALHERBE).
Texan Woodpecker.

Picus bairdi (SCL. MSS.) MALHERBE, Mon. Pic. I. 1861, 118, pl. 27.
Dryobates scalaris bairdi RIDGW. Man. N. Am. B. 1887, 285.

[B 79, C 297, R 363, C 434.]

GEOG. DIST.— Southern border of the United States, from Texas to California, north from western Arizona and southern Nevada to southwestern Utah, south to the tablelands of Mexico.

396 *a*. **Dryobates scalaris lucasanus** (XANTUS).
Saint Lucas Woodpecker.

Picus lucasanus XANTUS, Pr. Ac. Nat. Sci. Phila. 1859, 298.
Dryobates scalaris lucasanus RIDGW. Pr. U. S. Nat. Mus. VIII. 1885, 355.

[B —, C 297*b*, R 363*a*, C 436.]

GEOG. DIST.— Lower California, north to Lat. 34° in the Colorado Desert, California.

397. **Dryobates nuttallii** (GAMB.).
    Nuttall's Woodpecker.

Picus nuttallii GAMBEL, Pr. Ac. Nat. Sci. Phila. April, 1843, 259.
Dryobates nuttallii RIDGW. Pr. U. S. Nat. Mus. VIII. 1885, 355.

[B 78, C 297a, R 364, C 435.]

GEOG. DIST.—Southern Oregon, California, and northern Lower California.

398. **Dryobates arizonæ** (HARGITT).
    Arizona Woodpecker.

Picus arizonæ HARGITT, Ibis, April, 1886, 115.
Dryobates arizonæ RIDGW. Man. N. Am. B. 1887, 286.

[B —, C —, R 365, C 437.]

GEOG. DIST.—Southern Arizona, south into northern Mexico.

GENUS **XENOPICUS** BAIRD.

Xenopicus BAIRD, B. N. Am. 1858, 83. Type, *Leuconerpes albolarvatus* CASS.

399. **Xenopicus albolarvatus** (CASS.).
    White-headed Woodpecker.

Leuconerpes albolarvatus CASSIN, Pr. Ac. Nat. Sci. Phila. Oct. 1850, 106.
Xenopicus albolarvatus MALHERBE, Mon. Pic. II. 1862, 221.

[B 81, C 295, R 366, C 452.]

GEOG. DIST.—Mountains of the Pacific coast, from southern British Columbia to southern California (including the eastern slope of the Sierra Nevada), and east to the Blue Mountains of Oregon and west-central Idaho.

GENUS **PICOIDES** LACÉPÈDE.

Picoides LACÉPÈDE, Mém. de l'Inst. III. 1801, 509. Type *Picus tridactylus* LINN.

400. **Picoides arcticus** (Swains.).
Arctic Three-toed Woodpecker.

Picus (Apternus) arcticus Swains. in Sw. & Rich. Fauna Bor. Am. II. 1831, 313.
Picoides arcticus Gray, Gen. B. I. 1845, 434.

[B 82, C 300, R 367, C 443.]

Geog. Dist.— Northern North America, from the arctic regions south to the northern United States (New England, New York, Michigan, Minnesota, and Idaho), and in the Sierra Nevada to Lake Tahoe.

401. **Picoides americanus** Brehm.
American Three-toed Woodpecker.

Picoides americanus Brehm, Handb. Vög. Deutschl. 1831, 195.

[B 83, C 301, R 368, C 444.]

Geog. Dist.— Northern North America, east of the Rocky Mountains, from the arctic regions southward to the northern United States (Maine, Mass., New York).

401 *a*. **Picoides americanus alascensis** (Nels.).
Alaskan Three-toed Woodpecker.

Picoides tridactylus alascensis Nelson, Auk, I. April, 1884, 165.
Picoides americanus alascensis Ridgw. Pr. U. S. Nat. Mus. VIII. 1885, 355.

[B —, C —, R —, C —.]

Geog. Dist.— Alaska, south to northern Washington.

401 *b*. **Picoides americanus dorsalis** Baird.
Alpine Three-toed Woodpecker.

Picoides dorsalis Baird, B. N. Am. 1858, 100.
Picoides americanus dorsalis Baird, Orn. Calif. I. 1870, 386.

[B 84, C 301*a*, R 368*a*, C 445.]

Geog. Dist.— Rocky Mountain region, from British Columbia and Idaho south into New Mexico.

Genus **SPHYRAPICUS** Baird.

Sphyrapicus Baird, B. N. Am. 1858, 80, 101.   Type, *Picus varius* Linn.

402. **Sphyrapicus varius** (Linn.).
Yellow-bellied Sapsucker.

Picus varius Linn. S. N. ed. 12, I. 1766, 176.
Sphyrapicus varius Baird, B. N. Am. 1858, 103.

[B 85, C 302, R 369, C 446.]

Geog. Dist.— Eastern North America north to about Lat. 63° 30' (north of Fort Simpson), breeding from Massachusetts northward; south, in winter, to the West Indies, Mexico and Costa Rica.

402 a. **Sphyrapicus varius nuchalis** Baird.
Red-naped Sapsucker.

Sphyrapicus varius var. *nuchalis* Baird, B. N. Am. 1858, 103.

[B 86, C 302a, R 369a, C 447.]

Geog. Dist.— Rocky Mountain region, from British Columbia to the Sierra Bolaños, Jalisco, Mexico, and the Cape region of Lower California; and westward across the Great Basin to the eastern slope of the Sierra Nevada in northern California.

403. **Sphyrapicus ruber** (Gmel.).
Red-breasted Sapsucker.

Picus ruber Gmel. S. N. I. 1788, 429.
Sphyrapicus ruber Baird, B. N. Am. 1858, 104.

[B 87, C 302b, 303? R 369b, C 448.]

Geog. Dist.— Pacific coast region, from British Columbia south in the mountains and foothills of California to northern Lower California.

404. **Sphyrapicus thyroideus** (Cass.).
Williamson's Sapsucker.

Picus thyroideus Cassin, Pr. Ac. Nat. Sci. Phila. 1850–1851, 349.
Sphyrapicus thyroideus Baird, B. N. Am. 1858, 106.

[B 88, 89, C 304, 305, R 370, C 449.]

GEOG. DIST.— Rocky Mountain region of the United States, west to the Sierra Nevada, Cascades, and northern Coast Ranges; south on the tablelands of Mexico to the Sierra Bolaños, Jalisco.

GENUS **CEOPHLŒUS** CABANIS.

Ceophlœus CABANIS, J. f. O. 1862, 176. Type, *Picus pileatus* LINN.

405. **Ceophlœus pileatus** (LINN.).
Pileated Woodpecker.

Picus pileatus LINN. S. N. ed. 10, I. 1758, 113.
C[eophlœus] pileatus CABANIS, J. f. O. 1862, 176.

[B 90, C 294, R 371, C 432.]

GEOG. DIST.— Formerly the heavily wooded region of North America south of about Lat. 63°, except in the southern Rocky Mountains; now rare or extirpated in the more thickly settled parts of the Eastern States.

GENUS **MELANERPES** SWAINSON.

SUBGENUS **MELANERPES**.

Melanerpes SWAINS. in Sw. & RICH. Fauna Bor. Am. II. 1831, 316. Type, *Picus erythrocephalus* LINN.

406. **Melanerpes erythrocephalus** (LINN.).
Red-headed Woodpecker.

Picus erythrocephalus LINN. S. N. ed. 10, I. 1758, 113.
Melanerpes erythrocephalus SWAINS. in Sw. & RICH. Fauna Bor. Am. II. 1831, 316.

[B 94, C 309, R 375, C 453.]

GEOG. DIST.— United States, west to the Rocky Mountains, and north from Florida to about Lat. 50°, straggling westward to Salt Lake Valley and Arizona; rare or local east of the Hudson River.

407. **Melanerpes formicivorus bairdi** Ridgw.
Californian Woodpecker.

Melanerpes formicivorus bairdi Ridgw. Bull. No. 21 U. S. Nat. Mus. 1881, 34, 85.

[B 95, C 310, R, 377, C 454.]

Geog. Dist.— Pacific coast region of the United States, from southern Oregon south to northern Lower California and Mexico, east through Arizona to southern New Mexico and western Texas.

407 a. **Melanerpes formicivorus angustifrons** Baird.
Narrow-fronted Woodpecker.

Melanerpes formicivorus var. *angustifrons* Baird, Orn. Cal. I. 1870, 405.

[B —, C 310a, R 377a, C 455.]

Geog. Dist.— Southern Lower California.

Subgenus **ASYNDESMUS** Coues.

Asyndesmus Coues, Pr. Ac. Nat. Sci. Phila. 1866, 55. Type, *Picus torquatus* Wils.

408. **Melanerpes torquatus** (Wils.).
Lewis's Woodpecker.

Picus torquatus Wilson, Am. Orn. III. 1811, 31, pl. xx. fig. 3.
Melanerpes torquatus Bonap. Geog. & Comp. List, 1838, 40.

[B 96, C 311, R 376, C 456.]

Geog. Dist.— Western United States, from the Black Hills and the Rocky Mountains to the Pacific, and from southern British Columbia and southern Alberta south to Arizona, and (in winter) western Texas. Casual in Kansas.

Subgenus **CENTURUS** Swainson.

Centurus Swains. Classif. B. II. 1837, 310. Type, *Picus carolinus* Linn.

409. Melanerpes carolinus (LINN.).
　　Red-bellied Woodpecker.

Picus carolinus LINN. S. N. ed. 10. I. 1758, 113.
Melanerpes carolinus RIDGW. Ann. Lyc. N. Y. X. Jan. 1874, 378.

[B 91, C 306, R 372, C 450.]

GEOG. DIST.— Eastern and southern United States, north casually to Massachusetts, New York, Ontario, southern Michigan, and central Iowa, west to eastern Nebraska, eastern Kansas, Indian Territory and Texas.

410. Melanerpes aurifrons (WAGL.).
　　Golden-fronted Woodpecker.

Picus aurifrons WAGLER, Isis, 1829, 512.
Melanerpes aurifrons RIDGW. Pr. U. S. Nat. Mus. VIII. 1885, 355.

[B 92, C 307, R 373, C 451.]

GEOG. DIST.— Central and southern Texas, southward over the tablelands of Mexico to the City of Mexico, and from southern Tamaulipas west to Aguas Calientes and Jalisco.

411. Melanerpes uropygialis (BAIRD).
　　Gila Woodpecker.

Centurus uropygialis BAIRD, Pr. Ac. Nat. Sci. Phila. June, 1854, 120.
Melanerpes uropygialis RIDGW. Pr. U. S. Nat. Mus. VIII. 1885, 355.

[B 93, C 308, R 374, C 452.]

GEOG. DIST.— Southwestern New Mexico, and southern and western Arizona, from Lat. 35° southward through Lower California to Cape St. Lucas, and through western Mexico to Aguas Calientes and Jalisco.

GENUS **COLAPTES** SWAINSON.

Colaptes SWAINS. Zool. Journ. III. Dec. 1827, 353. Type, *Cuculus auratus* LINN.

412. Colaptes auratus (LINN.).
　　Flicker.

Cuculus auratus LINN. S. N. ed. 10, I. 1758, 112.
Colaptes auratus VIGORS, Zool. Journ. III. 1827, 444.

[B 97, C 312, R 378, C 457.]

GEOG. DIST.— Northern and eastern North America, west to the eastern slope of the Rocky Mountains and Alaska. Occasional on the Pacific slope, from California northward. Accidental in Europe.

413. Colaptes cafer (GMEL.).
Red-shafted Flicker.

Picus cafer GMEL. S. N. I. 1788, 431.
Colaptes cafer STEJN. Stand. Nat. Hist. IV. 1885, 428.

[B 98, C 314, R 378*b*, C 459.]

GEOG. DIST.— Rocky Mountain region, from British Columbia south to southern Mexico, and west to the Coast Ranges in Oregon and Washington, and to the Pacific coast from northern California southward.

413 *a*. Colaptes cafer saturatior (RIDGW.).
Northwestern Flicker.

Colaptes mexicanus saturatior RIDGW. Pr. Biol. Soc. Wash. II. April 10, 1884, 90.
Colaptes cafer saturatior A. O. U. Check-list, 1886, 218.

[B —, C —, R —, C —.]

GEOG. DIST.—Northwest coast, from northern California to Sitka.

414. Colaptes chrysoides (MALH.).
Gilded Flicker.

Geopicus chrysoides MALH. Rev. et Mag. Zool. IV. 1852, 553.
Colaptes chrysoides REICH. Handb. Spec. Ornith. Scansoriæ, 1854, 413.

[B 99, C 313, R 379, C 458.]

GEOG. DIST.— Central and southern Arizona, from Lat. 34° to southern Sonora, and Lower California south of Lat. 30°.

415. Colaptes rufipileus RIDGW.
Guadalupe Flicker.

Colaptes mexicanus rufipileus RIDGW. Bull. U. S. Geol. & Geog. Surv. Terr. II. No. 2, April 1, 1876, 191.
Colaptes rufipileus RIDGW. Bull. Nutt. Orn. Club, II. July, 1877, 60.

[B —, C —, R 380, C —.]

GEOG. DIST.— Guadalupe Island, Lower California.

Order MACROCHIRES. Goatsuckers, Swifts, etc.

Suborder CAPRIMULGI. Goatsuckers, etc.

Family **CAPRIMULGIDÆ**. Goatsuckers, etc.

Genus **ANTROSTOMUS** Gould.

Antrostomus Gould, Icones Avium, 1838. Type, *Caprimulgus carolinensis* Gmel.

416. Antrostomus carolinensis (Gmel.).
Chuck-will's-widow.

Caprimulgus carolinensis Gmel. S. N. I. ii. 1788, 1028.
Antrostomus carolinensis Gould, Icones Avium, 1838.

[B 111, C 264, R 353, C 396.]

Geog. Dist.— South Atlantic and Gulf States, from Virginia south through eastern Mexico to Central America ; Cuba. North, in the interior, to southern Illinois and Kansas. Accidental in Massachusetts.

417. Antrostomus vociferus (Wils.).
Whip-poor-will.

Caprimulgus vociferus Wils. Am. Orn. V. 1812, 71, pl. 41, figs. 1-3.
Antrostomus vociferus Bonap. Geog. & Comp. List, 1838, 8.

[B 112, C 265, R 354, C 397.]

Geog. Dist.— Eastern North America to the Plains, and from Lat. 50° south to Guatemala.

ORDER MACROCHIRES. 169

417 *a*. **Antrostomus vociferus macromystax** (WAGLER).
   Stephens's Whip-poor-will.

Caprimulgus macromystax WAGLER, Ibis, 1831, 533.
Caprimulgus vociferus macromystax HARTERT, Ibis, 1892, 286.
Antrostomus vociferus macromystax A. O. U. Check-List, 6th
   Suppl. Auk, XI. Jan. 1894, 48.

[B —, C —, R —, C 881.]

GEOG. DIST.— Arizona, New Mexico, and tablelands of Mexico south to Guatemala.

GENUS **PHALÆNOPTILUS** RIDGWAY.

Phalænoptilus RIDGW. Pr. U. S. Nat. Mus. III. 1880, 5. Type, *Caprimulgus nuttallii* AUD.

418. **Phalænoptilus nuttallii** (AUD.).
   Poor-will.

Caprimulgus nuttallii AUD. B. Am. VII. 1843, 350, pl. 495.
Phalænoptilus nuttalli RIDGW. Pr. U. S. Nat. Mus. III. 1880, 5.

[B 113, C 266, R 355, C 398.]

GEOG. DIST.— Western United States, from the Sierra Nevada eastward to eastern Nebraska and eastern Kansas, north to central Idaho and Montana, and south to southern Mexico.

418 *a*. **Phalænoptilus nuttallii nitidus** BREWST.
   Frosted Poor-will.

Phalænoptilus nuttalli nitidus BREWST. Auk, IV. April, 1877, 147.

[B 113, *part*, C 266, *part*, R 355, *part*, C 398, *part*.]

GEOG. DIST.— Texas to Arizona, and north to western Kansas.

418 *b*. **Phalænoptilus nuttallii californicus** RIDGW.
   Dusky Poor-will.

Phalænoptilus nuttalli californicus RIDGW. Man. N. Am. B. 1887, 588, foot-note.

[B 113, *part*, C 266, *part*, R 355, *part*, C 398, *part*.]

GEOG. DIST.— Coast of California.

GENUS **NYCTIDROMUS** GOULD.

Nyctidromus GOULD, Icones Avium, II. 1838, pl. ii. Type, *N. derbyanus* GOULD = *Caprimulgus albicollis* GMEL.

419. **Nyctidromus albicollis merrilli** SENN.
   Merrill's Parauque.

Nyctidromus albicollis merrilli SENN. Auk, V. Jan. 1888, 44.

[B —, C —, R 356, C 395.]

GEOG. DIST.— Valley of the Lower Rio Grande, north to the Nueces River, south into northeastern Mexico.

GENUS **CHORDEILES** SWAINSON.

Chordeiles SWAINS. in Sw. & RICH. Fauna Bor. Am. II. 1831, 496. Type, *Caprimulgus virginianus* GMEL.

420. **Chordeiles virginianus** (GMEL.).
   Nighthawk.

Caprimulgus virginianus GMEL. S. N. I. ii. 1788, 1028.
Chordeiles virginianus SWAINS. in Sw. & RICH. Fauna Bor. Am. II. 1831, 496.

[B 114, C 267, R 357, C 399.]

GEOG. DIST.— Northern and eastern North America, west to the Great Plains and central British Columbia, and from Labrador south through tropical America to the Argentine Republic.

420 *a*. **Chordeiles virginianus henryi** (CASS.).
   Western Nighthawk.

Chordeiles henryi CASS. Illustr. B. Cal. Tex. etc. I. 1855, 233.
Chordeiles virginianus var. *henryi* COUES, Key, 1872, 181.

[B 115, C 267*a*, R 357*a*, C 400.]

GEOG. DIST.— Western United States, from the Great Plains to the Pacific coast, and from British Columbia south to northern South America.

420 b. **Chordeiles virginianus chapmani** (COUES).
   Florida Nighthawk.

[*Chordeiles popetue*] *chapmani* (SENNET, MS.) COUES, Auk, V. Jan. 1888, 37.
Chordeiles virginianus chapmani SCOTT, Auk, V. April, 1888, 186.

[B —, C —, R 357b, C 401.]

GEOG. DIST.— Florida and the Gulf coast of Texas, south in winter to South America.

421. **Chordeiles acutipennis texensis** (LAWR.).
   Texan Nighthawk.

Chordeiles texensis LAWR. Ann. Lyc. N. Y. VI. Dec. 1856, 167.
Chordeiles acutipennis texensis RIDGW. in BAIRD, BREWER & RIDGWAY, N. Am. Birds, II. 1874, 406.

[B 116, C 268, R 358, C 402.]

GEOG. DIST.— Southern border of the United States, from Texas to southern California, north into southern Utah; south to Cape St. Lucas and Veragua.

SUBORDER CYPSELI. SWIFTS.

FAMILY **MICROPODIDÆ**. SWIFTS.

SUBFAMILY **CHÆTURINÆ**. SPINE-TAILED SWIFTS.

GENUS **CYPSELOIDES** STREUBEL.

Cypseloides STREUBEL, Isis, 1848, 366.   Type, *Hemiprocne fumigata* NATT. MS.

422. **Cypseloides niger** (GMEL.).
   Black Swift.

Hirundo nigra GMEL. S. N. I. ii. 1788, 1025.
Cypseloides niger SCL. P. Z. S. 1865, 615.

[B 108, C 270, R 350, C 404.]

GEOG. DIST.— Rocky Mountain region (Colorado), west to the Pacific coast; north to British Columbia, and south to Lower California, Mexico, Costa Rica, and the West Indies.

GENUS **CHÆTURA** STEPHENS.

Chætura STEPH. Gen. Zool. XIII. pt. ii. 1825, 76. Type, *Hirundo pelagica* LINN.

423. Chætura pelagica (LINN.).
Chimney Swift.

Hirundo pelagica LINN. S. N. ed. 10, I. 1758, 192.
Chætura pelasgia STEPH. Gen. Zool. XIII. pt. ii. 1825, 76.

[B 109, C 271, R 351, C 405.]

GEOG. DIST.— Eastern North America, north to Labrador and the Fur Countries, west to the Plains, and passing south of the United States in winter at least to Jalapa, Mexico, and Cozumel Island.

424. Chætura vauxii (TOWNS.).
Vaux's Swift.

Cypselus vauxii TOWNS. Journ. Ac. Nat. Sci. Phila. VIII. 1839, 148.
Chætura vauxii DEKAY, Zool. N. Y. II. 1844, 36.

[B 110, C 272, R 352, C 406.]

GEOG. DIST.— Pacific coast of the United States northward to British Columbia; migrating south in winter to Lower California and Mexico.

SUBFAMILY **MICROPODINÆ**. TYPICAL SWIFTS.

GENUS **AËRONAUTES** HARTERT.

Aëronautes HARTERT, Cat. Birds Brit. Mus. XVI, 1892, 459. Type, *Cypselus melanoleucus* BAIRD.

425. Aëronautes melanoleucus (BAIRD).
   White-throated Swift.

Cypselus melanoleucus BAIRD, Pr. Ac. Nat. Sci. Phila. June, 1854, 118.
Aëronautes melanoleucus HARTERT, Cat. Birds Brit. Mus. XVI, 1892, 459.

[B 107, C 269, R 349, C 403.]

GEOG. DIST.— Western United States, from the Black Hills, northern Wyoming, and southern Montana to the Pacific; south, in winter, to Guatemala.

SUBORDER TROCHILI. HUMMINGBIRDS.

FAMILY TROCHILIDÆ. HUMMINGBIRDS.

GENUS EUGENES GOULD.

Eugenes GOULD, Mon. Troch. pt. xii. 1856, pl. 59.   Type, *Trochilus fulgens* SWAINS.

426. Eugenes fulgens (SWAINS.).
   Rivoli Hummingbird.

Trochilus fulgens SWAINS. Phil. Mag. I. 1827, 441.
Eugenes fulgens GOULD, Mon. Troch. II. 1856, pl. 59.

[B —, C 274 *bis*, R 334, C 408.]

GEOG. DIST.— Southern Arizona and tablelands of Mexico to Nicaragua.

GENUS CŒLIGENA LESSON.

Cæligena LESS. Ind. & Synop. Gen. Troch. 1832, p. xviii.   Type, *Ornismya clemenciæ* LESS.

427. Cœligena clemenciæ LESS.
    Blue-throated Hummingbird.

Ornismya clemenciæ LESS. Ois. Mouch. 1829, 216, pl. 80.
Cæligena clemenciæ LESS. Ind. & Synop. Gen. Troch. 1832, p. xviii.

    [B —, C —, R —, C —.]

GEOG. DIST.— Southern Arizona, and the tablelands of Mexico to Guerrero and Oaxaca.

GENUS **TROCHILUS** LINNÆUS.

SUBGENUS **TROCHILUS**.

Trochilus LINN. S. N. ed. 10, I. 1758, 119. Type, by elimination, *T. colubris* LINN.

428. Trochilus colubris LINN.
    Ruby-throated Hummingbird.

Trochilus colubris LINN. S. N. ed. 10, I. 1758, 120.

    [B 101, C 275, R 335, C 409.]

GEOG. DIST.— Eastern North America to the Plains, north to the Fur Countries, breeding from Florida to Labrador, and south, in winter, to Cuba, Mexico, and Veragua.

429. Trochilus alexandri BOURC. & MULS.
    Black-chinned Hummingbird.

Trochilus alexandri BOURC. & MULS. Ann. Soc. Agric. Lyons, IX. 1846, 330.

    [B 102, C 276, R 336, C 410.]

GEOG. DIST.— Pacific coast region, from California to British Columbia, east to Utah and Arizona, and south to Lower California, the Valley of Mexico, and Guerrero.

429.1. Trochilus violajugulum JEFFRIES.
    Violet-throated Hummingbird.

Trochilus violajugulum JEFFRIES, Auk, V. April, 1888, 168.

    [B —, C —, R —, C —.]

GEOG. DIST.— Coast of southern California (Santa Barbara). Known only from the type specimen.

ORDER MACROCHIRES.

Genus **CALYPTE** Gould.

Calypte Gould, Mon. Troch. III. 1856, pl. 134. Type, *Ornismya costæ* Bourc.

430. Calypte costæ (Bourc.).
Costa's Hummingbird.
Ornismya costæ Bourc. Rev. Zool. 1839, 294.
Calypte costæ Gould, Mon. Troch. III. pt. xi, 1856, pl. 134.
[B 106, C 280, R 337, C 415.]

Geog. Dist.— Southern California, southern Nevada, Arizona, Lower California, and western Mexico.

431. Calypte anna (Less.).
Anna's Hummingbird.
Ornismya anna Less. Suppl. Ois. Mouch. 1831, 115, pl. vii.
Calypte annæ Gould, Mon. Troch. III. pt. xi, 1856, pl. 135.
[B 105, C 279, R 338, C 414.]

Geog. Dist.—Central and southern California, southern Arizona, and Lower California, casually to Guadalupe Island.

Genus **SELASPHORUS** Swainson.

Selasphorus Swains. in Sw. & Rich. Fauna Bor. Am. II. 1831, 324. Type, *Trochilus rufus* Gmel.

[431.1.] Selasphorus floresii Gould.
Floresi's Hummingbird.
Selasphorus floresii Gould, Mon. Troch. pt. xxiii. Sept. 1, 1861 (Vol. III. pl. 139).
[B —, C —, R —, C —.]

Geog. Dist.— Mexico (Bolaños, Jalisco); accidental at San Francisco, California.

432. Selasphorus platycercus (Swains.).
Broad-tailed Hummingbird.
Trochilus platycercus Swains. Phil. Mag. I. 1827, 441.
Selasphorus platycercus Bon. Consp. Av. I. 1850, 82.

[B 104, C 278, R 339, C 413.]

GEOG. DIST.— Rocky Mountain region (Idaho, Wyoming, and Colorado), west to the Sierra Nevada, and south through Arizona, New Mexico and Mexico to Guatemala.

433. Selasphorus rufus (GMEL.).
Rufous Hummingbird.

Trochilus rufus GMEL. S. N. I. i. 1788, 497.
Trochilus (Selasphorus) rufus SWAINS. in Sw. & RICH. Faun. Bor. Am. II. 1831, 324.

[B 103, C 277, R 340, C 411.]

GEOG. DIST.—Western Texas to Montana, west to the Pacific, and north to Mount St. Elias, Alaska; south in winter on the tablelands of Mexico to Vera Cruz and Oaxaca.

434. Selasphorus alleni HENSH.
Allen's Hummingbird.

Selasphorus alleni HENSH. Bull. Nutt. Orn. Club, II. 1877, 54.

[B —, C —, R 341, C 412.]

GEOG. DIST.— Pacific coast, north to British Columbia, east to southern Arizona.

GENUS **STELLULA** GOULD.

Stellula GOULD, Introd. Troch. 1861, 90.   Type, *Trochilus calliope* GOULD.

436. Stellula calliope GOULD.
Calliope Hummingbird.

Trochilus (Calothorax) calliope GOULD, P. Z. S. 1847, 11.
Stellula calliope GOULD, Introd. Troch. 1861, 90.

[B —, C 282, R 343, C 417.]

GEOG. DIST.— Mountains of the Pacific slope, from British Columbia to Montana, Nevada, and New Mexico; south to the Valley of Mexico and mountains of Guerrero.

Genus **CALOTHORAX** Gray.

Calothorax Gray, Gen. B. 1840, 13. Type, *Cynanthus lucifer* Swains.

437. **Calothorax lucifer** (Swains.).
Lucifer Hummingbird.

Cynanthus lucifer Swains. Phil. Mag. I. 1827, 442.
Calothorax lucifer Gray, Gen. B. I. 1844, 110.

[B —, C —, R 344, C 418.]

Geog. Dist.— Tablelands of Mexico, from Puebla and the Valley of Mexico north to southern Arizona.

Genus **AMAZILIA** Reichenbach.

Amazilia Reich. Syst. Av. 1849, pl. 39. Type, *Orthorhynchus amazili* Less.

438. **Amazilia fuscicaudata** (Fraser).
Rieffer's Hummingbird.

Trochilus fuscicaudatus Fras. P. Z. S. 1840, 17.
Amazilia fuscicaudata Ridgw. Pr. U. S. Nat. Mus. I. 1878, 118, 147.

[B —, C —, R 345, C 419.]

Geog. Dist.— Lower Rio Grande Valley in Texas, south through eastern Mexico to Central America and northern South America.

439. **Amazilia cerviniventris** Gould.
Buff-bellied Hummingbird.

Amazilius cerviniventris Gould, P. Z. S. 1856, 150.

[B—, C—, R 346, C 420.]

Geog. Dist.— Valley of the Lower Rio Grande and south in eastern Mexico to southern Vera Cruz.

Genus **BASILINNA** Boie.

Basilinna Boie, Isis, 1831, 546. Type, *Trochilus leucotis* Vieill

440. Basilinna xantusi (Lawr.).
Xantus's Hummingbird.

Amazilia xantusi Lawr. Ann. Lyc. N. Y. 1860, 109.
Basilinna xanthusi Elliot, Class. & Synop. Troch. March, 1879, 227.

[B—, C 273, R 347, C 407.]

Geog. Dist.— Lower California north to Lat. 29°.

440.1. Basilinna leucotis (Vieill.).
White-eared Hummingbird.

Trochilus leucotis Vieill. Nouv. Dict. d'Hist. Nat. XXIII. 1818, 428.
Basilinna leucotis Boie, Isis, 1831, 546.

[B—, C—, R—, C—.]

Geog. Dist.— Mexico and Nicaragua, north to the Chiricahua Mountains, Arizona.

Genus **IACHE** Elliot.

Iache Elliot, Class. & Synop. Troch. March, 1879, 234. Type, *Cynanthus latirostris* Swains.

441. Iache latirostris (Swains.).
Broad-billed Hummingbird.

Cynanthus latirostris Swains. Phil. Mag. I. 1827, 441.
Iache latirostris Elliot, Class. & Synop. Troch. March, 1879, 235.

[B—, C—, R 348, C 421.]

Geog. Dist.— Southern Arizona and south to the Valley of Mexico.

Order PASSERES. Perching Birds.

Suborder CLAMATORES. Songless Perching Birds.

Family COTINGIDÆ. The Cotingas.

Genus **Platypsaris** Sclater.

Platypsaris Scl. P. Z. S. 1857, 72 (ex Bonap., 1854, = nomen nudum). Type, *Pachyrhamphus latirostris* Bonap.

441.1. Platypsaris albiventris (Lawr.).
  Xantus's Becard.

Hadrostomus albiventris Lawr. Ann. Lyc. N. Y. VIII. 1867, 475.
Platypsaris albiventris Ridgw. Man. N. Am. B. 1887, 325.

[B —, C —, R —, C —.]

Geog. Dist.— Western and southern Mexico, north to southern Arizona (Huachuca Mts.).

Family TYRANNIDÆ. Tyrant Flycatchers.

Genus **MILVULUS** Swainson.

Milvulus Swainson, Zool. Journ. III. July, 1827, 165. Type, *Tyrannus savanna* Vieill. = *Muscicapa tyrannus* Linn.

[442.] **Milvulus tyrannus** (Linn.).
  Fork-tailed Flycatcher.

Muscicapa tyrannus Linn. S. N. ed. 12, I. 1766, 325.
Milvulus tyrannus Bonap. Geogr. & Comp. List, 1838, 25.

[B 122, C 240, R 302, C 366.]

GEOG. DIST.— Southern Mexico and southward throughout Central and most of South America. Accidental in the United States (Mississippi, Kentucky, New Jersey, southern California).

443. Milvulus forficatus (GMEL.).
Scissor-tailed Flycatcher.

Muscicapa forficata GMEL. S. N. I. ii. 1788, 931.
Milvulus forficatus SWAINS. Classif. B. II. 1827, 225.

[B 123, C 241, R 301, C 367.]

GEOG. DIST.— Texas, Oklahoma, Indian Territory, southern Kansas and southwestern Missouri, south through eastern Mexico to Costa Rica. Accidental in southern Florida (Key West), New Jersey, New England, and at York Factory, Hudson Bay.

GENUS **TYRANNUS** CUVIER.

Tyrannus CUVIER, Leç. d'An. Comp. I. 1799, tabl. ii. (*Cf.* Tabl. Elem. 1797, p. 201.) Type, *Lanius tyrannus* LINN.

444. Tyrannus tyrannus (LINN.).
Kingbird.

Lanius tyrannus LINN. S. N. ed. 10, I. 1758, 94.
Tyrannus tyrannus JORDAN, Man. Vert. ed. 4, 1884, 96.

[B 124, C 242, R 304, C 368.]

GEOG. DIST.— North America, from the British Provinces south, in winter, through eastern Mexico, Central and South America. Less common west of the Rocky Mountains. Not recorded from New Mexico and Arizona.

445. Tyrannus dominicensis (GMEL.).
Gray Kingbird.

Lanius tyrannus β. *dominicensis* GMEL. S. N. I. 1788, 302.
Tyrannus dominicensis RICHARDSON, Rep. Sixth Meet. Brit. Ass. V. 1837, 170.

[B 125, C 243, R 303, C 369.]

GEOG. DIST.— South Atlantic States (South Carolina, Georgia, Florida), West Indies, Atlantic coast of Central America, and northern South America. Accidental in Massachusetts.

446. **Tyrannus melancholicus couchii** (BAIRD).
Couch's Kingbird.

Tyrannus couchii BAIRD, B. N. Am. 1858, 175.
Tyrannus melancholicus var. *couchii* COUES, Check-list, ed. 1, Dec. 1873, 51.

[B 128, 129, C 246, R 305, C 372.]

GEOG. DIST.— Southern border of the United States (Texas), south to Guatemala.

447. **Tyrannus verticalis** SAY.
Arkansas Kingbird.

Tyrannus verticalis SAY, LONG'S Exp. II. 1823, 60.

[B 126, C 244, R 306, C 370.]

GEOG. DIST.— Western United States, from the Plains to the Pacific, and from British Columbia south through Lower California and western Mexico to Guatemala. Accidental in Maryland, New Jersey, New York, and Maine.

448. **Tyrannus vociferans** SWAINS.
Cassin's Kingbird.

Tyrannus vociferans SWAINS. Quart. Jour. Sci. XX. 1826, 273.

[B 127, C 245, R 307, C 371.]

GEOG. DIST.— Western United States from southern Wyoming, eastern Colorado, New Mexico, Arizona, western Texas and southern California, south to Guatemala.

GENUS **PITANGUS** SWAINSON.

Pitangus SWAINSON, Zool. Journ. III. July, 1827, 165. Type, *Tyrannus sulphuratus* VIEILL.

449. Pitangus derbianus (KAUP).
Derby Flycatcher.
Saurophagus derbianus KAUP, P. Z. S. 1851 (Oct. 1852), 44, pl. xxxvi.
Pitangus derbianus SCLATER, P. Z. S. 1856 (Jan. 1857), 297.
[B—, C—, R 308, C 364.]

GEOG. DIST.— Valley of the Lower Rio Grande in Texas, south to northern South America.

GENUS **MYIOZETETES** SCLATER.

Myiozetetes SCL. P. Z. S. 1859, 46. Type, *Muscicapa cayennensis* LINN.

[450.] **Myiozetetes texensis** (GIRAUD).
Giraud's Flycatcher.
Muscicapa texensis GIRAUD, Sixteen Sp. Texas B. 1841, pl. 1.
Myiozetetes texensis SCL. P. Z. S. 1859, 56.
[B—, C—, R 309, C—.]

GEOG. DIST.— "Texas" (GIRAUD), south to Central America and northern South America.

GENUS **MYIODYNASTES** BONAPARTE.

Myiodynastes BONAP. Bull. Soc. Linn. Normandée, II. 1857, 35 (ex BONAP. Comptes Rend. XXXVIII. 1854, 657, nomen nudum). Type, *Muscicapa audax* GMEL.

451. Myiodynastes luteiventris SCL.
Sulphur-bellied Flycatcher.
Myiodynastes luteiventris SCL. P. Z. S. 1859, 42 (ex BONAP. Comptes Rend. XXXVIII. 1854, 657, nomen nudum).
[B—, C—, R 310, C 365.]

GEOG. DIST.— Southern Arizona, south to Panama.

GENUS **MYIARCHUS** CABANIS.

Myiarchus CAB. Arch. f. Naturg. 1844, i, 272. Type, *Muscicapa ferox* GMEL.

452. **Myiarchus crinitus** (LINN.).
   Crested Flycatcher.
   Muscicapa crinita LINN. S. N. ed. 12, I. 1766, 325.
   Myiarchus crinitus LICHT. Nomencl. Mus. Berol. 1854, 16.
   [B 130, C 247, R 312, C 373.]

GEOG. DIST.— Eastern United States and southern Canada, west to Manitoba and the Plains, south through eastern Mexico to Costa Rica, Panama and Colombia. Breeds from Florida northward.

453. **Myiarchus mexicanus** (KAUP).
   Mexican Crested Flycatcher.
   Tyrannula mexicana KAUP, P. Z. S. 1851, 51.
   Myiarchus mexicanus BAIRD, B. N. Am. 1858, 179.
   [B 132, C —, R 311, C 374.]

GEOG. DIST.— Valley of the Lower Rio Grande in Texas, southward to Guatemala.

453 a. **Myiarchus mexicanus magister** RIDGW.
   Arizona Crested Flycatcher.
   Myiarchus mexicanus magister RIDGW. Pr. Biol. Soc. Wash. II. April 10, 1884, 90.
   [B —, C —, R —, C —.]

GEOG. DIST.— Southern Arizona, south into western Mexico.

454. **Myiarchus cinerascens** (LAWR.).
   Ash-throated Flycatcher.
   Tyrannula cinerascens LAWR. Ann. Lyc. N. Y. V. 1851, 121.
   Myiarchus cinerascens SCL. & SALV. Ibis, I. Apr. 1859, 121.
   [B 131, C 248, R 313, C 375.]

GEOG. DIST.— Western United States, north to Oregon, Nevada, Utah, and Colorado, south to Guatemala.

454 a. **Myiarchus cinerascens nuttingi** (RIDGW.).
   Nutting's Flycatcher.
   Myiarchus nuttingi RIDGW. Pr. U. S. Nat. Mus. V. 1882, 394.
   Myiarchus cinerascens nuttingi ALLEN, Bull. Am. Mus. Nat. Hist. IV. Dec. 1892, 346.

[B 131, *part*, C 248, *part*, R 313, *part*, C 375, *part*.]

GEOG. DIST.— Southern Arizona, southward through western Mexico to Costa Rica.

[455.] **Myiarchus lawrenceii** (GIRAUD).
Lawrence's Flycatcher.

Muscicapa lawrenceii GIRAUD, Sixteen Sp. Texas B. 1841, 9 (by actual counting, the text not being paged).
Myiarchus lawrencii BAIRD, B. N. Am. 1858, 181.

[B 133, C 248, R 314, C 376.]

GEOG. DIST.— "Texas" (GIRAUD) and eastern Mexico.

455 *a*. **Myiarchus lawrencei olivascens** RIDGW.
Olivaceous Flycatcher.

Myiarchus lawrencei olivascens RIDGW. Pr. Biol. Soc. Wash. II. April 10, 1884, 91.

[B —, C —, R —, C —.]

GEOG. DIST.— Arizona and western Mexico. Casual at Fort Lyon, Colorado.

GENUS **SAYORNIS** BONAPARTE.

Sayornis BONAP. Coll. Delattre, 1854, 87. Type, *Tyrannula nigricans* SWAINS.

456. **Sayornis phœbe** (LATH.).
Phœbe.

Muscicapa phœbe LATHAM, Ind. Orn. II. 1790, 489.
Sayornis phœbe STEJN. Auk, II. Jan. 1885, 51.

[B 135, C 252, R 315, C 379.]

GEOG. DIST.— Eastern North America, west to eastern Colorado and western Texas, and from the British Provinces south to eastern Mexico and Cuba, wintering from the South Atlantic and Gulf States southward. Breeds from South Carolina northward.

ORDER PASSERES. 185

457. **Sayornis saya** (BONAP.).
   Say's Phœbe.

Muscicapa saya BONAP. Am. Orn. I. 1825, 20.
Sayornis sayus BAIRD, B. N. Am. 1858, 185.

[B 136, C 250, R 316, C 377.]

GEOG. DIST.— Western United States, from the Plains (central North and South Dakota, Nebraska and Kansas) to the Pacific; north along the Yukon River to the Arctic Circle; south to Cape St. Lucas and over the Mexican Plateau to Puebla and central Vera Cruz. Accidental in Massachusetts.

458. **Sayornis nigricans** (SWAINS.).
   Black Phœbe.

Tyrannula nigricans SWAINS. Phil. Mag. I. May, 1827, 367.
Sayornis nigricans BONAP. Coll. Delattre, 1854, 87.

[B 134, C 251, R 317, C 378.]

GEOG. DIST.— Southwestern United States, from Texas through southern New Mexico and Arizona to California, and northward along the Pacific coast to Washington; south to Cape St. Lucas, Lower California, and in Mexico to Oaxaca.

GENUS **CONTOPUS** CABANIS.

Contopus CAB. J. f. O. III. Nov. 1855, 479. Type, *Muscicapa virens* LINN.

SUBGENUS **NUTTALLORNIS** RIDGW.

Nuttallornis RIDGW. Man. N. Am. B. 1887, 337. Type, *Tyrannus borealis* SWAINS.

459. **Contopus borealis** (SWAINS.).
   Olive-sided Flycatcher.

Tyrannus borealis SWAINS. in SW. & RICH. Faun. B. A. II. 1831, 141, pl. 35.
Contopus borealis BAIRD, B. N. Am. 1858, 188.

[B 137, C 253, R 318, C 380.]

GEOG. DIST.— North America, breeding from the northern and the higher mountainous parts of the United States northward to British Columbia and the Saskatchewan River. Accidental on the Lower Yukon and in Greenland. In winter, south to Central America, Colombia, and northern Peru.

SUBGENUS **CONTOPUS** CABANIS.

460. Contopus pertinax CAB.
Coues's Flycatcher.

Myiarchus pertinax LICHT. Nomen. Mus. Berol. 1854, 16 (nomen nudum).

Contopus pertinax CAB. Mus. Hein. II. Sept. 30, 1859, 72.

[B —, C 254, R 319, C 381.]

GEOG. DIST.— Mountains of southern and central Arizona, south through Mexico to Guatemala.

461. Contopus virens (LINN.).
Wood Pewee.

Muscicapa virens LINN. S. N. ed. 12, I. 1766, 327.

Contopus virens CAB. J. f. O. 1855, 479.

[B 139, C 255, R 320, C 382.]

GEOG. DIST.— Eastern North America, west to the Plains, and from southern Canada southward, migrating through eastern Mexico and Honduras to Colombia and Ecuador. Breeds from Florida to Newfoundland.

462. Contopus richardsonii (SWAINS.).
Western Wood Pewee.

Tyrannula richardsonii SWAINS. in SW. & RICH. F. B. A. II. 1831, 146, pl. 46, lower fig.

Contopus richardsonii BAIRD, B. N. Am. 1858, 189.

[B 138, C 255a, R 321, C 383.]

GEOG. DIST.— Western United States, from the Plains to the Pacific, north to British Columbia and the interior of British America, south through Central America to Colombia.

462 a. **Contopus richardsonii peninsulæ** BREWST.
    Large-billed Wood Pewee.

  Contopus richardsonii peninsulæ BREWST. Auk, VIII. April, 1891, 144.

  [B —, C —, R —, C —.]

  GEOG. DIST.— Sierra de la Laguna, Lower California.

GENUS **EMPIDONAX** CABANIS.

  Empidonax CAB. J. f. O. 1855, 480. Type, *Tyrannula pusilla* SWAINS.

463. **Empidonax flaviventris** BAIRD.
    Yellow-bellied Flycatcher.

  Tyrannula flaviventris BAIRD (W. M. & S. F.), Pr. Ac. Nat. Sci. Phila. July, 1843, 283.
  Empidonax flaviventris BAIRD, B. N. Am. 1858, 198.

  [B 144, C 259, R 322, C 388.]

  GEOG. DIST.— Eastern North America west to the Plains, and from southern Labrador south through eastern Mexico to Panama, breeding from the Northern States northward. Casual in Greenland.

464. **Empidonax difficilis** BAIRD.
    Western Flycatcher.

  Empidonax difficilis BAIRD, B. N. Am. 1858, 198 (in text).

  [B 144*a*, C 259, *part*, R 323, C 389.]

  GEOG. DIST.— Western United States, from the Plains to the Pacific; south to Cape St. Lucas and through western Mexico to Costa Rica; north to southern Alaska.

464.1. **Empidonax cineritius** BREWST.
    St. Lucas Flycatcher.

  Empidonax cineritius BREWST. Auk, V. Jan. 1888, 90.

  [B —, C —, R —, C —.]

  GEOG. DIST.— Lower California.

465. Empidonax virescens (VIEILL.).
Green-crested Flycatcher.

Platyrhynchos virescens VIEILL. Nouv. Dict. d'Hist. Nat. XXVII. 1818, 22.
Empidonax virescens BREWST. Auk, XII. April, 1895, 157.

[B 143, C 256, R 324, C 384.]

GEOG. DIST.— Eastern United States, north to southern New York and southern Michigan, west to the Plains, south to Cuba and Costa Rica. Rare or casual in southern New England (Hyde Park, Mass.).

466. Empidonax traillii (AUD.).
Traill's Flycatcher.

Muscicapa traillii AUD. Orn. Biog. I. 1832, 236.
Empidonax traillii BAIRD, Bds. N. Am. 1858, 193.

[B 141, C 257a, R 325, C 386.]

GEOG. DIST.— Western North America, from the Mississippi Valley (Ohio, Illinois, and Michigan) to the Pacific, and from the Fur Countries south into Mexico.

466 a. Empidonax traillii alnorum BREWST.
Alder Flycatcher.

Empidonax traillii alnorum BREWST. Auk, XII. April, 1895, 161.

[B 140, C 257, R 325a, C 385.]

GEOG. DIST.— Eastern North America, from the Maritime Provinces and New England westward at least to northern Michigan, etc., breeding from the southern edge of the Canadian Fauna northward; in winter south to Central America.

467. Empidonax minimus BAIRD.
Least Flycatcher.

Tyrannula minima BAIRD (W. M. & S. F.), Pr. Ac. Nat. Sci. Phila. July, 1843, 284.
Empidonax minimus BAIRD, B. N. Am. 1858, 195.

[B 142, C 258, R 326, C 387.]

GEOG. DIST.— Chiefly eastern North America, west to eastern Colorado and central Montana, south in winter to Central America. Breeds from the Northern States northward.

468. Empidonax hammondi (XANTUS).
        Hammond's Flycatcher.
    Tyrannula hammondi XANTUS, Pr. Ac. Nat. Sci. Phila. May, 1858, 117.
    Empidonax hammondi BAIRD, B. N. Am. 1858, 199.
        [B 145, C 260, R 327, C 390.]
    GEOG. DIST.— Western North America, from the western border of the Plains westward, north to Lesser Slave Lake and Alaska, and south to southern Mexico.

469. Empidonax wrightii BAIRD.
        Wright's Flycatcher.
    Empidonax wrightii BAIRD, B. N. Am. 1858, 200 (in text).
        [B 146, C 261, R 328, C 391.]
    GEOG. DIST.— Western United States, north to Oregon and Montana, and south to southern Mexico.

469.1. Empidonax griseus BREWST.
        Gray Flycatcher.
    Empidonax griseus BREWST. Auk, VI. April, 1889, 87.
        [B —, C —, R —, C —.]
    GEOG. DIST.— Lower California and portions of Sonora. (Arizona?)

[470.] Empidonax fulvifrons (GIRAUD).
        Fulvous Flycatcher.
    Muscicapa fulvifrons GIRAUD, Sixteen Sp. Tex. B. 1841, pl. ii.
    Empidonax fulvifrons SCL. P. Z. S. 1858, 301.
        [B —, C —, R 329, C —.]
    GEOG. DIST.— "Texas" (GIRAUD), and eastern Mexico.

470 a. Empidonax fulvifrons pygmæus (COUES).
        Buff-breasted Flycatcher.
    Empidonax pygmæus COUES, Ibis, 1865, 537.
    Empidonax fulvifrons pygmæus RIDGW. Pr. U. S. Nat. Mus. VIII. 1885, 356.
        [B —, C 262, R 329a, C 392.]
    GEOG. DIST.— Western New Mexico and southern Arizona, south into western Mexico.

Genus **PYROCEPHALUS** Gould.

Pyrocephalus Gould, Zool. Voy. Beag. 1841, 44. Types, "*Pyrocephalus parvirostris* (Gould), and *Muscicapa coronata* (Auct.)."

471. Pyrocephalus rubineus mexicanus (Scl.).
   Vermilion Flycatcher.

Pyrocephalus mexicanus Scl. P. Z. S. 1859, 45.
Pyrocephalus rubineus var. *mexicanus* Coues, Key, 1872, 177.

[B 147, C 263, R 330, C 394.]

Geog. Dist.— Southern and central Arizona, southwestern Utah, and the valley of the Lower Rio Grande in Texas, south to Lower California and Guatemala.

Genus **ORNITHION** Hartlaub.

Ornithion Hartlaub, J. f. O. 1853, 35. Type, *O. inerme* Hartl.

472. Ornithion imberbe (Scl.).
   Beardless Flycatcher.

Camptostoma imberbe Scl. P. Z. S. 1857, 203.
Ornithion imberbe Lawr. Ibis, 1876, 497.

[B —, C —, R 331, C 393.]

Geog. Dist.— Valley of the Lower Rio Grande in Texas, south into eastern Mexico, Guatemala, and Nicaragua.

472 a. Ornithion imberbe ridgwayi Brewst.
   Ridgway's Flycatcher.

Ornithium imberbe ridgwayi Brewst. Bull. Nutt. Orn. Cl. VII. Oct. 1882, 208.

[B —, C —, R —, C —.]

Geog. Dist.— Southern Arizona, south in Mexico to Puebla and Jalisco.

Suborder OSCINES. Song Birds.

Family ALAUDIDÆ. Larks.

Genus ALAUDA Linnæus.

Alauda Linn. S. N. ed. 10, I. 1758, 165.   Type, by elimination, *A. arvensis* Linn.

[473.] **Alauda arvensis** Linn.
   Skylark.

Alauda arvensis Linn. S. N. ed. 10, I. 1758, 165.

[B —, C 55 *bis*, R 299, C 88.]

Geog. Dist.— Europe and Asia.   Accidental in Greenland and Bermuda.

Genus OTOCORIS Bonaparte.

Otocoris Bonap. Nouvi Ann. Sci. Nat. Bologna, II. 1838, 407. Type, *Alauda alpestris* Linn.

474. **Otocoris alpestris** (Linn.).
   Horned Lark.

Alauda alpestris Linn. S. N. ed. 10, 1758, 166.
Otocoris alpestris Bonap. Nouvi Ann. Sci. Nat. Bologna, II. 1838. 407.

[B 302, C 53, R 300, C 82.]

Geog. Dist.— Northeastern North America, Greenland, and northern parts of the Old World; in winter south in eastern United States to the Carolinas, Illinois, etc.

474 a. Otocoris alpestris leucolæma (Coues).
   Pallid Horned Lark.

   Eremophila alpestris b. *leucolæma* Coues, B. N. W. 1875, 38 (part).
   Otocoris alpestris leucolæma Stejn. Pr. U. S. Nat. Mus. V.
      June 5, 1882, 34.

   [B —, C 53*b*, R 300*a*, C 83.]

   Geog. Dist.— Interior of British America, and Alaska, south in winter into western United States.

474 b. Otocoris alpestris praticola Hensh.
   Prairie Horned Lark.

   O[*tocorys*] *alpestris praticola* Hensh. Auk, I. July, 1884, 264.

   [B —, C —, R —, C —.]

   Geog. Dist.— Upper Mississippi Valley and the region of the Great Lakes to New England, breeding eastward to northeastern New York and western Massachusetts, New Hampshire and Vermont, and migrating south to South Carolina, Texas, etc.

474 c. Otocoris alpestris arenicola Hensh.
   Desert Horned Lark.

   O[*tocorys*] *alpestris arenicola* Hensh. Auk, I. July, 1884, 265.

   [B —, C —, R —, C —.]

   Geog. Dist.— Great Plains and Great Basin of the United States, south in winter to northern Mexico.

474 d. Otocoris alpestris giraudi Hensh.
   Texan Horned Lark.

   Otocorys alpestris giraudi Hensh. Auk, I. July, 1884, 266.

   [B —, C —, R —, C —.]

   Geog. Dist.— Eastern and southeastern Texas.

474 e. Otocoris alpestris chrysolæma (Wagl.).
   Mexican Horned Lark.

   Alauda chrysolæma Wagl. Isis, 1831, 530.
   Otocoris alpestris chrysolæma Stejn. Pr. U. S. Nat. Mus. V.
      June 5, 1882, 34.

[B—, C 53a, R 300b, C 84.]

GEOG. DIST.— Coast district of California (north to Nicasio), northern Lower California, and parts of Mexico (Mirador, Vera Cruz, Valley of Mexico, etc.).

474f. Otocoris alpestris rubea HENSH.
Ruddy Horned Lark.

O[tocorys] alpestris rubeus HENSH. Auk, I. July, 1884, 267.

[B—, C—, R—, C—.]

GEOG. DIST.— Sacramento and San Joaquin Valleys, California.

474g. Otocoris alpestris strigata HENSH.
Streaked Horned Lark.

O[tocorys] alpestris strigata HENSH. Auk, I. July, 1884, 267.

[B—, C—, R—, C—.]

GEOG. DIST.— Coast region of Washington, Oregon, and British Columbia. Islands off coast of southern California.

474h. Otocoris alpestris adusta DWIGHT.
Scorched Horned Lark.

Otocoris alpestris adusta DWIGHT, Auk, VII. April, 1890, 148.

[B—, C—, R—, C—.]

GEOG. DIST.— Southern Arizona and New Mexico, western Texas, and southward into Mexico.

474i. Otocoris alpestris merrilli DWIGHT.
Dusky Horned Lark.

Otocoris alpestris merrilli DWIGHT, Auk, VII. April, 1890, 153.

[B—, C—, R—, C—.]

GEOG. DIST.— Eastern Oregon, Washington, and British Columbia, between the Cascade and Rocky Mountains; southward in winter into Nevada and California.

474j. Otocoris alpestris pallida TOWNSEND.
Sonoran Horned Lark.

Otocoris alpestris pallida TOWNSEND, Proc. U. S. Nat. Mus., XIII, 1890, 138.

[B—, C—, R—, C—.]

GEOG. DIST.— Lower California and Sonora.

FAMILY **CORVIDÆ**. CROWS, JAYS, MAGPIES, ETC.

SUBFAMILY **GARRULINÆ**. MAGPIES AND JAYS.

GENUS **PICA** BRISSON.

Pica BRISS. Orn. II. 1760, 35. Type, *Corvus pica* LINN.

475. **Pica pica hudsonica** (SAB.).
American Magpie.

Corvus hudsonicus SAB. App. Frankl. Journ. 1823, 25, 671.
Pica pica hudsonica JORDAN, Man. Vert. ed. 4, 1884, 94.

[B 432, C 233, R 286, C 347.]

GEOG. DIST.— Northern and western North America, from the Plains to the Cascade Mountains and north to Alaska; casually east and south to Michigan (accidental in northern Illinois in winter), and in the Rocky Mountains to New Mexico and Arizona. Replaced in California, west of the Sierra Nevada, by the next species.

476. **Pica nuttalli** AUD.
Yellow-billed Magpie.

Pica nuttalli AUD. Orn. Biog. IV. 1838, 450, pl. 362.

[B 433, C 233*a*, R 287, C 348.]

GEOG. DIST.— California, west of the Sierra Nevada, from Sacramento Valley south to about latitude 34°, locally distributed.

GENUS **CYANOCITTA** STRICKLAND.

Cyanocitta STRICKL. Ann. Nat. Hist. XV. 1845, 261. Type, *Corvus cristatus* LINN.

477. **Cyanocitta cristata** (LINN.).
Blue Jay.

Corvus cristatus LINN. S. N. ed. 10, I. 1758, 106.
Cyanocitta cristata STRICKL. Ann. Nat. Hist. XV. 1845, 261.

ORDER PASSERES.

[B 434, C 234, R 289, C 349.]

GEOG. DIST.— Eastern North America to the Plains, and from the Fur Countries south to Florida and eastern Texas.

477 *a*. **Cyanocitta cristata florincola** COUES.
    Florida Blue Jay.

Cyanocitta cristata florincola COUES, Key, ed. 2, 1884, 421.

[B —, C —, R —, C —.]

GEOG. DIST.— Florida and the Gulf coast to southeastern Texas, casually along the coast to southwestern Texas.

478. **Cyanocitta stelleri** (GMEL.).
    Steller's Jay.

Corvus stelleri GMEL. S. N. I. 1788, 370.
Cyanocitta stelleri STRICKL. Ann. Nat. Hist. XV. 1845, 261.

[B 435, C 235, R 290, C 350.]

GEOG. DIST.— Pacific coast of North America, from Sitka south through the Cascade and Coast Ranges to Monterey Bay.

478 *a*. **Cyanocitta stelleri frontalis** (RIDGW.).
    Blue-fronted Jay.

Cyanura stelleri var. *frontalis* RIDGW. Am. Journ. Sc. & Arts, 3d ser. V. Jan. 1873, 41.
Cyanocitta stelleri var. *frontalis* BOUCARD, Cat. Av. 1876, 279.

[B —, C 235*b*, R 290*a*, C 353.]

GEOG. DIST.— Southern coast ranges and Sierra Nevada of California and western Nevada, from Fort Crook south to northern Lower California.

478 *b*. **Cyanocitta stelleri macrolopha** (BAIRD).
    Long-crested Jay.

Cyanocitta macrolopha BAIRD, Pr. Ac. Nat. Sci. Phila. 1854, 118.
Cyanocitta stelleri macrolopha COUES, Bull. Nutt. Orn. Cl. V. April, 1880, 98.

[B 436, C 235*a*, R 290*b*, 290*c*, C 352.]

GEOG. DIST.— Southern Rocky Mountains, southern Arizona and northwestern Mexico.

478 *c*. Cyanocitta stelleri annectens (BAIRD).
Black-headed Jay.

[*Cyanura stelleri*] var. *annectens* BAIRD, Hist. N. Am. B. II. 1874, 281, in text.
Cyanocitta stelleri annectens RIDGW. Proc. U. S. Nat. Mus. III. 1880, 184.

[B 436, *part*, C 255*a*, *part*, R 290*b*, C 352, *part*.]

GEOG. DIST.— Northern Rocky Mountains, south to Wahsatch range, west to eastern Oregon and Washington.

GENUS **APHELOCOMA** CABANIS.

Aphelocoma CABANIS, Mus. Hein. I. Oct. 15, 1851, 221. Type, *Garrulus californicus* VIG.

479. Aphelocoma floridana (BARTR.)
Florida Jay.

Corvus floridanus BARTR. Trav. Carol. 1791, 291.
Aphelocoma floridana CAB. Mus. Hein. I. 1851, 221.

[B 439, C 236, R 291, C 354.]

GEOG. DIST.— Florida, of local distribution.

480. Aphelocoma woodhouseii (BAIRD).
Woodhouse's Jay.

Cyanocitta woodhouseii BAIRD, B. N. Am. 1858, 585, pl. 59.
Aphelocoma woodhousii RIDGW. Field and Forest, June, 1877, 208.

[B 438, C 236*a*, R 292, C 355.]

GEOG. DIST.— Western United States, from the desert ranges of southern California north to eastern Oregon, east to Montana, Wyoming, Colorado and New Mexico, and south to northern Mexico.

480.1. Aphelocoma cyanotis RIDGW.
    Blue-eared Jay.

Aphelocoma cyanotis RIDGW. Man. N. Am. Bds. 1887, 357.

[B—, C—, R—, C—.]

GEOG. DIST.— Northern Mexico, ranging northward into western Texas.

481. Aphelocoma californica (VIG.).
    California Jay.

Garrulus californicus VIG. Zool. Beech. Voy. 1839, 21, pl. v.
Aphelocoma californica CAB. Mus. Hein. I. Oct. 15, 1851, 221.

[B 437, C 236*b*, R 293, C 356.]

GEOG. DIST.— Pacific coast region, including both slopes of the Sierra Nevada, from the Columbia River to northern Lower California.

481 *a*. Aphelocoma californica hypoleuca RIDGW.
    Xantus's Jay.

Aphelocoma californica hypoleuca RIDGW. Man. N. Am. B. 1887, 356.

[B 437, *part*, C 236*b*, *part*, R 293, *part*, C 356, *part*.]

GEOG. DIST.— Lower California, from Cape St. Lucas north to Lat. 28°.

481 *b*. Aphelocoma californica obscura ANTHONY.
    Belding's Jay.

Aphelocoma californica obscura ANTHONY, Proc. Cal. Ac. Sci. 2d ser. II. Oct. 11, 1889, 75.

[B—, C—, R—, C—.]

GEOG. DIST.— San Pedro Martir Mountains, Lower California.

481.1. Aphelocoma insularis HENSH.
    Santa Cruz Jay.

Aphelocoma insularis HENSH. Auk, III. Oct. 1886, 452.

[B—, C—, R—, C—.]

GEOG. DIST.— Santa Cruz Island, southern California.

482. Aphelocoma sieberii arizonæ RIDGW.
   Arizona Jay.

   Cyanocitta ultramarina var. *arizonæ* RIDGW. Bull. Essex Inst. V. Dec. 1873, 199.
   Aphelocoma sieberii arizonæ RIDGW. Pr. U. S. Nat. Mus. VIII. 1885, 355.

   [B 440, C 237, R 295, C 357.]

   GEOG. DIST.— Southern New Mexico and Arizona, and southward into Sonora and Chihuahua.

GENUS **XANTHOURA** BONAPARTE.

Xanthoura BONAP. Consp. Av. I. May 6, 1850, 380. Type, *Corvus yncas* BODD.

483. Xanthoura luxuosa (LESS.).
   Green Jay.

   Garrulus luxuosus LESS. Rev. Zool. 1839, 100.
   Xanthoura luxuosa BONAP. Consp. Av. I. 1850, 380.

   [B 442, C 238, R 296, C 358.]

   GEOG. DIST.— Valley of the Lower Rio Grande in Texas, and southward in eastern Mexico to Vera Cruz and Puebla.

GENUS **PERISOREUS** BONAPARTE.

Perisoreus BONAP. Saggio, 1831, 43. Type, *Corvus infaustus* LINN.

484. Perisoreus canadensis (LINN.).
   Canada Jay.

   Corvus canadensis LINN. S. N. ed. 12, I. 1766, 158.
   Perisoreus canadensis BONAP. Geog. & Comp. List, 1838, 27.

   [B 443, C 239, R 297, C 359.]

   GEOG. DIST.— Northern New York, northern New England, and northern Michigan, northward to Arctic America.

484 a. Perisoreus canadensis capitalis RIDGW.
Rocky Mountain Jay.

Perisoreus canadensis var. *capitalis* "BAIRD MS." RIDGW. Bull. Essex Inst. V. Nov. 1873, 193.

[B —, C 239*b*, R 297*a*, C 362.]

GEOG. DIST.— Rocky Mountain region of the United States, south to New Mexico and Arizona.

484 b. Perisoreus canadensis fumifrons RIDGW.
Alaskan Jay.

Perisoreus canadensis fumifrons RIDGW. Pr. U. S. Nat. Mus. III. March 27, 1880, 5.

[B —, C —, R 297*b*, C 360.]

GEOG. DIST.— Alaska, except southern coast district.

484 c. Perisoreus canadensis nigricapillus RIDGW.
Labrador Jay.

Perisoreus canadensis nigricapillus RIDGW. Pr. U. S. Nat. Mus. V. June 5, 1882, 15.

[B —, C —, R —, C —.]

GEOG. DIST.— Coast district of Labrador, north to Ungava Bay.

485. Perisoreus obscurus (RIDGW.).
Oregon Jay.

Perisoreus canadensis var. *obscurus* RIDGW. Bull. Essex Inst. Nov. 1873, 194.
Perisoreus obscurus SHARPE, Brit. Mus. Cat. B. III. 1877, 105.

[B —, C 239*a*, R 298, C 361.]

GEOG. DIST.— Northwest coast, from the northern Sierra Nevada and Humboldt Bay, in California, to British Columbia.

SUBFAMILY **CORVINÆ**. CROWS.

GENUS **CORVUS** LINNÆUS.

Corvus LINN. S. N. ed. 10, I. 1758, 105. Type, by elimination, *C. corax* LINN.

486. Corvus corax sinuatus (WAGL.).
American Raven.

Corvus sinuatus WAGLER, Isis, 1829, 748.
Corvus corax sinuatus RIDGW. Pr. U. S. Nat. Mus. VIII. 1885, 355.

[B 423, 424, C 226, R 280, C 338.]

GEOG. DIST.— Western United States, from the Rocky Mountains westward, and south to Guatemala.

486 a. Corvus corax principalis RIDGW.
Northern Raven.

Corvus corax principalis RIDGW. Man. N. Am. B. 1887, 361.

[B 423, *part*, C 226, *part*, R 280, *part*, C 338, *part*.]

GEOG. DIST.— Northern North America, south to British Columbia, northern Michigan, New Brunswick, Maine, New Jersey, North Carolina, etc.

487. Corvus cryptoleucus COUCH.
White-necked Raven.

Corvus cryptoleucus COUCH, Pr. Ac. Nat. Sci. Phila. April, 1854, 66.

[B 425, C 227, R 281, C 339.]

GEOG. DIST.— Southern border of the United States, from Texas to southern California, north to Colorado and western Kansas, south into northern Mexico.

488. Corvus americanus AUD.
American Crow.

Corvus americanus AUD. Orn. Biog. II. 1834, 317.

[B 426, C 228, R 282, C 340.]

GEOG. DIST.— North America, from the Fur Countries to the southern border of the United States. Locally distributed in the West.

488 a. Corvus americanus floridanus BAIRD.
Florida Crow.

Corvus americanus var. *floridanus* BAIRD, B. N. Am. 1858, 568.

[B 427, C 228a, R 282a, C 341.]

GEOG. DIST.— Florida.

489. **Corvus caurinus** BAIRD.
    Northwest Crow.

   Corvus caurinus BAIRD, B. N. Am. 1858, 569.

   [B 428, C 228*b*, R 282*b*, C 342.]

   GEOG. DIST.— Northwest coast, from California to Sitka.

490. **Corvus ossifragus** WILS.
    Fish Crow.

   Corvus ossifragus WILS. Am. Orn. V. 1812, 27, pl. 37, fig. 2.

   [B 429, C 229, R 283, C 343.]

   GEOG. DIST.— Atlantic and Gulf coasts, from southern Connecticut to Louisiana. Common in the lower Hudson Valley; casual in Massachusetts.

GENUS **NUCIFRAGA** BRISSON.

Nucifraga BRISSON, Orn. II. 1760, 58. Type, *N. caryocatactes*.

SUBGENUS **PICICORVUS** BONAPARTE.

Picicorvus BONAP. Consp. Av. I. 1850, 384. Type, *Corvus columbianus* WILS.

491. **Nucifraga columbiana** (WILS.).
    Clarke's Nutcracker.

   Corvus columbianus WILS. Am. Orn. III. 1811, 29, pl. 20, fig. 3.
   Nucifraga columbiana AUD. Orn. Biog. IV. 1834, 459.

   [B 430, C 230, R 284, C 344.]

   GEOG. DIST.— Higher coniferous forests of western North America, from the eastern slope of the Rocky Mountains to the Pacific, and from Putnam River, Alaska, south to Arizona and northern Lower California. Accidental in Kansas, Missouri and Arkansas.

GENUS **CYANOCEPHALUS** BONAPARTE.

Cyanocephalus BONAP. Oss. Stat. Zool. Eur. Vertebr. 1842, 17. Type, *Gymnorhinus cyanocephalus* WIED.

492. Cyanocephalus cyanocephalus (WIED).
   Piñon Jay.

   Gymnorhinus cyanocephalus WIED, Reise N. Amer. II. 1841, 21.
   Cyanocephalus cyanocephalus STEJN. Auk, I. 1884, 230.
   [B 431, C 231, R 285, C 345.]

   GEOG. DIST.— Rocky Mountains, west to the Cascade Range and the Sierra Nevada, and from British America south to northern Lower California. Accidental in eastern Kansas and eastern Nebraska.

FAMILY **STURNIDÆ**. STARLINGS.

GENUS **STURNUS** LINNÆUS.

Sturnus LINN. S. N. ed. 10, I. 1758, 167. Type, by elimination, *S. vulgaris* LINN.

[493.] **Sturnus vulgaris** LINN.
   Starling.

   Sturnus vulgaris LINN. S. N. ed. 10, I. 1758, 167.
   [B—, C—, R 279, C 363.]

   GEOG. DIST.— Europe and northern Asia; accidental in Greenland. Introduced and apparently well-established in the vicinity of New York city.

FAMILY **ICTERIDÆ**. BLACKBIRDS, ORIOLES, ETC.

GENUS **DOLICHONYX** SWAINSON.

Dolichonyx SWAINS. Phil. Mag. I. June, 1827, 435. Type, *Fringilla oryzivora* LINN.

494. Dolichonyx oryzivorus (LINN.).
   Bobolink.

   Fringilla oryzivora LINN. S. N. ed. 10, I. 1758, 179.
   Dolichonyx oryzivorus SWAINS. Zool. Jour. III. 1827, 351.

[B 399, C 210, R 257, C 312.]

GEOG. DIST.— Eastern North America, west to Montana, eastern Nevada, Utah, and Idaho; north to Ontario, and the southern parts of Manitoba, Assiniboia, and Alberta; south, in winter, to the West Indies and South America. Breeds from the Middle States northward, and winters south of the United States.

GENUS **MOLOTHRUS** SWAINSON.

Molothrus SWAINS. F. B. A. II. 1831, 277. Type, *Fringilla pecoris* GMEL. = *Oriolus ater* BODD.

495. **Molothrus ater** (BODD.).
Cowbird.

Oriolus ater BODD. Tabl. Pl. Enlum. 1783, 37.
Molothrus ater GRAY, Handl. B. II. 1870, 36.

[B 400, C 211, R 258, C 313.]

GEOG. DIST.— United States, from the Atlantic to the Pacific, north into southern British America, south, in winter, into Mexico.

495 a. **Molothrus ater obscurus** (GMEL.).
Dwarf Cowbird.

Sturnus obscurus GMEL. S. N. I. ii. 1788, 804.
M[*olothrus*] *ater* var. *obscurus* COUES, B. N. W. 1874, 180, in text.

[B —, C 211a, R 258a, C 314.]

GEOG. DIST.— Southern United States, from Texas to southern Arizona and Lower California, south into Mexico.

GENUS **CALLOTHRUS** CASSIN.

Callothrus CASS. Proc. Ac. Nat. Sci. Phil. 1866, 18. Type, *Psarocolius æneus* WAGL.

496. Callothrus robustus (CAB.).
    Red-eyed Cowbird.

Molothrus robustus CAB. Mus. Hein. I. Sept. 1851, 193, footnote.
Callothrus robustus RIDGW. Man. N. Am. B. 1887, 589.

[B —, C —, R 259, C 315.]

GEOG. DIST.— Valley of the Lower Rio Grande in Texas, and southward to Panama.

GENUS **XANTHOCEPHALUS** BONAPARTE.

Xanthocephalus BONAP. Consp. Av. I. 1850, 431. Type, *Icterus icterocephalus* BONAP. = *I. xanthocephalus* BONAP.

497. Xanthocephalus xanthocephalus (BONAP.).
    Yellow-headed Blackbird.

Icterus xanthocephalus BONAP. Journ. Ac. Nat. Sci. Phila. V. 1826, 223.
Xanthocephalus xanthocephalus JORDAN, Man. Vert. ed. 4, 1884, 92.

[B 404, C 213, R 260, C 319.]

GEOG. DIST.— Western North America, from Wisconsin, Illinois and Texas to the Pacific coast, and from British Columbia and the Saskatchewan River southward to the Valley of Mexico. Accidental in Ontario and the Atlantic States (Massachusetts, District of Columbia, South Carolina, Florida).

GENUS **AGELAIUS** VIEILLOT.

Agelaius VIEILL. Analyse, 1816, 33. Type, *Oriolus phœniceus* LINN.

498. Agelaius phœniceus (LINN.).
    Red-winged Blackbird.

Oriolus phœniceus LINN. S. N. ed. 12, I. 1766, 161.
Agelaius phœniceus VIEILL. Nouv. Dict. d'Hist. Nat. XXXIV. 1819, 539.

ORDER PASSERES. 205

[B 401, C 212, R 261, C 316.]

GEOG. DIST.— North America in general, from Great Slave Lake south to Costa Rica, excepting western Mexico and the lower Colorado Valley, southern Florida, the Gulf coast of Louisiana, and the lower Rio Grande Valley in Texas during the breeding season.

498 a. Agelaius phœniceus sonoriensis RIDGW.
Sonoran Red-wing.

Agelaius phœniceus sonoriensis RIDGW. Man. N. Am. B. 1887, 370.

[B 401, *part*, C 212, *part*, R 261, *part*, C 316, *part*.]

GEOG. DIST.— Northern Mexico and contiguous borders of the United States, from the Lower Rio Grande Valley and southern Arizona north to the lower Colorado Valley, California, and Chilliwack, British Columbia.

498 b. Agelaius phœniceus bryanti RIDGW.
Bahaman Red-wing.

Agelaius phœniceus bryanti RIDGW. Man. N. Am. B. 1887, 370.

[B 401, *part*, C 212, *part*, R 261, *part*, C 316, *part*.]

GEOG. DIST.— Bahamas and southern Florida, west to the Gulf coast of Louisiana (Lake Borgne), south to Yucatan and Nicaragua.

499. Agelaius gubernator (WAGL.).
Bicolored Blackbird.

Psarocolius gubernator WAGL. Isis, IV. 1832, 281.
Agelaius gubernator BONAP. P. Z. S. 1837 (June, 1838), 110.

[B 402, C 212a, R 261a, C 317.]

GEOG. DIST.— Pacific coast districts, from western Washington, south to Lower California, west of the Cascades and the Sierra Nevada. Casually to western Nevada and southeastern California (Inyo Co.).

500. Agelaius tricolor (AUD.).
Tricolored Blackbird.

Icterus tricolor "NUTT." AUD. Orn. Biog. V. 1839, pl. 388, fig. 1.
Agelaius tricolor BONAP. Geog. & Comp. List, 1838, 29.

[B 403, C 212b, R 262, C 318.]

GEOG. DIST.— Southwestern Oregon, south through California, west of the Sierra Nevada, to northern Lower California.

GENUS **STURNELLA** VIEILLOT.

Sturnella VIEILL. Analyse, 1816, 34. Type, *Alauda magna* LINN.

501. Sturnella magna LINN.).
Meadowlark.
Alauda magna LINN. S. N. ed. 10, I. 1758, 167.
Sturnella magna SWAINS. Phil. Mag. I. 1827, 436.
[B 406, C 214, R 263, C 320.]

GEOG. DIST.— Eastern United States and southern Canada to the Plains. Breeds from the Gulf of Mexico northward.

501 a. Sturnella magna mexicana (SCL.).
Mexican Meadowlark.
Sturnella mexicana SCL. Ibis, 1861, 179.
Sturnella magna var. *mexicana* B. B. & R. Hist. N. Am. B. II. 1874, 172.
[B—, C—, R 263a, C 321.]

GEOG. DIST.— Valley of the Lower Rio Grande and southern Arizona, and south through eastern and central Mexico to Panama.

501 b. Sturnella magna neglecta (AUD.).
Western Meadowlark.
Sturnella neglecta AUD. B. Am. VII. 1843, 339, pl. 487.
Sturnella magna var. *neglecta* ALLEN, Bull. M. C. Z. III. No. 2, July, 1872, 178.
[B 407, C 214a, R 264, C 322.]

GEOG. DIST.— Western United States, from Wisconsin, Illinois, Iowa, Texas, etc., west to the Pacific coast and north to British Columbia and Manitoba, south through central and western Mexico to Guanajuato and Jalisco.

GENUS **ICTERUS** BRISSON.

SUBGENUS **ICTERUS**.

Icterus BRISS. Orn. II. 1760, 85. Type, by elimination, *Oriolus icterus* LINN.

[502.] **Icterus icterus** (LINN.).
　　Troupial.

Oriolus icterus LINN. S. N. ed. 12, I. 1766, 161.
Icterus icterus RIDGW. Pr. U. S. Nat. Mus. VIII. 1885, 355.

[B 408, C —, R 265, C 323.]

GEOG. DIST.—West Indies (introduced) and northern South America. Accidental at Charleston, S. C. (AUDUBON).

503. **Icterus audubonii** GIRAUD.
　　Audubon's Oriole.

Icterus audubonii GIRAUD, Sixteen Sp. Texas B. 1841, 3.

[B 409, C 220, R 266, C 330.]

GEOG. DIST.— Valley of the Lower Rio Grande in Texas, and southward in Mexico to Oaxaca.

504. **Icterus parisorum** BONAP.
　　Scott's Oriole.

Icterus parisorum BONAP. P. Z. S. 1837 (June, 1838), 110.

[B 411, C 219, R 268, C 329.]

GEOG. DIST.— Southwestern United States, from western Texas to southern California; north to northern New Mexico, southwestern Utah, southern Nevada, and California to Lat. 38° east of the Sierra Nevada; south to Lower California and on the tablelands of Mexico to Puebla and Vera Cruz.

SUBGENUS **PENDULINUS** VIEILLOT.

Pendulinus VIEILL. Analyse, 1816, 33. Type, *Oriolus spurius* LINN.

505. **Icterus cucullatus** SWAINS.
　　Hooded Oriole.

Icterus cucullatus SWAINS. Phil. Mag. I. 1827, 436.

[B 413, C 218, R 269, C 328.]

GEOG. DIST.— Valley of the Lower Rio Grande in Texas, and southward through eastern and southern Mexico to British Honduras.

505 *a*. **Icterus cucullatus nelsoni** RIDGW.
Arizona Hooded Oriole.

Icterus cucullatus nelsoni RIDGW. Pr. U. S. Nat. Mus. Vol. VIII. April 20, 1885, 19.

[B —, C —, R —, C —.]

GEOG. DIST.— Southwestern New Mexico and southern Arizona, west to Santa Barbara, California, and south to Mazatlan and Cape St. Lucas.

506. **Icterus spurius** (LINN.).
Orchard Oriole.

Oriolus spurius LINN. S. N. ed. 12, I. 1766, 162.
Icterus spurius BONAP. Journ. Ac. Nat. Sci. Phila. III. 1823, 363.

[B 414, C 215, R 270, C 324.]

GEOG. DIST.— Eastern United States, north to the southern portions of New England, New York, Ontario, Michigan, and North Dakota, west to the Plains, south, in winter, to northern Colombia. Breeds throughout its United States range.

SUBGENUS **YPHANTES** VIEILLOT.

Yphantes VIEILL. Analyse, 1816, 33. Type, *Coracias galbula* LINN.

507. **Icterus galbula** (LINN.).
Baltimore Oriole.

Coracias galbula LINN. S. N. ed. 10, 1758, 108.
Icterus galbula COUES, Bull. Nutt. Orn. Cl. V. Apr. 1880, 98.

[B 415, C 216, R 271, C 326.]

GEOG. DIST.— Eastern United States, north to Ontario and Manitoba, west nearly to the Rocky Mountains, south, in winter, through Mexico to Colombia.

508. **Icterus bullocki** (SWAINS.).
Bullock's Oriole.

Xanthornus bullocki SWAINS. Phil. Mag. I. 1827, 436.
Icterus bullocki BONAP. Geog. & Comp. List, 1838, 29.

[B 416, C 217, R 272, C 327.]

GEOG. DIST.— Tablelands of Mexico, from Puebla and Valley of Mexico north through the western United States to Manitoba and British Columbia east of the Cascades, and from the western portion of the Plains to the Pacific.

GENUS **SCOLECOPHAGUS** SWAINSON.

Scolecophagus SWAINS. F. B. A. II. 1831, 286. Type, *Oriolus ferrugineus* GMEL. = *Turdus carolinus* MÜLL.

509. Scolecophagus carolinus (MÜLL.).
Rusty Blackbird.

Turdus carolinus MÜLLER, Syst. Nat. Suppl. 1776, 140.
Scolecophagus carolinus RIDGW. Pr. U. S. Nat. Mus. VIII. 1885, 356.

[B 417, C 221, R 273, C 331.]

GEOG. DIST.— Eastern North America, west to Alaska and the Plains. Breeds from northern New England, northern New York, and northern Michigan northward. Accidental in Lower California.

510. Scolecophagus cyanocephalus (WAGL.).
Brewer's Blackbird.

Psarocolius cyanocephalus WAGL. Isis, 1829, 758.
Scolecophagus cyanocephalus CAB. Mus. Hein. I. 1851, 193.

[B 418, C 222, R 274, C 332.]

GEOG. DIST.— Western North America, from the Plains to the Pacific, and from the Saskatchewan region south on the highlands of Mexico to Oaxaca.

GENUS **QUISCALUS** VIEILLOT.

SUBGENUS **QUISCALUS**.

Quiscalus VIEILL. Anal. 1816, 36. Type, *Gracula quiscula* LINN.

511. Quiscalus quiscula (LINN.).
   Purple Grackle.

   Gracula quiscula LINN. S. N. ed. 10, 1758, 109.
   Quiscalus quiscula JORDAN, Man. Vert. ed. 4, 1884, 93.
   [B 421, C 225, R 278, C 335.]

GEOG. DIST.— Northern Alabama, eastern Tennessee, and east of the Alleghanies from Georgia to Massachusetts.

511 a. Quiscalus quiscula aglæus (BAIRD).
   Florida Grackle.

   Quiscalus aglæus BAIRD, Am. Jour. Sci. & Arts, XLI. Jan. 1866, 84.
   Quiscalus quiscula aglæus STEJN. Auk, II. Jan. 1885, 43, foot-note.
   [B 422, C —, R 278a, C 336.]

GEOG. DIST.— Florida, and the southern part of the Gulf States to Texas; north along the Atlantic coast to Virginia.

511 b. Quiscalus quiscula æneus (RIDGW.).
   Bronzed Grackle.

   Quiscalus æneus RIDGW. Pr. Ac. Nat. Sci. Phila. June, 1869, 134.
   Quiscalus quiscula æneus STEJN. Auk, II. Jan. 1885, 43, foot-note.
   [B —, C 225a, R 278b, C 337.]

GEOG. DIST.— From the Alleghanies and southern New England north to Newfoundland and Great Slave Lake, west to the eastern base of the Rocky Mountains, and south to Louisiana and Texas. In migrations, the southeastern States, except Florida and the Atlantic coast district south of Virginia.

SUBGENUS **MEGAQUISCALUS** CASSIN.

   Megaquiscalus CASS. Pr. Ac. Nat. Sci. Phila. 1866, 409. Type, *Quiscalus major* VIEILL.

512. Quiscalus macrourus SWAINS.
   Great-tailed Grackle.

   Quiscalus macrourus SWAINS. Anim. in Menag. 1838, 299.
   [B 419, C 223, R 275, C 333.]

GEOG. DIST.— Eastern Texas, south to Central America.

513. Quiscalus major VIEILL.
   Boat-tailed Grackle.

Quiscalus major VIEILL. Nouv. Dict. d'Hist. Nat. XXVIII. 1819, 487.

[B 420, C 224, R 277, C 334.]

GEOG. DIST.— Coast region of the South Atlantic and Gulf States, from Virginia to Texas.

FAMILY **FRINGILLIDÆ**. FINCHES, SPARROWS, ETC.

GENUS **COCCOTHRAUSTES** BRISSON.

Coccothraustes BRISS. Orn. III. 1760, 218. Type, *Loxia coccothraustes* LINN.

SUBGENUS **HESPERIPHONA** BONAPARTE.

Hesperiphona BONAP. Compt. Rend. XXXI. Sept. 1850, 424. Type, *Fringilla vespertina* COOPER.

514. Coccothraustes vespertinus (COOP.).
   Evening Grosbeak.

Fringilla vespertina COOP. Ann. Lyc. N. Y. I. ii. 1825, 220.
Coccothraustes vespertina SW. & RICH. Fauna Bor. Am. II. 1831, 269, pl. 68.

[B 303, C 136, R 165, C 189.]

GEOG. DIST.— Western British Provinces, east to Lake Superior, and casually to Michigan, Ohio, Ontario, New York, and New England.

514 a. Coccothraustes vespertinus montanus (RIDGW.).
   Western Evening Grosbeak.

Hesperiphona vespertina var. *montana* RIDGW. in Hist. N. Am. Bds., Land Bds., I. 1874, 449.
Coccothraustes vespertina montana MEARNS, Auk, VII. July, 1890, 246.

[B 303, *part*, C 136, *part*, R 165, *part*, C 189, *part*.]

GEOG. DIST.— Western North America, from the Pacific coast eastward to the Rocky Mountains; southward over the tablelands of Mexico to Orizaba.

GENUS **PINICOLA** VIEILLOT.

Pinicola VIEILL. Ois. Am. Sept. I. 1807, p. iv. Type, *P. rubra* VIEILL. = *Loxia enucleator* LINN.

515. **Pinicola enucleator** (LINN.).
Pine Grosbeak.

Loxia enucleator LINN. S. N. ed. 10, I. 1758, 171.
Pinicola enucleator CAB. in ERSCH & GRUBER, Encycl. 1st Sect. I. 1849, 219.

[B 304, C 137, R 166, C 190.]

GEOG. DIST.— Northern parts of the northern hemisphere, breeding in North America from northern New England, Quebec, the Rocky Mountains in Colorado, and about Lat. 37° in the Sierra Nevada, northward nearly to the limit of trees; south in winter irregularly into northeastern United States.

GENUS **PYRRHULA** BRISSON.

Pyrrhula BRISS. Orn. III. 1760, 308. Type, *Loxia pyrrhula* LINN.

[516.] **Pyrrhula cassini** (BAIRD).
Cassin's Bullfinch.

Pyrrhula coccinea var. *cassini* BAIRD, Trans. Chicago Ac. Sci. I. 1869, 316.
Pyrrhula cassini TRISTRAM, Ibis, Apr. 1871, 231.

[B —, C 138, R 167, C 191.]

GEOG. DIST.— Eastern Siberia. Accidental at Nulato, Alaska.

GENUS **CARPODACUS** KAUP.

Carpodacus KAUP, Skizz. Entw.-Gesch. Eur. Thierw. 1829, 161. Type, *Loxia erythrina* PALL.

517. Carpodacus purpureus (GMEL.).
   Purple Finch.

Fringilla purpurea GMEL. S. N. I. ii. 1788, 923.
Carpodacus purpureus GRAY, Gen. B. II. 1844, 384.

[B 305, C 139, R 168, C 194.]

GEOG. DIST.— Eastern North America, from the Atlantic coast to the Plains. Breeds from the Middle States northward.

517 a. Carpodacus purpureus californicus BAIRD.
   California Purple Finch.

Carpodacus californicus BAIRD, B. N. Am. 1858, 413.
Carpodacus purpureus var. *californicus* B. B. & R. Hist. N. Am. B. I. 1874, 465.

[B 306, C —, R 168a, C —.]

GEOG. DIST.— Pacific coast region, from British Columbia south in winter to southern California.

518. Carpodacus cassini BAIRD.
   Cassin's Purple Finch.

Carpodacus cassini BAIRD, Pr. Ac. Nat. Sci. Phila. June, 1854, 119.

[B 307, C 140, R 169, C 195.]

GEOG. DIST.— Western United States, from the eastern base of the Rocky Mountains to the Pacific coast, and south over the plateau region of Mexico to Mt. Orizaba.

SUBGENUS **BURRICA** RIDGW.

Burrica RIDGW. Man. N. Am. B. 1887, 390. Type, *Fringilla mexicana* MÜLL.

519. Carpodacus mexicanus frontalis (SAY).
   House Finch.

Fringilla frontalis SAY, LONG's Exp. II. 1823, 40.
Carpodacus mexicanus frontalis RIDGW. Man. N. Am. B. 1887, 391.

[B 308, C 141, R 170, C 196.]

GEOG. DIST.— Colorado and western Texas, westward to Oregon and California, south into Lower California and western Mexico.

519 b. Carpodacus mexicanus ruberrimus RIDGW.
St. Lucas House Finch.

Carpodacus frontalis ruberrimus RIDGW. Man. N. Am. B. 1887, 391, foot-note.
Carpodacus mexicanus ruberrimus RIDGW. Man. N. Am. B. 1887, 594.

[B—, C 141a, R 170a, C 197.]

GEOG. DIST.— Lower California, and probably adjacent parts of Sonora.

520. Carpodacus amplus RIDGW.
Guadalupe House Finch.

Carpodacus amplus RIDGW. Bull. U. S. Geol. & Geog. Surv. Terr. II. No. 2, April 1, 1876, 187.

[B—, C—, R 171, C—.]

GEOG. DIST.— Guadalupe Island, Lower California.

GENUS **LOXIA** LINNÆUS.

Loxia LINN. S. N. ed. 10, I. 1758, 171. Type, by elimination, *Loxia curvirostra* LINN.

521. Loxia curvirostra minor (BREHM).
American Crossbill.

Crucirostra minor BREHM, Naumannia, 1853, 193.
Loxia curvirostra minor RIDGW. Pr. U. S. Nat. Mus. VIII. 1885, 354.

[B 318, C 143, R 172, C 199.]

GEOG. DIST.— Northern North America, resident sparingly south in the eastern United States to Maryland and Tennessee, and in the Alleghanies; irregularly abundant in winter. Casual at Charleston, S. C., and New Orleans, La.

521 a. **Loxia curvirostra stricklandi** RIDGW.
   Mexican Crossbill.

Loxia curvirostra stricklandi RIDGW. Pr. U. S. Nat. Mus. VIII. 1885, 354.

[B 318a, C 143a, R 172a, C 200.]

GEOG. DIST.— Mountains of Wyoming and Colorado, west to the Sierra Nevada, and south through New Mexico, Arizona, and the tablelands of Mexico to Guatemala.

522. **Loxia leucoptera** GMEL.
   White-winged Crossbill.

Loxia leucoptera GMEL. S. N. I. ii. 1788, 540.

[B 319, C 142, R 173, C 198.]

GEOG. DIST.— Northern parts of North America, south into the United States in winter. Breeds from northern New England northward.

GENUS **LEUCOSTICTE** SWAINSON.

Leucosticte SWAINS. in Sw. & RICH. Fauna Bor. Am. II. 1831, 265. Type, *Linaria tephrocotis* SWAINS.

523. **Leucosticte griseonucha** (BRANDT).
   Aleutian Leucosticte.

Fringilla (Linaria) griseonucha BRANDT, Bull. Ac. St. Pétersb. Nov. 1841, 36.
Leucosticte griseinucha BONAP. Consp. Av. I. 1850, 537.

[B 323, C 144a, R 174, C 205.]

GEOG. DIST.— Aleutian Islands, including Kadiak, Unalaska, Pribilof, and Commander Islands.

524. **Leucosticte tephrocotis** SWAINS.
   Gray-crowned Leucosticte.

Linaria (Leucosticte) tephrocotis SWAINS. in Sw. & RICH. Fauna Bor. Am. II. 1831, 265, pl. 50.
Leucosticte tephrocotis SWAINS. in Sw. & RICH. Fauna Bor. Am. II. 1831, 494.

[B 322, C 144, R 175, C 203.]

GEOG. DIST.— Interior of British America, south in winter throughout the entire Rocky Mountain region of the United States, but most abundant on the eastern slope. Known to breed only in the Sierra Nevada in California.

524 a. Leucosticte tephrocotis littoralis (BAIRD).
Hepburn's Leucosticte.

Leucosticte littoralis BAIRD, Trans. Chicago Ac. Sci. I. i. 1869, 318, pl. 28, fig. 1.
Leucosticte tephrocotis var. *littoralis* COUES, Key, 1872, 130.

[B —, C —, R 175a, C 204.]

GEOG. DIST.— In summer, probably the interior mountainous regions of British Columbia; in winter, northwest coast, from Kadiak southward, and eastward in the Rocky Mountain region to Colorado.

525. Leucosticte atrata RIDGW.
Black Leucosticte.

Leucosticte atrata RIDGW. American Sportsman, July 18, 1874, 241; Bull. U. S. Geol. & Geog. Surv. Terr. 2d ser. No. 2, May 11, 1875, 69.

[B —, C —, R 176, C 201.]

GEOG. DIST.— Breeds in the Salmon River Mountains, Idaho, and probably other northern ranges; in winter, mountains of Colorado and Utah.

526. Leucosticte australis RIDGW.
Brown-capped Leucosticte.

Leucosticte tephrocotis var. *australis* "ALLEN MS." RIDGW. Bull. Essex Inst. V. Dec. 1873, 197.
Leucosticte australis RIDGW. Bull. U. S. Geol. & Geog. Surv. Terr. 2d ser. No. 2, May 11, 1875, 79.

[B —, C —, R 177, C 203.]

GEOG. DIST.— Mountains of Colorado, breeding above timber-line, descending into the valleys in winter; New Mexico.

ORDER PASSERES.

GENUS **ACANTHIS** BECHSTEIN.

Acanthis BECHST. Orn. Tasch. Deutschl. 1803, 125. Type,
Fringilla linaria LINN.

527. Acanthis hornemannii (HOLB.).
Greenland Redpoll.
Linota hornemannii HOLBÖLL, Naturh. Tidskr. IV. 1843, 398.
Acanthis hornemannii STEJN. Auk, I. April, 1884, 152.

[B 321, C —, R 178, C 209.]

GEOG. DIST.— Greenland and eastern Arctic America.

527 a. Acanthis hornemannii exilipes (COUES).
Hoary Redpoll.
Ægiothus exilipes COUES, Pr. Ac. Nat. Sci. Phila. 1861, 385.
Acanthis hornemannii exilipes STEJN. Auk, I. April, 1884, 152.

[B —, C 146*b*, R 178*a*, C 210.]

GEOG. DIST.— Arctic America and northeastern Asia, south in winter (rarely?) to the northern border of the United States.

528. Acanthis linaria (LINN.).
Redpoll.
Fringilla linaria LINN. S. N. ed. 10, I. 1758, 182.
Acanthis linaria BONAP. & SCHLEG. Mon. Lox. 1850, 48.

[B 320, C 146, 146*a*, R 179, C 207.]

GEOG. DIST.— Northern portions of northern hemisphere, south irregularly in winter, in North America, to the middle United States (Virginia, Kansas, southeastern Oregon).

528 a. Acanthis linaria holbœllii (BREHM).
Holböll's Redpoll.
Linaria holbællii BREHM. Handb. Vög. Deutschl. 1831, 280.
Acanthis linaria β. *holbællii* DUBOIS, Consp. Av. Europ. 1871, 18.

[B —, C —, R 179*a*, *part*, C 208, *part.*]

GEOG. DIST.— Northern portions of northern hemisphere, near the seacoast, south in winter to northern New York and Massachusetts.

528 b. Acanthis linaria rostrata (COUES).
   Greater Redpoll.

Ægiothus rostratus COUES, Pr. Ac. Nat. Sci. Phila. 1861, 378.
Acanthis linaria rostrata STEJN. Auk, I. April, 1884, 153.

[B —, C —, R 179*a*, *part*, C 208, *part*.]

GEOG. DIST.— Greenland and northeastern North America, south irregularly in winter to New England, New York, and northern Illinois.

GENUS **SPINUS** KOCH.

Spinus KOCH, Bayr. Zool. 1816, 233. Type, *Fringilla spinus* LINN.

529. Spinus tristis (LINN.).
   American Goldfinch.

Fringilla tristis LINN. S. N. ed. 10, I. 1758, 181.
Spinus tristis STEJN. Auk, I. Oct. 1884, 362.

[B 313, C 149, R 181, C 213.]

GEOG. DIST.— Temperate North America generally, from southern Labrador, Manitoba and British Columbia south, in winter, to the northern boundary of Lower California; breeding southward to the middle districts of the United States (Virginia, Kentucky, Kansas, and California), and wintering mainly within the United States.

529 a. Spinus tristis pallidus MEARNS.
   Western Goldfinch.

Spinus tristis pallidus MEARNS, Auk, VII. July, 1890, 244.

[B 313, *part*, C 149, *part*, R 181, *part*, C 213, *part*.]

GEOG. DIST.— Arizona.

530. Spinus psaltria (SAY).
   Arkansas Goldfinch.

Fringilla psaltria SAY, LONG'S Exp. II. 1823, 40.
Spinus psaltria STEJN. Auk, I. Oct. 1884, 362.

[B 314, C 151, R 182, C 215.]

GEOG. DIST.— Western United States, from the Plains to the Pacific, and from southern Oregon, Colorado, and Utah southward to Cape St. Lucas and Sonora.

530 *a*. **Spinus psaltria arizonæ** (COUES).
Arizona Goldfinch.

Chrysomitris mexicana var. *arizonæ* COUES, Pr. Ac. Nat. Sci. Phila. 1866, 82.
Spinus psaltria arizonæ STEJN. Auk, I. Oct. 1884, 362.

[B—, C 151*a*, R 182*a*, C 216.]

GEOG. DIST.— Southern California, southwestern Utah, southern New Mexico and Arizona, southward into northern Mexico.

530 *b*. **Spinus psaltria mexicanus** (SWAINS.).
Mexican Goldfinch.

Carduelis mexicanus SWAINS. Phil. Mag. I. 1827, 435.
Spinus psaltria mexicanus STEJN. Auk, I. Oct. 1884, 362.

[B 315, C 159*b*, R 182*b*, C 217.]

GEOG. DIST.— Valley of the Lower Rio Grande in Texas, southward through Mexico.

531. **Spinus lawrencei** (CASS.).
Lawrence's Goldfinch.

Carduelis lawrencei CASS. Pr. Ac. Nat. Sci. Phila. 1851, 105, pl. v.
Spinus lawrencei STEJN. Auk, I. Oct. 1884, 362.

[B 316, C 150, R 183, C 214.]

GEOG. DIST.— California west of the Sierra Nevada, from Lat. 40° south to northern Lower California; Arizona (Fort Mohave and Fort Whipple) in winter.

[532.] **Spinus notatus** (DUBUS).
Black-headed Goldfinch.

Carduelis notata DUBUS, Bull. Ac. Brux. XIV. pt. 2, 1847, 106.
Spinus notatus STEJN. Auk, I. Oct. 1884, 362.

[B 310, C —, R 184, C 218.]

GEOG. DIST.— Mountains of Guatemala and southern Mexico, north at least to central Vera Cruz; accidental in Kentucky (AUDUBON).

533. **Spinus pinus** (WILS.).
Pine Siskin.

Fringilla pinus WILS. Am. Orn. II. 1810, 133, pl. 17, fig. 1.
Spinus pinus STEJN. Auk, I. Oct. 1884, 362.

[B 317, C 148, R 185, C 212.]

GEOG. DIST.— North America generally, breeding in the British Provinces, Rocky Mountains, Sierra Nevada, and high mountains of Arizona, south to Lower California and the mountains of Mexico to Orizaba. Also breeds sparingly in northeastern United States.

GENUS **PLECTROPHENAX** STEJNEGER.

Plectrophenax STEJN. Pr. U. S. Nat. Mus. V. June 5, 1882, 33.
Type, *Emberiza nivalis* LINN.

534. **Plectrophenax nivalis** (LINN.).
Snowflake.

Emberiza nivalis LINN. S. N. ed. 10, I. 1758, 176.
Plectrophenax nivalis STEJN. Pr. U. S. Nat. Mus. V. 1882, 33.

[B 325, C 152, R 186, C 219.]

GEOG. DIST.— Northern parts of the northern hemisphere, breeding in the arctic regions; in North America south in winter into the northern United States, irregularly to Georgia, southern Illinois, Kansas, and Oregon.

534 a. **Plectrophenax nivalis townsendi** RIDGW.
Pribilof Snowflake.

Plectrophenax nivalis townsendi RIDGW. Man. N. Am. B. 1887, 403.

ORDER PASSERES.

[B —, C —, R 186, *part*, C 219, *part.*]

GEOG. DIST.— Pribilof and Aleutian Islands, Alaska, and Commander Islands, Kamchatka.

535. Plectrophenax hyperboreus RIDGW.
McKay's Snowflake.

Plectrophenax hyperboreus RIDGW. Pr. U. S. Nat. Mus. VII. June 11, 1884, 68.

[B —, C —, R —, C —.]

GEOG. DIST.— Western Alaska, breeding on Hall Island (and propably St. Matthew Island), Bering Sea.

GENUS **CALCARIUS** BECHSTEIN.

Calcarius BECHST. Taschb. Vög. Deutschl. 1803, 130. Type, *Fringilla lapponica* LINN.

536. Calcarius lapponicus (LINN.).
Lapland Longspur.

Fringilla lapponica LINN. S. N. ed. 10, I. 1758, 180.
Calcarius lapponicus STEJN. Pr. U. S. Nat. Mus. V. June 5, 1882, 33.

[B 326, C 153, R 187, C 220.]

GEOG. DIST.— Northern portions of the northern hemisphere, breeding far north; in North America south in winter to the northern United States, irregularly to the Middle States, accidentally to South Carolina, and abundantly in the interior to Kansas and Colorado.

537. Calcarius pictus (SWAINS.).
Smith's Longspur.

Emberiza (Plectrophanes) picta SWAINS. in Sw. and RICH. Fauna Bor. Am. II. 1831, 250, pl. 49.
Calcarius pictus STEJN. Pr. U. S. Nat. Mus. V. June 5, 1882, 33.

[B 327, C 154, R 188, C 221.]

GEOG. DIST.— Interior of North America, from the Arctic coast to Illinois and Texas, breeding far north.

538. Calcarius ornatus (Towns.).
Chestnut-collared Longspur.

Plectrophanes ornatus Towns. Journ. Ac. Nat. Sci. Phila. VII. 1837, 189.
Calcarius ornatus STEJN. Pr. U. S. Nat. Mus. V. June 5, 1882, 33.

[B 328, 329, C 155, R 189, C 222.]

GEOG. DIST.— Interior of North America, from the Saskatchewan Plains south through Texas to Orizaba. Breeds from eastern Manitoba, western Minnesota and eastern Nebraska westward and northwestward into Montana and Assiniboia. Rare west of the Rocky Mountains. Accidental in Massachusetts.

GENUS **RHYNCHOPHANES** BAIRD.

Rhynchophanes BAIRD, B. N. Am. 1858, 432 (in text). Type, *Plectrophanes mccownii* LAWR.

539. Rhynchophanes mccownii (LAWR.).
McCown's Longspur.

Plectrophanes mccownii LAWR. Ann. Lyc. N. Y. V. 1851, 122.
Rhynchophanes maccownii RIDGW. Field & Forest, II. May, 1877, 197.

[B 330, C 156, R 190, C 223.]

GEOG. DIST.— Interior of North America, from the Sackatchewan Plains south to Texas and northern Mexico; breeds from about the northern border of western Kansas northward throughout Nebraska, western North and South Dakota, Wyoming, and Montana to the Plains of the Saskatchewan.

GENUS **POOCÆTES** BAIRD.

Poocætes BAIRD, B. N. Am. 1858, 447. Type, *Fringilla graminea* GMEL.

540. Poocætes gramineus (GMEL.).
Vesper Sparrow.

Fringilla graminea GMEL. S. N. I. ii. 1788, 992.
Poocætes gramineus BAIRD, B. N. Am. 1858, 447.

[B 337, *part*, C 161, R 197, C 232.]

GEOG. DIST.— Eastern North America to the Plains, from Nova Scotia and Ontario southward; breeds from Virginia, Kentucky, and Missouri northward.

540 *a*. **Poocætes gramineus confinis** BAIRD.
Western Vesper Sparrow.

Poocætes gramineus var. *confinis* BAIRD, B. N. Am. 1858, 448 (in text).

[B 337, *part*, C 161*a*, R 197*a*, C 232.]

GEOG. DIST.— Western United States, from the Plains to the Pacific, north into Manitoba and Assiniboia, south into Lower California and through Mexico as far as Jalapa, Vera Cruz.

540 *b*. **Poocætes gramineus affinis** MILLER.
Oregon Vesper Sparrow.

Poocætes gramineus affinis MILLER, Auk, V. Oct. 1888, 404.

[B 337, *part*, C 161*a*, *part*, R 197*a*, *part*, C 232, *part*.]

GEOG. DIST.— Northern California and western Oregon.

GENUS **AMMODRAMUS** SWAINSON.

Ammodramus SWAINS. Zool. Journ. III. 1827, 348. Type, *Fringilla caudacuta* WILSON.

SUBGENUS **PASSERCULUS** BONAPARTE.

Passerculus BONAP. Geog. & Comp. List, 1838, 33. Type, *Fringilla savanna* WILS.

541. **Ammodramus princeps** (MAYN.).
Ipswich Sparrow.

Passerculus princeps MAYN. Am. Nat. VI. 1872, 637.
Ammodramus princeps RIDGW. Pr. U. S. Nat. Mus. VIII. 1885, 354.

[B—, C 158, R 192, C 225.]

GEOG. DIST.— Atlantic coast, from Nova Scotia south, in winter, to Georgia. Breeds on Sable Island, Nova Scotia.

542. Ammodramus sandwichensis (GMEL.).
Sandwich Sparrow.

Emberiza sandwichensis GMEL. S. N. I. ii. 1788, 875.
Ammodramus sandwichensis RIDGW. Pr. U. S. Nat. Mus. VIII. 1885, 354.

[B 333, C 159*b*, R 193, C 226.]

GEOG. DIST.— Northwest coast, from the Columbia River to Unalaska.

542 *a*. Ammodramus sandwichensis savanna (WILS.).
Savanna Sparrow.

Fringilla savanna WILS. Am. Orn. III. 1811, 55, pl. 22, fig. 2.
Ammodramus sandwichensis savanna RIDGW. Pr. U. S. Nat. Mus. VIII. 1885, 354.

[B 332, C 159, R 193*a*, C 227.]

GEOG. DIST.— Eastern North America, breeding from the northern United States to Labrador and Hudson Bay Territory.

542 *b*. Ammodramus sandwichensis alaudinus (BONAP.).
Western Savanna Sparrow.

Passerculus alaudinus BONAP. Compt. Rend. XXXVII. 1853, 918.
Ammodramus sandwichensis alaudinus RIDGW. Pr. U. S. Nat. Mus. VIII. 1885, 354.

[B 335, C —, R 193*b*, C 229.]

GEOG. DIST.— Western North America, from the Plains to the Pacific coast region, north to the Arctic coast.

542 *c*. Ammodramus sandwichensis bryanti RIDGW.
Bryant's Marsh Sparrow.

Passerculus sandwichensis bryanti RIDGW. Pr. U. S. Nat. Mus. VII. Jan. 19, 1885, 517.
Ammodramus sandwichensis bryanti RIDGW. Pr. U. S. Nat. Mus. VIII. 1885, 354.

[B 334, *part*, C 159*a*, *part*, R 194, *part*, C 228, *part*.]

GEOG. DIST.— Salt marshes about San Francisco Bay, and south along the coast in winter to southern California.

543. **Ammodramus beldingi** RIDGW.
Belding's Marsh Sparrow.

Passerculus beldingi RIDGW. Pr. U. S. Nat. Mus. VII. Jan. 19, 1885, 516.
Ammodramus beldingi RIDGW. Pr. U. S. Nat. Mus. VIII. 1885, 354.

[B 334, *part*, C 159*a*, *part*, R 194, *part*, C 228, *part*.]

GEOG. DIST.— Salt marshes of the Pacific coast, from Santa Barbara south to Todos Santos Island, Lower California.

544. **Ammodramus rostratus** CASS.
Large-billed Sparrow.

Emberiza rostrata CASS. Pr. Ac. Nat. Sci. Phila. 1852, 348.
Ammodramus rostratus CASS. Illustr. B. Cal. Tex. etc. 1855, 226, pl. 38.

[B 336, C 160, R 196, C 230.]

GEOG. DIST.— Coast of southern California, south in winter to Cape St. Lucas and northwestern Mexico.

544 *a*. **Ammodramus rostratus guttatus** (LAWR.).
St. Lucas Sparrow.

Passerculus guttatus LAWR. Ann. Lyc. N. Y. VIII. 1867, 473.
Ammodramus rostratus guttatus RIDGW. Pr. U. S. Nat. Mus. VIII. 1885, 355.

[B—, C 160*a*, R 195, C 231.]

GEOG. DIST.— Southern Lower California.

SUBGENUS **CENTRONYX** BAIRD.

Centronyx BAIRD, B. N. Am. 1858, 440. Type, *Emberiza bairdii* AUD.

545. **Ammodramus bairdii** (AUD.).
Baird's Sparrow.

Emberiza bairdii AUD. B. Am. VII. 1843, 359, pl. 500.
Ammodramus bairdi GIEBEL, Thes. Orn. I. 1872, 328.

[B 331, C 157, 157*bis*, R 191, C 224.]

GEOG. DIST.— Interior of North America, from the plains of the Red River and Saskatchewan south to Texas, New Mexico, Arizona, and Chihuahua.

SUBGENUS **COTURNICULUS** BONAPARTE.

Coturniculus BONAP. Geog. & Comp. List, 1838, 32. Type, *Fringilla passerina* WILS.

546. **Ammodramus savannarum passerinus** (WILS.).
Grasshopper Sparrow.

Fringilla passerina WILS. Am. Orn. III. 1811, 76, pl. 26, fig. 5.
Ammodramus savannarum passerinus RIDGW. Pr. U. S. Nat. Mus. VIII. 1885, 355.

[B 338, *part*, C 162, R 198, C 234.]

GEOG. DIST.— Eastern United States and southern Canada, west to the Plains, south, in winter, to Florida, Cuba, Porto Rico, and coast of Central America.

546 *a*. **Ammodramus savannarum perpallidus** (COUES).
Western Grasshopper Sparrow.

Coturniculus passerinus var. *perpallidus* " RIDGW. MS." COUES, Key, 1872, 137.
Ammodramus savannarum perpallidus RIDGW. Pr. U. S. Nat. Mus. VIII. 1885, 355.

[B 338, *part*, C 162*a*, R 198*a*, C 235.]

GEOG. DIST.— Western United States, from the Plains to the Pacific coast, south to Cape St. Lucas and the tablelands of Mexico.

547. **Ammodramus henslowii** (AUD.).
Henslow's Sparrow.

Emberiza henslowii AUD. Orn. Biog. I. 1831, 360, pl. 77.
Ammodromus henslowi GRAY, Gen. B. II. June, 1849, 374.

[B 339, *part*, C 163, *part*, R 199, *part*, C 236, *part*.]

GEOG. DIST.— Eastern United States, west to the Plains, north to southern New England and Ontario.

547 *a*. **Ammodramus henslowii occidentalis** BREWST.
Western Henslow's Sparrow.

Ammodramus henslowii occidentalis BREWST. Auk, VIII. April, 1891, 145.

[B 339, *part*, C 163, *part*, R 199, *part*, C 236, *part*.]

GEOG. DIST.— South Dakota.

548. **Ammodramus leconteii** (AUD.).
Leconte's Sparrow.

Emberiza leconteii AUD. B. Am. VII. 1843, 338, pl. 488.
Ammodromus leconteii GRAY, Gen. B. II. June, 1849, 374.

[B 340, C 164, R 200, C 237.]

GEOG. DIST.— From the Plains eastward to Illinois and Indiana, and from Manitoba south in winter to South Carolina, Florida, and Texas.

SUBGENUS **AMMODRAMUS**.

Ammodramus SWAINS. Zool. Jour. III. 1827, 348. Type, *Oriolus caudacutus* GMEL.

549. **Ammodramus caudacutus** (GMEL.).
Sharp-tailed Sparrow.

Oriolus caudacutus GMEL. S. N. I. i. 1788, 394.
Ammodramus caudacuta SWAINS. Classif. B. II. 1837, 289.

[B 341, C 166, R 201, C 240.]

GEOG. DIST.— Salt marshes of the Atlantic coast, from southern New England to Maryland, and south in winter to the Gulf coast.

549 *a*. **Ammodramus caudacutus nelsoni** ALLEN.
Nelson's Sparrow.

Ammodromus caudacutus var. *nelsoni* ALLEN, Pr. Bost. Soc. Nat. Hist. XVII. March, 1875, 293.

[B —, C —, R 201*a*, C 241.]

GEOG. DIST.— Fresh marshes of the interior, from northern Illinois northward to North Dakota and Manitoba; south in winter to Texas; in migrations visits the Atlantic coast (New England and Lower Hudson Valley to Charleston, S. C.). Accidental in California.

549 *b*. Ammodramus caudacutus subvirgatus DWIGHT.
Acadian Sharp-tailed Sparrow.

Ammodramus caudacutus subvirgatus DWIGHT, Auk, IV. July, 1887, 233.

[B —, C —, R 201, *part*, C 240, *part*.]

GEOG. DIST.— Coast of southern New Brunswick, Prince Edward Island (and probably Nova Scotia), and southward in migration to South Carolina.

550. Ammodramus maritimus (WILS.).
Seaside Sparrow.

Fringilla maritima WILS. Am. Orn. VII. 1811, 68, pl. 24, fig. 2.
Ammodramus maritimus SWAINS. Classif. B. II. 1837, 289.

[B 342, C 165, R 202, C 238.]

GEOG. DIST.— Salt marshes of the Atlantic coast, from Connecticut southward to Georgia. Accidental in Massachusetts.

550 *a*. Ammodramus maritimus peninsulæ ALLEN.
Scott's Seaside Sparrow.

Ammodramus maritimus peninsulæ ALLEN, Auk, V. July, 1888, 284.

[B 342, *part*, C 165, *part*, R 202, *part*, C 238, *part*.]

GEOG. DIST.— South Carolina to northern Florida; Gulf coast from Florida to Texas.

550 *b*. Ammodramus maritimus sennetti ALLEN.
Texas Seaside Sparrow.

Ammodramus maritimus sennetti ALLEN, Auk, V. July, 1888, 286.

[B —, C —, R 202, *part*, C 238, *part*.]

GEOG. DIST.— Coast of Texas (Corpus Christi).

ORDER PASSERES.

551. Ammodramus nigrescens RIDGW.
Dusky Seaside Sparrow.

Ammodramus maritimus var. *nigrescens* RIDGW. Bull. Essex Inst. V. Dec. 1873, 198.
Ammodramus nigrescens RIDGW. Pr. U. S. Nat. Mus. III. Aug. 24, 1880, 178.

[B —, C 165*a*, R 203, C 239.]

GEOG. DIST.— Salt Lake and Merritt Island, eastern Florida.

GENUS **CHONDESTES** SWAINSON.

Chondestes SWAINS. Phil. Mag. I. 1827, 435. Type, *C. strigatus* SWAINS.

552. Chondestes grammacus (SAY).
Lark Sparrow.

Fringilla grammaca SAY, LONG'S Exp. II. 1823, 139.
Chondestes grammaca BONAP. Geog. & Comp. List, 1838, 32.

[B 344, *part*, C 186, *part*, R 204, C 281, *part*.]

GEOG. DIST.— Southern Ontario and Mississippi Valley region, from Ohio, Illinois, and Michigan to the Plains, south to eastern Texas and northwestern Alabama. Accidental near the Atlantic coast (Massachusetts, Long Island, New Jersey, Washington, D. C., Florida).

552 *a*. Chondestes grammacus strigatus (SWAINS.).
Western Lark Sparrow.

Chondestes strigatus SWAINS. Phil. Mag. I. 1827, 435.
Chondestes grammaca strigata RIDGW. Pr. U. S. Nat. Mus. III. Aug. 24, 1880, 179.

[B 344, *part*, C 186, *part*, R 204*a*, C 281, *part*.]

GEOG. DIST.—Western United States, from the Plains to the Pacific coast, north to British Columbia and Manitoba, south through Lower California and Mexico to Guatemala.

Genus **ZONOTRICHIA** Swainson.

Zonotrichia Swains. in Sw. & Rich. Fauna Bor. Am. II. 1831, 493. Type, by elimination, *Emberiza leucophrys* Forst.

553. Zonotrichia querula (Nutt.).
Harris's Sparrow.

Fringilla querula Nutt. Man. I. 2d ed. 1840, 555.
Zonotrichia querula Gamb. Journ. Ac. Nat. Sci. Phila. 2d ser. I. 1847, 51.

[B 348, C 185, R 205, C 280.]

Geog. Dist.— Middle United States, from Illinois, Missouri, and Iowa west to middle Kansas and the Dakotas, and from Texas north to Manitoba. Accidental on Vancouver Island and in British Columbia and Oregon.

554. Zonotrichia leucophrys (Forst.).
White-crowned Sparrow.

Emberiza leucophrys Forst. Philos. Trans. LXII. 1772, 426.
Z[onotrichia] leucophrys Swains. in Sw. & Rich. Fauna. Bor. Am. II. 1831, 493.

[B 345, C 183, R 206, C 276.]

Geog. Dist.— North America at large, breeding chiefly in the Rocky Mountains, the Sierra Nevada and northeast to Labrador. South in winter to the Valley of Mexico.

554a. Zonotrichia leucophrys intermedia Ridgw.
Intermediate Sparrow.

Zonotrichia leucophrys var. *intermedia* Ridgw. Bull. Essex Inst. V. Dec. 1873, 198.

[B 346, *part*, C 183*b*, R 207*a*, C 277.]

Geog. Dist.— Western North America, from the Rocky Mountains to the Pacific, and from Lower California and Mazatlan, Mexico, to Alaska. Breeds, so far as known, mainly north of the United States.

554 *b*. **Zonotrichia leucophrys gambelii** (NUTT.).
   Gambel's Sparrow.

Fringilla gambelii NUTT. Man. I. 2d ed. 1840, 556.
Zonotrichia leucophrys var. *gambeli* COUES, Key, 1872, 145.

[B 346, *part*, C 183*a*, R 207, C 278.]

GEOG. DIST.— Pacific coast region, from British Columbia southward into Lower California.

557. **Zonotrichia coronata** (PALL.).
   Golden-crowned Sparrow.

Emberiza coronata PALL. Zoog. Rosso-As. II. 1826, 44.
Zonotrichia coronata BAIRD, B. N. Am. 1858, 461.

[B 347, C 184, R 208, C 279.]

GEOG. DIST.— Pacific coast region, from Alaska to southern California. Casually to Guadalupe Island, and in Wisconsin.

558. **Zonotrichia albicollis** (GMEL.).
   White-throated Sparrow.

Fringilla albicollis GMEL. S. N. I. ii. 1788, 926.
Zonotrichia albicollis SWAINS. Classif. B. II. 1837, 288.

[B 349, C 182, R 209, C 275.]

GEOG. DIST.— Chiefly eastern North America, west to the Plains, north to Labrador and the Fur Countries. Breeds from Montana, northern Wyoming, northern Michigan, northern New York, and northern New England northward, and winters from Massachusetts southward. Accidental in Utah, California and Oregon.

GENUS **SPIZELLA** BONAPARTE.

Spizella BONAP. Saggio Distr. Met. 1832, 140. Type, *Fringilla pusilla* WILS.

559. **Spizella monticola** (GMEL.).
   Tree Sparrow.

Fringilla monticola GMEL. S. N. I. ii. 1788, 912.
Spizella monticola BAIRD, B. N. Am. 1858, 472.

[B 357, *part*, C 177, *part*, R 210, *part*, C 268, *part*.]

GEOG. DIST.— Eastern North America, west to the Plains, and from the Arctic Ocean south, in winter, to the Carolinas, Kentucky, and eastern Kansas. Breeds north of the United States, east of the Rocky Mountains.

559 a. Spizella monticola ochracea BREWST.
Western Tree Sparrow.

Spizella monticola ochracea BREWST. Bull. Nutt. Orn. Club, VII. Oct. 1882, 228.

[B 357, *part*, C 177, *part*, R 210, *part*, C 268, *part*.]

GEOG. DIST.— Western North America, east to the Dakotas and western Kansas, south in winter to New Mexico and Arizona, north to the arctic regions; breeds in Alaska.

560. Spizella socialis (WILS.).
Chipping Sparrow.

Fringilla socialis WILS. Am. Orn. II. 1810, 127, pl. 16, fig. 5.
Spizella socialis BONAP. Geog. & Comp. List, 1838, 33.

[B 359, *part*, C 178, R 211, C 269.]

GEOG. DIST.— Eastern North America, west to the Rocky Mountains, north to Great Slave Lake, and south to eastern Mexico, breeding from the Gulf States northward.

560 a. Spizella socialis arizonæ COUES.
Western Chipping Sparrow.

Spizella socialis var. *arizonæ* COUES, Key, 1872, 143.

[B 359, *part*, C 178a, R 211a, C 270.]

GEOG. DIST.— Western United States, from the Rocky Mountains to the Pacific, south in winter to central and western Mexico and Cape St. Lucas.

561. Spizella pallida (SWAINS.).
Clay-colored Sparrow.

Emberiza pallida SWAINS. in Sw. & RICH. Fauna Bor. Am. II. 1831, 251.
Spizella pallida BONAP. Geog. & Comp. List, 1838, 33.

ORDER PASSERES. 233

[B 360, C 180, R 212, C 272.]

GEOG. DIST.— Interior of North America, from Illinois and Iowa west to the Rocky Mountains, Arizona, and Cape St. Lucas, and from Guanajuato and Oaxaca north to the Saskatchewan Plains. Breeds from Iowa and Nebraska northward.

562. Spizella breweri CASS.
Brewer's Sparrow.

Spizella breweri CASS. Pr. Ac. Nat. Sci. Phila. Feb. 1856, 40.

[B 361, C 180a, R 213, C 273.]

GEOG. DIST.— Western United States, north to Montana and British Columbia, south to Cape St. Lucas and Durango. Breeds throughout its United States range. Accidental in Massachusetts.

563. Spizella pusilla (WILS.).
Field Sparrow.

Fringilla pusilla WILS. Am. Orn. II. 1810, 121, pl. 16, fig. 2.
Spizella pusilla BONAP. Geog. & Comp. List, 1838, 33.

[B 358, C 179, R 214, C 271.]

GEOG. DIST.— Eastern United States and southern Canada, west to the Plains, south to the Gulf States and Texas. Breeds from South Carolina, southern Illinois and Kansas northward.

563 a. Spizella pusilla arenacea CHADB.
Western Field Sparrow.

Spizella pusilla arenacea CHADB. Auk, III. April, 1886, 248.

[B —, C —, R —, C —.]

GEOG. DIST.— Great Plains, from Texas to Montana and Dakota. Casual at New Orleans, La.

564. Spizella wortheni RIDGW.
Worthen's Sparrow.

Spizella wortheni RIDGW. Pr. U. S. Nat. Mus. VII. Aug. 22, 1884, 259.

[B —, C —, R —, C —.]

GEOG. DIST.— New Mexico (Silver City), and Chalchicomula, Puebla.

565. Spizella atrigularis (CAB.).
Black-chinned Sparrow.
Spinites atrigularis CAB. Mus. Hein. I. 1851, 133.
Spizella atrigularis BAIRD, B. N. Am. 1858, 476.
[B 362, C 181, R 215, C 274.]

GEOG. DIST.— Southern California (north in the deserts to lat. 37°), Arizona, and southern New Mexico, south to Cape St. Lucas and on the tablelands of Mexico to Puebla.

GENUS JUNCO WAGLER.

Junco WAGLER, Isis, 1831, 526. Type, *J. phæonotus* WAGL. = *Fringilla cinerea* SWAINS.

566. Junco aikeni RIDGW.
White-winged Junco.
Junco hyemalis var. *aikeni* RIDGW. Am. Nat. VII. Oct. 1873, 612, 614.
Junco aikeni RIDGW. Field & Forest, May, 1877, 198.
[B —, C 174*a*, R 216, C 262.]

GEOG. DIST.— Colorado, north to the Black Hills, where it breeds.

567. Junco hyemalis (LINN.).
Slate-colored Junco.
Fringilla hyemalis LINN. S. N. ed. 10, I. 1758, 183.
Junco hyemalis SCL. P. Z. S. 1857, 7.
[B 354, C 174, R 217, C 261.]

GEOG. DIST.— North America, chiefly east of the Rocky Mountains, breeding from the higher parts of the Alleghanies, the Catskills, and the mountainous parts of southern New England northward. South in winter to the Gulf States. Casual in California and Arizona.

567 *a*. Junco hyemalis oregonus (TOWNS.).
Oregon Junco.
Fringilla oregana [err. typ.] TOWNS. Journ. Ac. Nat. Sci. Phila. VII. 1837, 188.
Junco hyemalis var. *oregonus* RIDGW. Am. Nat. VII. Oct. 1873, 612.

ORDER PASSERES. 235

[B 352, C 175, R 218, C 263.]

GEOG. DIST.— Pacific coast, from Oregon north to Alaska, south in winter into California and Arizona.

567 *b*. **Junco hyemalis shufeldti** COALE.
Shufeldt's Junco.

Junco hyemalis shufeldti COALE, Auk, IV. Oct. 1887, 330.

[B 352, *part*, C 175, *part*, R 218, *part*, C 263, *part*.]

GEOG. DIST.— Rocky Mountain region, west in the mountains of the Great Basin to California; in winter south to Arizona, New Mexico, Texas, and northern Mexico. Accidental in Michigan, Illinois, Massachusetts, Maryland, etc.

567 *c*. **Junco hyemalis thurberi** ANTHONY.
Thurber's Junco.

Junco hyemalis thurberi ANTHONY, Zoe, I. Oct. 1890, 238.

[B 352, *part*, C 175, *part*, R 218, *part*, C 263, *part*.]

GEOG. DIST.— Sierra Nevada, and deserts and southern coast ranges of California.

567 *d*. **Junco hyemalis pinosus** LOOMIS.
Point Pinos Junco.

Junco pinosus LOOMIS, Auk, X. April, 1893, 47.

[B—, C—, R—, C—.]

GEOG. DIST.— Vicinity of Monterey, California.

567 *e*. **Junco hyemalis carolinensis** BREWST.
Carolina Junco.

Junco hyemalis carolinensis BREWST. Auk, III. Jan. 1886, 108.

[B 354, *part*, C 174, *part*, R 217, *part*, C 261, *part*.]

GEOG. DIST.— Southern Alleghanies (Western North Carolina, etc.).

568. **Junco annectens** BAIRD.
Pink-sided Junco.

Junco annectens BAIRD, Orn. Cal. I. 1870, 564.

[B —, C —, R 219, C 264.]

GEOG. DIST.— Rocky Mountain region, from Idaho and Montana south, in winter, to Arizona, New Mexico and northern Mexico.

568.1. Junco ridgwayi MEARNS.
Ridgway's Junco.

Junco ridgwayi MEARNS, Auk, VII. July, 1890, 243.

[B —, C —, R —, C —.]

GEOG. DIST.— Wyoming, Colorado, Arizona, and New Mexico.

569. Junco caniceps (WOODH.).
Gray-headed Junco.

Struthus caniceps WOODH. Pr. Ac. Nat. Sci. Phila. Dec. 1852, 202.
Junco caniceps BAIRD, B. N. Am. 1858, 468.

[B 353, C 176, R 220, C 265.]

GEOG. DIST.— Rocky Mountain region, from the Black Hills to the Wahsatch and Uintah Mountains, south to New Mexico, Arizona, and northern Mexico.

570. Junco phæonotus palliatus RIDGW.
Arizona Junco.

Junco cinereus palliatus RIDGW. Auk, II. Oct. 1885, 364.
Junco phæonotus palliatus RIDGW. Auk, XII. Oct. 1895, 391.

[B 350, *part*, C —, R 222, *part*, C 267, *part*.]

GEOG. DIST.— Mountains of southern Arizona, and southward into northern Mexico.

570 a. Junco phæonotus dorsalis (HENRY).
Red-backed Junco.

Junco dorsalis HENRY, Pr. Ac. Nat. Sci. Phila. 1858, 117.
Junco phæonotus dorsalis RIDGW. Auk, XII. Oct. 1895, 391.

[B 351, C —, R 221, C 266.]

GEOG. DIST.— Mountains of New Mexico and eastern Arizona, south into northern Mexico.

571. Junco bairdi BELDING.
   Baird's Junco.

Junco bairdi BELDING, Pr. U. S. Nat. Mus. VI. Oct. 5, 1883, 155.

[B —, C —, R —, C —.]

GEOG. DIST.— Southern Lower California.

571.1. Junco townsendi ANTHONY.
   Townsend's Junco.

Junco townsendi ANTHONY, Pr. Cal. Ac. Sci. 2d. ser. II. Oct. 11, 1889, 76.

[B —, C —, R —, C —.]

GEOG. DIST.— San Pedro Martir Mountains, Lower California.

572. Junco insularis RIDGW.
   Guadalupe Junco.

Junco insularis RIDGW. Bull. U. S. Geol. & Geog. Surv. Terr. II. No. 2, April 1, 1876, 188.

[B —, C —, R 223, C —.]

GEOG. DIST.— Guadalupe Island, Lower California.

GENUS **AMPHISPIZA** COUES.

Amphispiza COUES, B. Northwest, 1875, 234. Type, *Emberiza bilineata* CASS.

573. Amphispiza bilineata (CASS.).
   Black-throated Sparrow.

Emberiza bilineata CASSIN, Pr. Ac. Nat. Sci. Phila. Oct. 1850, 104, pl. 3.
Amphispiza bilineata COUES, B. Northwest, 1875, 234.

[B 355, C 172, R 224, C 258.]

GEOG. DIST.— Western United States, from western Texas and Oklahoma west to the west slope of the Sierra Nevada, north throughout the Great Basin, and south in Mexico to Cape St. Lucas and San Luis Potosi. Breeds throughout its range.

574. Amphispiza belli (CASS.).
   Bell's Sparrow.

Emberiza belli CASSIN, Pr. Ac. Nat. Sci. Phila. Oct. 1850, 104, pl. 4.
Amphispiza bellii COUES, B. Northwest, 1875, 234.

[B 356, C 173, R 225, C 259.]

GEOG. DIST.— California west of the Sierra Nevada, north to about Lat. 38°, south to Lower California. Breeds throughout most of its range.

574 a. Amphispiza belli nevadensis (RIDGW.).
   Sage Sparrow.

Poospiza belli var. *nevadensis* RIDGW. Bull. Essex Inst. V. Nov. 1873, 191.
Amphispiza bellii var. *nevadensis* COUES, B. Northwest, 1875, 234.

[B —, C 173a, R 225a, C 260.]

GEOG. DIST.— Great Basin, from Oregon and Idaho south to southern Arizona and New Mexico, breeding throughout its range.

574 b. Amphispiza belli cinerea TOWNSEND.
   Gray Sage Sparrow.

Amphispiza belli cinerea TOWNSEND, Pr. U. S. Nat. Mus. XIII. 1890, 136.

[B —, C —, R —, C —.]

GEOG. DIST.— Lower California.

GENUS **PEUCÆA** AUDUBON.

Peucæa AUD. Synop. 1839, 112. Type, *Fringilla bachmanii* AUD.

575. Peucæa æstivalis (LICHT.).
   Pine-woods Sparrow.

Fringilla æstivalis LICHT. Verz. Doubl. 1823, 25.
Peucæa æstivalis CAB. Mus. Hein. I. 1850, 132.

[B 370, *part*, C 170, *part*, R 226, C 251.]

GEOG. DIST.— Florida and southern Georgia, migrating to southern Florida in winter.

575 a. **Peucæa æstivalis bachmanii** (AUD.).
　　Bachman's Sparrow.

Fringilla bachmanii AUD. Orn. Biog. II. 1834, 366, pl. 165.
Peucæa æstivalis bachmani BREWST. Auk, II. Jan. 1885, 106.

　　[B 370, *part*, C 170, *part*, R 226 a, C 252.]

GEOG. DIST.— North and South Carolina, Georgia, and Alabama, west to Texas, and north to southern Illinois and southern Indiana. Florida in winter.

576. **Peucæa arizonæ** RIDGW.
　　Arizona Sparrow.

Peucæa æstivalis var. *arizonæ* RIDGW. Am. Nat. VII. Oct. 1873, 615.
Peucæa arizonæ RIDGW. Pr. U. S. Nat. Mus. I. Aug. 15, 1878, 127.

　　[B —, C 170 a, R 227, C 253.]

GEOG. DIST.— Southern Arizona and Sonora.

577. **Peucæa mexicana** (LAWR.).
　　Mexican Sparrow.

Coturniculus mexicanus LAWR. Ann. Lyc. N. Y. VIII. May, 1867, 474. (Mts. of Colima.)
Peucæa mexicana RIDGW. Pr. U. S. Nat. Mus. VIII. No. 7, May 23, 1885, 99.

　　[B —, C —, R —, C —.]

GEOG. DIST.— Valley of the Lower Rio Grande in Texas south into central and western Mexico.

578. **Peucæa cassini** (WOODH.).
　　Cassin's Sparrow.

Zonotrichia cassini WOODH. Pr. Ac. Nat. Sci. Phila. April, 1852, 60.
Peucæa cassini BAIRD, B. N. Am. 1858, 485.

　　[B 371, C 170 bis, R 228, C 254.]

GEOG. DIST.— Central and western Kansas, southward and westward through Texas, New Mexico, Arizona and southern Nevada.

579. **Peucæa carpalis** Coues.
   Rufous-winged Sparrow.

   Peucæa carpalis Coues, Am. Nat. VII. June, 1873, 322.

   [B—, C 171 *bis*, R 229, C 257.]

   Geog. Dist.— Arizona and Sonora.

580. **Peucæa ruficeps** (Cass.).
   Rufous-crowned Sparrow.

   Ammodromus ruficeps Cass. Pr. Ac. Nat. Sci. Phila. Oct. 1852, 184.
   Peucæa ruficeps Baird, B. N. Am. 1858, 486.

   [B 372, C 171, R 230, C 255.]

   Geog. Dist.— Coast of California, from Lat. 40° south to Cape St. Lucas.

580 *a*. **Peucæa ruficeps boucardi** (Scl.).
   Boucard's Sparrow.

   Zonotrichia boucardi Sclater, P. Z. S. 1867, 1, pl. i.
   Peucæa ruficeps boucardi Ridgw. Hist. N. Am. B. II. 1874, 38.

   [B—, C—, R 230*a*, C 256.]

   Geog. Dist.— Southern New Mexico and southern Arizona, south into Mexico to Puebla.

580 *b*. **Peucæa ruficeps eremœca** Brown.
   Rock Sparrow.

   Peucæa ruficeps eremœca Brown, Bull. Nutt. Orn. Cl. VII. Jan. 1882, 26.

   [B—, C—, R—, C—.]

   Geog. Dist.— Southwestern Texas, south in eastern Mexico to Orizaba.

Genus **MELOSPIZA** Baird.

Melospiza Baird, B. N. Am. 1858, 478. Type, *Fringilla melodia* Wils. = *F. fasciata* Gmel.

ORDER PASSERES.

581. Melospiza fasciata (GMEL.).
Song Sparrow.
Fringilla fasciata GMEL. S. N. I. ii. 1788, 922.
Melospiza fasciata SCOTT, Am. Nat. X. 1876, 18.
[B 363, C 169, R 231, C 244.]

GEOG. DIST.— Eastern United States to the Plains, breeding from Virginia and the southern portion of the Lake States northward to the Fur Countries.

581 a. Melospiza fasciata fallax (BAIRD).
Desert Song Sparrow.
Zonotrichia fallax BAIRD, Pr. Ac. Nat. Sci. Phila. June, 1854, 119 (nec *Melospiza fallax* auctorum plurimorum !).
Melospiza fasciata fallax HENSH. Auk, I. July, 1884, 224.
[B 367, C 169a, *part*, R 231a, *part*, C 245, *part*.]

GEOG. DIST.— Parts of New Mexico, Arizona, southern Nevada, and southwestern Utah.

581 b. Melospiza fasciata montana HENSH.
Mountain Song Sparrow.
Melospiza fasciata montana HENSHAW, Auk, I. July, 1884, 224.
[B —, C 169a, *part*, R 231a, *part*, C 245, *part*.]

GEOG. DIST.— Northern Mexico, mountains of New Mexico, Colorado, Utah, Nevada, and northward.

581 c. Melospiza fasciata heermanni (BAIRD).
Heerman's Song Sparrow.
Melospiza heermanni BAIRD, B. N. Am. 1858, 478.
Melospiza fasciata δ. *heermanni* RIDGW. Bull. Nutt. Orn. Cl. III. April, 1878, 66.
[B 364, C 169d, R 231b, C 248.]

GEOG. DIST.— California, east into western Nevada.

581 d. Melospiza fasciata samuelis (BAIRD).
Samuels's Song Sparrow.
Ammodromus samuelis BAIRD, B. N. Am. 1858, 455.
Melospiza fasciata samuelis RIDGW. Pr. U. S. Nat. Mus. III. Mar. 1880, 3.

[B 343, 365, C 169*e*, R 231*c*, C 249.]

GEOG. DIST.— Coast region of California.

581*e*. Melospiza fasciata guttata (NUTT.).
Rusty Song Sparrow.

Fringilla guttata NUTTALL, Man. Orn. I. ed. 2, 1840, 581.
Melospiza fasciata β. guttata RIDGW. Bull. Nutt. Orn. Cl. III. April, 1878, 66.

[B —, C 169*b*, R 231*d*, C 246.]

GEOG. DIST.— Coast region of Washington and Oregon, south in winter to San Francisco, California.

581*f*. Melospiza fasciata rufina (BONAP.).
Sooty Song Sparrow.

Passerella rufina BONAP. Consp. Av. I. July 15, 1850, 477.
Melospiza fasciata rufina RIDGW. Pr. U. S. Nat. Mus. III. Mar. 1880, 3.

[B 366, C 169*c*, R 231*e*, C 247.]

GEOG. DIST.— Coast region of British Columbia, north to Sitka.

581*g*. Melospiza fasciata rivularis BRYANT.
Brown's Song Sparrow.

Melospiza fasciata rivularis BRYANT, Proc. Cal. Ac. Sci. 2d ser. I. Sept. 29, 1888, 197.

[B —, C —, R —, C —.]

GEOG. DIST.— Lower California, from Comondu northward.

581*h*. Melospiza fasciata graminea TOWNSEND.
Santa Barbara Song Sparrow.

Melospiza fasciata graminea TOWNSEND, Pr. U. S. Nat. Mus. XIII. 1890, 139.

[B —, C —, R —, C —.]

GEOG. DIST.— Santa Barbara Island, and, in winter, adjacent mainland of California.

581 *i*. Melospiza fasciata clementæ TOWNSEND.
   San Clemente Song Sparrow.

Melospiza fasciata clementæ TOWNSEND, Pr. U. S. Nat. Mus. XIII. 1890, 139.

[B —, C —, R —, C --.]

GEOG. DIST.— San Clemente and Santa Rosa Islands, California.

581.1. Melospiza insignis BAIRD.
   Bischoff's Song Sparrow.

Melospiza insignis BAIRD, Trans. Chicago Acad. Sci. I. 1869, 319, pl. xxix, fig. 2.

[B —, C 169 *f*, R 232, *part*, C 250, *part*.]

GEOG. DIST.— Kadiak Island, Alaska.

582. Melospiza cinerea (GMEL.).
   Aleutian Song Sparrow.

Fringilla cinerea GMEL. S. N. I. ii. 1788, 922.
Melospiza cinerea FINSCH, Abhandl. Nat. Ver. Bremen, III. 1872, 20.

[B —, C 169 *f*, R 232, C 250.]

GEOG. DIST. — Aleutian and Pribilof Islands (except Kadiak Island), and east to Fort Kenai, Alaska.

583. Melospiza lincolnii (AUD.).
   Lincoln's Sparrow.

Fringilla lincolnii AUD. Orn. Biog. II. 1834, 539, pl. 193.
Melospiza lincolni BAIRD, B. N. Am. 1858, 482.

[B 368, C 167, R 234, C 242.]

GEOG. DIST.— North America at large, breeding chiefly north of the United States (as far north as Fort Yukon) and in the higher parts of the Rocky Mountains and Sierra Nevada; south, in winter, to Panama.

583 *a*. Melospiza lincolnii striata BREWST.
   Forbush's Sparrow.

Melospiza lincolni striata BREWST. Auk, VI. April, 1889, 89.

[B 368, *part*, C 167, *part*, R 234, *part*, C 242, *part*.]

GEOG. DIST.— British Columbia.

584. Melospiza georgiana (LATH.).
Swamp Sparrow.

Fringilla georgiana LATH. Ind. Orn. I. 1790, 460.
Melospiza georgiana RIDGW. Pr. U. S. Nat. Mus. VIII. 1885, 355.

[B 369, C 168, R 233, C 243.]

GEOG. DIST.— Eastern North America to the Plains, accidentally to Utah, north to the British Provinces, including Newfoundland and Labrador. Breeds from the Northern States northward, and winters from Massachusetts southward to the Gulf States.

GENUS **PASSERELLA** SWAINSON.

Passerella SWAINS. Classif. B. II. 1837, 288. Type, *Fringilla iliaca* MERR.

585. Passerella iliaca (MERR.).
Fox Sparrow.

Fringilla iliaca MERREM, " Beitr. zur besond. Gesch. der Vögel, II. 1786–87, 40, pl. x."
Passerella iliaca SWAINS. Classif. B. II. 1837, 288.

[B 374, C 188, R 235, C 282.]

GEOG. DIST.— Eastern North America, west to the Plains and Alaska (valley of the Yukon to the Pacific), and from the Arctic coast south to the Gulf States. Breeds north of the United States; winters chiefly south of the Potomac and Ohio Rivers. Accidental in winter in California.

585 *a*. Passerella iliaca unalaschcensis (GMEL.).
Townsend's Sparrow.

Emberiza unalaschcensis GMEL. S. N. I. ii. 1788, 875.
Passerella iliaca unalaschcensis RIDGW. Pr. U. S. Nat. Mus. III. Mar. 1880, 3.

ORDER PASSERES. 245

[B 375, C 189, R 235*a*, C 283.]

GEOG. DIST.— Pacific coast region, from Kadiak south, in winter, to southern California, and casually to Guadalupe Island, Lower California. Breeds north of the United States.

585 *b*. **Passerella iliaca megarhyncha** (BAIRD).
Thick-billed Sparrow.

Passerella megarhynchus BAIRD, B. N. Am. 1858, 925.
Passerella iliaca δ. *megarhyncha* BELDING, Pr. U. S. Nat. Mus. I. Mar. 1879, 418.

[B 376*a*, C —, R 235*b*, C 285.]

GEOG. DIST.— Sierra Nevada and Coast Range, California.

585 *c*. **Passerella iliaca schistacea** (BAIRD).
Slate-colored Sparrow.

Passerella schistacea BAIRD, B. N. Am. 1858, 490.
Passerella iliaca var. *schistacea* ALLEN, Bull. M. C. Z. III. 1872, 168.

[B 376, C 189*a*, R 235*c*, C 284.]

GEOG. DIST.— Rocky Mountain region of the United States, east in winter, to the Plains (Kansas), west to Nevada and California.

GENUS **EMBERNAGRA** LESSON.

Embernagra LESS. Traité, 1831, 465. Type, *E. dumetorum* LESS. = *Emberiza platensis* GMEL.

586. **Embernagra rufivirgata** LAWR.
Texas Sparrow.

Embernagra rufivirgata LAWR. Ann. Lyc. N. Y. V. May, 1851, 112, pl. 5, fig. 2.

[B 373, C 209, R 236, C 311.]

GEOG. DIST.— Valley of the Lower Rio Grande in Texas and eastern Mexico; casually north to the coast of Louisiana.

GENUS **PIPILO** VIEILLOT.

Pipilo VIEILL. Analyse, 1816, 32. Type, *Fringilla erythrophthalma* LINN.

587. Pipilo erythrophthalmus (LINN.).
Towhee.

Fringilla erythrophthalma LINN. S. N. ed. 10, I. 1758, 180.
Pipilo erythrophthalmus VIEILL. Gal. Ois. I. 1824, 109, pl. 80.

[B 391, C 204, R 237, C 301.]

GEOG. DIST.— Eastern United States and southern Canada, west to the Plains, breeding from the lower Mississippi Valley and Georgia northward; in winter from the middle districts southward.

587 a. Pipilo erythrophthalmus alleni COUES.
White-eyed Towhee.

Pipilo erythrophthalmus var. *alleni* COUES, Am. Nat. V. Aug. 1871, 366.

[B—, C 204a, R 237a, C 302.]

GEOG. DIST.— Florida, and northward along the Atlantic coast to Charleston, South Carolina.

588. Pipilo maculatus arcticus (SWAINS.).
Arctic Towhee.

Pyrgita (*Pipilo*) *arctica* SWAINS. in SW. & RICH. Fauna Bor. Am. II. 1831, 260, pll. 51, 52.
Pipilo maculatus var. *arcticus* COUES, Key, 1872, 152.

[B 393, C 205a, R 238, C 304.]

GEOG. DIST.— Plains of the Platte, Upper Missouri, Yellowstone and Saskatchewan Rivers, west to the eastern slope of the Rocky Mountains, south in winter to Kansas, Colorado, and Texas.

588 a. Pipilo maculatus megalonyx (BAIRD).
Spurred Towhee.

Pipilo megalonyx BAIRD, B. N. Am. 1858, 515.
Pipilo maculatus var. *megalonyx* COUES, Key, 1872, 152.

[B 394, C 205b, R 238a, C 305.]

GEOG. DIST.— Rocky Mountain region of the United States, west to the Sierra Nevada and southern California, south into northern Mexico and Lower California.

588 *b*. **Pipilo maculatus oregonus** (BELL).
Oregon Towhee.

Pipilo oregonus BELL, Ann. Lyc. N. Y. V. 1852, 6.
Pipilo maculatus var. *oregonus* COUES, Key, 1872, 152.

[B 392, C 205, R 238*b*, C 303.]

GEOG. DIST.— Pacific coast region, from British Columbia south to San Francisco, and, in winter, to southern California.

589. **Pipilo consobrinus** RIDGW.
Guadalupe Towhee.

Pipilo maculatus consobrinus RIDGW. Bull. U. S. Geol. & Geog. Surv. Terr. II. No. 2, April 1, 1876, 189.
Pipilo consobrinus RIDGW. Bull. Nutt. Orn. Club, II. July, 1877, 60.

[B—, C—, R 238*c*, C—.]

GEOG. DIST.— Guadalupe Island, Lower California.

590. **Pipilo chlorurus** (TOWNS.).
Green-tailed Towhee.

Fringilla chlorura TOWNS. in AUD. Orn. Biog. V. 1839, 336.
Pipilo chlorurus BAIRD, B. N. Am. 1858, 519.

[B 398, C 208, R 239, C 310.]

GEOG. DIST.— Interior Plateau region of the United States, from the western border of the Plains to the Sierra Nevada, from central Idaho and Yellowstone National Park south to Cape St. Lucas, and on the tablelands of Mexico to Guanajuato.

591. **Pipilo fuscus mesoleucus** (BAIRD).
Cañon Towhee.

Pipilo mesoleucus BAIRD, Pr. Ac. Nat. Sci. Phila. June, 1854, 119.
Pipilo fuscus var. *mesoleucus* RIDGW. Bull. Essex Inst. V. Nov. 1873, 183.

[B 397, C 206, R 240, C 306.]

GEOG. DIST.— Southern border of the United States, from the valley of the Upper Rio Grande west to the valley of the Gila, south into Sonora and Chihuahua.

591 a. Pipilo fuscus albigula (BAIRD).
  Saint Lucas Towhee.

Pipilo albigula BAIRD, Pr. Ac. Nat. Sci. Phila. Nov. 1859, 305.
Pipilo fuscus var. *albigula* COUES, Key, 1872, 152.

[B —, C 206*a*, R 240*a*, C 307.]

GEOG. DIST.— Lower California, north to Lat. 30°.

591 b. Pipilo fuscus crissalis (VIG.).
  California Towhee.

Fringilla crissalis VIG. Zool. Blos. 1839, 19.
Pipilo fuscus var. *crissalis* COUES, Key, 1872, 153.

[B 396, C 206*b*, R 240*b*, C 308.]

GEOG. DIST.—Pacific coast region west of the Cascades and Sierra Nevada, from the Umpqua Valley, Oregon, south to northern Lower California.

591 c. Pipilo fuscus senicula ANTHONY.
  Anthony's Towhee.

Pipilo fuscus senicula ANTHONY, Auk, XII. April, 1895, 111.

[B 396, *part*, C 206*b*, *part*, R 240*b*, *part*, C 308, *part*.]

GEOG. DIST.— Southern California, and Lower California, south to Lat. 29°.

592. Pipilo aberti BAIRD.
  Abert's Towhee.

Pipilo aberti BAIRD, STANSBURY'S Rep. Exped. Utah, 1852, 325.

[B 395, C 207, R 241, C 309.]

GEOG. DIST.— New Mexico and Arizona, north into southern Colorado, southwestern Utah, and southern Nevada.

GENUS **CARDINALIS** BONAPARTE.

Cardinalis BONAP. P. Z. S. 1837 (June, 1838), 111. Type, *C. virginianus* BONAP. = *Loxia cardinalis* LINN.

593. Cardinalis cardinalis (LINN.).
   Cardinal.

Loxia cardinalis LINN. S. N. ed. 10, 1758, 172.
Cardinalis cardinalis LICHT. Nomencl. Mus. Berol. 1854, 44.

[B 390, C 203, R 242, C 299.]

GEOG. DIST.— Eastern United States, north to the lower Hudson Valley and the Great Lakes, casually further north, and west to the Plains. Resident in Bermuda.

593 a. Cardinalis cardinalis superbus RIDGW.
   Arizona Cardinal.

Cardinalis cardinalis superbus RIDGW. Auk, II. Oct. 1885, 344.

[B —, C 203a, *part,* R 242a, *part,* C 300, *part.*]

GEOG. DIST.— Southern Arizona and western Mexico, south to Mazatlan.

593 b. Cardinalis cardinalis igneus (BAIRD).
   Saint Lucas Cardinal.

Cardinalis igneus BAIRD, Pr. Ac. Nat. Sci. Phila. 1859, 305.
Cardinalis cardinalis igneus STEJN. Auk, I. 1884, 171.

[B —, C 203a, *part,* R 242a, *part,* C 300, *part.*]

GEOG. DIST.— Lower California, north to Lat. 29°.

593 c. Cardinalis cardinalis canicaudus CHAPM.
   Gray-tailed Cardinal.

Cardinalis cardinalis canicaudus CHAPM. Bull. Am. Mus. Nat. Hist. III. Aug. 1891, 324.

[B 390, *part,* C 203, *part,* R 242, *part,* C 299, *part.*]

GEOG. DIST.— Southwestern Texas, south into northeastern Mexico.

GENUS **PYRRHULOXIA** BONAPARTE.

Pyrrhuloxia BONAP. Consp. Av. I. 1850, 500. Type, *Cardinalis sinuatus* BONAP.

594. Pyrrhuloxia sinuata BONAP.
Texas Cardinal.

Cardinalis sinuatus BONAP. P. Z. S. 1837 (June, 1838), 111.
Pyrrhuloxia sinuata BONAP. Consp. Av. I. 1850, 500.

[B 389, C 202, R 243, C 298.]

GEOG. DIST.— Southern border of the United States, from the valley of the Lower Rio Grande south to San Luis Potosi, Puebla, etc. North casually to the coast of Louisiana.

594 *a*. Pyrrhuloxia sinuata beckhami RIDGW.
Arizona Pyrrhuloxia.

Pyrrhuloxia sinuata beckhami RIDGW. Auk, IV. Oct. 1887, 347.

[B 389, *part*, C 202, *part*, R 243, *part*, C 298, *part.*]

GEOG. DIST.— Southern Arizona to western Texas, and south into northwestern Mexico.

594 *b*. Pyrrhuloxia sinuata peninsulæ RIDGW.
Saint Lucas Pyrrhuloxia.

Pyrrhuloxia sinuata peninsulæ RIDGW. Auk, IV. Oct. 1887, 347.

[B 389, *part*, C 202, *part*, R 243, *part*, C 298, *part.*]

GEOG. DIST.— Lower California.

GENUS **HABIA** REICHENBACH.

Habia REICH. Syst. Av. June 1, 1850, pl. lxxviii. Type, *Guiraca melanocephala* SWAINS.

595. Habia ludoviciana (LINN.).
Rose-breasted Grosbeak.

Loxia ludoviciana LINN. S. N. ed. 12, I. 1766, 306.
Habia ludoviciana STEJN. Auk, I. Oct. 1884, 367.

[B 380, C 193, R 244, C 289.]

GEOG. DIST.— Eastern United States and southern Canada, west to Manitoba and the eastern border of the Plains, breeding from Kansas and the mountains of the Carolinas northward; south, in winter, to Cuba, Central America, and northern South America.

596. Habia melanocephala (SWAINS.).
Black-headed Grosbeak.

Guiraca melanocephala SWAINS. Philos. Mag. I. 1827, 438.
Habia melanocephala STEJN. Auk, I. Oct. 1884, 367.

[B 381, C 194, R 245, C 290.]

GEOG. DIST.— Western United States, from middle Kansas to the Pacific coast, north to British Columbia and Montana, and south in Mexico to Oaxaca and the Cape region of Lower California.

GENUS **GUIRACA** SWAINSON.

Guiraca SWAINS. Zool. Jour. III. Nov. 1827, 350. Type, *Loxia cærulea* LINN.

597. Guiraca cærulea (LINN.).
Blue Grosbeak.

Loxia cærulea LINN. S. N. ed. 10, I. 1758, 175.
Guiraca cærulea SWAINS. Phil. Mag. I. 1827, 438.

[B 382, C 195, R 246, C 291.]

GEOG. DIST.— Eastern United States, from southern New Jersey, southern Illinois and central Nebraska, south to Cuba and Mexico. Casual northward to New England.

597 a. Guiraca cærulea eurhyncha COUES.
Western Blue Grosbeak.

Guiraca cærulea, var. *eurhyncha* COUES, Am. Nat. VIII. Sept. 1874, 563.

[B 382, *part*, C 195, *part*, R 246, *part*, C 291, *part*.]

GEOG. DIST.— Southwestern United States, from South Dakota, Colorado, southern Utah, southern Nevada and California to Lower California and southern Mexico.

GENUS **PASSERINA** VIEILLOT.

Passerina VIEILL. Analyse, 1816, 30. Type, by elimination, *Tanagra cyanea* LINN.

598. Passerina cyanea (LINN.).
Indigo Bunting.

Tanagra cyanea LINN. S. N. ed. 12, I. 1766, 315.
Passerina cyanea VIEILL. Nouv. Dict. d'Hist. Nat. XXV. 1817, 7.

[B 387, C 199, R 248, C 295.]

GEOG. DIST.— Eastern United States, west to Kansas, north to New Brunswick, southern Ontario and Minnesota; south in winter to Central America.

599. Passerina amœna (SAY).
Lazuli Bunting.

Emberiza amœna SAY, LONG'S EXP. II. 1823, 47.
Passerina amœna GRAY, Handl. II. 1870, 97.

[B 386, C 200, R 249, C 296.]

GEOG. DIST.— Western United States, from the Plains to the Pacific, north to the dry interior of British Columbia and Idaho, south to the Valley of Mexico.

600. Passerina versicolor (BONAP.).
Varied Bunting.

Spiza versicolor BONAP. P. Z. S. 1837 (June, 1838), 120.
Passerina versicolor GRAY, Handl. II. 1870, 97.

[B 385, C 197, R 250, C 293.]

GEOG. DIST.— From the valley of the Lower Rio Grande in Texas southward to Guatemala. Accidental in southern Michigan.

600 a. Passerina versicolor pulchra RIDGW.
Beautiful Bunting.

Passerina versicolor pulchra RIDGW. Man. N. Am. B. 1887, 448.

[B 385, *part*, C 197, *part*, R 250, *part*, C 293, *part*.]

GEOG. DIST.— Lower California and northwestern Mexico.

601. Passerina ciris (LINN.).
Painted Bunting.

Emberiza ciris LINN. S. N. ed. 10, I. 1758, 179.
Passerina ciris VIEILL. Nouv. Dict. d'Hist. Nat. XXV. 1817, 17.

[B 384, C 196, R 251, C 292.]

GEOG. DIST.— South Atlantic and Gulf States to western Texas, north to North Carolina and southern Illinois, and south to Panama.

GENUS **SPOROPHILA** CABANIS.

Sporophila CABANIS, Arch. f. Naturg. X. i. 1844, 291.

602. Sporophila morelleti sharpei LAWR.
Sharpe's Seed-eater.

Sporophila morelleti sharpei LAWR. Auk, VI. Jan. 1889, 53.

[B 388, C 200, R 252, C 296.]

GEOG. DIST.— Southeastern Texas and adjacent parts of Mexico.

GENUS **EUETHEIA** REICHENBACH.

Euetheia REICH. Av. Syst. Nat. June 1, 1850, pl. lxxix. Type, *Emberiza lepida* LINN.

[603.] Euetheia bicolor (LINN.).
Grassquit.

Fringilla bicolor LINN. S. N. ed. 12, I. 1766, 324.
Euetheia bicolor GUNDLACH, J. f. O. XXII. 1874, 312.

[B —, C 201, R 253, C 297.]

GEOG. DIST.— West Indies. Accidental or casual in southern Florida.

[603.1.] Euetheia canora (GMEL.).
Melodious Grassquit.

Loxia canora GMEL. S. N. I. ii. 1788, 858.
Euetheia canora BREWER, Proc. Bost. Soc. Nat. Hist. VII. 1860, 307.

[B —, C —, R —, C —.]

GEOG. DIST.— Cuba. Accidental in southern Florida (Sombrero Key).

GENUS **SPIZA** BONAPARTE.

Spiza BONAP. Journ. Ac. Nat. Sci. Phila. IV. i. Aug. 1824, 45. Type, *Emberiza americana* GMEL.

604. Spiza americana (GMEL.).
Dickcissel.

Emberiza americana GMEL. S. N. I. ii. 1788, 872.
Spiza americana RIDGW. Pr. U. S. Nat. Mus. III. March 27, 1880, 3.

[B 378, C 191, R 254, C 287.]

GEOG. DIST.— Eastern United States to the Rocky Mountains, breeding from Texas north to Massachusetts, New York, southern Ontario, Wisconsin, Minnesota, and North Dakota; south in winter through Central America to northern South America; southwest in migrations to Arizona. Now rare or entirely absent east of the Alleghanies.

GENUS **CALAMOSPIZA** BONAPARTE.

Calamospiza BONAP. Geog. & Comp. List, 1838, 30. Type, *Fringilla bicolor* TOWNS. = *Calamospiza melanocorys* STEJN.

605. Calamospiza melanocorys STEJN.
Lark Bunting.

Calamospiza melanocorys STEJN. Auk, II. Jan. 1885, 49.

[B 377, C 190, R 256, C 286.]

GEOG. DIST.— From the Plains of middle Kansas north to Manitoba and Assiniboia, west to the Rocky Mountains, less commonly to the Pacific in southern California, and south to Guanajuato and Lower California. Accidental in Massachusetts, New York, and South Carolina.

FAMILY **TANAGRIDÆ**. TANAGERS.

GENUS **EUPHONIA** DESMAREST.

Euphonia DESM. Hist. Nat. Tang. 1805, pl. xix. Type, *Pipra musica* GMEL.?

ORDER PASSERES.

[606.] **Euphonia elegantissima** (BONAP.).
Blue-headed Euphonia.

Pipra elegantissima BONAP. P. Z. S. 1837 (June, 1838), 112.
Euphonia elegantissima GRAY, Gen. B. App. 1849, 17.

[B 224, C —, R 160, C —.]

GEOG. DIST.— Eastern Mexico, and south to Veragua. Texas (GIRAUD).

GENUS **PIRANGA** VIEILLOT.

Piranga VIEILL. Ois. Am. Sept. I. 1807, p. iv. Type, *Muscicapa rubra* LINN. 1766 = *Fringilla rubra* LINN. 1758.

607. **Piranga ludoviciana** (WILS.).
Louisiana Tanager.

Tanagra ludoviciana WILS. Am. Orn. III. 1811, 27, pl. 20, fig. 1.
Pyranga ludoviciana RICHARDSON, Rep. Brit. Ass. Adv. Sci. V. 1837, 175.

[B 223, C 110, R 162, C 158.]

GEOG. DIST.— Western United States, from the Great Plains to the Pacific, north to South Dakota and British Columbia. In winter south to Guatemala. Accidental in New York and New England.

[607.1.] **Piranga rubriceps** GRAY.
Gray's Tanager.

Pyranga rubriceps GRAY, Gen. B. II. 1844, pl. 89.

[B —, C —, R —, C —.]

GEOG. DIST.— Colombia. Accidental in California (Dos Pueblos, Santa Barbara Co.).

608. **Piranga erythromelas** VIEILL.
Scarlet Tanager.

Pyranga erythromelas VIEILL. Nouv. Dict. d'Hist. Nat. XXVIII. 1819, 293 (= *Pyranga rubra* AUCT, nec *Fringilla rubra* LINN.).

[B 220, C 107, R 161, C 154.]

GEOG. DIST.— Eastern United States, west to the Plains, and north to southern Ontario and Manitoba. In winter the West Indies, eastern Mexico, Central America and northern South America.

609. **Piranga hepatica** SWAINS.
Hepatic Tanager.

Pyranga hepatica SWAINS. Phil. Mag. I. 1827, 438.

[B 222, C 109, R 163, C 157.]

GEOG. DIST.— Southern New Mexico and southern Arizona southward to Guatemala.

610. **Piranga rubra** (LINN.).
Summer Tanager.

Fringilla rubra LINN. S. N. ed. 10, I. 1758, 181.
Piranga rubra VIEILL. Ois. Am. Sept. I. 1807, p. iv.

[B 221, C 108, R 164, C 155.]

GEOG. DIST.— Eastern United States, to the Plains, north to southern New Jersey and southern Illinois, casually north to Massachusetts and Ontario, and accidentally to Nova Scotia. In winter, Cuba, eastern Mexico, Central America, and northern South America to Peru.

610 *a*. **Piranga rubra cooperi** RIDGW.
Cooper's Tanager.

Pyranga cooperi RIDGW. Pr. Ac. Nat. Sci. Phila. 1869, 130.
Piranga rubra cooperi RIDGW. Pr. U. S. Nat. Mus. VIII. 1885, 354.

[B —, C 108*a*, R 164*a*, C 156.]

GEOG. DIST.— New Mexico and Arizona, south in western Mexico to Colima.

FAMILY **HIRUNDINIDÆ**. SWALLOWS.

GENUS **PROGNE** BOIE.

Progne BOIE, Isis, 1826, 971. Type, *Hirundo subis* LINN.

ORDER PASSERES.

611. Progne subis (LINN.).
   Purple Martin.
Hirundo subis LINN. S. N. ed. 10, I. 1758, 192.
Progne subis BAIRD, Rev. Am. B. I. May, 1865, 274.
   [B 231, C 117, R 152, C 165.]

GEOG. DIST.— Temperate North America, north to Ontario and the Saskatchewan, south to the higher parts of Mexico, wintering in South America.

611 a. Progne subis hesperia BREWST.
   Western Martin.
Progne subis hesperia BREWST. Auk, VI. April, 1889, 92.
   [B 231, *part*, C 117, *part*, R 152, *part*, C 165, *part*.]

GEOG. DIST.— California, south of Latitude 40°, and southern Arizona; in winter, south to Nicaragua.

611.1. Progne cryptoleuca BAIRD.
   Cuban Martin.
Progne cryptoleuca BAIRD, Rev. Am. B. I. May, 1865, 277.
   [B 231*a*, C—, R 152*a*, C—.]

GEOG. DIST.— Cuba, and southern Florida.

GENUS **PETROCHELIDON** CABANIS.

Petrochelidon CAB. Mus. Hein. I. 1850, 47. Type, *Hirundo melanogastra* SWAINS.

612. Petrochelidon lunifrons (SAY).
   Cliff Swallow.
Hirundo lunifrons SAY, LONG'S Exp. II. 1823, 47.
Petrochelidon lunifrons CASSIN, Cat. Hirun. Mus. Phila. Acad. Nat. Sci. 1853, 4.
   [B 226, C 114, R 153, C 162.]

GEOG. DIST.— North America, north to the limit of trees, breeding south to the valleys of the Potomac and the Ohio, southern Texas, southern Arizona, and California; Central and South America in winter. Not recorded from Florida or the West Indies.

[612.1.] **Petrochelidon fulva** (VIEILL.).
Cuban Cliff Swallow.

Hirundo fulva VIEILL. Ois. Am. Sept. I. 1807, 62, pl. 30.
Petrochelidon fulva CAB. Mus. Hein. I. 1850, 47.

[B—, C—, R—, C—.]

GEOG. DIST.—Greater Antilles and coast of Central America. Accidental on the Dry Tortugas, Florida.

GENUS **CHELIDON** FORSTER.

Chelidon FORST. Synop. Cat. Brit. B. 1817, 55. Type, *Hirundo rustica* LINN.

613. **Chelidon erythrogastra** (BODD.).
Barn Swallow.

Hirundo erythrogaster BODD. Tabl. P. E. 1783, 45.
Chelidon erythrogastra STEJN. Pr. U. S. Nat. Mus. V. June 5, 1882, 31.

[B 225, C 111, R 154, C 159.]

GEOG. DIST.—North America in general, breeding from the Fur Countries south into Mexico; visits the West Indies in migrations, and winters in Central America and South America.

GENUS **TACHYCINETA** CABANIS.

Tachycineta CAB. Mus. Hein. I. 1850, 48. Type, *Hirundo thalassina* SWAINS.

614. **Tachycineta bicolor** (VIEILL.).
Tree Swallow.

Hirundo bicolor VIEILL. Ois. Am. Sept. I. 1807, 61, pl. 31.
Tachycineta bicolor CAB. Mus. Hein. I. 1850, 48.

[B 227, C 112, R 155, C 160.]

GEOG. DIST.—North America at large, breeding from the Fur Countries south to New Jersey, the Ohio Valley, Kansas, and Colorado, etc., wintering from South Carolina and the Gulf States southward to the West Indies and Guatemala.

ORDER PASSERES.

615. Tachycineta thalassina (SWAINS.).
   Violet-green Swallow.

Hirundo thalassinus SWAINS. Phil. Mag. I. 1827, 366.
Tachycineta thalassina CAB. Mus. Hein. I. 1850, 48.
   [B 228, C 113, R 156, C 161.]

GEOG. DIST.— Western United States, from the eastern base of the Rocky Mountains to the Pacific, north to British Columbia, south, in winter, to Guatemala and Costa Rica.

GENUS **CALLICHELIDON** BAIRD.

Callichelidon BRYANT, MS. BAIRD, Rev. Am. Bds. I. 1865, 303.
Type, *Hirundo cyaneoviridis* BRYANT.

[615.1.] Callichelidon cyaneoviridis (BRYANT).
   Bahaman Swallow.

Hirundo cyaneoviridis BRYANT, Pr. Boston Soc. Nat. Hist., VII. 1859, 111.
Callichelidon cyaneoviridis BRYANT, MS. BAIRD, Rev. Am. Birds, I. 1865, 303.
   [B —, C —, R —, C —.]

GEOG. DIST.— Bahamas. Accidental on the Dry Tortugas, Florida.

GENUS **CLIVICOLA** FORSTER.

Clivicola FORST. Synop. Cat. Brit. B. 1817, 55. Type, *Hirundo riparia* LINN.

616. Clivicola riparia (LINN.).
   Bank Swallow.

Hirundo riparia LINN. S. N. ed. 10, I. 1758, 192.
Clivicola riparia STEJN. Pr. U. S. Nat. Mus. V. 1882, 32.
   [B 229, C 115, R 157, C 163.]

GEOG. DIST.— Northern hemisphere; in America, south to the West Indies, Central America, and northern South America, breeding from the middle districts of the United States northward to about the limit of trees.

Genus **STELGIDOPTERYX** Baird.

Stelgidopteryx Baird, B. N. Am. 1858, 312.   Type, *Hirundo serripennis* Aud.

617. Stelgidopteryx serripennis (Aud.).
Rough-winged Swallow.

Hirundo serripennis Aud. Orn. Biog, IV. 1838, 593.
Stelgidopteryx serripennis Baird, B. N. Am. 1858, 312.

[B 230, C 116, R 158, C 164.]

Geog. Dist.— United States at large, north to Connecticut, southern Ontario, southern Minnesota, southern Montana, and British Columbia, south through Mexico to Costa Rica. Breeds throughout its United States range and south into Mexico.

Family **AMPELIDÆ**.   Waxwings, etc.

Subfamily **AMPELINÆ**.   Waxwings.

Genus **AMPELIS** Linnæus.

Ampelis Linn. S. N. ed. 12, I. 1766, 297.   Type, by elimination, *Lanius garrulus* Linn.

618. Ampelis garrulus Linn.
Bohemian Waxwing.

Lanius garrulus Linn. S. N. ed. 10, I. 1758, 95.
Ampelis garrulus Linn. S. N. ed. 12, I. 1766, 297.

[B 232, C 118, R 150, C 166.]

Geog. Dist.— Northern parts of the northern hemisphere. In North America, south in winter, irregularly, to Pennsylvania, Illinois, Kansas, southern Colorado, and northern California. Accidental at Fort Mohave, Arizona. Breeds north of the United States.

619. Ampelis cedrorum (Vieill.).
Cedar Waxwing.

Bombycilla cedrorum Vieill. Ois. Am. Sept. I. 1807, 88, pl. 57.
Ampelis cedrorum Gray, Gen. B. I. 1846, 278.

ORDER PASSERES. 261

[B 233, C 119, R 151, C 167.]

GEOG. DIST.—North America at large, from the Fur Countries southward. In winter, from the northern border of the United States south to the West Indies and Costa Rica. Breeds from Virginia, the southern Alleghanies, Kentucky, Kansas, Arizona, etc., northward.

SUBFAMILY **PTILIOGONATINÆ**.

GENUS **PHAINOPEPLA** SCLATER.

Phainopepla SCL. P. Z. S. 1858, 543.   Type, *Ptiliogonys nitens* SWAINS.

620. **Phainopepla nitens** (SWAINS.).
Phainopepla.

Ptiliogonys nitens SWAINS. Anim. in Menag. 1838, 285.
Phainopepla nitens SCL. P. Z. S. 1858, 543.

[B 234, C 120, R 26, C 168.]

GEOG. DIST.—Southwestern United States, from southwestern Texas westward; north to southern Utah, Nevada, Fort Crook, California, and south to Cape St. Lucas and the Valley of Mexico.

FAMILY **LANIIDÆ**.   SHRIKES.

GENUS **LANIUS** LINNÆUS.

Lanius LINN. S. N. ed. 10, I. 1758, 93.   Type, by elimination, *L. excubitor* LINN.

621. **Lanius borealis** VIEILL.
Northern Shrike.

Lanius borealis VIEILL. Ois. Am. Sept. 1. 1807, 80, pl. 50.

[B 236, C 134, R 148, C 186.]

GEOG. DIST.—Northern North America, south in winter to the middle portions of the United States (Virginia, Kentucky, Kansas, Colorado, Arizona, northern California). Breeds north of the United States.

622. Lanius ludovicianus LINN.
Loggerhead Shrike.

Lanius ludovicianus LINN. S. N. ed. 12, I. 1766, 134.

[B 237, C 135, R 149, C 187.]

GEOG. DIST.— Eastern United States, west to the Plains; north to northern New England. Breeds from the Gulf States to Virginia and casually north, on the Atlantic coast, to southern New Jersey; in the interior, northward to the Great Lakes, and through western Pennsylvania and New York to New Hampshire, Vermont, and Maine.

622 *a*. Lanius ludovicianus excubitorides (SWAINS.).
White-rumped Shrike.

Lanius excubitorides SWAINS. in Sw. & RICH. Fauna Bor. Am. II. 1831, 115, pl. 34.
Lanius ludovicianus var. *excubitoroides* COUES, Key, 1872, 125.

[B 238, C 135*a*, R 149*a*, C 188.]

GEOG. DIST.— Western North America, from the eastern border of the Plains to the Pacific, except coast of California, and from Manitoba and the Plains of the Saskatchewan south over the tablelands of Mexico.

622 *b*. Lanius ludovicianus gambeli RIDGW.
California Shrike.

Lanius ludovicianus gambeli RIDGW. Man. N. Am. B. 1887, 467.

[B 238, *part*, C 153*a*, *part*, R 149*a*, *part*, C 188, *part*.]

GEOG. DIST.— Coast of California.

FAMILY **VIREONIDÆ**. VIREOS.

GENUS **VIREO** VIEILLOT.

SUBGENUS **VIREOSYLVA** BONAPARTE.

Vireosylva BONAP. Geog. & Comp. List, 1838, 26. Type, *Muscicapa olivacea* LINN.

ORDER PASSERES.

623. Vireo calidris barbatulus (CAB.).
Black-whiskered Vireo.

Phyllomanes barbatulus CAB. J. f. O. 1855, 467.
Vireo calidris barbatulus COUES, B. Col. Vall. 1878, 491.

[B 243, C 123, R 137, C 172.]

GEOG. DIST.— Bahamas, Cuba, and southern Florida.

624. Vireo olivaceus (LINN.).
Red-eyed Vireo.

Muscicapa olivacea LINN. S. N. ed. 12, I. 1766, 327.
Vireo olivaceus BONAP. Ann. Lyc. N. Y. II. 1826, 71.

[B 240, C 122, R 135, C 170.]

GEOG. DIST.— Eastern North America, west to Colorado, Utah, and British Columbia; north to the arctic regions; south, in winter, from Florida to northern South America. Breeds nearly throughout its North American range.

625. Vireo flavoviridis (CASS.).
Yellow-green Vireo.

Vireosylvia flavoviridis CASS. Pr. Ac. Nat. Sci. Phila. V. Feb. 1851, 152.
Vireo flavoviridis BAIRD, B. N. Am. 1858, 332.

[B 241, C —, R 136, C 171.]

GEOG. DIST.— Valley of the Lower Rio Grande in Texas, southward to Panama, Ecuador, Peru and Upper Amazon. Accidental at Godbout, Province of Quebec, and at Riverside, California.

626. Vireo philadelphicus (CASS.).
Philadelphia Vireo.

Vireosylvia philadelphica CASS. Pr. Ac. Nat. Sci. Phila. V. Feb. 1851, 153, pl. 10, fig. 2.
Vireo philadelphicus BAIRD, B. N. Am. 1858, 335.

[B 244, C 124, R 138, C 173.]

GEOG. DIST.— Eastern North America, north to Hudson Bay; south, in winter, to Costa Rica and Panama. Not recorded from Mexico or the West Indies. Breeds from Maine, New Hampshire, and Manitoba northward.

627. Vireo gilvus (VIEILL.).
Warbling Vireo.

Muscicapa gilva VIEILL. Ois. Am. Sept. I. 1807, 65, pl. 34.
Vireo gilvus BONAP. Journ. Ac. Nat. Sci. Phila. IV. 1824, 176.

[B 245, C 125, 125*a*, R 139, 139*a*, C 174, 175.]

GEOG. DIST.— North America in general, from the Fur Countries to Oaxaca, Mexico. Breeds throughout the greater part of its range.

SUBGENUS **LANIVIREO** BAIRD.

Lanivireo BAIRD, Rev. Am. B. I. May, 1866, 345. Type, *Vireo flavifrons* VIEILL.

628. Vireo flavifrons VIEILL.
Yellow-throated Vireo.

Vireo flavifrons VIEILL. Ois. Am. Sept. I. 1807, 85, pl. 54.

[B 252, C 126, R 140, C 176.]

GEOG. DIST.— Eastern United States, north to Ontario and Manitoba; south, in winter, to Colombia. Breeds from Florida and the Gulf States northward.

629. Vireo solitarius (WILS.).
Blue-headed Vireo.

Muscicapa solitaria WILS. Am. Orn. II. 1810, 43, pl. 17, fig. 6.
Vireo solitarius VIEILL. Nouv. Dict. d'Hist. Nat. XXXVI. 1819, 103.

[B 250, C 127, R 141, C 177.]

GEOG. DIST.— Eastern North America to the Plains, north to Hudson Bay and Fort Simpson. South, in winter, to Guatemala. Breeds from southern New England and the northern part of the Lake States northward.

629*a*. Vireo solitarius cassinii (XANTUS).
Cassin's Vireo.

Vireo cassinii XANT. Pr. Ac. Nat. Sci. Phila. 1858, 117.
Vireo solitarius var. *cassini* HENSH. Rep. Orn. Spec. (Wheeler's Exp.), 1874, 105.

ORDER PASSERES.

[B 251, C —, R 141*a*, C 178.]

GEOG. DIST.— Western United States; confined to the Pacific slope, from British Columbia southward, during the breeding season.

629 *b*. Vireo solitarius plumbeus (COUES).
Plumbeous Vireo.

Vireo plumbeus COUES, Pr. Ac. Nat. Sci. Phila. 1866, 74.
Vireo solitarius var. *plumbeus* ALLEN, Bull. M. C. Z. III. 1872, 176.

[B —, C 127*a*, R 141*b*, C 179.]

GEOG. DIST.— Southern Rocky Mountain region from the eastern base of the mountains westward to the desert ranges of the Great Basin, and from southern Wyoming south, in winter, to Oaxaca, Mexico. Accidental in New York.

629 *c*. Vireo solitarius alticola BREWST.
Mountain Solitary Vireo.

Vireo solitarius alticola BREWST. Auk, III. Jan. 1886, 111.

[B 250, *part*, C 127, *part*, R 141, *part*, C 177, *part*.]

GEOG. DIST.— Southern Alleghanies (western North Carolina, etc.), south in winter to Florida.

629 *d*. Vireo solitarius lucasanus BREWST.
St. Lucas Solitary Vireo.

Vireo solitarius lucasanus BREWST. Auk, VIII. April, 1891, 147.

[B —, C —, R —, C —.]

GEOG. DIST.— Lower California.

SUBGENUS **VIREO** VIEILLOT.

Vireo VIEILL. Ois. Am. Sept. I. 1807, 83. Type, *V. musicus* VIEILL. = *Muscicapa noveboracensis* GMEL.

630. Vireo atricapillus WOODH.
Black-capped Vireo.

Vireo atricapillus WOODH. Pr. Ac. Nat. Sci. Phila. 1852, 60.

[B 427, C 133, R 142, C 185.]

GEOG. DIST.— Central and western Texas, from the Rio Grande north to southwestern Kansas.

631. Vireo noveboracensis (GMEL.).
White-eyed Vireo.

Muscicapa noveboracensis GMEL. S. N. I. ii. 1788, 947.
Vireo noveboracensis BONAP. Journ. Ac. Nat. Sci. Phila. IV. 1824, 176.

[B 248, C 129, R 143, C 181.]

GEOG. DIST.— Eastern United States, west to the Rocky Mountains; north to southern New England and Minnesota; south in winter, from Florida to Guatemala and Honduras. Breeds from Florida and the Gulf States northward. Resident in Bermuda.

631 a. Vireo noveboracensis maynardi BREWST.
Key West Vireo.

Vireo noveboracensis maynardi BREWST. Auk, IV. April, 1887, 148.

[B —, C —, R —, C —.]

GEOG. DIST.— Southern Florida.

632. Vireo huttoni CASS.
Hutton's Vireo.

Vireo huttoni CASS. Pr. Ac. Nat. Sci. Phila. 1851, 150, pl. 10, fig. 1.

[B 249, C 130, R 144, C 182.]

GEOG. DIST.— Southern and central California, west of the Sierra Nevada.

632 a. Vireo huttoni stephensi BREWST.
Stephens's Vireo.

Vireo huttoni stephensi BREWST. Bull. Nutt. Orn. Club, VII. July, 1882, 142.

[B —, C —, R —, C —.]

GEOG. DIST.— Arizona, western Mexico, and Lower California.

632 c. Vireo huttoni obscurus ANTHONY.
Anthony's Vireo.

Vireo huttoni obscurus ANTHONY, Zoe, I. Dec. 1890, 306.

[B—, C—, R—, C—.]

GEOG. DIST.— Pacific coast, from Oregon to southern British Columbia, south in winter to California.

633. Vireo bellii AUD.
Bell's Vireo.

Vireo bellii AUD. B. Am. VII. 1844, 333, pl. 485.

[B 246, C 131, R 145, C 183.]

GEOG. DIST.— Upper Mississippi Valley and Great Plains, from Dakota, Minnesota, Illinois, and western Indiana, southwestward to Mexico.

633 *a*. Vireo bellii pusillus (COUES).
Least Vireo.

Vireo pusillus COUES, Pr. Ac. Nat. Sci. Phila. 1866, 76.
Vireo bellii pusillus RIDGW. Pr. U. S. Nat. Mus. VIII. 1885, 354.

[B—, C 132, R 146, C 184.]

GEOG. DIST.— Arizona and California, south to Cape St. Lucas, and throughout western Mexico.

634. Vireo vicinior COUES.
Gray Vireo.

Vireo vicinior COUES, Pr. Ac. Nat. Sci. Phila. 1866, 75.

[B—, C 128, R 147, C 180.]

GEOG. DIST.— Southern border of the United States, from western Texas and New Mexico to southern and Lower California and northwestern Mexico, north to southern Nevada (Grapevine Mts., Lat. 37°) and the Grand Cañon of the Colorado in Arizona.

FAMILY **CŒREBIDÆ**. HONEY CREEPERS.

GENUS **CŒREBA** VIEILLOT.

Cœreba VIEILLOT, Ois. Am. Sept. I. 1807, 70. Type, *Certhia flaveola* LINN.

685. Cœreba bahamensis (REICH.).
   Bahama Honey Creeper.

Certhiola bahamensis REICH. Handb. I. 1853, 253.
Cæreba bahamensis A. O. U. Code and Check-List, Suppl. 1889, 23.

[B 301, C 106, R 159, C 153.]

GEOG. DIST.— Bahamas, and the Keys of the southern coast of Florida.

FAMILY **MNIOTILTIDÆ**. WOOD WARBLERS.

GENUS **MNIOTILTA** VIEILLOT.

Mniotilta VIEILL. Analyse, 1816, 45. Type, *Motacilla varia* LINN.

636. Mniotilta varia (LINN.).
   Black and White Warbler.

Motacilla varia LINN. S. N. ed. 12, I. 1766, 333.
Mniotilta varia VIEILL. Nouv. Dict. d'Hist. Nat. XXI. 1818, 230.

[B 167, C 57, R 74, 74*a*, C 91, 92.]

GEOG. DIST.— Eastern United States to the Plains, north to Fort Simpson, south, in winter, through Central America and the West Indies to Venezuela and Colombia. Breeds from Virginia and southern Kansas northward, and winters from Florida and the Gulf States southward.

GENUS **PROTONOTARIA** BAIRD.

Protonotaria BAIRD, B. N. Am. 1858, 239. Type, *Motacilla citrea* BODD.

637. Protonotaria citrea (BODD.).
   Prothonotary Warbler.

Motacilla citrea BODD. Tabl. P. E. 1783, 44.
Protonotaria citrea BAIRD, B. N. Am. 1858, 239.

[B 169, C 59, R 75, C 95.]

GEOG. DIST.— Eastern United States, west to Nebraska and Kansas, north to Virginia, southern Michigan, and Iowa, casually to New England, Ontario, and Minnesota; in winter Cuba and northern South America. Breeds throughout its United States range.

GENUS **HELINAIA** AUDUBON.

Helinaia AUD. Synop. 1839, 66. Type, *Sylvia swainsonii* AUD.

638. Helinaia swainsonii AUD.
Swainson's Warbler.

Sylvia swainsonii AUD. Orn. Biog. II. 1834, 563, pl. 198.
Helinaia swainsonii AUD. Synop. 1839, 66.

[B 179, C 61, R 76, C 97.]

GEOG. DIST.— Southeastern United States, north to southern Virginia (Dismal Swamp), southwestern Indiana, southeastern Missouri, and west to Texas; in winter, south to Vera Cruz, Mexico, and Jamaica.

GENUS **HELMITHERUS** RAFINESQUE.

Helmitherus RAFIN. Journ. de Phys. LXXXVIII. 1819, 417.
Type, *Motacilla vermivora* GMEL.

639. Helmitherus vermivorus (GMEL.).
Worm-eating Warbler.

Motacilla vermivora GMEL. S. N. I. ii. 1788, 951.
Helmitheros vermivora BONAP. Consp. Av. I. April 20, 1850, 314.

[B 178, C 60, R 77, C 96.]

GEOG. DIST.— Eastern United States, north to southern New York and southern New England, west to eastern Nebraska and Texas; south, in winter, to Cuba and northern South America. Breeds throughout its United States range.

GENUS **HELMINTHOPHILA** RIDGWAY.

Helminthophila RIDGW. Bull. Nutt. Orn. Club, VII. Jan. 1882. 53.
Type, *Sylvia ruficapilla* WILS.

640. Helminthophila bachmanii (AUD.).
   Bachman's Warbler.

   Sylvia bachmanii AUD. Orn. Biog. II. 1834, 483, pl. 183.
   Helminthophila bachmani RIDGW. Bull. Nutt. Orn. Club, VII. Jan. 1882, 53.
   [B 182, C 64, R 78, C 103.]

   GEOG. DIST.— South Atlantic States (southern Virginia to Florida), and westward to Louisiana; Cuba, in winter.

641. Helminthophila pinus (LINN.).
   Blue-winged Warbler.

   Certhia pinus LINN. S. N. ed. 12, I. 1766, 187.
   Helminthophila pinus RIDGW. Bull. Nutt. Orn. Club, VII. Jan. 1882, 53.
   [B 180, C 62, R 79, C 98.]

   GEOG. DIST.— Eastern United States, from southern New York, southern New England, and southern Minnesota southward, and west to Nebraska and Texas. In winter, south to Mexico, Guatemala and Nicaragua.

642. Helminthophila chrysoptera (LINN.).
   Golden-winged Warbler.

   Motacilla chrysoptera LINN. S. N. ed. 12, I. 1766, 333.
   Helminthophila chrysoptera RIDGW. Bull. Nutt. Orn. Club, VII. Jan. 1882, 53.
   [B 181, C 63, R 81, C 102.]

   GEOG. DIST.— Eastern United States, north to southern New England, southwestern Ontario, and southern Minnesota; breeding from northern New Jersey and northern Indiana northward, and southward along the Alleghanies to South Carolina. Central America and northern South America in winter.

643. Helminthophila luciæ (COOPER).
   Lucy's Warbler.

   Helminthophaga luciæ COOPER, Pr. Cal. Ac. Sci. July, 1862, 120.
   Helminthophila luciæ RIDGW. Bull. Nutt. Orn. Club, VII. Jan. 1882, 54.

[B—, C 65, R 83, C 104.]

GEOG. DIST.— Arizona and extreme southwestern Utah, from the Santa Clara Valley southward to Sonora, Mexico.

644. Helminthophila virginiæ (BAIRD).
Virginia's Warbler.

Helminthophaga virginiæ BAIRD, B. N. Am. ed. 1860, Atlas, p. xi. foot-note, pl. 79, fig. 1.
Helminthophila virginiæ RIDGW. Bull. Nutt. Orn. Club, VII. Jan. 1882, 54.

[B—, C 66, R 84, C 105.]

GEOG. DIST.— Rocky Mountain region of the United States, from Wyoming, Colorado, Utah, and Nevada southward on the tableland of Mexico to Guanajuato.

645. Helminthophila ruficapilla (WILS.).
Nashville Warbler.

Sylvia ruficapilla WILS. Am. Orn. III. 1811, 120, pl. 27, fig. 3.
Helminthophila ruficapilla RIDGW. Bull. Nutt. Orn. Club, VII. Jan. 1882, 54.

[B 183, *part*, C 67, *part*, R 85, *part*, C 106, *part*.]

GEOG. DIST.— Eastern North America to the Plains, north to the Fur Countries, breeding from the northern United States northward. Mexico and Guatemala in winter.

645 a. Helminthophila ruficapilla gutturalis RIDGW.
Calaveras Warbler.

Helminthophaga ruficapilla var. *gutturalis* RIDGW. in Hist. N. Am. B. I. Jan. 1874, 191.
Helminthophila ruficapilla gutturalis RIDGW. Pr. U. S. Nat. Mus. VIII. 1885, 354.

[B 183, *part*, C 67, *part*, R 85, *part*, C 106, *part*.]

GEOG. DIST.— Pacific coast of North America, eastward, during migrations, to the Rocky Mountains, northward to Kadiak, Alaska, and southward to Lower California and western Mexico.

646. Helminthophila celata (SAY).
   Orange-crowned Warbler.

Sylvia celata SAY, LONG'S Exp. I. 1823, 169.
Helminthophila celata RIDGW. Bull. Nutt. Orn. Club, VII. Jan. 1882, 54.

[B 184, *part*, C 68, R 86, C 107.]

GEOG. DIST.— Eastern North America, breeding as far northward as the Yukon and Mackenzie River districts, and southward through the Rocky Mountains, and wintering in the south Atlantic and Gulf States and Mexico. Rare east of the Alleghanies, north of Virginia.

646 a. Helminthophila celata lutescens (RIDGW.).
   Lutescent Warbler.

Helminthophaga celata var. *lutescens* RIDGW. Am. Jour. Sci. & Arts, 1872, 457.
Helminthophila celata lutescens BREWST. Bull. Nutt. Orn. Club, VII. April, 1882, 85.

[B 184, *part*, C 68*a*, R 86*a*, C 108.]

GEOG. DIST.— Western United States, from the Rocky Mountains to the Pacific.

646 b. Helminthophila celata sordida TOWNSEND.
   Dusky Warbler.

Helminthophila celata sordida TOWNSEND, Pr. U. S. Nat. Mus. XIII. 1890, 139.

[B —, C —, R —, C —.]

GEOG. DIST.— San Clemente, Santa Cruz, and Santa Rosa Islands, California.

647. Helminthophila peregrina (WILS.).
   Tennessee Warbler.

Sylvia peregrina WILS. Am. Orn. III. 1811, 83, pl. 25, fig. 2.
Helminthophila peregrina RIDGW. Bull. Nutt. Orn. Club, VII. Jan. 1882, 54.

[B 185, C 69, R 87, C 109.]

GEOG. DIST.— Eastern North America, breeding from northern New York and northern New England northward to Hudson Bay Territory; in winter south through eastern Mexico to Costa Rica and Colombia.

ORDER PASSERES.

GENUS **COMPSOTHLYPIS** CABANIS.

Compsothlypis CAB. Mus. Hein. I. 1850, 20.   Type, *Parus americanus* LINN.

648. Compsothlypis americana (LINN.).
Parula Warbler.

Parus americanus LINN. S. N. ed. 10, I. 1758, 190.
Compsothlypis americana CAB. Mus. Hein. I. 1850, 20.

[B 168, C 58, R 88, C 93.]

GEOG. DIST.— Eastern United States, west to the Plains, north to Canada, and south in winter to the West Indies, Eastern Mexico and Nicaragua. Breeds locally throughout its United States range.

649. Compsothlypis nigrilora (COUES).
Sennett's Warbler.

Parula nigrilora COUES, Bull. U. S. Geol. & Geog. Surv. Terr. IV. 1878, 11.
Compsothlypis nigrilora STEJN. Auk, I. April, 1884, 170.

[B—, C—, R 89*a*, C 94.]

GEOG. DIST.— Valley of the Lower Rio Grande in Texas, and southward in Nuevo Leon, Tamaulipas, and southeastern San Luis Potosi.

GENUS **DENDROICA** GRAY.

SUBGENUS **PERISSOGLOSSA** BAIRD.

Perissoglossa BAIRD, Rev. Am. B. I. April, 1865, 180.   Type, *Motacilla tigrina* GMEL.

650. Dendroica tigrina (GMEL.).
Cape May Warbler.

Motacilla tigrina GMEL. S. N. I. ii. 1788, 985.
Dendroica tigrina BAIRD, B. N. Am. 1858, 286.

[B 206, C 85, R 90, C 126.]

GEOG. DIST.— Eastern North America, north to Lake Winnipeg and Hudson Bay Territory, west to the Plains. Breeds from northern New England northward; winters in the West Indies.

SUBGENUS **PEUCEDRAMUS** COUES.

Peucedramus COUES, in Zool. Wheeler's Exp. 1876, 201.   Type, *Sylvia olivacea* GIRAUD.

651. **Dendroica olivacea** (GIRAUD).
Olive Warbler.

Sylvia olivacea GIRAUD, Sixteen Sp. Tex. B. 1841, 29, pl. 7, fig. 2.
Dendroica olivacea BAIRD, B. N. Am. 1858, 305.

[B—, C—, R 92, C 110.]

GEOG. DIST.— Highlands of Guatemala and Mexico, north to southern New Mexico and Mt. Graham, Arizona.

SUBGENUS **DENDROICA** GRAY.

Dendroica GRAY, List Gen. B. App. 1842, 8.   Type, *Motacilla coronata* LINN.

652. **Dendroica æstiva** (GMEL.).
Yellow Warbler.

Motacilla æstiva GMEL. S. N. I. ii. 1788, 996.
Dendroica æstiva BAIRD, B. N. Am. 1858, 282.

[B 203, C 70, R 93, C 111.]

GEOG. DIST.— North America at large, except southwestern part, south in winter to Central America and northern South America. Breeds nearly throughout its North American range.

652 *a*. **Dendroica æstiva sonorana** BREWST.
Sonora Yellow Warbler.

Dendroica æstiva sonorana BREWST. Auk, V. April, 1888, 137.

ORDER PASSERES.

[B 203, *part*, C 70, *part*, R 93, *part*, C 111, *part*.]

GEOG. DIST.— Southern Arizona to western Texas and northwestern Mexico.

653. **Dendroica bryanti castaneiceps** RIDGW.
Mangrove Warbler.

Dendroica bryanti castaneiceps RIDGW. Pr. U. S. Nat. Mus. VIII. Sept. 2, 1885, 350.

[B—, C—, R—, C —.]

GEOG. DIST.— Western Mexico, and southern part of Lower California.

654. **Dendroica cærulescens** (GMEL.).
Black-throated Blue Warbler.

Motacilla cærulescens GMEL. S. N. I. 1788, 960.
Dendroica cærulescens BAIRD, Rev. Am. B. I. April, 1865, 186.

[B 193, C 76, R 94, C 117.]

GEOG. DIST.— Eastern North America to the Plains, breeding from northern New England and northern New York northward to Labrador, and in the Alleghanies south to northern Georgia; West Indies and Guatemala in winter. Accidental on the Farallon Islands, California.

655. **Dendroica coronata** (LINN.).
Myrtle Warbler.

Motacilla coronata LINN. S. N. ed. 12, I. 1766, 333.
Dendroica coronata GRAY, List Gen. B. App. 1842, 8.

[B 194, C 78, R 95, C 119.]

GEOG. DIST.— Eastern North America, chiefly, straggling more or less commonly westward to the Pacific; breeds from the northern United States northward, and winters from southern New England and the Ohio valley southward to the West Indies, and through Mexico to Panama.

656. **Dendroica auduboni** (TOWNS.).
Audubon's Warbler.

Sylvia auduboni TOWNS. Journ. Ac. Nat. Sci. Phila. VII. 1837, 191.
Dendroica audubonii BAIRD, B. N. Am. 1858, 273.

[B 195, C 79, R 96, C 120.]

GEOG. DIST.— Western United States, east to the western border of the Plains and north to British Columbia; south in winter to Guatemala. Accidental in Pennsylvania and Massachusetts.

657. Dendroica maculosa (GMEL.).
Magnolia Warbler.

Motacilla maculosa GMEL. S. N. I. ii. 1788, 984.
Dendroica maculosa BAIRD, B. N. Am. 1858, 284.

[B 204, C 84, R 97, C 125.]

GEOG. DIST.— Eastern North America, west to the base of the Rocky Mountains, and casually to British Columbia; breeding from northern New England, northern New York, and northern Michigan, to Hudson Bay Territory and southward in the Alleghanies to Pennsylvania. In winter, Bahamas, Cuba, and south through eastern Mexico to Panama.

658. Dendroica cærulea (WILS.).
Cerulean Warbler.

Sylvia cærulea WILS. Am. Orn. II. 1810, 141, pl. 17, fig. 5.
Dendroica cærulea BAIRD, B. N. Am. 1858, 280.

[B 201, C 77, R 98, C 118.]

GEOG. DIST.— Eastern United States and southern Ontario, west to the Plains. Rare or casual east of central New York and the Alleghanies. In winter south to Cuba (rare), southeastern Mexico, Central America, Colombia, Peru, and Bolivia. Breeds from West Virginia, Tennessee, Missouri, and Kansas northward to Minnesota.

659. Dendroica pensylvanica (LINN.).
Chestnut-sided Warbler.

Motacilla pensylvanica LINN. S. N. ed. 12, I. 1766, 333.
Dendroica pennsylvanica BAIRD, B. N. Am. 1858, 279.

[B 200, C 83, R 99, C 124.]

GEOG. DIST.— Eastern United States and southern Ontario, west to Manitoba and the Plains, breeding southward to central Illinois and northern New Jersey, and in the Appalachian highlands probably to northern Georgia. Visits the Bahamas, eastern Mexico, Central America and Panama in winter.

660. Dendroica castanea (WILS.).
   Bay-breasted Warbler.

Sylvia castanea WILS. Am. Orn. II. 1810, 97, pl. 14, fig. 4.
Dendroica castanea BAIRD, B. N. Am. 1858, 276.

[B 197, C 82, R 100, C 123.]

GEOG. DIST.— Eastern North America, north to Hudson Bay. Breeds from northern New England and northern Michigan northward; in winter south through eastern Mexico (rare) and Guatemala to Colombia.

661. Dendroica striata (FORST.).
   Black-poll Warbler.

Muscicapa striata FORST. Philos. Trans. LXII. 1772, 406, 428.
Dendroica striata BAIRD, B. N. Am. 1858, 280.

[B 202, C 81, R 101, C 122.]

GEOG. DIST.— Eastern North America, west to the Rocky Mountains, north to Greenland, the Barren Grounds, and Alaska, breeding from northern New England and the Catskills northward. South in winter to northern South America, but not recorded from Mexico or Central America.

662. Dendroica blackburniæ (GMEL.).
   Blackburnian Warbler.

Motacilla blackburniæ GMEL. S. N. I. ii. 1788, 977.
Dendroica blackburniæ BAIRD, B. N. Am. 1858, 274.

[B 196, C 80, R 102, C 121.]

GEOG. DIST.— Eastern North America, west to eastern Kansas and Manitoba, breeding from the southern Alleghanies, Massachusetts, and Michigan northward to Labrador. In winter, south to the Bahamas, eastern Mexico, Central America, Colombia, Ecuador, and Peru.

663. Dendroica dominica (LINN.).
   Yellow-throated Warbler.

Motacilla dominica LINN. S. N. ed. 12, I. 1766, 334.
Dendroica dominica BAIRD, Rev. Am. B. I. April, 1865, 209.

[B 209, *part*, C 88, R 103, C 129.]

GEOG. DIST.— Southeastern United States, north to southern Maryland and Virginia, and casually to southern New England; south to the West Indies.

663 *a*. Dendroica dominica albilora RIDGW.
Sycamore Warbler.

Dendroica dominica var. *albilora* BAIRD MSS. RIDGW. Am. Nat. VII. Oct. 1873, 606.

[B 209, *part*, C 88*a*, R 103*a*, C 130.]

GEOG. DIST.— Mississippi Valley, west to the Plains, north to Lake Erie and southern Michigan, and east to western North Carolina; in winter south to southern Mexico, Honduras, Guatemala and Nicaragua.

664. Dendroica graciæ BAIRD.
Grace's Warbler.

Dendroica graciæ "COUES MSS." BAIRD, Rev. Am. B. I. April, 1865, 210.

[B —, C 87, R 104, C 128.]

GEOG. DIST.— Southern New Mexico and Arizona, and southward into Sonora.

665. Dendroica nigrescens (TOWNS.).
Black-throated Gray Warbler.

Sylvia nigrescens TOWNS. Journ. Ac. Nat. Sci. Phila. VII. 1837, 191.
Dendroica nigrescens BAIRD, B. N. Am. 1858, 270.

[B 192, C 75, R 105, C 116.]

GEOG. DIST.— Western United States, north to Colorado, Oregon, and British Columbia west of the Cascades, migrating to southern Mexico in winter.

666. Dendroica chrysoparia SCL. & SALV.
Golden-cheeked Warbler.

Dendræca chrysoparia SCL. & SALV. P. Z. S. 1860, 298.

[B—, C 74, R 106, C 115.]

GEOG. DIST.— Southern Texas, and southward to Guatemala.

667. Dendroica virens (GMEL.).
Black-throated Green Warbler.

Motacilla virens GMEL. S. N. I. ii. 1788, 985.
Dendroica virens BAIRD, B. N. Am. 1858, 267.

[B 189, C 71, R 107, C 112.]

GEOG. DIST.— Eastern North America to the Plains, north to Hudson Bay Territory, breeding from Connecticut and northern Illinois northward, and south along the Alleghanies to South Carolina. In winter, south to Cuba and Panama. Accidental in Greenland and Europe.

668. Dendroica townsendi (TOWNS.).
Townsend's Warbler.

Sylvia townsendi "NUTT." TOWNS. Journ. Ac. Nat. Sci. Phila. VII. 1837, 191.
Dendroica townsendi BAIRD, B. N. Am. 1858, 269.

[B 191, C 73, R 108, C 114.]

GEOG. DIST.— Western North America, east to central Colorado, north to Sitka, south in winter to Mexico and Guatemala. Accidental near Philadelphia. Breeds from the southern border of the United States northward.

669. Dendroica occidentalis (TOWNS.).
Hermit Warbler.

Sylvia occidentalis TOWNS. Journ. Ac. Nat. Sci. Phila. VII. 1837, 190.
Dendroica occidentalis BAIRD, B. N. Am. 1858, 268.

[B 190, C 72, R 109, C 113.]

GEOG. DIST.— Western United States, from the Rocky Mountains to the Pacific coast, and from Washington southward; in winter, Lower California and Mexico to the highlands of Guatemala.

670. Dendroica kirtlandi BAIRD.
Kirtland's Warbler.

Sylvicola kirtlandi BAIRD, Ann. Lyc. N. Y. V. 1852, 216, pl. 6.
Dendroica kirtlandii BAIRD, B. N. Am. 1858, 286.

[B 205, C 89, R 110, C 131.]

GEOG. DIST.— Eastern United States (South Carolina, Virginia, Ohio, Indiana, Illinois, Missouri, Michigan, Wisconsin, Minnesota), and the Bahamas in winter.

671. Dendroica vigorsii (AUD.).
Pine Warbler.

Sylvia vigorsii AUD. Orn. Biog. I. 1832, 153, pl. 30.
Dendroica vigorsii STEJN. Auk, II. Oct. 1885, 343.

[B 198, C 91, R 111, C 134.]

GEOG. DIST.— Eastern United States, west to the Plains, north to Manitoba, Ontario, and New Brunswick, wintering in the South Atlantic and Gulf States, and the Bahamas.

672. Dendroica palmarum (GMEL.).
Palm Warbler.

Motacilla palmarum GMEL. S. N. I. ii. 1788, 951.
Dendroica palmarum BAIRD, B. N. Am. 1858, 288.

[B 208, *part*, C 90, *part*, R 113, C 132.]

GEOG. DIST.— Northern interior to Great Slave Lake; in winter South Atlantic and Gulf States, the West Indies and Mexico. Of rare but regular occurrence in the Atlantic States in migrations.

672 a. Dendroica palmarum hypochrysea RIDGW.
Yellow Palm Warbler.

Dendrœca palmarum hypochrysea RIDGW. Bull. Nutt. Orn. Club, I. Nov. 1876, 85.

[B 208, *part*, C 90, *part*, R 113a, C 133.]

GEOG. DIST.— Atlantic States, north to Hudson Bay. Breeds from eastern Maine, New Brunswick, and Nova Scotia northward; winters in the South Atlantic and Gulf States.

673. Dendroica discolor (VIEILL.).
Prairie Warbler.

Sylvia discolor VIEILL. Ois. Am. Sept. I. 1807, 37, pl. 98.
Dendroica discolor BAIRD, B. N. Am. 1858, 290.

[B 210, C 86, R 114, C 127.]

GEOG. DIST.— Eastern United States to the Plains, breeding from Florida north to Michigan and southern New England. Winters in southern Florida and the West Indies.

GENUS **SEIURUS** SWAINSON.

Seiurus SWAINS. Phil. Mag. I. May, 1827, 369. Type, *Motacilla aurocapilla* LINN.

674. Seiurus aurocapillus (LINN.).
Oven-bird.

Motacilla aurocapilla LINN. S. N. ed. 12, I. 1766, 334.
Seiurus aurocapillus SWAINS. Zool. Journ. III. 1827, 171.

[B 186, C 92, R 115, C 135.]

GEOG. DIST.— Eastern North America, north to Hudson Bay Territory and Alaska, breeding from Kansas, the Ohio Valley, and Virginia northward. In winter, Florida, the West Indies, southern Mexico, and Central America to Panama.

675. Seiurus noveboracensis (GMEL.).
Water-Thrush.

Motacilla noveboracensis GMEL. S. N. I. ii. 1788, 958.
Seiurus noveboracensis BONAP. Geog. & Comp. List, 1838, 21.

[B 187, *part*, C 93, *part*, R 116, C 136.]

GEOG. DIST.— Eastern United States to Illinois, and northward to Arctic America, breeding from the northern United States northward. South in winter to the West Indies, Central America, and northern South America.

675 a. Seiurus noveboracensis notabilis (RIDGW.).
Grinnell's Water-Thrush.

Seiurus nævius notabilis "GRINNELL," RIDGW. Pr. U. S. Nat. Mus. III. 1880, 12.
Seiurus noveboracensis notabilis RIDGW. Pr. U. S. Nat. Mus. VIII. 1885, 354.

[B 187, *part*, C 93, *part*, R 116a, C 137.]

GEOG. DIST.— Western United States, from Indiana and Illinois westward to California, and north into British America. Casual in migrations eastward to the Atlantic coast. Winters from the southern border of the United States southward to Lower California, Mexico, and northern South America.

676. Seiurus motacilla (VIEILL.).
Louisiana Water-Thrush.

Turdus motacilla VIEILL. Ois. Am. Sept. II. 1807, 9, pl. 65.
Seiurus motacilla BONAP. Consp. Av. I. 1850, 306.

[B 188, C 94, R 117, C 138.]

GEOG. DIST.— Eastern United States, north to southern New England and southern Michigan, casually north to Lake George, northeastern New York, west to the Plains. In winter, West Indies, southern Mexico, and Central America to Panama.

GENUS **GEOTHLYPIS** CABANIS.

SUBGENUS **OPORORNIS** BAIRD.

Oporornis BAIRD, B. N. Am. 1858, 246. Type, *Sylvia agilis* WILS.

677. Geothlypis formosa (WILS.).
Kentucky Warbler.

Sylvia formosa WILS. Am. Orn. III. 1811, 85, pl. 25, fig. 3.
Geothlypis formosa RIDGW. Pr. U. S. Nat. Mus. VIII. 1885, 354.

[B 175, C 96, R 119, C 140.]

GEOG. DIST.— Eastern United States, west to the Plains, breeding from the Gulf States north to southern New England and southern Michigan. In winter, West Indies, eastern Mexico, and Central America to Panama.

678. Geothlypis agilis (WILS.).
Connecticut Warbler.

Sylvia agilis WILS. Am. Orn. V. 1812, 64, pl. 39, fig. 4.
Geothlypis agilis GREGG, Pr. Elmira Acad. 1870,—(p. 7 of reprint).

[B 174, C 95, R 118, C 139.]

GEOG. DIST.— Eastern North America, breeding north of the United States (Manitoba, Ontario). Northern South America in winter.

SUBGENUS **GEOTHLYPIS** CABANIS.

Geothlypis CAB. Wiegm. Archiv, 1847, i. 316, 349. Type, *Turdus trichas* LINN.

679. Geothlypis philadelphia (WILS.).
Mourning Warbler.

Sylvia philadelphia WILS. Am. Orn. II. 1810, 101, pl. 14, fig. 6.
Geothlypis philadelphia BAIRD, B. N. Am. 1858, 243.

[B 172, C 98, R 120, C 142.]

GEOG. DIST.— Eastern North America to the Plains, breeding from the mountainous portions of Pennsylvania, New England, New York, and northern Michigan northward. Central America and northern South America in winter. Accidental in Greenland.

680. Geothlypis macgillivrayi (AUD.).
Macgillivray's Warbler.

Sylvia macgillivrayi AUD. Orn. Biog. V. 1839, 75, pl. 399, figs, 4, 5.
Geothlypis macgillivrayi BAIRD, B. N. Am. 1858, 244.

[B 173, C 99, R 121, C 143.]

GEOG. DIST.— Western United States, from the eastern foothills of the Rocky Mountains to the Pacific coast, north into British Columbia. Lower California, Mexico, and Central America to Colombia in winter.

681. Geothlypis trichas (LINN.).
Maryland Yellow-throat.

Turdus trichas LINN. S. N. ed. 12, I. 1766, 293.
Geothlypis trichas CAB. Mus. Hein. I. 1850, 16.

[B 170, *part*, C 97, *part*, R 122, *part*, C 141, *part*.]

GEOG. DIST.— Eastern United States, north to Ontario, Nova Scotia, and southern Labrador, breeding from Georgia northward. In winter, South Atlantic and Gulf States, the West Indies, eastern Mexico, and Central America; casually northward to Massachusetts.

681 a. Geothlypis trichas occidentalis BREWST.
Western Yellow-throat.

Geothlypis trichas occidentalis BREWST. Bull. Nutt. Orn. Club, VIII. July, 1883, 159.

[B 170, *part,* C 97, *part,* R 122, *part,* C 141, *part.*]

GEOG. DIST.— Western United States, from the Mississippi Valley west to the Pacific coast, and north to British Columbia; south, in winter, to Central America.

681 b. Geothlypis trichas ignota CHAPM.
Florida Yellow-throat.

Geothlypis trichas ignota CHAPM. Auk, VII. Jan. 1890, 11.

[B 170, *part,* C 97, *part,* R 122, *part,* C 141, *part.*]

GEOG. DIST.— Florida, north to southern Georgia.

682. Geothlypis beldingi RIDGW.
Belding's Yellow-throat.

Geothlypis beldingi RIDGW. Pr. U. S. Nat. Mus. V. 1882, 344.

[B —, C —, R —, C —.]

GEOG. DIST.— Southern portion of Lower California, north to San Ignacio (Lat. 27°).

682.1. Geothlypis poliocephala ralphi RIDGW.
Rio Grande Yellow-throat.

Geothlypis poliocephala ralphi RIDGW. Proc. U. S. Nat. Mus. 1893, 692.

[B —, C —, R —, C —.]

GEOG. DIST.— Lower Rio Grande Valley.

GENUS ICTERIA VIEILLOT.

Icteria VIEILL. Ois. Am. Sept. I. 1807, pp. iii. 85. Type, *Muscicapa viridis* GMEL. = *Turdus virens* LINN.

683. Icteria virens (LINN.).
   Yellow-breasted Chat.

Turdus virens LINN. S. N. ed. 10, I. 1758, 171.
Icteria virens BAIRD, Rev. Am. B. I. April, 1865, 228.

[B 176, C 100, R 123, C 144.]

GEOG. DIST.— Eastern United States to the Plains, breeding north to Ontario and southern New England; south, in winter, to eastern Mexico, Guatemala, Nicaragua, and Costa Rica.

683 a. Icteria virens longicauda (LAWR.).
   Long-tailed Chat.

Icteria longicauda LAWR. Ann. Lyc. N. Y. VI. 1853, 4.
Icteria virens var. *longicauda* COUES, Key, 1872, 108.

[B 177, C 100a, R 123a, C 145.]

GEOG. DIST.— Western United States, from the Plains to the Pacific, north to southern Montana, Washington, and the dry interior of British Columbia, south into Lower California and Mexico.

GENUS **SYLVANIA** NUTTALL.

Sylvania NUTT. Man. Land Birds, I. 1832, 290. Type, by elimination, *Muscicapa selbii* AUD. = *Motacilla mitrata* GMEL.

684. Sylvania mitrata (GMEL.).
   Hooded Warbler.

Motacilla mitrata GMEL. S. N. I. ii. 1788, 977.
Sylvania mitrata NUTT. Man. Land B. ed. 1840, 333.

[B 211, C 101, R 124, C 146.]

GEOG. DIST.— Eastern United States, west to the Plains, north and east to southern Michigan, southern Ontario, western and southeastern New York, and southern New England. Breeds from the Gulf of Mexico northward. In winter, West Indies, eastern Mexico, and Central America to Panama.

685. Sylvania pusilla (WILS.).
   Wilson's Warbler.

Muscicapa pusilla WILS. Am. Orn. III. 1811, 103, pl. 26, fig. 4.
Sylvania pusilla NUTT. Man. Land B. ed. 1840, 335.

[B 213, *part*, C 102, R 125, C 147.]

GEOG. DIST.— Eastern North America, west to and including the Rocky Mountains, north to Labrador, Hudson Bay Territory, and Alaska. Breeds chiefly north of the United States, migrating south to eastern Mexico and Central America.

685 a. Sylvania pusilla pileolata (PALL.).
Pileolated Warbler.

Motacilla pileolata PALL. Zoog. Rosso-As. I. 1826, 497.
Sylvania pusilla pileolata RIDGW. Pr. U. S. Nat. Mus. VIII. 1885, 354.

[B 213, *part*, C 102*a*, R 125*a*, C 148.]

GEOG. DIST.— Western North America, from the Great Basin to the Pacific, north to Alaska (Kadiak), and south, in winter, to Costa Rica.

686. Sylvania canadensis (LINN.).
Canadian Warbler.

Muscicapa canadensis LINN. S. N. ed. 12, I. 1766, 327.
Sylvania canadensis RIDGW. Pr. U. S. Nat. Mus. VIII. 1885, 354.

[B 214, 215, C 103, R 127, C 149.]

GEOG. DIST.— Eastern North America, west to the Plains, and north to Newfoundland, southern Labrador, and Lake Winnipeg, south, in winter, to Central America and northern South America. Breeds from the higher parts of the Alleghanies, and the more elevated parts of southern New York and southern New England, northward.

GENUS **SETOPHAGA** SWAINSON.

Setophaga SWAINS. Phil. Mag. I. May, 1827, 368. Type, *Motacilla ruticilla* LINN.

687. Setophaga ruticilla (LINN.).
American Redstart.

Motacilla ruticilla LINN. S. N. ed. 10, I. 1758, 186.
Setophaga ruticilla SWAINS. Phil. Mag. I. May, 1827, 368.

[B 217, C 104, R 128, C 152.]

GEOG. DIST.— North America, north to Fort Simpson, west regularly to the Great Basin, casually to California and Lower California, breeding from the middle portion of the United States northward. In winter, the West Indies, southern Mexico, Central America and northern South America.

688. **Setophaga picta** SWAINS.
Painted Redstart.

Setophaga picta SWAINS. Zool. Illustr. 2d ser. I. 1829, pl. 3.

[B 218, C 105, R 129, C 151.]

GEOG. DIST.— Mountains of Mexico, north to southern Arizona.

[689.] **Setophaga miniata** SWAINS.
Red-bellied Redstart.

Setophaga miniata SWAINS. Phil. Mag. I. 1827, 368.

[B 219, C —, R 130, C —.]

GEOG. DIST.— Highlands of Mexico. Texas (GIRAUD).

GENUS **CARDELLINA** DU BUS.

Cardellina DU BUS, Esq. Orn. 1850, pl. 25. Type, *C. amicta* DU BUS = *Muscicapa rubrifrons* GIRAUD.

690. **Cardellina rubrifrons** (GIRAUD).
Red-faced Warbler.

Muscicapa rubrifrons GIRAUD, Sixteen Sp. Texas B. 1841, pl. 7, fig. 1.
Cardellina rubrifrons SCL. P. Z. S. 1855, 66.

[B —, C —, R 131, C 150.]

GEOG. DIST.— Southern Arizona and southwestern New Mexico, through Mexico, to Guatemala. Texas (GIRAUD).

GENUS **ERGATICUS** BAIRD.

Ergaticus BAIRD, Rev. Am. B. I. April, 1865, 237. Type, *Setophaga rubra* SWAINS.

[691.] **Ergaticus ruber** (SWAINS.).
Red Warbler.

Setophaga rubra SWAINS. Phil. Mag. I. 1827, 368.
Ergaticus ruber SCL. & SALV. Nom. Neotr. 1873, 11.

[B 216, C —, R 132, C —.]

GEOG. DIST.— Highlands of Mexico. Texas (GIRAUD).

GENUS **BASILEUTERUS** CABANIS.

Basileuterus CAB. in SCHOMB. Guiana, III. 1848, 666. Type, *Sylvia vermivora* VIEILL. = *Setophaga auricapilla* SWAINS.

[692.] **Basileuterus culicivorus** (LICHT.).
Brasher's Warbler.

Sylvia culicivora (LICHT.) Preis-Verzeich. 1830, no. 78.
Basileuterus culicivorus BONAP. Consp. Av. I. 1850, 313.

[B —, C —, R 133, C —.]

GEOG. DIST.— Central America, from Panama north to eastern Mexico. Texas (GIRAUD.)

[693.] **Basileuterus belli** (GIRAUD).
Bell's Warbler.

Muscicapa belli GIRAUD, Sixteen Sp. Texas B. 1841, pl. 4, fig. 1.
Basileuterus belli SCL. P. Z. S. 1855, 65.

[B —, C —, R 134, C —.]

GEOG. DIST.— Guatemala and Mexico, north to the temperate regions of Vera Cruz. Texas (GIRAUD).

FAMILY **MOTACILLIDÆ**. WAGTAILS.

GENUS **MOTACILLA** LINNÆUS.

Motacilla LINN. S. N. ed. 10, I. 1758, 184. Type, by elimination, *M. alba* LINN.

ORDER PASSERES.

[694.] Motacilla alba LINN.
    White Wagtail.

Motacilla alba LINN. S. N. ed. 10, I. 1758, 185.

[B—, C—, R 69, C 86.]

GEOG. DIST.— Northern Europe and northern Asia, south, in winter, to North Africa and India. Accidental in Greenland.

[695.] Motacilla ocularis SWINH.
    Swinhoe's Wagtail.

Motacilla ocularis SWINH. Ibis, Jan. 1860, 55.

[B—, C—, R—, C—.]

GEOG. DIST.— Eastern Asia. Accidental in Lower California. Aleutian Islands?

GENUS **BUDYTES** CUVIER.

Budytes CUV. Règne An. I. 1817, 371. Type, *Motacilla flava* LINN.

696. Budytes flavus leucostriatus (HOM.).
    Siberian Yellow Wagtail.

Budytes leucostriatus HOMEYER, J. f. O. 1878, 128.
Budytes flavus leucostriatus STEJN. Orn. Expl. Kamtsch. 1885, 280.

[B—, C 54, R 70, C 87.]

GEOG. DIST.— Alaska and northern Siberia to China, wintering in the Moluccas.

GENUS **ANTHUS** BECHSTEIN.

SUBGENUS **ANTHUS**.

Anthus BECHST. Gem. Naturg. Deutschl. III. 1807, 704. Type, by elimination, *A. aquaticus* = *Alauda spinoletta* LINN.

697. Anthus pensilvanicus (LATH.).
    American Pipit.

Alauda pensilvanica LATH. Synop. Suppl. I. 1787, 287.
Anthus pensilvanicus THIENEM. Rhea, II. 1849, 171.

[B 165, C 55, R 71, C 89.]

GEOG. DIST.— North America at large, breeding in the higher parts of the Rocky Mountains and subarctic districts, and wintering in the Gulf States, Mexico, and Central America. Accidental in Europe.

[698.] **Anthus pratensis** (LINN.).
Meadow Pipit.

Alauda pratensis LINN. S. N. ed. 10, I. 1758, 166.
Anthus pratensis BECHST. Gem. Naturg. Deutschl. III. 1807, 732.

[B —, C 55 *bis*, R 72, C 88.]

GEOG. DIST.— Europe, straggling to Greenland (and Alaska?).

[699.] **Anthus cervinus** (PALLAS).
Red-throated Pipit.

Motacilla cervina PALLAS, Zoog. Rosso-As. I. 1826, 511.
Anthus cervinus KEYS. & BLAS. Wirb. Eur. I. 1840, p. xlviii.

[B —, C —, R —, C —.]

GEOG. DIST.— Northern parts of the Old World. Accidental in Lower California. St. Michael and Aleutian Islands, Alaska?

SUBGENUS **NEOCORYS** SCLATER.

Neocorys SCL. P. Z. S. 1857, 5. Type, *Alauda spragueii* AUD.

700. **Anthus spragueii** (AUD.).
Sprague's Pipit.

Alauda spragueii AUD. B. Am. VII. 1843, 335, pl. 486.
Anthus spraguei BAIRD, Rev. Am. B. I. Oct. 1864, 155.

[B 166, C 56, R 73, C 90.]

GEOG. DIST.— Interior plains of North America, breeding from the plains of the Yellowstone northward to the Saskatchewan district, and from the Red River westward (probably to the Rocky Mountains). South in winter on the tablelands of Mexico to Puebla. Accidental in South Carolina.

FAMILY **CINCLIDÆ**. DIPPERS.

GENUS **CINCLUS** BECHSTEIN.

Cinclus BECHST. Orn. Taschenb. Deutschl. 1802, 205. Type, *Sturnus cinclus* LINN.

701. Cinclus mexicanus SWAINS.
American Dipper.

Cinclus mexicanus SWAINS. Phil. Mag. I. 1827, 368.

[B 164, C 19, R 19, C 30.]

GEOG. DIST.— The mountainous parts of central and western North America, from the Yukon Valley and Unalaska to Guatemala; east, in the United States, to the eastern base of the Rocky Mountains. Apparently resident throughout its range.

FAMILY **TROGLODYTIDÆ**. WRENS, THRASHERS, ETC.

SUBFAMILY **MIMINÆ**. THRASHERS.

GENUS **OROSCOPTES** BAIRD.

Oroscoptes BAIRD, B. N. Am. 1858, 346. Type, *Orpheus montanus* TOWNS.

702. Oroscoptes montanus (TOWNS.).
Sage Thrasher.

Orpheus montanus TOWNS. Journ. Ac. Nat. Sci. Phila. VII. 1837, 193.

Oroscoptes montanus BAIRD, B. N. Am. 1858, 347.

[B 255, C 7, R 10, C 14.]

GEOG. DIST.— Western United States, from the western part of the Plains (western South Dakota, western Nebraska, and eastern Colorado), north to Montana, west to the Cascades and Sierra Nevada, south into northern Mexico, Lower California, and casually to Guadalupe Island.

GENUS **MIMUS** BOIE.

Mimus BOIE, Isis, Oct. 1826, 972. Type, *Turdus polyglottos* LINN.

703. **Mimus polyglottos** (LINN.).
Mockingbird.

Turdus polyglottos LINN. S. N. ed. 10, I. 1758, 169.
Mimus polyglottus BONAP. Geog. & Comp. List, 1838, 17.

[B 253, 253*a*, C 8, R 11, C 15.]

GEOG. DIST.— United States, south into Mexico. Rare and of irregular distribution from Maryland northward to Massachusetts, and north of southern Ohio, Colorado, and southern California. Bahamas. Casual on Guadalupe Island, Lower California.

GENUS **GALEOSCOPTES** CABANIS.

Galeoscoptes CAB. Mus. Hein. I. 1850, 82. Type, *Muscicapa carolinensis* LINN.

704. **Galeoscoptes carolinensis** (LINN.).
Catbird.

Muscicapa carolinensis LINN. S. N. ed. 12, I. 1766, 328.
Galeoscoptes carolinensis CAB. Mus. Hein. I. 1850, 82.

[B 254, C 9, R 12, C 16.]

GEOG. DIST. — Eastern United States and British Provinces, west to and including the Rocky Mountains; occasional on the Pacific coast, from British Columbia south to central California. Breeds from the Gulf States northward to the Saskatchewan. Winters in the Southern States, Cuba, and Middle America to Panama. Bermuda, resident. Accidental in Europe.

GENUS **HARPORHYNCHUS** CABANIS.

SUBGENUS **METHRIOPTERUS** REICHENBACH.

Methriopterus REICH. Syst. Nat. 1850, pl. iv. Type, *Turdus rufus* LINN.

705. **Harporhynchus rufus** (LINN.).
   Brown Thrasher.

Turdus rufus LINN. S. N. ed. 10, I. 1758, 169.
Harporhynchus rufus CAB. Mus. Hein. I. 1850, 82.

[B 261, 261a, C 10, R 13, C 17.]

GEOG. DIST.— Eastern United States, west to the Rocky Mountains, north to southern Maine, Ontario, and Manitoba. Breeds from the Gulf States, including eastern Texas, northward. Accidental in Europe.

706. **Harporhynchus longirostris sennetti** (RIDGW.).
   Sennett's Thrasher.

Harporhynchus longirostris sennetti RIDGW. Proc. U. S. Nat. Mus. X. Aug. 6, 1888, 506.

[B 260, C 10a, R 13a, C 18.]

GEOG. DIST.— Southeastern Texas, from Corpus Christi and Laredo southward to central Nuevo Leon and Tamaulipas.

707. **Harporhynchus curvirostris** (SWAINS.).
   Curve-billed Thrasher.

Orpheus curvirostris SWAINS. Phil. Mag. I. 1827, 369.
Harporhynchus curvirostris CAB. Mus. Hein. I. 1850, 81.

[B 259, 259a, C —, R 15, C 19.]

GEOG. DIST.— Tablelands of Mexico, from Oaxaca and Puebla northward to southern New Mexico and southeastward in Texas to the mouth of the Rio Grande.

707 a. **Harporhynchus curvirostris palmeri** COUES.
   Palmer's Thrasher.

Harporhynchus curvirostris var. *palmeri* "RIDGW." COUES, Key, 1872, 351.

[B —, C 11, R 15a, C 20.]

GEOG. DIST.— Southern Arizona, from about fifty miles northwest of Phœnix south to Guaymas, Sonora.

708. **Harporhynchus bendirei** COUES.
   Bendire's Thrasher.

Harporhynchus bendirei COUES, Am. Nat. VII. 1873, 330.

[B —, C 11 *bis*, R 14*a*, C 21.]

GEOG. DIST.— Arizona, from Phœnix and the Painted Desert south to Guaymas, Sonora. Westward casually to Agua Caliente, California. Accidental (?) at Colorado Springs, Colorado.

709. Harporhynchus cinereus XANTUS.
St. Lucas Thrasher.

Harporhynchus cinereus XANTUS, Pr. Ac. Nat. Sci. Phila. 1859, 298.

[B —, C 12, R 14, C 22.]

GEOG. DIST.— Lower California, from Cape St. Lucas north to San Quintin (Lat. 30° 30').

709 *a*. Harporhynchus cinereus mearnsi ANTHONY.
Mearns's Thrasher.

Harporhynchus cinereus mearnsi ANTHONY, Auk, XII. Jan. 1895, 53.

[B —, C —, R —, C —.]

GEOG. DIST.— Northern Lower California.

SUBGENUS **HARPORHYNCHUS** CABANIS.

Harporhynchus CAB. Wiegm. Archiv, 1848, i. 98. Type, *Harpes rediviva* GAMB.

710. Harporhynchus redivivus (GAMB.).
Californian Thrasher.

Harpes rediviva GAMB. Pr. Ac. Nat. Sci. Phila. 1845, 264.
Harporhynchus redivivus CAB. Wiegm. Archiv, 1848, i. 98.

[B 256, C 13, R 16, C 23.]

GEOG. DIST.— Coast region of California, from the heads of the Sacramento and Russian River valleys south to El Rosario, Lower California (Lat. 30°).

711. Harporhynchus lecontei (LAWR.).
Leconte's Thrasher.

Toxostoma lecontei LAWR. Ann. Lyc. N. Y. V. 1852, 121.
Harporhynchus lecontii BONAP. Notes Coll. Delattre, 1854, 39.

[B 257, C 13a, R 16a, C 24.]

GEOG. DIST.— Desert region of southern California, Nevada, and extreme southwestern Utah, from Benton, Cal. (Lat. 38°), southeastward through Arizona to Sonora (Lat. 30°). Local in the southern San Joaquin Valley.

712. Harporhynchus crissalis (HENRY).
Crissal Thrasher.

Toxostoma crissalis HENRY, Pr. Ac. Nat. Sci. Phila. 1858, 117.
Harporhynchus crissalis BAIRD, B. N. Am. 1858, 350.

[B 258, C 14, R 17, C 25.]

GEOG. DIST.— Southwestern United States, from western Texas to the Colorado Desert, California, and northern Lower California; north to the Charleston Mountains, Nevada, and St. George, Utah.

SUBFAMILY **TROGLODYTINÆ**. WRENS.

GENUS **HELEODYTES** CABANIS.

Heleodytes CABANIS, Mus. Hein. I. 1850, 80. Type, *Furnarius griseus* SWAIN.

713. Heleodytes brunneicapillus (LAFR.).
Cactus Wren.

Picolaptes brunneicapillus LAFR. Mag. de Zool. 1835, 61, pl. 47.
Heleodytes brunneicapillus FISHER, N. Am. Fauna, No. 7, May 31, 1893, 130.

[B 262, C 43, R 56, C 63.]

GEOG. DIST.— Southern border of the United States, from the Lower Rio Grande in Texas to southern California, north to southwestern Utah, and south to central Mexico.

713 a. Heleodytes brunneicapillus bryanti ANTHONY.
Bryant's Cactus Wren.

Heleodytes brunneicapillus bryanti ANTHONY, Auk, XI. July, 1894, 212.

[B 262, *part*, C 43, *part*, R 56, *part*, C 63, *part*.]

GEOG. DIST.— Northern Lower California, north into southern California.

713 b. **Heleodytes brunneicapillus affinis** (XANTUS).
    St. Lucas Cactus Wren.

Campylorhynchus affinis XANTUS, Pr. Ac. Nat. Sci. Phila. 1859, 298.
Heleodytes brunneicapillus affinis ANTHONY, Auk, XII. July, 1895, 280.

[B —, C 44, R 57, C 64.]

GEOG. DIST.— Southern Lower California.

GENUS **SALPINCTES** CABANIS.

Salpinctes CAB. Wiegm. Archiv, 1847, i. 323. Type, *Troglodytes obsoletus* SAY.

715. **Salpinctes obsoletus** (SAY).
    Rock Wren.

Troglodytes obsoletus SAY, LONG'S Exp. II. 1823, 4.
Salpinctes obsoletus CAB. Wiegm. Archiv, 1847, i. 323.

[B 264, C 45, R 58, C 65.]

GEOG. DIST.— Western United States, from the western border of the Plains to the Pacific, north to Dakota, Montana, and British Columbia; south on the tablelands of Mexico and Guatemala to Salvador. Breeds throughout its range, and is resident from about the southern border of the United States southward.

716. **Salpinctes guadeloupensis** RIDGW.
    Guadalupe Rock Wren.

Salpinctes obsoletus guadeloupensis RIDGW. Bull. U. S. Geol. & Geog. Serv. Terr. II. No. 2, April, 1876, 185.
Salpinctes guadalupensis RIDGW. Bull. Nutt. Orn. Club, II. July, 1877, 60.

[B —, C—, R 58*a*, C —.]

GEOG. DIST.— Guadalupe Island, Lower California.

GENUS **CATHERPES** BAIRD.

Catherpes BAIRD, B. N. Am. 1858, 356. Type, *Thryothorus mexicanus* SWAINS.

[717.] **Catherpes mexicanus** (SWAINS.).
Whlte-throated Wren.

Thryothorus mexicanus SWAINS. Zool. Ill. 2d ser. I. 1829, pl. 11.
Catherpes mexicanus BAIRD, B. N. Am. 1858, 356.

[B 263, C —, R 59, C 66.]

GEOG. DIST.— Mexico, from Oaxaca and Orizaba northward on the tablelands. Texas (GIRAUD).

717 *a*. **Catherpes mexicanus conspersus** RIDGW.
Cañon Wren.

Catherpes mexicanus var. *conspersus* RIDGW. Am. Nat. VII. Oct. 1873, 602.

[B 263,*part*, C 46, R 59*a*, C 67.]

GEOG. DIST.— Great Basin and Rocky Mountain region, from the Sierra Nevada and Cascades eastward to southern Idaho, Wyoming, Colorado, and western Texas; south on the tablelands of Mexico to Aguas Calientes. Breeds nearly throughout its range; resident in the southern parts of its United States distribution.

717 *b*. **Catherpes mexicanus punctulatus** RIDGW.
Dotted Cañon Wren.

Catherpes mexicanus punctulatus RIDGW. Proc. U. S. Nat. Mus. V. Sept. 5, 1882, 343.

[B 263, *part*, C 46, *part*, R 59, *part*, C 67, *part*.]

GEOG. DIST.— Oregon and California, west of the Cascades and Sierra Nevada, and Lower California. Resident from central California southward.

GENUS **THRYOTHORUS** VIEILLOT.

SUBGENUS **THRYOTHORUS**.

Thryothorus VIEILL. Analyse, 1816, 45. Type, *Troglodytes arundinaceus* VIEILL. = *Sylvia ludoviciana* LATH.

718. Thryothorus ludovicianus (LATH.).
Carolina Wren.

Sylvia ludoviciana LATH. Ind. Orn. II. 1790, 548.
Thryothorus ludovicianus BONAP. Geog. & Comp. List, 1838, 11.

[B 265, C 47, R 60, C 68.]

GEOG. DIST.— Eastern United States, north to southern New York, southern Michigan, and southern Nebraska; west to the Plains. Rare or casual in southern New England and southern Ontario. Resident nearly throughout its range.

718 a. Thryothorus ludovicianus miamensis RIDGW.
Florida Wren.

Thryothorus ludovicianus var. *miamensis* RIDGW. Am. Nat. IX. Aug. 1875, 469.

[B 265, *part*, C 47, *part*, R 60b, C 69.]

GEOG. DIST.— Southern Florida.

718 b. Thryothorus ludovicianus lomitensis SENN.
Lomita Wren.

Thryothorus ludovicianus lomitensis SENN. Auk, VII. Jan. 1890, 58.

[B 265, *part*, C 47, *part*, R 60, *part*, C 68, *part*.]

GEOG. DIST.— Southeastern Texas.

SUBGENUS **THRYOMANES** SCLATER.

Thryomanes SCL. Cat. Am. B. 1861, 22. Type, *Troglodytes bewickii* AUD.

719. Thryothorus bewickii (AUD.).
Bewick's Wren.

Troglodytes bewickii AUD. Orn. Biog. I. 1831, 96, pl. 18.
Thryothorus bewickii BONAP. Geog. & Comp. List, 1838, 11.

[B 267, C 48, R 61, C 71.]

GEOG. DIST.— Eastern United States, west to the eastern border of the Plains and eastern Texas; rare east of the Alleghanies north of Maryland and Delaware; north irregularly in the Mississippi Valley to southern Minnesota. Migratory only along the northern border of its range.

719 a. Thryothorus bewickii spilurus (VIG.).
Vigors's Wren.

Troglodytes spilurus VIG. Zool. Voy. Bloss. 1839, 18, pl. 4, fig. 1.
Thryothorus bewickii var. *spilurus* BAIRD, Rev. Am. B. I. 1864, 126.

[B —, C 48*b*, R 61*a*, C 73.]

GEOG. DIST.— Pacific coast region of North America, from British Columbia southward to Lower California and western Mexico. Breeds nearly throughout its range; resident from central California southward.

719 b. Thryothorus bewickii bairdi (SALV. & GODM.).
Baird's Wren.

Thryothorus bairdi SALV. & GODM. Biol. Centr.-Am. Aves, I. April, 1880, 95.
Thryothorus bewickii bairdi RIDGW. Pr. U. S. Nat. Mus. VIII. 1885, 354.

[B —, C 48*a*, R 61*b*, C 72.]

GEOG. DIST.— Southern Texas, Arizona, and California east of the Sierra Nevada, north to middle Kansas, Colorado, and southern Utah, south into Mexico. Breeds throughout its range; resident from Arizona and Kansas southward.

719.1. Thryothorus leucophrys ANTHONY.
San Clementê Wren.

Thryothorus leucophrys ANTHONY, Auk, XII. Jan. 1895, 52.

[B —, C —, R —, C —.]

GEOG. DIST.— San Clemente Island, California.

720. Thryothorus brevicauda (RIDGW.).
Guadalupe Wren.

Thryomanes brevicauda RIDGW. Bull. U. S. Geol. & Geog. Surv. Terr. II. No. 2, April 1, 1876, 186.
Thryothorus brevicauda SHARPE, Cat. B. Brit. Mus. VI. 1881, 227.

[B—, C —, R 62, C —.]

GEOG. DIST.— Guadalupe Island, Lower California.

Genus **TROGLODYTES** Vieillot.

Subgenus **TROGLODYTES**.

Troglodytes Vieill. Ois. Am. Sept. II. 1807, 52. Type, *T. aëdon* Vieill.

721. **Troglodytes aëdon** Vieill.
House Wren.

Troglodytes aëdon Vieill. Ois. Am. Sept. II. 1807, 52, pl. 107.

[B 270, 272, C 49, R 63, C 74.]

Geog. Dist.— Eastern United States and southern Ontario, west to Indiana and Louisiana. Resident from the middle districts southward.

721 a. **Troglodytes aëdon parkmanii** (Aud.).
Parkman's Wren.

Troglodytes parkmanii Aud. Orn. Biog. V. 1839, 310.
Troglodytes ædon var. *parkmanni* Coues, Key, 1872, 87.

[B 271, C 49a, R 63a, C 75.]

Geog. Dist.— Pacific coast region of British Columbia, Washington, Oregon, and northern California.

721 b. **Troglodytes aëdon aztecus** Baird.
Western House Wren.

Troglodytes ædon var. *aztecus* Baird, Rev. Am. B. I. Sept. 1864, 139.

[B 271, *part*, C 49a, *part*, R 63a, *part*, C 75, *part*.]

Geog. Dist.— Western United States, except Pacific coast, east to Manitoba and Illinois, south into Mexico.

Subgenus **ANORTHURA** Rennie.

Anorthura Rennie, Mont. Orn. Dict. ed. 2, 1831, 570. Type, *Motacilla troglodytes* Linn.

ORDER PASSERES. 301

722. Troglodytes hiemalis VIEILL.
Winter Wren.

Troglodytes hiemalis VIEILL. Nouv. Dict. d'Hist. Nat. XXXIV. 1819, 514.

[B 273, C 50, R 65, C 76.]

GEOG. DIST.— Eastern North America generally, breeding from the northern parts of the United States northward, and in the Alleghanies south to North Carolina, and wintering from about its southern breeding limit southward.

722 a. Troglodytes hiemalis pacificus BAIRD.
Western Winter Wren.

Troglodytes hyemalis var. *pacificus* BAIRD, Rev. Am. B. I. Sept. 1864, 145.

[B 273, *part*, C 50, *part*, R 65a, C 77.]

GEOG. DIST.— Pacific coast, from Sitka to southern California, and eastward to the mountains of Idaho; south, in winter, to Mexico.

723. Troglodytes alascensis BAIRD.
Alaskan Wren.

Troglodytes alascensis BAIRD, Trans. Chic. Ac. Sci. I. 1869, 315, pl. 30, fig. 3.

[B—, C 50a, R 66, C 78.]

GEOG. DIST.— Aleutian and Pribilof Islands, Alaska.

GENUS **CISTOTHORUS** CABANIS.

SUBGENUS **CISTOTHORUS**.

Cistothorus CAB. Mus. Hein. I. 1850, 77. Type, *Troglodytes stellaris* LICHT.

724. Cistothorus stellaris (LICHT.).
Short-billed Marsh Wren.

Troglodytes stellaris LICHT. in NAUM. Vög. Deutschl. III. 1823, tab. ad p. 724.

Cistothorus stellaris CAB. Mus. Hein. I. 1850, 77.

[B 269, C 52, R 68, C 81.]

GEOG. DIST.— Eastern United States, north to southern New Hampshire, southern Ontario, southern Michigan, and southern Manitoba, and west to the Plains. Winters in the South Atlantic and Gulf States.

SUBGENUS **TELMATODYTES** CABANIS.

Telmatodytes CAB. Mus. Hein. I. 1850, 78. Type, *Certhia palustris* WILS.

725. **Cistothorus palustris** (WILS.).
Long-billed Marsh Wren.

Certhia palustris WILS. Am. Orn. II. 1810, 58, pl. 12, fig. 4.
Cistothorus (Telmatodytes) palustris BAIRD, B. N. Am. 1858, 364.

[B 268, C 51, R 67, C 79.]

GEOG. DIST.— Eastern United States, north to Massachusetts, Ontario, and southern Manitoba, wintering from the Gulf States south to eastern Mexico, and locally as far north as southern New England. Breeds throughout its United States and British American range.

725 *a*. **Cistothorus palustris paludicola** BAIRD.
Tulé Wren.

Cistothorus palustris, var. *paludicola* BAIRD, Rev. Am. B. I. Sept. 1864, 148.

[B 268, *part*, C 51, *part*, R 67*a*, C 80.]

GEOG. DIST.— Western United States, east to the Rocky Mountains and north to British Columbia; south to southern Mexico. Breeds nearly throughout its range, and winters from Oregon southward.

725 *b*. **Cistothorus palustris griseus** BREWST.
Worthington's Marsh Wren.

Cistothorus palustris griseus BREWST. Auk, X. July, 1893, 216.

[B 268, *part*, C 51, *part*, R 67, *part*, C 79, *part*.]

GEOG. DIST.— Coast region of South Carolina and Georgia.

ORDER PASSERES. 303

725.1. Cistothorus marianæ Scott.
Marian's Marsh Wren.
Cistothorus marianæ Scott, Auk, V. April, 1888, 188.

[B —, C —, R —, C —.]

Geog. Dist.— Western Florida.

Family **CERTHIIDÆ**. Creepers.

Genus **CERTHIA** Linnæus.

Certhia Linn. S. N. ed. 10, I. 1758, 118. Type, by elimination, *C. familiaris* Linn.

726. Certhia familiaris americana (Bonap.).
Brown Creeper.
Certhia americana Bonap. Geog. & Comp. List, 1838, 11.
Certhia familiaris var. *americana* Ridgw. Bull. Essex Inst. V. 1873, 180.

[B 275, C 42, R 55, C 62.]

Geog. Dist.— Eastern North America, breeding from the northern and more elevated parts of the United States northward, and casually further south, migrating southward in winter.

726 a. Certhia familiaris alticola Miller.
Mexican Creeper.
Certhia familiaris alticola Miller, Auk, XII. April, 1895, 186.

[B 276, C —, R 55*a*, C —.]

Geog. Dist.— Guatemala, Mexico, and southern Arizona.

726 b. Certhia familiaris montana Ridgw.
Rocky Mountain Creeper.
[*Certhia familiaris*] *montana* Ridgw. Proc. U. S. Nat. Mus. V. July 8, 1882, 114.

[B 275, *part*, C 42, *part*, R 55, *part*, C 62, *part*.]

Geog. Dist.— Rocky Mountains, from northern Mexico to Alaska.

726 c. Certhia familiaris occidentalis RIDGW.
    Californian Creeper.

[*Certhia familiaris*] *occidentalis* RIDGW. Proc. U. S. Nat. Mus. V. July 8, 1882, 114.

[B 275, *part*, C 42, *part*, R 55, *part*, C 62, *part*.]

GEOG. DIST.— Pacific coast, from California to southern Alaska.

FAMILY **PARIDÆ**. NUTHATCHES AND TITS.

SUBFAMILY **SITTINÆ**. NUTHATCHES.

GENUS **SITTA** LINNÆUS.

Sitta LINN. S. N. ed. 10, I. 1758, 115. Type, *S. europœa* LINN.

727. Sitta carolinensis LATH.
    White-breasted Nuthatch.

Sitta carolinensis LATH. Ind. Orn. I. 1790, 262.

[B 277, C 38, R 51, C 57.]

GEOG. DIST.— Eastern United States, from Georgia north to the southern British Provinces, and west to the Rocky Mountains.

727 a. Sitta carolinensis aculeata (CASS.).
    Slender-billed Nuthatch.

Sitta aculeata CASS. Pr. Ac. Nat. Sci. Phila. Oct. 1856, 254.
Sitta carolinensis var. *aculeata* ALLEN, Bull. M. C. Z. III. No. 6, July, 1872, 161.

[B 278, C 38*a*, R 51*a*, C 58.]

GEOG. DIST.— Western North America, east to the Plains, and south into Mexico.

727 b. Sitta carolinensis atkinsi SCOTT.
    Florida White-breasted Nuthatch.

Sitta carolinensis atkinsi SCOTT, Auk, VII. April, 1890, 118.

[B 277, *part*, C 38, *part*, R 51, *part*, C 57, *part*.]

GEOG. DIST.— Florida, and northward along the coast to South Carolina.

728. Sitta canadensis LINN.
Red-breasted Nuthatch.

Sitta canadensis LINN. S. N. ed. 12, I. 1766, 177.

[B 279, C 39, R 52, C 59.]

GEOG. DIST.— North America at large, breeding from northern New England, northern New York, and northern Michigan northward, and southward in the Alleghanies, Rocky Mountains, and Sierra Nevada; in winter south to about the southern border of the United States.

729. Sitta pusilla LATH.
Brown-headed Nuthatch.

Sitta pusilla LATH. Ind. Orn. I. 1790, 263.

[B 280, C 40, R 53, C 60.]

GEOG. DIST.— South Atlantic and Gulf States, north to southern Maryland and (casually?) Ohio, Missouri, etc.

730. Sitta pygmæa VIG.
Pygmy Nuthatch.

Sitta pygmæa VIG. Zool. Beechey's Voy. 1839, 25, pl. 4.

[B 281, C 41, R 54, C 61.]

GEOG. DIST.— Western United States, from New Mexico, Colorado, and Montana to southern California, Washington, and eastern British Columbia; southward in Mexico to Mt. Orizaba.

730 *a*. Sitta pygmæa leuconucha ANTHONY.
White-naped Nuthatch.

Sitta pygmæa leuconucha ANTHONY, Proc. Cal. Ac. Sci. 2d ser. II. Oct. 11, 1889, 77.

[B 281, *part*, C 41, *part*, R 54, *part*, C 61, *part*.]

GEOG. DIST.— San Pedro Mountains, Lower California.

Subfamily **PARINÆ**. Titmice.

Genus **PARUS** Linnæus.

Subgenus **LOPHOPHANES** Kaup.

Lophophanes Kaup, Entw. Gesch. Eur. Thierw. 1829, 92. Type, *Parus cristatus* Linn.

731. **Parus bicolor** Linn.
Tufted Titmouse.

Parus bicolor Linn. S. N. ed. 12, I. 1766, 340.

[B 285, C 27, R 36, C 40.]

Geog. Dist.— Eastern United States to the Plains, north to northern New Jersey and southern Iowa; casual in southern New England. Resident throughout its breeding range.

731 a. **Parus bicolor texensis** Senn.
Texan Tufted Titmouse.

Parus bicolor texensis Senn. Auk, IV. Jan. 1887, 29.

[B —, C —, R —, C —.]

Geog. Dist.— Southeastern Texas (Bee and Cameron Counties).

732. **Parus atricristatus** Cass.
Black-crested Titmouse.

Parus atricristatus Cass. Pr. Ac. Nat. Sci. Phila. 1850, 103, pl. 2.

[B 286, C 29, R 37, C 42.]

Geog. Dist.— Southeastern Texas and eastern Mexico.

733. **Parus inornatus** Gamb.
Plain Titmouse.

Parus inornatus Gamb. Pr. Ac. Nat. Sci. Phila. Aug. 1845, 265.

[B 287, *part*, C 28, *part*, R 38, *part*, C 41, *part*.]

Geog. Dist.— Pacific coast of California and western Oregon.

733 *a*. **Parus inornatus griseus** RIDGW.
   Gray Titmouse.

   Lophophanes inornatus griseus RIDGW. Pr. U. S. Nat. Mus. V. Sept. 5, 1882, 344.
   Parus inornatus griseus RIDGW. Pr. U. S. Nat. Mus. VIII. 1885, 354.

   [B 287, *part,* C 28, *part,* R 38, *part,* C 41, *part.*]

   GEOG. DIST.— New Mexico and Colorado to Arizona, Nevada and California east of the Sierra Nevada.

733 *b*. **Parus inornatus cineraceus** RIDGW.
   Ashy Titmouse.

   Lophophanes inornatus cineraceus RIDGW. Pr. U. S. Nat. Mus. VI. Oct. 5, 1883, 154.
   Parus inornatus cineraceus RIDGW. Pr. U. S. Nat. Mus. VIII. 1885, 354.

   [B —, C —, R —, C —.]

   GEOG. DIST.— Lower California.

734. **Parus wollweberi** (BONAP.).
   Bridled Titmouse.

   Lophophanes wollweberi BONAP. Compt. Rend. XXXI. Sept. 1850, 478.
   Parus wollweberi HENRY, Pr. Ac. Nat. Sci. Phila. 1855, 309.

   [B 288, C 30, R 39, B 43.]

   GEOG. DIST.— Western Texas, southern New Mexico, southern Arizona, and southward on the tableland of Mexico to Orizaba.

SUBGENUS **PARUS** LINNÆUS.

Parus LINN. S. N. ed. 10, I. 1758, 189. Type, by elimination, *P. major* LINN.

735. **Parus atricapillus** LINN.
   Chickadee.

   Parus atricapillus LINN. S. N. ed. 12, I. 1766, 341.

[B 290, C 31, R 41, C 44.]

GEOG. DIST.— Eastern North America, north of the Potomac and Ohio Valleys.

735 a. Parus atricapillus septentrionalis (HARRIS).
Long-tailed Chickadee.

Parus septentrionalis HARRIS, Pr. Ac. Nat. Sci. Phila. 1845, 300.
Parus atricapillus var. *septentrionalis* ALLEN, Bull. M. C. Z. III. 1872, 174.

[B 289, 289a, C 31a, R 41a, C 45.]

GEOG. DIST.— Rocky Mountain Plateau region, east to Manitoba and the Plains.

735 b. Parus atricapillus occidentalis (BAIRD).
Oregon Chickadee.

Parus occidentalis BAIRD, B. N. Am. 1858, 391.
Parus atricapillus var. *occidentalis* COUES, Key, 1872, 81.

[B 291, C 31c, R 41b, C 46.]

GEOG. DIST.— Northwest coast region, from northern California to Sitka.

736. Parus carolinensis AUD.
Carolina Chickadee.

Parus carolinensis AUD. Orn. Biog. II. 1834, 341, pl. 160.

[B 293, C 31b, R 42, C 47.]

GEOG. DIST.— Southeastern States, north to New Jersey and Illinois, west to Missouri.

736 a. Parus carolinensis agilis SENN.
Plumbeous Chickadee.

Parus carolinensis agilis SENN. Auk, V. Jan. 1888, 46.

[B —, C —, R —, C —.]

GEOG. DIST.— Eastern and central Texas (Bee, Victoria, Cook, and Concho Counties, etc.).

787. Parus meridionalis SCL.
Mexican Chickadee.

Parus meridionalis SCL. P. Z. S. 1856, 293.

[B 292, C —, R 43, C 879.]

GEOG. DIST.— Mountains of Mexico, from Orizaba north to southern Arizona.

738. Parus gambeli RIDGW.
Mountain Chickadee.

Parus gambeli RIDGW. in A. O. U. Check-List, 1886, 335.

[B 294, C 32, R 40, C 48.]

GEOG. DIST.— Mountainous parts of the western United States, from the eastern base of the Rocky Mountains to the Sierra Nevada, north to British Columbia, Idaho, etc., and south to northern Lower California.

739. Parus cinctus obtectus (CAB.).
Siberian Chickadee.

Parus (Pœcila) obtectus CAB. J. f. O. 1871, 237.
Parus cinctus obtectus RIDGW. Pr. U. S. Nat. Mus. VIII. 1885, 354.

[B —, C —, R 44, C 52.]

GEOG. DIST.— Northern Alaska and eastern Siberia.

740. Parus hudsonicus FORST.
Hudsonian Chickadee.

Parus hudsonicus FORST. Phil. Trans. LXII. 1772, 383, 430.

[B 296, C 33, R 45, C 49.]

GEOG. DIST.— Northern North America, from the more elevated parts of the northern United States (northern New England, northern New York, northern Michigan, etc.) northward.

740 a. Parus hudsonicus stoneyi (RIDGW.).
Kowak Chickadee.

Parus stoneyi RIDGW. Man. N. Am. B. Aug. 1887, 591.
Parus hudsonicus stoneyi A. O. U. Check-List, 1st Suppl. 1889, 17.

[B—, C—, R—, C—.]

GEOG. DIST.— Valley of the Kowak River, northwestern Alaska.

740 b. Parus hudsonicus columbianus RHOADS.
Columbian Chickadee.

Parus hudsonicus columbianus RHOADS, Auk, X. Jan. 1893, 23.

[B 296, *part*, C 33, *part*, R 45, *part*, C 49, *part*.]

GEOG. DIST.— Rocky Mountains, from Liard River south into Montana.

741. Parus rufescens TOWNS.
Chestnut-backed Chickadee.

Parus rufescens TOWNS. Journ. Ac. Nat. Sci. Phila. VII. ii. 1837, 190.

[B 295, *part*, C 34, *part*, R 46, C 50.]

GEOG. DIST.— Coast district of Oregon, Washington, British Columbia, and southern Alaska.

741 a. Parus rufescens neglectus RIDGW.
California Chickadee.

Parus rufescens β. *neglectus* RIDGW. Pr. U. S. Nat. Mus. I. April 25, 1879, 485.

[B 295, *part*, C 34, *part*, R 46a, C 51.]

GEOG. DIST.— Coast of California, from Monterey County northward.

SUBFAMILY **CHAMÆINÆ**. WREN-TITS AND BUSH-TITS.

GENUS **CHAMÆA** GAMBEL.

Chamæa GAMB. Pr. Ac. Nat. Sci. Phila. 1847, 154. Type, *Parus fasciatus* GAMB.

742. Chamæa fasciata GAMB.
Wren-Tit.

Parus fasciatus GAMB. Pr. Ac. Nat. Sci. Phila. Aug. 1845, 265.
Chamæa fasciata GAMB. Pr. Ac. Nat. Sci. Phila. 1847, 154.

[B 274, *part*, C 26, *part*, R 35, *part*, C 39, *part*.]

GEOG. DIST.— Coast region of California north at least to Humboldt Bay.

742 a. Chamæa fasciata henshawi RIDGW.
Pallid Wren-Tit.

Chamæa fasciata henshawi RIDGW. Pr. U. S. Nat. Mus. V. June 5, 1882, 13.

[B 274, *part*, C 26, *part*, R 35, *part*, C 39, *part*.]

GEOG. DIST.— Interior of California, including the western slope of the Sierra Nevada, from the head of the Sacramento Valley south to northern Lower California.

GENUS **PSALTRIPARUS** BONAPARTE.

Psaltriparus BONAP. Compt. Rend. XXXI. 1850, 478. Type, *Parus melanotis* HARTL.

743. Psaltriparus minimus (TOWNS.).
Bush-Tit.

Parus minimus TOWNS. Journ. Ac. Nat. Sci. Phila. VII. ii. 1837, 190.
Psaltriparus minimus BONAP. Compt. Rend. XXXVIII. 1854, 62.

[B 298, *part*, C 35, *part*, R 47, *part*, C 53, *part*.]

GEOG. DIST.— Pacific coast region, from northern California to Washington.

743 a. Psaltriparus minimus californicus RIDGW.
California Bush-Tit.

Psaltriparus minimus californicus RIDGW. Pr. Biol. Soc. Wash. II. April 10, 1884, 89.

[B 298, *part*, C 35, *part*, R 47, *part*, C 53, *part*.]

GEOG. DIST.— California, except the northern coast district.

743 b. Psaltriparus minimus grindæ (BELDING).
Grinda's Bush-Tit.

Psaltriparus grindæ BELD. Pr. U. S. Nat. Mus. VI. Oct. 5, 1883, 155.
Psaltriparus minimus grindæ RIDGW. Pr. U. S. Nat. Mus. VIII. 1885, 354.

[B —, C —, R —, C —.]

GEOG. DIST.— Lower California.

744. Psaltriparus plumbeus BAIRD.
Lead-colored Bush-Tit.

Psaltria plumbea BAIRD, Pr. Ac. Nat. Sci. Phila. June, 1854, 118.
Psaltriparus plumbeus BAIRD, B. N. Am. 1858, 398.

[B 299, C 36, R 48, C 54.]

GEOG. DIST.— New Mexico and Arizona, north to eastern Oregon and western Wyoming.

744.1. Psaltriparus santaritæ RIDGW.
Santa Rita Bush-Tit.

Psaltriparus santaritæ RIDGW. Proc. U. S. Nat. Mus. X. Sept. 19, 1888, 697.

[B —, C —, R —, C —.]

GEOG. DIST.— Santa Rita Mountains, southern Arizona.

745. Psaltriparus lloydi SENNETT.
Lloyd's Bush-Tit.

Psaltriparus lloydi SENN. Auk, V. Jan. 1888, 43.

[B 297, C —, R 49, C 55.]

GEOG. DIST.— Western Texas (mountains between Pecos River and Rio Grande), and west to eastern Sonora.

GENUS **AURIPARUS** BAIRD.

Auriparus BAIRD, Rev. Am. B. I. July, 1864, 85. Type, *Ægithalus flaviceps* SUND.

746. Auriparus flaviceps (SUND.).
   Verdin.
   Ægithalus flaviceps SUND. Öfv. Vet. Ak. Förh. VII. 1850, 129.
   Auriparus flaviceps BAIRD, Rev. Am. B. I. July, 1864, 85.
   [B 300, C 37, R 50, C 56.].

GEOG. DIST.— Southern border of the United States, from the Valley of the Rio Grande to Arizona and southern California, north to southern Nevada and southwestern Utah, and south to Lower California, Zacatecas, and southern Tamaulipas. Resident nearly throughout its range.

FAMILY **SYLVIIDÆ**. WARBLERS, KINGLETS, GNATCATCHERS.

SUBFAMILY **SYLVIINÆ**. WARBLERS.

GENUS **PHYLLOPSEUSTES** MEYER.

Phyllopseustes MEYER, Vög. Lifl. Estl. 1815, 122. Type, *Sylvia sibilatrix* BECHST.

747. Phyllopseustes borealis (BLAS.).
   Kennicott's Willow Warbler.
   Phyllopneuste borealis BLASIUS, Naumannia, 1858, 313.
   Phyllopseustes borealis MEVES, J. f. O. 1875, 429.
   [B —, C 20, R 34, C 32.]

GEOG. DIST.— Northeastern Asia and Alaska.

SUBFAMILY **REGULINÆ**. KINGLETS.

GENUS **REGULUS** CUVIER.

Regulus CUV. Leç. d'Anat. Comp. I. 1799–1800, tab. ii. Type, *Motacilla regulus* LINN.

748. Regulus satrapa LICHT.
   Golden-crowned Kinglet.
   Regulus satrapa LICHT. Verz. Doubl. 1823, 35.

[B 162, *part*, C 22, *part*, R 33, C 34.]

GEOG. DIST.— North America generally, breeding in the northern and elevated parts of the United States and northward, migrating south in winter to Guatemala.

748 *a*. **Regulus satrapa olivaceus** BAIRD.
Western Golden-crowned Kinglet.

Regulus satrapa var. *olivaceus* BAIRD, Rev. Am. B. I. July, 1864, 65 (in text under *R. satrapa*).

[B 162, *part*, C 22, *part*, R 33*a*, C 35.]

GEOG. DIST.— Pacific coast region of North America, from California northward.

749. **Regulus calendula** (LINN.).
Ruby-crowned Kinglet.

Motacilla calendula LINN. S. N. ed. 12, I. 1766, 337.
Regulus calendula LICHT. Verz. Doubl. 1823, 35.

[B 161, C 21, R 30, C 33.]

GEOG. DIST.— North America, south to Guatemala, north to the Arctic coast, breeding chiefly north of the United States, and in the Rocky Mountains, the Sierra Nevada, and the mountains of Arizona.

750. **Regulus obscurus** RIDGW.
Dusky Kinglet.

Regulus calendula obscurus RIDGW. Bull. U. S. Geol. & Geog. Surv. Terr. II. No. 2, April 1, 1876, 184.
Regulus obscurus RIDGW. Bull. Nutt. Orn. Club, II. July, 1877, 59.

[B —, C —, R 31, C —.]

GEOG. DIST.— Guadalupe Island, Lower California.

SUBFAMILY **POLIOPTILINÆ**. GNATCATCHERS.

GENUS **POLIOPTILA** SCLATER.

Polioptila SCL. P. Z. S. 1855, 11. Type, *Motacilla cærulea* LINN.

751. Polioptila cærulea (LINN.).
   Blue-gray Gnatcatcher.

Motacilla cærulea LINN. S. N. ed. 12, I. 1766, 337.
Polioptila cærulea SCL. P. Z. S. 1855, 11.

[B 282, C 23, R 27, C 36.]

GEOG. DIST.— Middle and southern portions of the eastern United States, south, in winter, to Guatemala, Cuba, and the Bahamas; rare north toward the Great Lakes, southern New York, and southern New England, accidental north to Massachusetts and Maine. Breeds throughout its United States range, and winters from the South Atlantic and Gulf States southward.

751 a. Polioptila cærulea obscura RIDGW.
   Western Gnatcatcher.

Polioptila cærula obscura RIDGW. Proc. U. S. Nat. Mus. V. March 21, 1883, 535, foot-note.

[B 282, *part*, C 23, *part*, R 27, *part*, C 36, *part*.]

GEOG. DIST.— Arizona, California, Lower California, and western Mexico.

752. Polioptila plumbea BAIRD.
   Plumbeous Gnatcatcher.

Culicivora plumbea BAIRD, Pr. Ac. Nat. Sci. Phila. June, 1854, 118.
Polioptila plumbea BAIRD, B. N. A. 1858, 382.

[B 283, C 25, R 28, C 38.]

GEOG. DIST.— Western Texas to eastern edge of Mohave Desert and eastern coast of Lower California.

753. Polioptila californica BREWST.
   Black-tailed Gnatcatcher.

Polioptila californica BREWST. Bull. Nutt. Orn. Club, VI. April, 1881, 103.

[B 284, C 24, R 29, C 37.]

GEOG. DIST.— Southern California and Pacific coast of Lower California.

Family TURDIDÆ. Thrushes, Solitaires, Stonechats, Bluebirds, etc.

Subfamily MYADESTINÆ. Solitaires.

Genus MYADESTES Swainson.

Myadestes Swains. Nat. Libr. XIII. Flycatchers, 1838, 132. Type, *M. genibarbis* Swains.

754. Myadestes townsendii (Aud.).
Townsend's Solitaire.

Ptiliogonys townsendii Aud. Orn. Biog. V. 1839, 206, pl. 419, fig. 2.
Myiadestes townsendi Cab. Wiegm. Archiv, 1847, i. 208.

[B 235, C 121, R 25, C 169.]

Geog. Dist.— Western United States, from the Plains westward to the Pacific coast, north to British Columbia, and south, in winter, to the southern border of Arizona and northern Lower California. Breeds from the mountains of New Mexico, southern Arizona, and central California northward.

Subfamily TURDINÆ. Thrushes.

Genus TURDUS Linnæus.

Subgenus HYLOCICHLA Baird.

Hylocichla Baird, Rev. Am. B. I. June, 1864, 12. Type, *Turdus mustelinus* Gmel.

755. Turdus mustelinus Gmel.
Wood Thrush.

Turdus mustelinus Gmel. S. N. I. ii. 1788, 817.

ORDER PASSERES.

[B 148, C 3, R 1, C 6.]

GEOG. DIST.— Eastern United States to the Plains, north to southern Michigan, Ontario, and Massachusetts, south, in winter, to Guatemala and Cuba. Breeds from Virginia, Kentucky, and Kansas northward.

756. Turdus fuscescens STEPH.
Wilson's Thrush.

Turdus fuscescens STEPH. Gen. Zool. X. i. 1817, 182.

[B 151, C 6, R 2, C 7.]

GEOG. DIST.— Eastern United States to the Plains, north to Manitoba, Ontario, Anticosti, and Newfoundland. Breeds from northern New Jersey and the northern part of the Lake States northward; winters sparingly in Florida, but chiefly south of the United States.

756 a. Turdus fuscescens salicicola (RIDGW.).
Willow Thrush.

Hylocichla fuscescens salicicola RIDGW. Pr. U. S. Nat. Mus. IV. April 6, 1882, 374.

Turdus fuscescens salicicola COUES, Key, ed. 2, 1884, 246.

[B —, C —, R —, C —.]

GEOG. DIST.— Rocky Mountain region, north to British Columbia, east to Dakota, occasionally to Illinois, casually to South Carolina; in winter south to southern Brazil.

757. Turdus aliciæ BAIRD.
Gray-cheeked Thrush.

Turdus aliciæ BAIRD, B. N. Am. 1858, 217.

[B 154, C 5a, R 3, C 12.]

GEOG. DIST.— Eastern North America, west to the Plains, Alaska, and eastern Siberia, north to the Arctic coast, south, in winter, to Costa Rica. Breeds chiefly north of the United States.

757 a. Turdus aliciæ bicknelli (RIDGW.).
Bicknell's Thrush.

Hylocichla aliciæ bicknelli RIDGW. Pr. U. S. Nat. Mus. IV. April 6, 1882, 377.

Turdus aliciæ bicknelli COUES, Key, ed. 2, 1884, 248.

[B 154, *part*, C 5*a*, *part*, R 3, *part*, C 12, *part*.]

GEOG. DIST.—Mountainous parts of the northeastern States (Catskills, White Mountains, etc.) and Nova Scotia, migrating south in winter.

758. **Turdus ustulatus** NUTT.
Russet-backed Thrush.

Turdus ustulatus NUTT. Man. Orn. Land. B. ed. 2, 1840, 830 (*cestulatus*, err. typ. p. 400).

[B 152, C 5*b*, R 4, C 11.]

GEOG. DIST.—Pacific coast region of North America, from Alaska to California, south in winter to northern Lower California, Mexico, and Guatemala.

758 *a*. **Turdus ustulatus swainsonii** (CAB.).
Olive-backed Thrush.

Turdus swainsonii CAB. Fauna Per. 1845–46, 187.
Turdus ustulatus β. *swainsoni* RIDGW. Field & Forest, II. May, 1877, 195.

[B 153, C 5, R 4*a*, C 13.]

GEOG. DIST.—Eastern North America, and westward to the Upper Columbia River and East Humboldt Mountains, straggling to the Pacific coast. Southward in winter to Cuba, Guatemala, Nicaragua, Colombia, Ecuador and Peru. Casual in Bermuda. Breeds in the northern Alleghanies, the Catskills, the mountainous parts of southern New England, southern Sierra Nevada, and northward.

759. **Turdus aonalaschkæ** GMEL.
Dwarf Hermit Thrush.

Turdus aonalaschkæ GMEL. S. N. I. ii. 1788, 808.

[B 150, C 4*b*, R 5, C 8.]

GEOG. DIST.—Pacific Coast region, from Alaska to Lower California and western Mexico, east during migrations, to Nevada and Arizona. Breeds from the southern Sierra Nevada in California northward.

759 a. Turdus aonalaschkæ auduboni (BAIRD).
Audubon's Hermit Thrush.

Turdus auduboni BAIRD, Rev. Am. B. June, 1864, 16.
Turdus aonalaschkæ auduboni RIDGW. Pr. U. S. Nat. Mus. III. March 27, 1880, 1.

[B 149*a*, C 4*a*, R 5*a*, C 9.]

GEOG. DIST.— Rocky Mountain region, from near the northern border of the United States south to the highlands of Mexico and Guatemala, west to the mountains of Arizona and southern California.

759 b. Turdus aonalaschkæ pallasii (CAB.).
Hermit Thrush.

Turdus pallasii CAB. Wiegm. Archiv. 1847, i. 205.
Turdus aonalaschkæ pallasi RIDGW. Pr. U. S. Nat. Mus. III. March 27, 1880, 1.

[B 149, C 4, R 5*b*, C 10.]

GEOG. DIST.— Eastern North America, breeding from the northern Alleghanies, the mountainous parts of southern New England, southern New York, and northern Michigan, etc., northward, and wintering from the Northern States southward.

SUBGENUS **TURDUS** LINNÆUS.

Turdus LINN. S. N. ed. 10, I. 1758, 168. Type, by elimination, *T. viscivorus* LINN.

[760.] **Turdus iliacus** LINN.
Red-winged Thrush.

Turdus iliacus LINN. S. N. ed. 10, I. 1758, 168.

[B —, C —, R 6, C 4.]

GEOG. DIST.— Northern parts of the Old World; accidental in Greenland.

GENUS **MERULA** LEACH.

Merula LEACH, Syst. Cat. Brit. Mam. & B. 1816, 20. Type, *Turdus merula* LINN.

761. Merula migratoria (LINN.).
American Robin.

Turdus migratorius LINN. S. N. ed. 12, I. 1766, 292.
Merula migratoria SWAINS. Phil. Mag. I. 1827, 368.

[B 155, *part*, C 1, *part*, R 7, C 1.]

GEOG. DIST.— Eastern North America to the Rocky Mountains, including eastern Mexico and Alaska. Breeds from Virginia and Kansas northward to the Arctic coast; winters from southern Canada and the Northern States (irregularly) southward. Casual in Bermuda. Accidental in Europe.

761 a. Merula migratoria propinqua RIDGW.
Western Robin.

T[urdus] propinquus RIDGW. Bull. Nutt. Orn. Club, II. Jan. 1877, 9.
Merula migratoria propinqua RIDGW. Pr. U. S. Nat. Mus. III. Aug. 24, 1880, 166.

[B 155, *part*, C 1, *part*, R 7a, C 2.]

GEOG. DIST.— Western United States, from the eastern base of the Rocky Mountains westward, and south to northern Lower California and the tablelands of Mexico.

762. Merula confinis (BAIRD).
St. Lucas Robin.

Turdus confinis BAIRD, Rev. Am. B. I. June, 1864, 29.
Merula confinis RIDGW. Pr. U. S. Nat. Mus. III. Aug. 24, 1880, 166.

[B —, C 1a, R 8, C 3.]

GEOG. DIST.— Cape region of Lower California; accidental at Hayward, California.

GENUS HESPEROCICHLA BAIRD.

Hesperocichla BAIRD, Rev. Am. B. I. June, 1864, 12. Type, *Turdus nævius* GMEL.

763. Hesperocichla nævia (GMEL.).
Varied Thrush.

Turdus nævius GMEL. S. N. I. ii. 1788, 817.
Hesperocichla nævia RIDGW. Pr. U. S. Nat. Mus. III. Aug. 24, 1880, 166.

[B 156, C 2, R 9, C 5.]

GEOG. DIST.— Pacific coast of North America, from Bering Strait to southern California. Accidental on Guadalupe Island, Lower California, and in New Jersey, Long Island, and Massachusetts.

Genus CYANECULA BREHM.

Cyanecula BREHM, Isis, 1828, 1280. Type, *Motacilla suecica* LINN.

[764.] Cyanecula suecica (LINN.).
Red-spotted Bluethroat.

Motacilla suecica LINN. S. N. ed. 10, I. 1758, 187.
Cyanecula suecica BREHM, Isis, 1828, 1280.

[B —, C —, R 20, C 31.]

GEOG. DIST.— Northern parts of the Old World; casual in Alaska.

Genus SAXICOLA BECHSTEIN.

Saxicola BECHST. Orn. Taschb. 1803, 216. Type, *Motacilla œnanthe* LINN.

765. Saxicola œnanthe (LINN.).
Wheatear.

Motacilla œnanthe LINN. S. N. ed. 10, I. 1758, 186.
Saxicola œnanthe BECHST. Orn. Taschb. 1803, 217.

[B 157, C 15, R 21, C 26.]

GEOG. DIST.— Europe, North Africa, Asia, Alaska, Greeenland, and Labrador, straggling southward to Nova Scotia, Maine, Long Island, and Bermuda. Accidental at New Orleans, La.

Genus **SIALIA** Swainson.

Sialia Swains. Phil. Mag. I. May, 1827, 369. Type, *Motacilla sialis* Linn.

766. **Sialia sialis** (Linn.).
Bluebird.

Motacilla sialis Linn. S. N. ed. 10, I. 1758, 187.
Sialia sialis Haldem. Trego's Geog. Penn. 1843, 77.

[B 158, C 16, R 22, C 27.]

Geog. Dist.— Eastern United States to the eastern base of the Rocky Mountains, north to Manitoba, Ontario, and Nova Scotia, south, in winter, from the Middle States to the Gulf States and Cuba. Bermuda, resident.

766 *a*. **Sialia sialis azurea** (Swains.).
Azure Bluebird.

Sialia azurea Baird, Rev. Am. B. July, 1884, 62.
Sialia sialis var. *azurea* B. B. & R. Hist. N. Am. B. I. Jan. 1874, 62.

[B —, C —, R —, C —.]

Geog. Dist.— Southern Arizona and eastern Mexico.

767. **Sialia mexicana occidentalis** (Towns.).
Western Bluebird.

Sialia occidentalis Towns. Journ. Acad. Nat. Sci. Phila. VII. 1837, 188.
Sialia mexicana occidentalis Ridgw. Auk, XI. April, 1894, 151, 154.

[B 159, *part*, C 17, *part*, R 23, *part*, C 28, *part*.]

Geog. Dist.— Pacific coast, from British Columbia to southern California, east to western Nevada, and casually, during migrations, to New Mexico.

767 *a*. **Sialia mexicana bairdi** RIDGW.
   Chestnut-backed Bluebird.

   Sialia mexicana bairdi RIDGW. Auk, XI. April, 1894, 151, 157.

   [B 159, *part*, C 17, *part*, R 23, *part*, C 28, *part*.]

   GEOG. DIST.— Rocky Mountain district, south to northern Mexico.

767 *b*. **Sialia mexicana anabelæ** ANTHONY.
   San Pedro Bluebird.

   Sialia mexicana anabelæ ANTHONY, Proc. Cal. Acad. Sci. 2d Ser. II. Oct. 1889, 79.

   [B —, C —, R —, C —.]

   GEOG. DIST.— San Pedro Martir Mountains, Lower California.

768. **Sialia arctica** SWAINS.
   Mountain Bluebird.

   Erythaca (*Sialia*) *arctica* SWAINS. in Sw. & RICH. Fauna Bor. Am. II. 1831, 209, pl. 39.

   [B 160, C 18, R 24, C 29.]

   GEOG. DIST.— Western North America (chiefly the interior), from the western parts of the Plains to the Pacific, north to Great Slave Lake, south to northern Mexico.

HYPOTHETICAL LIST.[1]

FAMILY **PODICIPIDÆ**.

1. **Æchmophorus clarkii** (LAWR.).
    Clark's Grebe.

    Podiceps clarkii LAWR. in BAIRD'S B. N. Am. 1858, 895.
    Æchmophorus clarkii COUES, Pr. Ac. Nat. Sci. Phila. 1862, 229.

    [B 705, C 608a, R 730, C 846.]

    Probably the female of *Æ. occidentalis* (LAWR.). (*Cf.* HENSHAW, Bull. Nutt. Orn. Club, VI. 1881, pp. 214–218; B. B. & R., Water B. N. Am. II. p. 423; and especially BRYANT, Auk, II. 1885, pp. 313, 314.)

FAMILY **ALCIDÆ**.

2. **Cepphus motzfeldi** (BENICK.).
    Black-winged Guillemot.

    Uria motzfeldi BENICK. Isis, Aug. 1824, 889.
    Cepphus motzfeldi STEJN. Pr. U. S. Nat. Mus. VII. Aug. 5, 1884, 210.

    [B —, C —, R —, C —.]

    North American, but its specific validity not satisfactorily established. (*Cf.* STEJN. *l. c.*, and Water B. N. Am. II. 1884, pp. 497, 498.)

[1] Consisting of species which have been recorded as North American, but whose status as North American birds is doubtful, either from lack of positive evidence of their occurrence within the prescribed limits of the present Check-List, or from absence of satisfactory proof of their validity as species.

3. Cepphus carbo PALL.
Sooty Guillemot.

Cepphus carbo PALL. Zoog. Rosso-As. II. 1826, 350.

[B 728, C 633, R 762, C 873.]

No evidence of its occurrence in North America. (*Cf.* STEJN. Proc. U. S. Nat. Mus. VII. 1884, pp. 225–227.)

FAMILY LARIDÆ.

GENUS CREAGRUS BON.

Creagrus BON. Naumannia, 1854, 211. Type, *Larus furcatus* NEBOUX.

4. Creagrus furcatus (NEB.).
Swallow-tailed Gull.

Larus furcatus NEB. Voy. 'Venus,' Atlas, pl. 10 (1846).
Creagrus furcatus BONAP. Naumannia, 1854, 213.

[B 679, C 559, R 678, C 791.]

In all probability erroneously accredited to North America. At least nine examples are now known,— the type, said to be from Monterey, Cal., three from the Galapagos, one from the coast of Peru, and four from Malpelo Island (Lat. 3° 59′ N., Long. 81° 34½′ W.).

FAMILY DIOMEDEIDÆ.

4.1. Diomedea exulans LINN.
Wandering Albatross.

Diomedea exulans LINN. S. N. ed. 10, I. 1758, 132.

[B —, C —, R —, C —.]

GEOG. DIST.— Southern oceans; said to have occurred in Tampa Bay, Florida, and off coast of Washington. (*Cf.* COUES, Auk, II. Oct. 1885, 387; XII. April, 1895, 178; RIDGWAY, Man. N. Am. B. 1887, 51. The Florida record is open to question, and the others are unsatisfactory.)

Family PROCELLARIIDÆ.

5. Puffinus kuhlii (BOIE).
Cinereous Shearwater.

Procellaria kuhlii BOIE, Isis, 1835, 257.
Puffinus kuhlii BONAP. Consp. II. 1856, 202.

[B 651, C 596, R 708, C 831.]

An Eastern Atlantic species, of which no American specimens are known to exist in collections.

6. Oceanodroma hornbyi (GRAY).
Hornby's Petrel.

Thalassidroma hornbyi GRAY, P. Z. S. 1853, 62.
Oceanodroma hornbyi BONAP. Consp. II. 1856, 195.

[B 641, C 592, R 727, C 827.]

A very distinct species, of which only one specimen has been obtained, the alleged locality being the "northwest coast of America."

Family PHALACROCORACIDÆ.

7. Phalacrocorax perspicillatus PALL.
Pallas's Cormorant.

Phalacrocorax perspicillatus PALL. Zoog. Rosso-As. II. 1826, 305.

[B 621, C 533, R 648, C 756.]

Believed, on good evidence, to be now extinct, as it unquestionably is in the locality (Bering Island) where originally discovered. Only four specimens are known to exist in collections, — two in the St. Petersburgh Museum and one each in the Leyden and British Museums. Even if existing, it has no valid claim to a place in the North American fauna. (*Cf.* STEJN. Pr. U. S. Nat. Mus. VI. 1883, p. 65.)

Family ARDEIDÆ.

9. Ardea wuerdemanni BAIRD.
Würdemann's Heron.

Ardea würdemanni BAIRD, B. N. Am. 1858, 669.

[B 488, C 450, R 486, *part*, C 656, *part*.]

Believed to be either the colored phase of *A. occidentalis* AUD., or an abnormal specimen of *A. wardi* RIDGW. (*Cf.* RIDGW. Bull. U. S. Geol. & Geog. Surv. Terr. IV. No. 1, 1878, pp. 229–236; Bull. Nutt. Orn. Club, VII. 1882, pp. 1–6; Auk, I. 1884, pp. 161–163; Water B. N. Am. I. 1884, pp. 7–13.)

10. Ardea (Dichromanassa) pealei BONAP.
Peale's Egret.

Ardea pealei BONAP. Ann. Lyc. N. Y. II. 1826, 154.

[B 482, C 355, *part*, R 491, *part*, C 661, *part*.]

Supposed to be the white phase of *A. rufescens* GMEL., but possibly entitled to recognition as a local or geographical race.

FAMILY **SCOLOPACIDÆ**.

11. Tringa (Actodromas) cooperi BAIRD.
Cooper's Sandpiper.

Tringa cooperi BAIRD, B. N. Am. 1858, 716.

[B 527, C 422, R 535, C 618.]

Known only from the single specimen from which the species was originally described, taken on Long Island, in May, 1833, and still extant in the National Museum. The status of the species is in doubt.

11.1. Numenius arquatus (LINN.).
European Curlew.

Scolopax arquata LINN. Syst. Nat. I. 1758, 145.
Numenius arquatus LATH. Gen. Syn. Suppl. I. 1787, 291.

[B —, C —, R —, C —.]

GEOG. DIST.— Northern Europe, migrating to southern Africa. Recorded as occurring on Long Island, N. Y. (*Cf.* MARSHALL and DUTCHER, Auk, IX. Oct. 1892, 390–392.) While there is no question as to the proper identification of the specimen, the evidence that it was taken on Long Island is not considered entirely satisfactory.

Family CATHARTIDÆ.

Genus GYPAGUS Vieillot.

Gypagus Vieill. Analyse, 1816, 21. Type, by elimination, *Vultur papa* Linn.

12. Gypagus papa (Linn.).
King Vulture.

Vultur papa Linn. S. N. ed. 10, I. 1758, 86.
Gypagus papa Vieill. Nouv. Dict. d'Hist. Nat. XXXVI. 1819, 456.

[B —, C —, R —, C —.]

Geog. Dist.— Tropical continental America. Recorded as occurring on the Rio Verde, Arizona, but its identity not satisfactorily determined. (*Cf.* Coues, Bull. Nutt. Orn. Club, VI. 1881, p. 248.)

13. Cathartes burrovianus Cass.
Burroughs's Turkey Vulture.

Cathartes burrovianus Cass. Pr. Ac. Nat. Sci. Phila. II. 1845, 212.

[B 4, C —, R —, C —.]

Geog. Dist.— Mexico and eastern South America. Reported as having been seen near Brownsville, Texas. (*Cf.* Dresser, Ibis, 1865, p. 322.)

Family FALCONIDÆ.

14. Buteo cooperi Cass.
Cooper's Henhawk.

Buteo cooperi Cass. Pr. Ac. Nat. Sci. Phila. VIII. 1856, 253.

[B 29, C 349, R 437, C 514.]

Probably the light phase of *B. harlani* Aud. (*Cf.* Ridgw. Auk, I. 1884, pp. 253, 254; *ibid.*, II. 1885, pp. 165, 166.)

Family PSITTACIDÆ.

Genus RHYNCHOPSITTA Bonaparte.

Rhynchopsitta Bonap. Rev. et Mag. Zool. VI. 1854, 149. Type, *Macrocercus pachyrhynchus* Swains.

16. Rhynchopsitta pachyrhyncha (Swains.).
   Thick-billed Parrot.

Macrocercus pachyrhynchus Swains. Phil. Mag. I. 1827, 439.
Rhynchopsitta pachyrhyncha Bonap. Rev. et Mag. Zool. VI. 1854, 149.

[B 64, C —, R 391, C —.]

Geog. Dist.— Mexico. There is said to be a specimen in "the collection of the Philadelphia Academy of Natural Sciences, labelled Rio Grande, Texas, J. W. Audubon," but there is doubt as to whether the specimen was really taken within the limits of the United States. (*Cf.* Baird, Birds N. Am. 1858, p. 66, foot-note; Ridgw. Man. N. Am. B. 1887, 269.) Its occurrence in Texas is not improbable but the evidence is unsatisfactory.

Family CAPRIMULGIDÆ.

16.1. Chordeiles virginianus sennetti (Coues).
   Sennett's Nighthawk.

Chordiles popetue sennetti Coues, Auk, V. Jan. 1888, 37.
Chordeiles virginianus sennetti Chamberlain, Systematic Table of Canadian Birds, 1888, Appendix A. p. 14.

[B 115, *part*, C 267*a*, *part*, R 367*a*, *part*, C 400, *part*.]

Geog. Dist.— "Dakota to Texas, in any treeless country."

Family FRINGILLIDÆ.

17. Acanthis brewsterii Ridgw.
   Brewster's Linnet.

Ægiothus (*flavirostris* var.) *brewsterii* Ridgw. Am. Nat. July, 1872, 433.
Acanthis brewsterii Ridgw. Pr. U. S. Nat. Mus. VIII. 1885, 354.

[B —, C 147, R 180, C 211.]

The type-specimen, taken at Waltham, Mass., remains unique. It cannot be identified with any known species, but may be a hybrid between *Acanthis linaria* and *Spinus pinus*. (*Cf.* BREWST. Bull. Nutt. Orn. Club, VI. 1881, p. 225.)

18. Spiza townsendii (AUD.).
Townsend's Bunting.

Emberiza townsendii AUD. Orn. Biog. II. 1834, 183.

Spiza townsendii RIDGW. Pr. U. S. Nat. Mus. III. Aug. 24, 1880, 182.

[B 379, C 192, R 255, C 288.]

The original specimen, taken May 11, 1833, in Chester County, Pa., by Mr. J. K. Townsend, remains unique. Its peculiarities cannot be accounted for by hybridism, nor probably by individual variation.

FAMILY VIREONIDÆ.

GENUS HYLOPHILUS TEMMINCK.

Hylophilus TEMM. Pl. Col. III. Livr. 29, 1823, text, and pl. 173, fig. 1. Type, *H. thoracicus* TEMM.

19. Hylophilus decurtatus (BONAP.).
Short-winged Hylophilus.

Sylvicola decurtata BONAP. P. Z. S. 1837, 118.

Hylophilus decurtatus BAIRD, Rev. Am. B. I. 1866, 380.

[B —, C —, R —, C —.]

GEOG. DIST.— Mexico and Central America, to Isthmus of Panama. Southern Texas? (*Helinai brevipennis* GIRAUD, Ann. Lyc. N. Y. 1850, 40. "Mexico and Texas.")

FAMILY MNIOTILTIDÆ.

20. Helminthophila lawrencei (HERRICK).
Lawrence's Warbler.

Helminthophaga lawrencei HERRICK, Pr. Ac. Nat. Sci. Phila. 1874, 220, pl. 15.

Helminthophila lawrencei RIDGW. Bull. Nutt. Orn. Club. VII. Jan. 1882, 53.

[B —, C —, R 80, C 99.]

About a dozen specimens have been taken, chiefly in New Jersey and southern Connecticut. Supposed to be a hybrid between *H. pinus* and *H. chrysoptera*. (*Cf.* RIDGW. Ibis, 1876, p. 169; BREWST. Bull. Nutt. Orn. Club, VI. 1881, pp. 218-225; EAMES, Auk, VI. 1889, pp. 305-310.)

21. Helminthophila leucobronchialis (BREWST.).
Brewster's Warbler.

Helminthophaga leucobronchialis BREWST. Bull. Nutt. Orn. Club, I. Jan. 1876, 1, plate.
Helminthophila leucobronchialis RIDGW. Bull. Nutt. Orn. Club, VII. Jan. 1882, 53.

[B —, C —, R 82, C 100.]

Known from numerous specimens, taken in Southern New England, Lower Hudson Valley, New Jersey, Virginia, Michigan, etc. Supposed to be a hybrid between *H. pinus* and *H. chrysoptera*. (*Cf.* BREWST. Bull. Nutt. Orn. Club, VI. 1881, pp. 218-225; RIDGW. Auk, II. Oct. 1885, pp. 359-363; EAMES, Auk, VI. 1889, pp. 305-310.)

22. Helminthophila cincinnatiensis (LANGD.).
Cincinnati Warbler.

Helminthophaga cincinnatiensis LANGD. Jour. Cinc. Soc. N. H. July, 1880, 119, 120, pl. 4.
Helminthophila cincinnatiensis RIDGW. Pr. U. S. Nat. Mus. VIII. 1885, 354.

[B —, C —, R —, C 101.]

One specimen taken near Cincinnati, Ohio. Probably a hybrid between *H. pinus* and *Geothlypis* (*Oporornis*) *formosa*. (*Cf.* RIDGW. Bull. Nutt. Orn. Club, V. 1880, p. 237.)

23. Dendroica (Perissoglossa ?) carbonata (AUD.).
Carbonated Warbler.

Sylvia carbonata AUD. Orn. Biog. I. 1831, 308, pl. 60.
Dendroica carbonata BAIRD, B. N. Am. 1858, 287.
Perissoglossa carbonata B. B. & R. Hist. N. Am. B. I. Jan. 1874, 214.

[B 207, C —, R 91, C —.]

Known only from Audubon's plate and description of two specimens killed near Henderson, Kentucky, in May, 1811.

24. Dendroica montana (WILS.).
Blue Mountain Warbler.

Sylvia montana WILS. Am. Orn. V. 1812, 113, pl. 44, fig. 2.
Dendroica montana BAIRD, B. N. Am. 1858, 278.

[B 199, C —, R 112, C —.]

Known only from the works of Wilson and Audubon. Taken in the Blue Mountains of Virginia. Not as yet satisfactorily identified with any other species.

25. Sylvania (?) microcephala RIDGW.
Small-headed Warbler.

Sylvania microcephala RIDGW. Pr. U. S. Nat. Mus. VIII. 1885, 354. (= *Muscicapa minuta* WILS. Am. Orn. VI. 1812, 62, pl. 1, fig. 5, nec GMEL., 1788.)

[B 212, C —, R 126, C —.]

Known only from the works of Wilson and Audubon. Claimed to have been taken in New Jersey and Kentucky.

FAMILY **SYLVIIDÆ**.

26. Regulus cuvierii AUD.
Cuvier's Kinglet.

Regulus cuvierii AUD. Orn. Biog. I. 1832, 288, pl. 55.

[B 163, C —, R 32, C —.]

Known only from Audubon's description and figure of the original specimen, killed in June, 1812, on the banks of the Schuylkill River, in Pennsylvania.

THE FOSSIL BIRDS OF NORTH AMERICA.

A. — JURASSIC.

1. **Laopteryx priscus** MARSH.

   Laopteryx priscus MARSH, Am. Journ. Sci. XXI. 1881, 341.

   Upper Jurassic beds of Wyoming.

B. — CRETACEOUS.[1]

2. **Apatornis celer** MARSH.

   Ichthyornis celer MARSH, Am. Journ. Sci. V. 1873, 74.
   Apatornis celer MARSH, Am. Journ. Sci. V. 1873, 162.

   Middle Cretaceous of western Kansas.

3. **Baptornis advenus** MARSH.

   Baptornis advenus MARSH, Am. Journ. Sci. XIV. 1877, 86.

   Cretaceous of western Kansas, in the same beds with Odontornithes and Pteranodontia.

4. **Cimolopteryx rarus** MARSH.

   Cimolopteryx rarus MARSH, Am. Journ. Sci. XLIV. 1892, 175, pl. iii, fig. 2.

   Laramie beds of Wyoming.

5. **Cimolopteryx retusus** MARSH.

   Cimolopteryx retusus MARSH, Am. Journ. Sci. XLIV. 1892, 175.

   Laramie beds of Wyoming.

[1] The genera alphabetically arranged.

6. Coniornis altus MARSH.

Coniornis altus MARSH, Am. Journ. Sci. XLV. 1893, 82.

Cretaceous of Montana, near mouth of Judith River.

7. Graculavus velox MARSH.

Graculavus velox MARSH, Am. Journ. Sci. III. 1872, 363.

Greensand of the middle marl bed, or Upper Cretaceous, near Hornerstown, New Jersey.

8. Graculavus pumilus MARSH.

Graculavus pumilus MARSH, Am. Journ. Sci. III. 1872, 364.

Greensand of the middle marl bed, or Upper Cretaceous, near Hornerstown, New Jersey.

9. Hesperornis regalis MARSH.

Hesperornis regalis MARSH, Am. Journ. Sci. III. 1872, 56.

Pteranodon beds of western Kansas.

10. Hesperornis crassipes MARSH.

Lestornis crassipes MARSH, Am. Journ. Sci. XI. 1876, 509.
Hesperornis crassipes MARSH, Odontornithes, 1880, 196, figs. 40 *a–d*, pls. vii, xvii.

Yellow chalk of the Pteranodon beds, western Kansas.

11. Hesperornis gracilis MARSH.

Hesperornis gracilis MARSH, Am. Journ. Sci. XI. 1876, 510.

Yellow chalk of the Pteranodon beds, western Kansas.

12. Ichthyornis dispar MARSH.

Ichthyornis dispar MARSH, Am. Journ. Sci. IV. 1872, 344.

Pteranodon beds, Middle Cretaceous, northwestern Kansas.

13. Ichthyornis agilis MARSH.

Graculavus agilis MARSH, Am. Journ. Sci. V. 1873, 230.
Ichthyornis agilis MARSH, Odontornithes, 1880, 197.

Pteranodon beds, Middle Cretaceous, western Kansas.

14. Ichthyornis anceps MARSH.

Graculavus anceps MARSH, Am. Journ. Sci. III. 1872, 364.
Ichthyornis anceps MARSH, Odontornithes, 1880, 198.

Gray shale of the Middle Cretaceous, Smoky Hill River, western Kansas.

15. Ichthyornis lentus MARSH.

Graculavus lentus MARSH, Am. Journ. Sci. XIV. 1877, 253.
Ichthyornis lentus MARSH, Odontornithes, 1880, 198.

Middle Cretaceous beds, near Fort McKinney, Texas.

16. Ichthyornis tener MARSH.

Ichthyornis tener MARSH, Odontornithes, 1880, 198, pl. xxx. fig. 8.

Pteranodon beds, Middle Cretaceous, Wallace County, Kansas.

17. Ichthyornis validus MARSH.

Ichthyornis validus MARSH, Odontornithes, 1880, 198, pl. xxx. figs. 11–14.

Yellow chalk of the Middle Cretaceous, near Solomon River, northwestern Kansas.

18. Ichthyornis victor MARSH.

Ichthyornis victor MARSH, Am. Journ. Sci. XI. 1876, 511.

Middle Cretaceous of Kansas, in various localities.

19. Laornis edvardsianus MARSH.

Laornis edvardsianus MARSH, Pr. Ac. Nat. Sci. Phila. 1870, 5.

Middle marl bed, Upper Cretaceous, Birmingham, New Jersey.

20. **Palæotringa littoralis** MARSH.

Palæotringa littoralis MARSH, Pr. Ac. Nat. Sci. Phila. 1870, 5.

Greensand of the Upper Cretaceous, near Hornerstown, New Jersey.

21. **Palæotringa vagans** MARSH.

Palæotringa vagans MARSH, Am. Journ. Sci. III. 1872, 365.

Greensand of the Upper Cretaceous, near Hornerstown, New Jersey.

22. **Palæotringa vetus** MARSH.

Scolopax MORTON, Syn. Organic Remains of the Cret. U. S. 1834, 32.
Palæotringa vetus MARSH, Pr. Ac. Nat. Sci. Phila. 1870, 5.

Lower marl bed of the Cretaceous formation, near Arneytown, New Jersey.

23. **Telmatornis priscus** MARSH.

Telmatornis priscus MARSH, Pr. Ac. Nat. Sci. Phila. 1870, 5.

Middle marl bed of the Upper Cretaceous, near Hornerstown, New Jersey.

24. **Telmatornis affinis** MARSH.

Telmatornis affinis MARSH, Pr. Ac. Nat. Sci. Phila. 1870, 5.

Middle marl beds of the Upper Cretaceous, near Hornerstown, New Jersey.

C. — TERTIARY.

SUBCLASS RATITÆ.

25. **Gastornis giganteus** (COPE).

Diatryma gigantea COPE, Pr. Ac. Nat. Sci. Phila. 1876, 11.
Gastornis giganteus COUES, Key N. A. Birds, 2d ed. 1884, 825.

Wahsatch Epoch, Eocene of New Mexico.

26. **Barornis regens** MARSH.

> *Barornis regens* MARSH, Am. Journ. Sci. XLVIII. 1894, 344.

Eocene of New Jersey, near Squantum, N. J.

SUBCLASS CARINATÆ.

ORDER PYGOPODES.

27. **Uria antiqua** (MARSH).

> *Catarractes antiqua* MARSH, Am. Journ. Sci. XLIX. 1870, 213.
> *Uria antiqua* COUES, in A. O. U. Check-List, ed. 1, 1886, 363.

Miocene of North Carolina.

28. **Uria affinis** (MARSH).

> *Catarractes affinis* MARSH, Am. Journ. Sci. IV. 1872, 259.
> *Uria affinis* COUES, in A. O. U. Check-List, ed. 1, 1886, 363.

Post-pliocene of Maine.

ORDER LONGIPENNES.

29. **Larus robustus** SHUFELDT.

> *Larus robustus* SHUFELDT, Journ. Ac. Nat. Sci. Phila. XI. 1892, 398, pl. xv, fig. 1, 2.

Pliocene of Oregon.

30. **Larus oregonus** SHUFELDT.

> *Larus oregonus* SHUFELDT, Journ. Ac. Nat. Sci. Phila. XI. 1892, 398.

Pliocene of Oregon.

Order TUBINARES.

31. Puffinus conradii MARSH.

Puffinus conradii MARSH, Am. Journ. Sci. XLIX. 1870, 212.

Miocene of Maryland.

Order STEGANOPODES.

32. Sula loxostyla COPE.

Sula loxostyla COPE, Tr. Amer. Philos. Soc. XIV. 1870, 236.

Miocene of North Carolina.

33. Phalacrocorax idahensis (MARSH).

Graculus idahensis MARSH, Am. Journ. Sci. XLIX. 1870, 216.
Phalacrocorax idahensis COUES, Key N. A. Birds, 2d ed. 1884, 824.

Pliocene of Idaho.

34. Phalacrocorax macropus (COPE).

Graculus macropus COPE, Bull. U. S. Geol. Surv. Terr. IV. No. 2, 1878, 386.
Phalacrocorax macropus COUES, Key N. A. Birds, 2d ed. 1884, 824.

Pliocene of Oregon.

Order ANSERES.

35. **Anser condoni** SHUFELDT.

Anser condoni SHUFELDT, Journ. Ac. Nat. Sci. Phila. XI. 1892, 406.

Pliocene of Oregon.

36. **Branta hypsibatus** (COPE).

Anser hypsibatus COPE, Bull. U. S. Geol. Surv. Terr. IV. No. 2, 1878, 387.

Branta hypsibates COUES, in A. O. U. Check-List, ed. 1, 1886, 364.

87. **Branta propinqua** SHUFELDT.

Branta propinqua SHUFELDT, Journ. Ac. Nat. Sci. Phila. XI. 1892, 407, pl. xv, fig. 17.

Pliocene of Oregon.

38. **Cygnus paloregonus** COPE.

Cygnus paloregonus COPE, Bull. U. S. Geol. Surv. Terr. IV. No. 2, 1878, 388.

Pliocene of Oregon.

Order ODONTOGLOSSÆ.

39. **Phœnicopterus copei** SHUFELDT.

Phœnicopterus copei SHUFELDT, Journ. Ac. Nat. Sci. Phila. XI. 1892, 410, pl. xv, fig. 41–43, pl. xvii, fig. 28, 29, 38.

Pliocene of Oregon.

Order HERODIONES.

40. **Ardea paloccidentalis** SHUFELDT.

Ardea paloccidentalis SHUFELDT, Journ. Ac. Nat. Sci. Phila. XI. 1892, 411, pl. xvii. fig. 31.

Pliocene of Oregon.

Order PALUDICOLÆ.

41. Grus haydeni MARSH.

Grus haydeni MARSH, Am. Journ. Sci. XLIX. 1870, 214.

Pliocene of Nebraska.

42. Grus proavus MARSH.

Grus proavus MARSH, Am. Journ. Sci. IV. 1872, 261.

Post-pliocene of New Jersey.

43. Fulica minor SHUFELDT.

Fulica minor SHUFELDT, Journ. Ac. Nat. Sci. Phila. XI. 1892, 412, pl. xvii. fig. 32.

Pliocene of Oregon.

44. Aletornis nobilis MARSH.

Aletornis nobilis MARSH, Am. Journ. Sci. IV. 1872, 256.

Eocene of Wyoming.

45. Aletornis pernix MARSH.

Aletornis pernix MARSH, Am. Journ. Sci. IV. 1872, 256.

Eocene of Wyoming.

46. Aletornis venustus MARSH.

Aletornis venustus MARSH, Am. Journ. Sci. IV. 1872, 257.

Eocene of Wyoming.

47. Aletornis gracilis MARSH.

Aletornis gracilis MARSH, Am. Journ. Sci. IV. 1872, 258.

Eocene of Wyoming.

FOSSIL BIRDS. 343

48. **Aletornis bellus** MARSH.

Aletornis bellus MARSH, Am. Journ. Sci. IV. 1872, 258.

Eocene of Wyoming.

ORDER LIMICOLÆ.

49. **Charadrius sheppardianus** COPE.

Charadrius sheppardianus COPE, Bull. U. S. Geol. Surv. Terr. VI. No. 1, 1881, 83.

(Formation and locality not given.)

ORDER GALLINÆ.

50. **Palæotetrix gilli** SHUFELDT.

Palæotetrix gilli SHUFELDT, Journ. Ac. Nat. Sci. Phila. XI. 1892, 415, pl. xvii. fig. 37.

Pliocene of Oregon.

51. **Pediocætes lucasi** SHUFELDT.

Pediocætes lucasi SHUFELDT, Journ. Ac. Nat. Sci. Phila. XI. 1892, 414, pl. xvii. fig. 30.

Pliocene of Oregon.

52. **Pediocætes nanus** SHUFELDT.

Pediocætes nanus SHUFELDT, Journ. Ac. Nat. Sci. Phila. XI. 1892, 414, pl. xvii. fig. 36, 37.

Pliocene of Oregon.

53. **Meleagris antiquus** MARSH.

Meleagris antiquus MARSH, Am. Journ. Sci. II. 1871, 126.

Miocene of Colorado.

54. **Meleagris altus** MARSH.

Meleagris altus MARSH, Pr. Ac. Nat. Sci. Phila. 1870, 11.

Post-pliocene of New Jersey.

55. **Meleagris celer** MARSH.

Meleagris celer MARSH, Am. Journ. Sci. 1872, 261.

Post-pliocene of New Jersey.

ORDER RAPTORES.

56. **Palæoborus umbrosus** COPE.

Cathartes umbrosus COPE, Pr. Ac. Nat. Sci. Phila. 1874, 151.
Palæoborus umbrosus COUES, Key N. A. Birds, 2d ed. 1884, 822.

Pliocene of New Mexico.

57. **Bubo leptosteus** MARSH.

Bubo leptosteus MARSH, Am. Journ. Sci. II. 1871, 126.

Lower Tertiary of Wyoming.

58. **Aquila danana** MARSH.

Aquila danana MARSH, Am. Journ. Sci. II. 1871, 125.

Pliocene of Nebraska.

59. **Aquila pliogryps** SHUFELDT.

Aquila pliogryps SHUFELDT, Journ. Ac. Nat. Sci. Phila. XI. 1892, 416, pl. xvii. fig. 33.

Pliocene of Oregon.

60. **Aquila sodalis** SHUFELDT.

Aquila sodalis SHUFELDT, Journ. Ac. Nat. Sci. Phila. XI. 1892, 417.

Pliocene of Oregon.

Order COCCYGES.

61. Uintornis lucaris MARSH.

Uintornis lucaris MARSH, Am. Journ. Sci. IV. 1872, 259.

Lower Tertiary formation of Wyoming.

Order PASSERES.

62. Corvus annectens SHUFELDT.

Corvus annectens SHUFELDT, Journ. Ac. Nat. Sci. Phila. XI. 1892, 419, pl. xv. fig. 14–16.

Pliocene of Oregon.

63. Scolecophagus affinis SHUFELDT.

Scolecophagus affinis SHUFELDT, Journ. Ac. Nat. Sci. Phila. XI. 1892, 418, pl. xv. fig. 10.

Pliocene of Oregon.

64. Palæospiza bella ALLEN.

Palæospiza bella ALLEN, Bull. U. S. Geol. Surv. Terr. IV. No. 2, 1878, 443, pl. i. figs. 1, 2.

Insect-bearing shales of Florissant, Colorado.

INDEX.

ACANTHIS, 217.
   brewsterii, 330.
   hornemannii, 217.
   hornemannii exilipes, 217.
   linaria, 217.
   linaria holbœllii, 217.
   linaria rostrata, 218.
Accipiter, 128.
   atricapillus, 129.
   atricapillus striatulus, 129.
   cooperi, 128.
   velox, 128.
Accipitrinæ, 126.
Actitis, 96.
   macularia, 97.
Actochelidon, 23.
Actodromas, 87.
Æchmophorus, 1.
   clarkii, 325.
   occidentalis, 1.
Ægialitis, 100.
   dubia, 101.
   hiaticula, 101.
   meloda, 101.
   meloda circumcincta, 101.
   mongola, 102.
   montana, 103.
   nivosa, 102.
   semipalmata, 100.
   vocifera, 100.
   wilsonia, 102.
Aëronautes, 172.
   melanoleucus, 172.
Æsalon, 138.
Æstrelata, 34.
   fisheri, 34.
   hasitata, 34.
   scalaris, 34.
Agelaius, 204.
   gubernator, 205.
   phœniceus, 204.
   phœniceus bryanti, 205.
   phœniceus sonoriensis, 205.
   tricolor, 205.

Aix, 52.
Aix sponsa, 52.
Ajaja, 66.
   ajaja, 67.
Alauda, 191.
   arvensis, 191.
Alaudidæ, 191.
Albatross, Black-footed, 28.
   Short-tailed, 28.
   Sooty, 29.
   Wandering, 326.
   Yellow-nosed, 28.
Alca, 12.
   torda, 12.
Alcedinidæ, 156.
Alcidæ, 5, 325.
Alcinæ, 11.
Alcyones, 156.
Aletornis bellus, 343.
   gracilis, 342.
   nobilis, 342.
   pernix, 342.
   venustus, 342.
Alle, 13.
   alle, 13.
Allinæ, 13.
Amazilia, 177.
   cerviniventris, 177.
   fuscicaudata, 177.
Ammodramus, 223, 227.
   bairdii, 226.
   beldingi, 225.
   caudacutus, 227.
   caudacutus nelsoni, 227.
   caudacutus subvirgatus, 228.
   henslowii, 226.
   henslowii occidentalis, 227.
   leconteii, 227.
   maritimus, 228.
   maritimus peninsulæ, 228.
   maritimus sennetti, 228.
   nigrescens, 229.
   princeps, 223.
   rostratus, 225.

Ammodramus rostratus guttatus, 225.
    sandwichensis, 224.
    sandwichensis alaudinus, 224.
    sandwichensis bryanti, 224.
    sandwichensis savanna, 224.
    savannarum passerinus, 226.
    savannarum perpallidus, 226.
Ampelidæ, 260.
Ampelinæ, 260.
Ampelis, 260.
    cedrorum, 260.
    garrulus, 260.
Amphispiza, 237.
    belli, 238.
    belli cinerea, 238.
    belli nevadensis, 238.
    bilineata, 237.
Anas, 48.
    americana, 49.
    boschas, 48.
    carolinensis, 50.
    crecca, 50.
    cyanoptera, 51.
    discors, 50.
    fulvigula, 48.
    fulvigula maculosa, 49.
    obscura, 48.
    penelope, 49.
    strepera, 49.
Anatidæ, 47.
Anatinæ, 48.
Ancylocheilus, 90.
Anhinga, 41.
    anhinga, 41.
Anhingidæ, 41.
Ani, 153.
    Groove-billed, 153.
Anorthura, 300.
Anous, 27.
    stolidus, 27.
Anser, 61.
    albifrons, 61.
    albifrons gambeli, 61.
    condoni, 340.
Anseres, 47.
Anserinæ, 60.
Anthus, 289.
    cervinus, 290.
    pensilvanicus, 289.
    pratensis, 290.
    spragueii, 290.
Antrostomus, 168.
    carolinensis, 168.
    vociferus, 168.
    vociferus macromystax, 169.
Apatornis celer, 335.
Aphelocoma, 196.

Aphelocoma californica, 197.
    californica hypoleuca, 197.
    californica obscura, 197.
    cyanotis, 197.
    floridana, 196.
    insularis, 197.
    sieberii arizonæ, 198.
    woodhousei, 196.
Aphriza, 103.
    virgata, 103.
Aphrizidæ, 103.
Aphrizinæ, 103.
Aquila, 135.
    chrysaëtos, 135.
    danana, 344.
    pliogryps, 344.
    sodalis, 344.
Aramidæ, 76.
Aramus, 76.
    giganteus, 76.
Archibuteo, 134.
    ferrugineus, 135.
    lagopus, 134.
    lagopus sancti-johannis, 134.
Arctonetta, 56.
    fischeri, 56.
Ardea, 70.
    candidissima, 72.
    cinerea, 71.
    cærulea, 73.
    egretta, 71.
    herodias, 71.
    occidentalis, 71.
    paloccidentalis, 341.
    pealei, 328.
    rufescens, 72.
    tricolor ruficollis, 72.
    virescens, 73.
    virescens frazari, 73.
    wardi, 71.
    wuerdemanni, 327.
Ardeidæ, 69, 327.
Ardeinæ, 70.
Ardetta, 70.
    exilis, 70.
    neoxena, 70.
Arenaria, 103.
    interpres, 103.
    melanocephala, 104.
Arenariinæ, 103.
Arquatella, 87.
Asio, 142.
    accipitrinus, 142.
    wilsonianus, 142.
Astur, 128.
Asturina, 134.
    plagiata, 134.

INDEX.   349

Asyndesmus, 165.
Auk, Great, 13.
    Razor-billed, 12.
Auklet, Cassin's, 7.
    Crested, 7.
    Least, 8.
    Paroquet, 7.
    Rhinoceros, 6.
    Whiskered, 8.
Auriparus, 312.
    flaviceps, 313.
Avocet, American, 83.
Aythya, 52.
    affinis, 53.
    americana, 52.
    collaris, 53.
    marila nearctica, 53.
    vallisneria, 53.

BALDPATE, 49.
Baptornis advenus, 335.
Barornis regens, 339.
Bartramia, 96.
    longicauda, 96.
Basileuterus, 288.
    belli, 288.
    culicivorus, 288.
Basilinna, 178.
    leucotis, 178.
    xantusi, 178.
Becard, Xantus's, 179.
Bird, Man-of-War, 46.
    Red-billed Tropic, 39.
    Surf, 103.
    Yellow-billed Tropic, 39.
Bittern, American, 70.
    Cory's Least, 70.
    Least, 70.
Blackbird, Bicolored, 205.
    Brewer's, 209.
    Red-winged, 204.
    Rusty, 209.
    Tricolored, 205.
    Yellow-headed, 204.
Bluebird, 322.
    Azure, 322.
    Chestnut-backed, 323.
    Mountain, 323.
    San Pedro, 322.
    Western, 322.
Bluethroat, Red-spotted, 321.
Bobolink, 202.
Bob-white, 106.
    Florida, 106.
    Masked, 107.
    Texan, 107.

Bonasa, 112.
    umbellus, 112.
    umbellus sabini, 112.
    umbellus togata, 112.
    umbellus umbelloides, 112.
Booby, 40.
    Blue-faced, 40.
    Blue-footed, 40.
    Brewster's, 40.
    Red-footed, 40.
Botaurinæ, 69.
Botaurus, 69.
    lentiginosus, 70.
Brachyramphus, 9.
    craveri, 10.
    hypoleucus, 9.
    kittlitzii, 9.
    marmoratus, 9.
Brant, 63.
    Black, 63.
Branta, 62.
    bernicla, 63.
    canadensis, 62.
    canadensis hutchinsii, 62.
    canadensis minima, 63.
    canadensis occidentalis, 62.
    hypsibatus, 341.
    leucopsis, 63.
    nigricans, 63.
    propinqua, 341.
Bubo, 147.
    leptosteus, 344.
    virginianus, 148.
    virginianus arcticus, 148.
    virginianus saturatus, 148.
    virginianus subarcticus, 148.
Bubonidæ, 142.
Budytes, 289.
    flavus leucostriatus, 289.
Buffle-head, 54.
Bullfinch, Cassin's, 212.
Bulweria, 34.
    bulweri, 35.
Bunting, Beautiful, 252.
    Indigo, 252.
    Lark, 254.
    Lazuli, 252.
    Painted, 252.
    Townsend's, 331.
    Varied, 252.
Burrica, 213.
Bush-Tit, 311.
    Californian, 311.
    Grinda's, 312.
    Lead-colored, 312.
    Lloyd's, 312.
    Santa Rita, 312.

Buteo, 130.
    abbreviatus, 132.
    albicaudatus sennetti, 132.
    borealis, 130.
    borealis calurus, 130.
    borealis harlani, 131.
    borealis krideríi, 130.
    borealis lucasanus, 131.
    brachyurus, 133.
    buteo, 130.
    cooperi, 329.
    latissimus, 133.
    lineatus, 131.
    lineatus alleni, 131.
    lineatus elegans, 132.
    swainsoni, 132.
Buteola, 133.
Butorides, 73.
Buzzard, European, 130.

CALAMOSPIZA, 254.
    melanocorys, 254.
Calcarius, 221.
    lapponicus, 221.
    ornatus, 222.
    pictus, 221.
Calidris, 91.
    arenaria, 91.
Callichelidon, 259.
    cyaneoviridis, 259.
Callipepla, 108.
    californica, 109.
    californica vallicola, 109.
    gambeli, 109.
    squamata, 108.
    squamata castanogastris, 108.
Callothrus, 203.
    robustus, 204.
Calothorax, 177.
    lucifer, 177.
Calypte, 175.
    anna, 175.
    costæ, 175.
Campephilus, 157.
    principalis, 158.
Camptolaimus, 56.
    labradorius, 56.
Canachites, 111.
Canvas-back, 53.
Caprimulgi, 168.
Caprimulgidæ, 168, 330.
Caracara, Audubon's, 141.
    Guadalupe, 141.
Cardellina, 287.
Cardellina rubrifrons, 287.
Cardinal, 249.

Cardinal, Arizona, 249.
    Gray-tailed, 249.
    Saint Lucas, 249.
    Texas, 250.
Cardinalis, 248.
    cardinalis, 249.
    cardinalis canicaudus, 249.
    cardinalis igneus, 249.
    cardinalis superbus, 249.
Carinatæ, 339.
Carpodacus, 212.
    amplus, 214.
    cassini, 213.
    mexicanus frontalis, 213.
    mexicanus ruberrimus, 214.
    purpureus, 213.
    purpureus californicus, 213.
Catbird, 292.
Catharista, 125.
    atrata, 125.
Cathartes, 125.
    aura, 125.
    burrovianus, 329.
Cathartidæ, 124, 329.
Catherpes, 296.
    mexicanus, 297.
    mexicanus conspersus, 297.
    mexicanus punctulatus, 297.
Centrocercus, 117.
    urophasianus, 117.
Centronyx, 225.
Centurus, 165.
Ceophlœus, 164.
    pileatus, 164.
Cepphi, 3.
Cepphus, 10.
    carbo, 326.
    columba, 11.
    grylle, 10.
    mandtii, 10.
    motzfeldi, 325.
Cerorhinca, 6.
    monocerata, 6.
Certhia, 303.
    familiaris alticola, 303.
    familiaris americana, 303.
    familiaris occidentalis, 304.
Certhiidæ, 303.
Ceryle, 156.
    alcyon, 156.
    americana septentrionalis, 157.
    torquata, 157.
Chachalaca, 119.
Chætura, 172.
    pelagica, 172.
    vauxii, 172.
Chæturinæ, 171.

Chamæa, 310.
    fasciata, 310.
    fasciata henshawi, 311.
Chamæinæ, 310.
Charadriidæ, 98.
Charadrius, 99.
    apricarius, 99.
    dominicus, 99.
    dominicus fulvus, 100.
    sheppardianus, 343.
    squatarola, 99.
Charitonetta, 54.
    albeola, 54.
Chat, Long-tailed, 285.
    Yellow-breasted, 285.
Chaulelasmus, 49.
Chelidon, 258.
    erythrogaster, 258.
Chen, 60.
    cærulescens, 61.
    hyperborea, 60.
    hyperborea nivalis, 60.
    rossii, 61.
Chickadee, 307.
    California, 310.
    Carolina, 308.
    Chestnut-backed, 310.
    Columbian, 310.
    Hudsonian, 309.
    Kowak, 309.
    Long-tailed, 308.
    Mexican, 309.
    Mountain, 309.
    Oregon, 308.
    Plumbeous, 308.
    Siberian, 309.
Chloroceryle, 157.
Chondestes, 229.
    grammacus, 229.
    grammacus strigatus, 229.
Chordeiles, 170.
    acutipennis texensis, 171.
    virginianus, 170.
    virginianus chapmani, 171.
    virginianus henryi, 170.
    virginianus sennetti, 330.
Chuck-will's-widow, 168.
Ciceronia, 8.
Ciconiæ, 68.
Ciconiidæ, 68.
Ciconiinæ, 69.
Cimolopteryx rarus, 335.
    retusus, 335.
Cinclidæ, 291.
Cinclus, 291.
    mexicanus, 291.
Circus, 127.

Circus hudsonius, 128.
Cistothorus, 301.
    marianæ, 303.
    palustris, 302.
    palustris griseus, 302.
    palustris paludicola, 302.
    stellaris, 301.
Clamatores, 179.
Clangula, 55.
    hyemalis, 55.
Clivicola, 259.
    riparia, 259.
Coccothraustes, 211.
    vespertinus, 211.
    vespertinus montanus, 211.
Coccyges, 153.
Coccyginæ, 153.
Coccyzus, 154.
    americanus, 154.
    americanus occidentalis, 155.
    erythrophthalmus, 155.
    minor, 154.
    minor maynardi, 154.
Cœligena, 173.
    clemenciæ, 174.
Cœreba, 267.
    bahamensis, 268.
Cœrebidæ, 267.
Colaptes, 166.
    auratus, 166.
    cafer, 167.
    cafer saturatior, 167.
    chrysoides, 167.
    rufipileus, 167.
Colinus, 106.
    ridgwayi, 107.
    virginianus, 106.
    virginianus floridanus, 106.
    virginianus texanus, 107.
Columba, 119.
    fasciata, 119.
    fasciata vioscæ, 120.
    flavirostris, 120.
    leucocephala, 120.
Columbæ, 119.
Columbidæ, 119.
Columbigallina, 122.
    passerina pallescens, 123.
    passerina terrestris, 122.
Colymbus, 1.
    auritus, 2.
    dominicus, 2.
    holbœlii, 1.
Colymbus nigricollis californicus, 2.
Compsohalieus, 43.
Compsothlypis, 273.
    americana, 273.

Compsothlypis nigrilora, 273.
Coniornis altus, 336.
Contopus, 185.
    borealis, 185.
    pertinax, 186.
    richardsonii, 186.
    richardsonii peninsulæ, 187.
    virens, 186.
Conurus, 152.
    carolinensis, 152.
Coot, American, 81.
    European, 81.
Cormorant, 42.
    Baird's, 44.
    Brandt's, 44.
    Double-crested, 42.
    Farallone, 43.
    Florida, 42.
    Mexican, 43.
    Pallas's, 327.
    Pelagic, 44.
    Red-faced, 45.
    Violet-green, 44.
    White-crested, 43.
Corvidæ, 194.
Corvinæ, 199.
Corvus, 199.
    americanus, 200.
    americanus floridanus, 200.
    caurinus, 201.
    corax principalis, 200.
    corax sinuatus, 200.
    cryptoleucus, 200.
    ossifragus, 201.
Cotingidæ, 179.
Coturnicops, 79.
Coturniculus, 226.
Cowbird, 203.
    Dwarf, 203.
    Red-eyed, 204.
Cracidæ, 119.
Crake, Corn, 80.
    Spotted, 78.
Crane, Little Brown, 75.
    Sandhill, 75.
    Whooping, 75.
Creagrus, 326.
    furcatus, 326.
Creciscus, 79.
Creeper, Bahama Honey, 268.
    Brown, 303.
    California, 304.
    Mexican, 303.
    Rocky Mountain, 303.
Crex, 80.
    crex, 80.
Crossbill, American, 214.
    Mexican, 215.

Crossbill, White-winged, 215.
Crotophaga, 153.
    ani, 153.
    sulcirostris, 153.
Crotophaginæ, 153.
Crow, American, 200.
    Fish, 201.
    Florida, 200.
    Northwest, 201.
Crymophilus, 82.
    fulicarius, 82.
Cuckoo, Black-billed, 155.
    California, 155.
    Kamchatkan, 155.
    Mangrove, 154.
    Maynard's, 154.
    Yellow-billed, 154.
Cuculi, 153.
Cuculidæ, 153.
Cuculus, 155.
    canorus telephonus, 155.
Curlew, Bristle-thighed, 98.
    Eskimo, 97.
    European, 328.
    Hudsonian, 97.
    Long-billed, 97.
Cyanecula, 321.
    suecica, 321.
Cyanocephalus, 201.
    cyanocephalus, 202.
Cyanocitta, 194.
    cristata, 194.
    cristata florincola, 195.
    stelleri, 195.
    stelleri annectens, 196.
    stelleri frontalis, 195.
    stelleri macrolopha, 195.
Cyclorrhynchus, 7.
    psittaculus, 7.
Cygninæ, 65.
Cygnus paloregonus, 341.
Cymodroma, 38.
    grallaria, 38.
Cypseli, 171.
Cypseloides, 171.
    niger, 171.
Cyrtonyx, 109.
    montezumæ, 110.
Cyrtopelicanus, 45.

DAFILA, 51.
    acuta, 51.
Daption, 35.
    capensis, 35.
Dendragapus, 110.
    canadensis, 111.
    franklinii, 111.

Fulmar, Rodgers's, 30.
    Slender-billed, 31.
Fulmarus, 30,
    glacialis, 30.
    glacialis glupischa, 30.
    glacialis minor, 30.
    glacialis rodgersii, 30.
    glacialoides, 31.

GADWALL, 49.
Galeoscoptes, 291.
    carolinensis, 291.
Gallinæ, 106.
Gallinago, 85.
    delicata, 85.
    gallinago, 85.
Gallinula, 81.
    galeata, 81.
Gallinule, Florida, 81.
    Purple, 80.
Gallinulinæ, 80.
Gannet, 41.
Garrulinæ, 194.
Garzetta, 72.
Gastornis giganteus, 338.
Gavia, 15.
    alba, 15.
Gelochelidon, 22.
    nilotica, 22.
Geococcyx, 153.
    californianus, 154.
Geothlypis, 282, 283.
    agilis, 282.
    beldingi, 284.
    formosa, 282.
    macgillivrayi, 283.
    philadelphia, 283.
    trichas, 283.
    trichas ignota, 284.
    trichas occidentalis, 284.
    poliocephala ralphi, 284.
Geotrygon, 123.
    martinica, 123.
    montana, 124.
Glaucidium, 150.
    gnoma, 150.
    gnoma californicum, 151.
    hoskinsii, 151.
    phalænoides, 151.
Glaucionetta, 54.
    clangula americana, 54.
    islandica, 54.
Glottis, 93.
Gnatcatcher, Black-tailed, 315.
    Blue-gray, 315.
    Plumbeous, 315.

Gnatcatcher, Western, 315.
Godwit, Black-tailed, 92.
    Hudsonian, 92.
    Marbled, 91.
    Pacific, 92.
Golden-eye, American, 54.
    Barrow's, 54.
Goldfinch, American, 218.
    Arizona, 219.
    Arkansas, 218.
    Black-headed, 219.
    Lawrence's, 219.
    Mexican, 219.
    Western, 218.
Goose, American White-fronted, 61.
    Barnacle, 63.
    Blue, 61.
    Cackling, 63.
    Canada, 62.
    Emperor, 64.
    Greater Snow, 60.
    Hutchins's, 62.
    Lesser Snow, 60.
    Ross's Snow, 61.
    White-cheeked, 62.
    White-fronted, 61.
Goshawk, American, 129.
    Mexican, 134.
    Western, 129.
Grackle, Boat-tailed, 211.
    Bronzed, 210.
    Florida, 210.
    Great-tailed, 210.
    Purple, 210.
Graculavus pumilus, 336.
    velox, 336.
Grassquit, 253.
    Melodius, 253.
Grebe, American Eared, 2.
    Clark's, 325.
    Holbœll's, 1.
    Horned, 2.
    Pied-billed, 3.
    St. Domingo, 2.
    Western, 1.
Green-shank, 93.
Grosbeak, Black-headed, 251.
    Blue, 251.
    Evening, 211.
    Pine, 212.
    Rose-breasted, 251.
    Western Blue, 250.
    Western Evening, 211.
Grouse, Canada, 111.
    Canadian Ruffed, 112.
    Columbian Sharp-tailed, 116.
    Dusky, 110.

Grouse, Franklin's, 111.
    Gray Ruffed, 112.
    Oregon Ruffed, 112.
    Prairie Sharp-tailed, 117.
    Richardson's, 111.
    Ruffed, 112.
    Sage, 117.
    Sharp-tailed, 116.
    Sooty, 110.
Grues, 75.
Gruidæ, 75.
Grus, 75.
    americana, 75.
    canadensis, 75.
    haydeni, 342.
    mexicana, 75.
    proavus, 342.
Guara, 67.
    alba, 67.
    rubra, 67.
Guillemot, Black, 10.
    Black-winged, 325.
    Mandt's, 10.
    Pigeon, 11.
    Sooty, 326.
Guiraca, 251.
    cærulea, 251.
    cærulea euryncha, 251.
Gull, American Herring, 19.
    Bonaparte's, 21.
    California, 19.
    Franklin's, 20.
    Glaucous, 16.
    Glaucous-winged, 17.
    Great Black-backed, 18.
    Herring, 18.
    Heermann's, 20.
    Iceland, 17.
    Ivory, 15.
    Kumlien's, 17.
    Laughing, 20.
    Little, 21.
    Mew, 20.
    Nelson's, 17.
    Pallas's, 89.
    Point Barrow, 16.
    Ring-billed, 19.
    Ross's, 21.
    Sabine's, 22.
    Short-billed, 20.
    Siberian, 18.
    Slaty-backed, 18.
    Swallow-tailed, 326.
Gull, Vega, 19.
    Western, 18.
Gypagus, 329.
    papa, 329.

Gyrfalcon, 137.
    Black, 137.
    Gray, 137.
    White, 136.

HABIA, 250.
    ludoviciana, 250.
    melanocephala, 251.
Hæmatopodidæ, 104.
Hæmatopus, 104.
    bachmani, 105.
    frazari, 105.
    ostralegus, 104.
    palliatus, 104.
Haliplana, 26.
Halocyptena, 35.
    microsoma, 35.
Haliæetus, 136.
    albicilla, 136.
    leucocephalus, 136.
Harporhynchus, 292, 294.
    bendirei, 293.
    cinereus, 294.
    cinereus mearnsi, 294.
    crissalis, 295.
    curvirostris, 293.
    curvirostris palmeri, 293.
    lecontei, 294.
    longirostris sennetti, 293.
    redivivus, 294.
    rufus, 293.
Hawk, American Rough-legged, 134.
    American Sparrow, 140.
    Desert Sparrow, 140.
    Broad-winged, 133.
    Cooper's, 128.
    Cuban Sparrow, 140.
    Duck, 138.
    Florida Red-shouldered, 131.
    Harlan's, 131.
    Harris's, 129.
    Krider's, 130.
    Marsh, 128.
    Mexican Black, 133.
    Pigeon, 138.
    Red-bellied, 132.
    Red-shouldered, 131.
    Red-tailed, 130.
    Rough-legged, 134.
    Sennett's White-tailed, 132.
    Sharp-shinned, 128.
    Short-tailed, 133.
    St. Lucas Sparrow, 140.
    Swainson's, 132.
    Zone-tailed, 132.
Heleodytes, 295.

Dendragapus obscurus, 110.
    obscurus fuliginosus, 110.
    obscurus richardsonii, 111.
Dendrocygna, 64.
    autumnalis, 64.
    fulva, 64.
Dendroica, 273, 274.
    æstiva, 274.
    æstiva sonorana, 274.
    auduboni, 275.
    blackburniæ, 277.
    bryanti castaneiceps, 275.
    cærulea, 276.
    cærulescens, 275.
    carbonata, 332.
    castanea, 277.
    chrysoparia, 278.
    coronata, 275.
    discolor, 281.
    dominica, 277.
    dominica albilora, 278.
    graciæ, 278.
    kirtlandi, 280.
    maculosa, 276.
    montana, 333.
    nigrescens, 278.
    occidentalis, 279.
    olivacea, 274.
    palmarum, 280.
    palmarum hypochrysea, 280.
    pensylvanica, 276.
    striata, 277.
    tigrina, 273.
    townsendi, 279.
    vigorsii, 280.
    virens, 279.
Dichromanassa, 72.
Dickcissel, 254.
Diomedea, 28.
    albatrus, 28.
    exulans, 326.
    nigripes, 28.
Diomedeidæ, 28, 326.
Dipper, American, 291.
Dolichonyx, 202.
    oryzivorus, 202.
Dove, Ground, 122.
    Inca, 123.
    Mexican Ground, 123.
    Mourning, 121.
    White-fronted, 122.
    White-winged, 122.
    Zenaida, 121.
Dovekie, 13.
Dowitcher, 85.
    Long-billed, 86.
Dryobates, 158.

Dryobates arizonæ, 161.
    borealis, 160.
    nuttallii, 161.
    pubescens, 159.
    pubescens gairdnerii, 159.
    pubescens oreœcus, 160.
    scalaris bairdi, 160.
    scalaris lucasanus, 160.
    villosus, 158.
    villosus audubonii, 158.
    villosus harrisii, 159.
    villosus hyloscopus, 159.
    villosus leucomelas, 158.
Duck, American Scaup, 53.
    Black, 48.
    Florida, 48.
    Harlequin, 55.
    Labrador, 56.
    Lesser Scaup, 53.
    Masked, 60.
    Mottled, 49.
    Ring-necked, 53.
    Ruddy, 59.
    Rufous-crested, 52.
    Steller's, 55.
    Wood, 52.
Dunlin, 89.
Dysporus, 41.
Dytes, 2.

EAGLE, Bald, 136.
    Golden, 135.
    Gray Sea, 136.
    Harpy, 135.
Ectopistes, 120.
    migratorius, 120.
Egret, American, 71.
    Peale's, 328.
    Reddish, 72.
Eider, American, 57.
    King, 58.
    Northern, 57.
    Pacific, 57.
    Spectacled, 56.
Elanoides, 126.
    forficatus, 126.
Elanus, 126.
    leucurus, 126.
Embernagra, 245.
    rufivirgata, 245.
Empidonax, 187.
    cineritius, 187.
    difficilis, 187.
    flaviventris, 187.
    fulvifrons, 189.
    fulvifrons pygmæus, 189.

Empidonax griseus, 189.
    hammondi, 189.
    minimus, 188.
    traillii, 188.
    traillii alnorum, 188.
    virescens, 188.
    wrightii, 189.
Eniconetta, 56.
    stelleri, 56.
Ereunetes, 90.
    occidentalis, 91.
    pusillus, 90.
Erionetta, 57.
Ergaticus, 287.
    ruber, 288.
Erismatura, 59.
    rubida, 59.
Euetheia, 253.
    bicolor, 253.
    canora, 253.
Eugenes, 173.
    fulgens, 173.
Euphonia, 254.
    elegantissima, 255.
Euphonia, Blue-headed, 255.
Eurynorhynchus, 90.
    pygmæus, 90.

FALCO, 136.
    columbarius, 138.
    columbarius suckleyi, 139.
    dominicensis, 140.
    fusco-cœrulescens, 139.
    islandus, 136.
    mexicanus, 137.
    peregrinus anatum, 138.
    peregrinus pealei, 138.
    regulus, 139.
    richardsonii, 139.
    rusticolus, 137.
    rusticolus gyrfalco, 137.
    rusticolus obsoletus, 137.
    sparverius, 140.
    sparverius deserticolus, 140.
    sparverius peninsularis, 140.
    tinnunculus, 140.
Falcon, Aplomado, 139.
    Peale's, 138.
    Prairie, 137.
Falcones, 126.
Falconidæ, 126, 329.
Falconinæ, 136.
Finch, California Purple, 213.
    Cassin's Purple, 213.
    Guadalupe House, 214.
    House, 213.

Finch, Purple, 213.
    St. Lucas House, 214.
Flamingo, American, 66.
Flicker, 166.
    Gilded, 167.
    Guadalupe, 167.
    Northwestern, 167.
    Red-shafted, 167.
Florida, 73.
Flycatcher, Alder, 188.
    Arizona Crested, 183.
    Ash-throated, 183.
    Beardless, 190.
    Buff-breasted, 189.
    Coues's, 186.
    Crested, 183.
    Derby, 182.
    Fork-tailed, 179.
    Fulvous, 189.
    Giraud's, 182.
    Gray, 189.
    Green-crested, 188.
    Hammond's, 189.
    Lawrence's, 184.
    Least, 188.
    Mexican Crested, 183.
    Nutting's, 183.
    Olivaceous, 184.
    Olive-sided, 185.
    Ridgway's, 190.
    St. Lucas, 187.
    Scissor-tailed, 180.
    Sulphur-bellied, 182.
    Traill's, 188.
    Vermilion, 190.
    Western, 187.
    Wright's, 189.
    Yellow-bellied, 187.
Fratercula, 5.
    arctica, 5.
    arctica glacialis, 5.
    corniculata, 6.
Fraterculinæ, 5.
Fregata, 46.
    aquila, 46.
Fregatidæ, 46.
Fringillidæ, 211.
Fulica, 81.
    americana, 81.
    atra, 81.
    minor, 342.
Fulicinæ, 81.
Fuligula, 53.
Fulmar, 30.
    Giant, 29.
    Lesser, 30.
    Pacific, 30.

Heleodytes brunneicapillus, 295.
    brunneicapillus affinis, 296.
    brunneicapillus bryanti, 295.
Helinaia, 269.
    swainsonii, 269.
Helminthophila, 269.
    bachmani, 270.
    celata, 272.
    celata lutescens, 272.
    celata sordida, 272.
    chrysoptera, 270.
    cincinnatiensis, 332.
    lawrencei, 331.
    leucobronchialis, 332.
    luciæ, 270.
    peregrina, 272.
    pinus, 270.
    ruficapilla, 271.
    ruficapilla gutturalis, 271.
    virginiæ, 271.
Helmitherus, 269.
    vermivorus, 269.
Helodromas, 93.
Hen, Attwater's Prairie, 115.
    Heath, 115.
    Lesser Prairie, 116.
    Prairie, 115.
Henhawk, Cooper's, 329.
Herodias, 71.
Herodii, 69.
Herodiones, 66.
Heron, Black-crowned Night, 74.
    European Blue, 71.
    Frazar's Green, 73.
    Great Blue, 71.
    Great White, 71.
    Green, 73.
    Little Blue, 73.
    Louisiana, 72.
    Snowy, 72.
    Ward's, 71.
    Würdemann's, 327.
    Yellow-crowned Night, 74.
Hesperiphona, 211.
Hesperocichla, 320.
    nævia, 321.
Hesperornis crassipes, 336.
    gracilis, 336.
    regalis, 336.
Heteractitis, 95.
    incana, 95.
Hierofalco, 136.
Himantopus, 83.
    mexicanus, 84.
Hirundinidæ, 256.
Histrionicus, 55.
    histrionicus, 55.

Hummingbird, Allen's, 176.
    Anna's, 175.
    Black-chinned, 174.
    Blue-throated, 174.
    Broad-billed, 178.
    Broad-tailed, 175.
    Buff-bellied, 177.
    Calliope, 176.
    Costa's, 175.
    Floresi's, 175.
    Lucifer, 177.
    Rieffer's, 177.
    Rivoli, 173.
    Ruby-throated, 174.
    Rufous, 176.
    Violet-throated, 174.
    White-eared, 178.
    Xantus's, 178.
Hydranassa, 72.
Hydrochelidon, 26.
    leucoptera, 27.
    nigra surinamensis, 26.
Hylocichla, 316.
Hylophilus, 331.
    decurtatus, 331.
Hylophilus, Short-winged, 331.

IACHE, 178.
    latirostris, 178.
Ibides, 66.
Ibididæ, 67.
Ibis, Glossy, 68.
    Scarlet, 67.
    White, 67.
    White-faced Glossy, 68.
    Wood, 69.
Ichthyornis agilis, 336.
    anceps, 337.
    dispar, 337.
    lentus, 337.
    tener, 337.
    validus, 337.
    victor, 337.
Icteria, 284.
    virens, 285.
    virens longicauda, 285.
Icteridæ, 202.
Icterus, 206.
    audubonii, 207.
    bullocki, 208.
    cucullatus, 207.
    cucullatus nelsoni, 208.
    galbula, 208.
    icterus, 207.
    parisorum, 207.
    spurius, 208.

Ictinia, 127.
  mississippiensis, 127.
Ionornis, 80.
  martinica, 80.

JABIRU, 69.
Jacana, 105.
  spinosa, 105.
Jaçana, Mexican, 105.
Jacanidæ, 105.
Jaeger, Parasitic, 14.
  Pomarine, 14.
  Long-tailed, 15.
Jay, Alaskan, 199.
  Arizona, 198.
  Belding's, 197.
  Black-headed, 196.
  Blue, 194.
  Blue-eared, 197.
  Blue-fronted, 195.
  California, 197.
  Canada, 198.
  Florida, 196.
  Florida Blue, 195.
  Green, 198.
  Labrador, 199.
  Long-crested, 195.
  Oregon, 199.
  Piñon, 202.
  Rocky Mountain, 199.
  Santa Cruz, 197.
  Steller's, 195.
  Woodhouse's, 196.
  Xantus's, 197.
Junco, 234.
  aikeni, 234.
  annectens, 235.
  bairdi, 237.
  caniceps, 236.
  phæonotus dorsalis, 236.
  phæonotus palliatus, 236.
  hyemalis, 234.
  hyemalis carolinensis, 235.
  hyemalis oregonus, 234.
  hyemalis pinosus, 235.
  hyemalis shufeldti, 235.
  hyemalis thurberi, 235.
  insularis, 237.
  ridgwayi, 236.
  townsendi, 237.
Junco, Arizona, 236.
  Baird's, 237.
  Carolina, 235.
  Gray-headed, 236.
  Guadalupe, 237.
  Oregon, 234.

Junco, Pink-sided, 235.
  Point Pinos, 235.
  Red-backed, 236.
  Ridgway's, 236.
  Slate-colored, 234.
  Shufeldt's, 236.
  Thurber's, 235.
  Townsend's, 237.
  White-winged, 234.

KESTREL, 140.
Killdeer, 100.
Kingbird, 180.
  Arkansas, 181.
  Cassin's, 181.
  Couch's, 181.
  Gray, 180.
Kingfisher, Belted, 156.
  Ringed, 157.
  Texan, 157.
Kinglet, Cuvier's, 333.
  Dusky, 314.
  Golden-crowned, 313.
  Ruby-crowned, 314.
  Western Golden-crowned, 314.
Kite, Everglade, 127.
  Mississippi, 127.
  Swallow-tailed, 126.
  White-tailed, 126.
Kittiwake, 15.
  Pacific, 16.
  Red-legged, 16.
Knot, 86.

LAGOPUS, 113.
  lagopus, 113.
  lagopus alleni, 113.
  leucurus, 114.
  rupestris, 113.
  rupestris atkhensis, 114.
  rupestris nelsoni, 114.
  rupestris reinhardi, 114.
  welchi, 114.
Laniidæ, 261.
Lanius, 261.
  borealis, 261.
  ludovicianus, 262.
  ludovicianus gambeli, 262.
  ludovicianus excubitorides, 262.
Lanivireo, 297.
Laopteryx priscus, 335.
Laornis edvardsianus, 337.
Lapwing, 98.
Laridæ, 15, 326.
Larinæ, 15.

INDEX.   359

Lark, Desert Horned, 192.
   Dusky Horned, 193.
   Horned, 191.
   Mexican Horned, 192.
   Pallid Horned, 192.
   Prairie Horned, 192.
   Ruddy Horned, 193.
   Scorched Horned, 193.
   Sonoran Horned, 193.
   Streaked Horned, 193.
   Texan Horned, 192.
Larus, 16.
   affinis, 18.
   argentatus, 18.
   argentatus smithsonianus, 19.
   atricilla, 20.
   barrovianus, 16.
   brachyrhynchus, 20.
   cachinnans, 19.
   californicus, 89.
   canus, 20.
   delawarensis, 19.
   franklinii, 20.
   glaucescens, 17.
   glaucus, 16.
   heermanni, 20.
   kumlieni, 17.
   leucopterus, 17.
   marinus, 18.
   minutus, 21.
   nelsoni, 17.
   occidentalis, 18.
   oregonus, 339.
   philadelphia, 21.
   robustus, 339.
   schistisagus, 18.
   vegæ, 19.
Leptopelicanus, 46.
Leptotila, 121.
   fulviventris brachyptera, 122.
Leucosticte, 215.
   atrata, 216.
   australis, 216.
   griseonucha, 215.
   tephrocotis, 215.
   tephrocotis littoralis, 216.
Leucosticte, Aleutian, 215.
   Black, 216.
   Brown-capped, 216.
   Gray-crowned, 215.
   Hepburn's, 216.
Limicolæ, 82.
Limosa, 91.
   fedoa, 91.
   hæmastica, 92.
   lapponica baueri, 92.
   limosa, 92.

Limpkin, 76.
Linnet, Brewster's, 330.
Longipennes, 13.
Longspur, Chestnut-collared, 222.
   Lapland, 221.
   McCown's, 222.
   Smith's, 221.
Loon, 3.
   Black-throated, 4.
   Pacific, 4.
   Red-throated, 4.
   Yellow-billed, 4.
Lophodytes, 47.
   cucullatus, 48.
Lophophanes, 306.
Lophortyx, 109.
Loxia, 214.
   curvirostra minor, 214.
   curvirostra stricklandi, 215.
   leucoptera, 215.
Lunda, 5.
   cirrhata, 5.

MACROCHIRES, 168.
Macrorhamphus, 85.
   griseus, 85.
   scolopaceus, 86.
Magpie, American, 194.
   Yellow-billed, 194.
Mallard, 48.
Man-o'-War Bird, 46.
Mareca, 49.
Martin, Cuban, 257.
   Purple, 257.
   Western, 257.
Meadowlark, 206.
   Mexican, 206.
   Western, 206.
Megalestris, 13.
   skua, 14.
Megaquiscalus, 210.
Megascops, 145.
   asio, 145.
   asio aikeni, 147.
   asio bendirei, 146.
   asio cineraceus, 146.
   asio floridanus, 145.
   asio kennicottii, 146.
   asio macfarlanei, 147.
   asio maxwelliæ, 146.
   asio trichopsis, 145.
   flammeola, 147.
   flammeola idahoensis, 147.
Melanerpes, 164.
   aurifrons, 166.
   carolinus, 166.

Melanerpes erythrocephalus, 164.
    formicivorus angustifrons, 165.
    formicivorus bairdi, 165.
    torquatus, 165.
    uropygialis, 166.
Melanitta, 58.
Meleagrinæ, 117.
Meleagris, 117.
    altus, 344.
    antiquus, 343.
    celer, 344.
    gallopavo, 118.
    gallopavo ellioti, 118.
    gallopavo mexicana, 118.
    gallopavo osceola, 118.
Melopelia, 122.
    leucoptera, 122.
Melospiza, 240.
    cinerea, 243.
    fasciata, 241.
    fasciata clementæ, 243.
    fasciata fallax, 241.
    fasciata graminea, 242.
    fasciata guttata, 242.
    fasciata heermanni, 241.
    fasciata montana, 241.
    fasciata rivularis, 242.
    fasciata rufina, 242.
    fasciata samuelis, 241.
    georgiana, 244.
    insignis, 243.
    lincolni, 243.
    lincolni striata, 243.
Merganser, 47.
    americanus, 47.
    serrator, 47.
Merganser, American, 47.
    Hooded, 48.
    Red-breasted, 47.
Merginæ, 47.
Merlin, 139.
    Black, 139.
    Richardson's, 139.
Merula, 319.
    confinis, 320.
    migratoria, 320.
    migratoria propinqua, 320.
Methriopterus, 292.
Micropalama, 86.
    himantopus, 86.
Micropallas, 151.
    whitneyi, 151.
Micropodidæ, 171.
Micropodinæ, 172.
Milvulus, 179.
    forficatus, 180.
    tyrannus, 179.

Miminæ, 291.
Mimus, 291.
    polyglottos, 292.
Mniotilta, 268.
    varia, 268.
Mniotiltidæ, 268, 331.
Mockingbird, 292.
Molothrus, 203.
    ater, 203.
    ater obscurus, 203.
Motacilla, 288.
    alba, 289.
    ocularis, 289.
Motacillidæ, 288.
Murre, 11.
    Brünnich's, 12.
    California, 11.
    Pallas's, 12.
Murrelet, Ancient, 8.
    Craveri's, 10.
    Kittlitz's, 9.
    Marbled, 9.
    Xantus's, 9.
Myadestes, 316.
    townsendii, 316.
Myadestinæ, 316.
Mycteria, 69.
    americana, 69.
Myiarchus, 182.
    cinerascens, 183.
    cinerascens nuttingi, 183.
    crinitus, 183.
    lawrenceii, 184.
    lawrenceii olivascens, 184.
    mexicanus, 183.
    mexicanus magister, 183.
Myiozetetes, 182.
    texensis, 182.
Myiodynastes, 182.
    luteiventris, 182.

NEOCORYS, 290.
Netta, 52.
    rufina, 52.
Nettion, 50.
Nighthawk, 170.
    Florida, 171.
    Sennett's, 330.
    Texan, 171.
    Western, 170.
Noddy, 27.
Nomonyx, 60.
    dominicus, 60.
Nucifraga, 201.
    columbianus, 201.
Numenius, 97.

INDEX. 361

Numenius arquatus, 328.
  borealis, 97.
  hudsonicus, 97.
  longirostris, 97.
  phæopus, 98.
  tahitiensis, 98.
Nutcracker, Clarke's, 201.
Nuthatch, Brown-headed, 305.
  Florida White-breasted, 304.
  Pygmy, 305.
  Red-breasted, 305.
  Slender-billed, 304.
  White-breasted, 304.
  White-naped, 305.
Nuttallornis, 185.
Nyctala, 144.
  acadica, 145.
  tengmalmi richardsoni, 144.
Nyctanassa, 74.
Nyctea, 149.
  nyctea, 149.
Nycticorax, 74.
  nycticorax nævius, 74.
  violaceus, 74.
Nyctidromus, 170.
  albicollis merrilli, 170.

OCEANITES, 37.
  oceanicus, 37.
Oceanitinæ, 37.
Oceanodroma, 36.
  furcata, 36.
  homochroa, 37.
  hornbyi, 327.
  leucorhoa, 36.
  macrodactyla, 37.
  melania, 37.
Ochthodromus, 102.
Odontoglossæ, 66.
Oidemia, 58.
  americana, 58.
  deglandi, 59.
  fusca, 58.
  perspicillata, 59.
Old-squaw, 55.
Olor, 65.
  buccinator, 65.
  columbianus, 65.
  cygnus, 65.
Oporornis, 282.
Oreortyx, 107.
  pictus, 107.
  pictus confinis, 108.
  pictus plumiferus, 107.
Oriole, Arizona Hooded, 208.
  Audubon's, 207.

Oriole, Baltimore, 208.
  Bullock's, 208.
  Hooded, 207.
  Orchard, 208.
  Scott's, 207.
Ornithion, 190.
  imberbe, 190.
  imberbe ridgwayi, 190.
Oroscoptes, 291.
  montanus, 291.
Ortalis, 119.
  vetula maccali, 119.
Oscines, 238.
Osprey, American, 141.
Ossifraga, 29.
  gigantea, 29.
Otocoris, 191.
  alpestris, 191.
  alpestris adusta, 193.
  alpestris arenicola, 192.
  alpestris chrysolæma, 192.
  alpestris giraudi, 192.
  alpestris leucolæma, 192.
  alpestris merrilli, 193.
  alpestris pallida, 193.
  alpestris praticola, 192.
  alpestris rubea, 193.
  alpestris strigata, 193.
Oven-bird, 281.
Owl, American Barn, 142.
  Aiken's Screech, 147.
  American Hawk, 149.
  American Long-eared, 142.
  Arctic Horned, 148.
  Barred, 143.
  Burrowing, 150.
  California Pygmy, 151.
  California Screech, 146.
  Dusky Horned, 148.
  Dwarf Screech, 147.
  Elf, 151.
  Ferruginous Pygmy, 151.
  Flammulated Screech, 147.
  Florida Barred, 143.
  Florida Burrowing, 150.
  Florida Screech, 145.
  Great Gray, 144.
  Great Horned, 148.
  Hawk, 149.
  Hoskins's Pygmy, 151.
  Kennicott's Screech, 146.
  Lapp, 144.
  MacFarlane's Screech, 147.
  Mexican Screech, 146.
  Pygmy, 150.
  Richardson's, 144.
  Rocky Mountain Screech, 145.

Owl, Saw-whet, 145.
   Screech, 145.
   Short-eared, 142.
   Snowy, 149.
   Spotted, 143.
   Texas Screech, 145.
   Western Horned, 148.
Oxyechus, 100.
Oyster-catcher, 104.
   American, 104.
   Black, 105.
   Frazar's, 105.

PALÆOBORUS umbrosus, 344.
Palæospiza bella, 345.
Palæotetrix gilli, 343.
Palæotringa littoralis, 337.
   vagans, 338.
   vetus, 338.
Paludicolæ, 75.
Pandion, 141.
   haliaëtus carolinensis, 141.
Pandioninæ, 141.
Parabuteo, 129.
   unicinctus harrisi, 129.
Parauque, Merrill's, 170.
Paridæ, 304.
Parinæ, 332.
Paroquet, Carolina, 152.
Parrot, Thick-billed, 330.
Partridge, California, 109.
   Chestnut-bellied Scaled, 108.
   Gambel's, 109.
   Massena, 110.
   Mountain, 107.
   Plumed, 107.
   San Pedro, 108.
   Scaled, 108.
   Valley, 109.
Parus, 306.
   atricapillus, 307.
   atricapillus occidentalis, 308.
   atricapillus septentrionalis, 308.
   atricristatus, 306.
   bicolor, 306.
   bicolor texensis, 306.
   carolinensis, 308.
   carolinensis agilis, 308.
   cinctus obtectus, 309.
   gambeli, 309.
   hudsonicus, 309.
   hudsonicus columbianus, 310.
   hudsonicus stoneyi, 309.
   inornatus, 306.
   inornatus cineraceus, 307.
   inornatus griseus, 307.

Parus meridionalis, 309.
   rufescens, 310.
   rufescens neglectus, 310.
   wollweberi, 307.
Passerculus, 223.
Passerella, 244.
   iliaca, 244.
   iliaca megarhyncha, 245.
   iliaca schistacea, 245.
   iliaca unalaschensis, 244.
Passeres, 179.
Passerina, 251.
   amœna, 252.
   ciris, 252.
   cyanea, 252.
   versicolor, 252.
   versicolor pulchra, 252.
Pavoncella, 95.
   pugnax, 95.
Pediocætes, 116.
   lucasi, 343.
   nanus, 343.
   phasianellus, 116.
   phasianellus campestris, 117.
   phasianellus columbianus, 116.
Pelagodroma, 38.
   marina, 38.
Pelecanidæ, 45.
Pelecanus, 45.
   californicus, 46.
   erythrorhynchos, 45.
   fuscus, 46.
Pelican, American White, 45.
   Brown, 46.
   California Brown, 46.
Pelidna, 89.
Pelionetta, 59.
Pendulinus, 207.
Penelopes, 118.
Penelopinæ, 118.
Perdicinæ, 106.
Perisoreus, 198.
   canadensis, 198.
   canadensis capitalis, 199.
   canadensis fumifrons, 199.
   canadensis nigricapillus, 199.
   obscurus, 199.
Perissoglossa, 273.
Petrel, Ashy, 37.
   Black, 37.
   Black-capped, 34.
   Bulwer's, 35.
   Fisher's, 34.
   Fork-tailed, 36.
   Guadalupe, 37.
   Hornby's, 327.
   Leach's, 36.

Petrel, Least, 35.
    Pintado, 35.
    Scaled, 34.
    Stormy, 36.
    White-bellied, 38.
    White-faced, 38.
    Wilson's, 37.
Petrochelidon, 257.
    fulva, 258.
    lunifrons, 257.
Peucæa, 238.
    æstivalis, 238.
    æstivalis bachmanii, 239.
    arizonæ, 239.
    carpalis, 240.
    cassini, 239.
    mexicana, 239.
    ruficeps, 240.
    ruficeps boucardi, 240.
    ruficeps eremœca, 240.
Peucedramus, 274.
Pewee, Large-billed, 187.
    Western Wood, 186.
    Wood, 186.
Phaëthon, 39.
    æthereus, 39.
    flavirostris, 39.
Phaëthontidæ, 39.
Phainopepla, 261.
    nitens, 261.
Phalacrocoracidæ, 42, 327.
Phalacrocorax, 42.
    carbo, 42.
    dilophus, 42.
    dilophus albociliatus, 43.
    dilophus cincinatus, 43.
    dilophus floridanus, 42.
    idahensis, 340.
    macropus, 340.
    mexicanus, 43.
    pelagicus, 44.
    pelagicus resplendens, 44.
    pelagicus robustus, 44.
    penicillatus, 44.
    perspicillatus, 327.
    urile, 45.
Phalænoptilus, 169.
    nuttallii, 169.
    nuttallii californicus, 169.
    nuttallii nitidus, 169.
Phalarope, Northern, 82.
    Red, 82.
    Wilson's, 83.
Phalaropodidæ, 82.
Phalaropus, 82.
    lobatus, 82.
    tricolor, 83.

Phalerinæ, 6.
Phaleris, 8.
Phasiani, 106.
Phasianidæ, 117.
Philacte, 64.
    canagica, 64.
Philohela, 84.
    minor, 84.
Phœbe, 184.
    Black, 185.
    Say's, 185.
Phœbetria, 29.
    fuliginosa, 29.
Phœnicopteridæ, 66.
Phœnicopterus, 66.
    copei, 341.
    ruber, 66.
Phyllopseustes, 313.
    borealis, 313.
Pica, 194.
    nuttalli, 194.
    pica hudsonica, 194.
Pici, 157.
Picidæ, 157.
Picoides, 161.
    americanus, 162.
    americanus alascensis, 162.
    americanus dorsalis, 162.
    arcticus, 162.
Picicorvus, 201.
Pigeon, Band-tailed, 119.
    Passenger, 120.
    Red-billed, 120.
    Viosca's, 119.
    White-crowned, 120.
Pinicola, 212.
    enucleator, 212.
Pintail, 51.
Pipilo, 245.
    alberti, 248.
    chlorurus, 247.
    consobrinus, 247.
    erythrophthalmus, 246.
    erythrophthalmus alleni, 246.
    fuscus albigula, 248.
    fuscus crissalis, 248.
    fuscus mesoleucus, 247.
    fuscus senicula, 248.
    maculatus arcticus, 246.
    maculatus megalonyx, 246.
    maculatus oregonus, 247.
Pipit, American, 289.
    Meadow, 291.
    Red-throated, 290.
    Sprague's, 290.
Piranga, 255.
    erythromelas, 255.

Piranga hepatica, 256.
    ludoviciana, 255.
    rubra, 256.
    rubra cooperi, 256.
    rubriceps, 255.
Pitangus, 181.
    derbianus, 182.
Plataleidæ, 66.
Platypsaris, 179.
    albiventris, 179.
Plautus, 12.
    impennis, 13.
Plectrophenax, 220.
    hyperboreus, 221.
    nivalis, 220.
    nivalis townsendi, 220.
Plegadis, 68.
    autumnalis, 68.
    guarauna, 68.
Plover, American Golden, 99.
    Belted Piping, 101.
    Black-bellied, 99.
    Golden, 99.
    Little Ring, 101.
    Mongolian, 102.
    Mountain, 103.
    Pacific Golden, 100.
    Piping, 101.
    Ring, 101.
    Semipalmated, 100.
    Snowy, 102.
    Wilson's, 102.
Podasocys, 102.
Podiceps, 2.
Podicipedes, 1.
Podicipidæ, 1, 325.
Podilymbus, 3.
    podiceps, 3.
Polioptila, 314.
    cærulea, 315.
    cærulea obscura, 315.
    californica, 315.
    plumbea, 315.
Polioptilinæ, 314.
Polyborus, 141.
    cheriway, 141.
    lutosus, 141.
Poocætes, 222.
    gramineus, 222.
    gramineus affinis, 223.
    gramineus confinis, 223.
Poor-will, 169.
    Dusky, 169.
    Frosted, 169.
Porzana, 78.
    carolina, 79.
    coturniculus, 80.

Porzana jamaicensis, 79.
    noveboracensis, 79.
    porzana, 78.
Priocella, 31.
Priofinus, 33.
Procellaria, 36.
    pelagica, 36.
Procellariidæ, 29, 327.
Procellariinæ, 29.
Progne, 256.
    cryptoleuca, 257.
    subis, 257.
    subis hesperia, 257.
Protonotaria, 268.
    citrea, 268.
Psaltriparus, 311.
    lloydi, 312.
    minimus, 311.
    minimus californicus, 311.
    minimus grindæ, 312.
    plumbeus, 312.
    santaritæ, 312.
Pseudogryphus, 124.
    californianus, 125.
Psittaci, 152.
Psittacidæ, 152, 330.
Ptarmigan, Allen's, 113.
    Nelson's, 114.
    Reinhardt's, 114.
    Rock, 113.
    Turner's, 114.
    Welch's, 114.
    White-tailed, 114.
    Willow, 113.
Ptiliogonatinæ, 261.
Ptychoramphus, 6.
    aleuticus, 7.
Puffin, 5.
    Horned, 6.
    Large-billed, 5.
    Tufted, 5.
Puffinus, 31.
    auduboni, 32.
    borealis, 31.
    cinereus, 33.
    conradii, 340.
    creatopus, 32.
    gavia, 32.
    griseus, 33.
    kuhlii, 327.
    major, 31.
    puffinus, 32.
    stricklandi, 32.
    tenuirostris, 33.
Pygopodes, 1.
Pyrocephalus, 190.
    rubineus mexicanus, 190.

Pyrrhula, 212.
   cassini, 212.
Pyrrhuloxia, 249.
   sinuata, 250.
   sinuata beckhami, 250.
   sinuata peninsulæ, 250.
Pyrrhuloxia, Arizona, 250.
   Saint Lucas, 250.

Quail-Dove, Blue-headed, 124.
   Key West, 123.
   Ruddy, 124.
Querquedula, 50.
Quiscalus, 209.
   macrourus, 210.
   major, 211.
   quiscula, 210.
   quiscula æneus, 210.
   quiscula aglæus, 210.

Rail, Belding's, 77.
   Black, 79.
   California Clapper, 77.
   Caribbean Clapper, 78.
   Clapper, 77.
   Farallone, 80.
   Florida Clapper, 78.
   King, 76.
   Louisiana Clapper, 77.
   Virginia, 78.
   Yellow, 79.
Ralli, 76.
Rallidæ, 76.
Rallinæ, 76.
Rallus, 76.
   beldingi, 77.
   elegans, 76.
   crepitans, 77.
   crepitans saturatus, 77.
   longirostris caribæus, 78.
   obsoletus, 77.
   scottii, 78.
   virginianus, 78.
Raptores, 124.
Raven, American, 200.
   Northern, 200.
   White-necked, 200.
Ratitæ, 338.
Recurvirostra, 83.
   americana, 83.
Recurvirostridæ, 83.
Redhead, 52.
Redpoll, 217.
   Greenland, 217.

Redpoll, Greater, 218.
   Hoary, 217.
   Holbœll's, 217.
Redstart, American, 286.
   Painted, 287.
   Red-bellied, 287.
Red-tail, St. Lucas, 131.
   Western, 130.
Regulinæ, 313.
Regulus, 313.
   calendula, 314.
   cuvieri, 333.
   obscurus, 314.
   satrapa, 313.
   satrapa olivaceus, 314.
Rhodostethia, 21.
   rosea, 21.
Rhynchodon, 138.
Rhynchofalco, 139.
Rhynchophanes, 222.
   mccownii, 222.
Rhynchopsitta, 330.
   pachyrhynca, 330.
Rissa, 15.
   brevirostris, 16.
   tridactyla, 15.
   tridactyla pollicaris, 16.
Road-runner, 154.
Robin, American, 320.
   St. Lucas, 320.
   Western, 320.
Rostrhamus, 127.
   sociabilis, 127.
Rough-leg, Ferruginous, 135.
Ruff, 95.
Rynchopidæ, 27.
Rynchops, 27.
   nigra, 27.

Salpinctes, 296.
   guadeloupensis, 296.
   obsoletus, 296.
Sanderling, 91.
Sandpiper, Aleutian, 87.
   Baird's, 88.
   Bartramian, 96.
   Buff-breasted, 96.
   Cooper's, 328.
   Curlew, 90.
   Green, 94.
   Least, 89.
   Pectoral, 88.
   Pribilof, 87.
   Purple, 87.
   Red-backed, 89.
   Semipalmated, 90.

Sandpiper, Sharp-tailed, 88.
　Solitary, 94.
　Spoonbill, 90.
　Spotted, 97.
　Stilt, 86.
　Western, 91.
　Western Solitary, 94.
　White-rumped, 88.
Sapsucker, Red-breasted, 163.
　Red-naped, 163.
　Williamson's, 163.
　Yellow-bellied, 163.
Sarcorhamphi, 124.
Saxicola, 321.
　œnanthe, 321.
Sayornis, 184.
　nigricans, 185.
　phœbe, 184.
　saya, 185.
Scardafella, 123.
　inca, 123.
Scolecophagus, 209.
　affinis, 345.
　carolinus, 209.
　cyanocephalus, 209.
Scolopacidæ, 84, 328.
Scolopax, 84.
　rusticola, 84.
Scoter, American, 58.
　Surf, 59.
　Velvet, 58.
　White-winged, 59.
Scotiaptex, 144.
　cinerea, 144.
　cinerea lapponica, 144.
Seed-eater, Sharpe's, 253.
Seiurus, 281.
　aurocapillus, 281.
　motacilla, 282.
　noveboracensis, 281.
　noveboracensis notabilis, 281.
Selasphorus, 175.
　alleni, 176.
　floresii, 175.
　platycercus, 175.
　rufus, 176.
Setophaga, 286.
　miniata, 287.
　picta, 287.
　ruticilla, 286.
Shearwater, Audubon's, 32.
　Black-tailed, 33.
　Black-vented, 32.
　Cinereous, 327.
　Cory's, 31.
　Dark-bodied, 33.
　Greater, 31.

Shearwater, Manx, 32.
　Pink-footed, 32.
　Slender-billed, 33.
　Sooty, 32.
Shoveller, 51.
Shrike, California, 262.
　Loggerhead, 262.
　Northern, 261.
　White-rumped, 262.
Sialia, 322.
　arctica, 323.
　mexicana anabelæ, 322.
　mexicana bairdi, 323.
　mexicana occidentalis, 322.
　sialis, 322.
　sialis azurea, 322.
Simorhynchus, 7.
　cristatellus, 7.
　pusillus, 8.
　pygmæus, 8.
Siskin, Pine, 220.
Sitta, 304.
　canadensis, 305.
　carolinensis, 304.
　carolinensis aculeata, 304.
　carolinensis atkinsi, 304.
　pusilla, 305.
　pygmæa, 305.
　pygmæa leuconucha, 305.
Sittinæ, 304.
Skimmer, Black, 27.
Skua, 14.
Skylark, 191.
Snipe, European, 85.
　Wilson's, 85.
Snowflake, 220.
　McKay's, 221.
　Pribilof, 220.
Solitaire, Townsend's, 316.
Somateria, 57.
　dresseri, 57.
　mollissima borealis, 57.
　spectabilis, 58.
　v-nigra, 57.
Sora, 79.
Sparrow, Acadian Sharp-tailed, 228.
　Aleutian Song, 243.
　Arizona, 239.
　Bachman's, 239.
　Baird's, 226.
　Belding's Marsh, 225.
　Bell's, 238.
　Bischoff's Song, 242.
　Black-chinned, 234.
　Black-throated, 237.
　Boucard's, 240.
　Brewer's, 233.

Sparrow, Brown's Song, 242.
 Bryant's Marsh, 224.
 Cassin's, 239.
 Chipping, 232.
 Clay-colored, 232.
 Desert Song, 241.
 Dusky Seaside, 229.
 Field, 233.
 Forbush's, 243.
 Fox, 244.
 Gambel's, 231.
 Golden-crowned, 231.
 Grasshopper, 226.
 Gray Sage, 238.
 Harris's, 230.
 Heermann's, 241.
 Henslow's, 226.
 Intermediate, 230.
 Ipswich, 223.
 Large-billed, 225.
 Lark, 229.
 Leconte's, 227.
 Lincoln's, 243.
 Mexican, 239.
 Mountain Song, 241.
 Nelson's, 227.
 Oregon Vesper, 223.
 Pine-woods, 238.
 Rock, 240.
 Rufous-crowned, 240.
 Rufous-winged, 240.
 Rusty Song, 242.
 Sage, 238.
 St. Lucas, 225.
 Samuels's Song, 241.
 San Clemente Song, 243.
 Sandwich, 224.
 Santa Barbara Song, 242.
 Savanna, 224.
 Scott's Seaside, 228.
 Seaside, 228.
 Sharp-tailed, 227.
 Slate-colored, 245.
 Song, 241.
 Sooty Song, 242.
 Swamp, 244.
 Texas, 245.
 Texas Seaside, 228.
 Thick-billed, 245.
 Townsend's, 244.
 Tree, 231.
 Vesper, 222.
 Western Chipping, 232.
 Western Field, 233.
 Western Grasshopper, 226.
 Western Henslow's, 227.
 Western Lark, 229.

Sparrow, Western Savanna, 224.
 Western Tree, 232.
 Western Vesper, 223.
 White-crowned, 230.
 White-throated, 231.
 Worthen's, 233.
Spatula, 51.
 clypeata, 51.
Speotyto, 150.
 cunicularia floridana, 150.
 cunicularia hypogæa, 150.
Sphyrapicus, 163.
 ruber, 163.
 thyroideus, 163.
 varius, 163.
 varius nuchalis, 163.
Spinus, 218.
 lawrencei, 219.
 notatus, 219.
 pinus, 220.
 psaltria, 218.
 psaltria arizonæ, 219.
 psaltria mexicanus, 219.
 tristis, 218.
 tristis pallidus, 218.
Spiza, 254.
 americana, 254.
 townsendi, 331.
Spizella, 231.
 atrigularis, 234.
 breweri, 233.
 monticola, 231.
 monticola ochracea, 232.
 pallida, 232.
 pusilla, 233.
 pusilla arenacea, 233.
 socialis, 232.
 socialis arizonæ, 232.
 wortheni, 233.
Spoonbill, Roseate, 67.
Sporophila, 253.
 morelleti sharpei, 253.
Squatarola, 99.
Starling, 202.
Starnœnas, 124.
 cyanocephala, 124.
Steganopodes, 39.
Steganopus, 83.
Stelgidopteryx, 260.
 serripennis, 260.
Stellula, 176.
 calliope, 176.
Stercorariidæ, 13.
Stercorarius, 14.
 longicaudus, 15.
 parasiticus, 14.
 pomarinus, 14.

Sterna, 23, 24.
    aleutica, 25.
    anæthetus, 26.
    antillarum, 26.
    dougalli, 25.
    elegans, 23.
    forsteri, 24.
    fuliginosa, 26.
    hirundo, 24.
    maxima, 23.
    paradisæa, 25.
    sandvicensis acuflavida, 24.
    trudeaui, 24.
    tschegrava, 23.
Sterninæ, 22.
Sternula, 25.
Stilt, Black-necked, 84.
Stint, Long-toed, 89.
Streptoceryle, 156.
Striges, 142.
Strigidæ, 142.
Strix, 142.
    pratincola, 142.
Sturnella, 206.
    magna, 206.
    magna mexicana, 206.
    magna neglecta, 206.
Sturnidæ, 202.
Sturnus, 202.
    vulgaris, 202.
Sula, 39.
    bassana, 41.
    brewsteri, 40.
    cyanops, 40.
    gossi, 40.
    loxostyla, 340.
    piscator, 40.
    sula, 40.
Sulidæ, 39.
Surnia, 149.
    ulula, 149.
    ulula caparoch, 149.
Swallow, Bahaman, 259.
    Bank, 259.
    Barn, 258.
    Cliff, 257.
    Cuban Cliff, 258.
    Rough-winged, 260.
    Tree, 257.
    Violet-green, 259.
Swan, Trumpeter, 65.
    Whistling, 65.
    Whooping, 65.
Swift, Black, 171.
    Chimney, 172.
    Vaux's, 172.
    White-throated, 173.

Sylvania, 285.
    canadensis, 286.
    microcephala, 333.
    mitrata, 285.
    pusilla, 285.
    pusilla pileolata, 286.
Sylviidæ, 313, 333.
Sylviinæ, 313.
Symphemia, 94.
    semipalmata, 94.
    semipalmata inornata, 95.
Synthliboramphus, 8.
    antiquus, 8.
Syrnium, 143.
    nebulosum, 143.
    nebulosum alleni, 143.
    occidentale, 143.

TACHYCINETA, 258.
    bicolor, 258.
    thalassina, 259.
Tachytriorchis, 132.
Tanager, Cooper's, 256.
    Gray's, 255.
    Hepatic, 256.
    Louisiana, 255.
    Scarlet, 255.
    Summer, 256.
Tanagridæ, 254.
Tantalinæ, 68.
Tantalus, 68.
    loculator, 69.
Tatler, Wandering, 95.
Teal, Blue-winged, 50.
    Cinnamon, 51.
    European, 50.
    Green-winged, 50.
Telmatodytes, 302.
Telmatornis affinis, 338.
    priscus, 338.
Tern, Aleutian, 25.
    Arctic, 25.
    Black, 26.
    Bridled, 26.
    Cabot's, 24.
    Caspian, 23.
    Common, 24.
    Elegant, 23.
    Forster's, 24.
    Gull-billed, 22.
    Least, 26.
    Roseate, 25.
    Royal, 23.
    Sooty, 26.
    Trudeau's, 24.
    White-winged Black, 27.

Tetraonidæ, 106.
Tetraoninæ, 110.
Thalasseus, 23.
Thalassogeron, 28.
    culminatus, 28.
Thrasaëtos, 135.
    harpyia, 135.
Thrasher, Bendire's, 293.
    Brown, 293.
    California, 294.
    Crissal, 295.
    Curve-billed, 293.
    Leconte's, 294.
    Mearns's, 294.
    Palmer's, 293.
    Sage, 291.
    St. Lucas, 294.
    Sennett's, 293.
Thrush, Audubon's Hermit, 319.
    Bicknell's, 317.
    Dwarf Hermit, 318.
    Gray-cheeked, 317.
    Hermit, 319.
    Olive-backed, 318.
    Red-winged, 319.
    Russet-backed, 318.
    Varied, 321.
    Willow, 317.
    Wilson's, 317.
    Wood, 316.
Thryomanes, 298.
Thryothorus, 297.
    bewickii, 298.
    bewickii bairdi, 299.
    bewickii spilurus, 299.
    brevicaudus, 299.
    leucophrys, 299.
    ludovicianus, 298.
    ludovicianus lomitensis, 298.
    ludovicianus miamensis, 298.
Tinnunculus, 140.
Titmouse, Ashy, 307.
    Black-crested, 306.
    Bridled, 307.
    Gray, 307.
    Plain, 306.
    Texas Tufted, 306.
    Tufted, 306.
Totanus, 92.
    flavipes, 93.
    melanoleucus, 93.
    nebularius, 93.
    ochropus, 94.
    solitarius, 94.
    solitarius cinnamomeus, 94.
Towhee, 246.
    Abert's, 248.

Towhee, Anthony's, 248.
    Arctic, 246.
    California, 248.
    Cañon, 247.
    Green-tailed, 247.
    Guadalupe, 247.
    Oregon, 247.
    Saint Lucas, 248.
    Spurred, 246.
    White-eyed, 246.
Tree-duck, Black-bellied, 64.
    Fulvous, 64.
Tringa, 86.
    acuminata, 88.
    alpina, 89.
    alpina pacifica, 89.
    bairdii, 88.
    canutus, 86.
    cooperi, 328.
    couesi, 87.
    damacensis, 89.
    ferruginea, 90.
    fuscicollis, 88.
    maculata, 88.
    maritima, 87.
    minutilla, 89.
    ptilocnemis, 87.
Trochili, 173.
Trochilidæ, 173.
Trochilus, 174.
    alexandri, 174.
    colubris, 174.
    violajugulum, 174.
Troglodytes, 300.
    aëdon, 300.
    aëdon aztecus, 300.
    aëdon parkmanii, 300.
    alascensis, 301.
    hiemalis, 301.
    hiemalis pacificus, 301.
Troglodytidæ, 291.
Troglodytinæ, 295.
Trogon, 156.
    ambiguus, 156.
    Coppery-tailed, 156.
Trogones, 156.
Trogonidæ, 156.
Troupial, 207.
Tryngites, 96.
    subruficollis, 96.
Tubinares, 28.
Turdidæ, 316.
Turdinæ, 316.
Turdus, 316.
    aliciæ, 317.
    aliciæ bicknelli, 317.
    aonalaschkæ, 318.

Turdus aonalaschkæ auduboni, 319.
    aonalaschkæ pallasi, 319.
    fuscescens, 317.
    fuscescens salicicolus, 317.
    iliacus, 319.'
    mustelinus, 316.
    ustulatus, 318.
    ustulatus swainsoni, 318.
Turkey, Florida Wild, 118.
    Mexican, 118.
    Rio Grande Wild, 118.
    Wild, 118.
Turnstone, 103.
    Black, 104.
Tympanuchus, 115.
    americanus, 115.
    americanus attwateri, 115.
    cupido, 115.
    pallidicinctus, 116.
Tyrannidæ, 179.
Tyrannus, 180.
    dominicensis, 180.
    melancholicus couchii, 181.
    tyrannus, 180.
    verticalis, 181.
    vociferans, 181.

UINTORNIS lucaris, 345.
Uria, 11.
    affinis, 339.
    antiqua, 339.
    lomvia, 12.
    lomvia arra, 12.
    troile, 11.
    troile californica, 11.
Urile, 44.
Urinator, 3.
    adamsii, 4.
    arcticus, 4.
    imber, 3.
    lumme, 4.
    pacificus, 4.
Urinatoridæ, 3.
Urubitinga, 133.
    anthracina, 133.

VANELLUS, 98.
    vanellus, 98.
Verdin, 313.
Vireo, 272, 265.
    atricapillus, 265.
    bellii, 267.
    bellii pusillus, 267.
    calidris barbatulus, 263.

Vireo flavifrons, 264.
    flavoviridis, 263.
    gilvus, 264.
    hutttoni, 266.
    huttoni obscurus, 266.
    huttoni stephensi, 266.
    noveboracensis, 266.
    noveboracensis maynardi, 266.
    olivaceus, 263.
    philadelphicus, 263.
    solitarius, 264.
    solitarius alticola, 265.
    solitarius cassinii, 264.
    solitarius lucasanus, 265.
    solitarius plumbeus, 265.
    vicinior, 267.
Vireo, Anthony's, 266.
    Bell's, 267.
    Black-capped, 265.
    Black-whiskered, 263.
    Blue-headed, 264.
    Cassin's, 264.
    Gray, 267.
    Hutton's, 266.
    Key West, 266.
    Least, 267.
    Mountain Solitary, 265.
    Philadelphia, 263.
    Plumbeous, 265.
    Red-eyed, 263.
    St. Lucas Solitary, 265.
    Stephens's, 266.
    Warbling, 264.
    White-eyed, 266.
    Yellow-green, 263.
    Yellow-throated, 264.
Vireonidæ, 262, 331.
Vireosylva, 262.
Vulture, Black, 125.
    Burroughs's Turkey, 329.
    California, 125.
    King, 329.
    Turkey, 125.

WAGTAIL, Siberian Yellow, 289.
    Swinhoe's, 289.
    White, 289.
Warbler, Audubon's, 275.
    Bachman's, 270.
    Bay-breasted, 277.
    Bell's, 288.
    Black and White, 268.
    Blackburnian, 277.
    Black-poll, 277.
    Black-throated Blue, 275.
    Black-throated Gray, 278.

Warbler, Black-throated Green, 279.
  Blue Mountain, 333.
  Blue-winged, 270.
  Brasher's, 288.
  Brewster's, 332.
  Calaveras, 271.
  Canadian, 286.
  Cape May, 273.
  Carbonated, 332.
  Cerulean, 276.
  Chestnut-sided, 276.
  Cincinnati, 332.
  Connecticut, 282.
  Dusky, 272.
  Golden-cheeked, 278.
  Golden-winged, 270.
  Grace's, 278.
  Hermit, 279.
  Hooded, 285.
  Kennicott's Willow, 313.
  Kentucky, 282.
  Kirtland's, 280.
  Lawrence's, 331.
  Lucy's, 270.
  Lutescent, 272.
  Macgillivray's, 283.
  Magnolia, 276.
  Mangrove, 275.
  Mourning, 283.
  Myrtle, 275.
  Nashville, 271.
  Olive, 274.
  Orange-crowned, 272.
  Palm, 280.
  Parula, 273.
  Pileolated, 286.
  Pine, 280.
  Prairie, 281.
  Prothonotary, 268.
  Red, 288.
  Red-faced, 287.
  Sennett's, 273.
  Small-headed, 333.
  Sonora Yellow, 274.
  Swainson's, 269.
  Sycamore, 278.
  Tennessee, 272.
  Townsend's, 279.
  Virginia's, 271.
  Wilson's, 285.
  Worm-eating, 269.
  Yellow, 274.
  Yellow Palm, 280.
  Yellow-throated, 277.
Water-Thrush, 281.
  Grinnell's, 281.
  Louisiana, 282.
Waxwing, Bohemian, 260.
  Cedar, 260.
Wheatear, 321.
Whimbrel, 98.
Whip-poor-will, 168.
  Stephens's, 169.
Widgeon, 49.
Willet, 94.
  Western, 95.
Woodcock, American, 84.
  European, 84.
Woodpecker, Alaskan Three-toed, 162.
  Alpine Three-toed, 162.
  American Three-toed, 162.
  Arctic Three-toed, 162.
  Arizona, 161.
  Batchelder's, 160.
  Cabanis's, 159.
  Californian, 164.
  Downy, 159
  Gairdner's, 159.
  Gila, 166.
  Golden-fronted, 166.
  Hairy, 158.
  Harris's, 159.
  Ivory-billed, 158.
  Lewis's, 164.
  Narrow-fronted, 164.
  Northern Hairy, 158.
  Nuttall's, 161.
  Pileated, 164.
  Red-bellied, 165.
  Red-cockaded, 160.
  Red-headed, 164.
  Saint Lucas, 160.
  Southern Hairy, 158.
  Texan, 160.
  White-headed, 161.
  Williamson's, 163.
Wren, Alaskan, 301.
  Baird's, 299.
  Bewick's, 298.
  Bryant's Cactus, 295.
  Cactus, 295.
  Cañon, 297.
  Carolina, 298.
  Dotted Cañon, 295.
  Florida, 298.
  Guadalupe, 299.
  Guadalupe Rock, 296.
  House, 300.
  Lomita, 298.
  Long-billed Marsh, 302.
  Marian's Marsh, 303.
  Parkman's, 300.
  Rock, 296.
  St. Lucas Cactus, 296.

Wren, San Clemente, 299.
    Short-billed Marsh, 301.
    Tulé, 302.
    Vigors's, 299.
    Western House, 300.
    Western Winter, 301.
    White-throated, 297.
    Winter, 301.
    Worthington's Marsh, 302.
Wren-Tit, 310.
    Pallid, 311.

XANTHOCEPHALUS, 204.
    xanthocephalus, 204.
Xanthoura, 198.
    luxuosa, 198.
Xema, 22.
    sabinii, 22.
Xenopicus, 161.
    albolarvatus, 161.

YELLOW-LEGS, 93.
    Greater, 93.
Yellow-throat, Belding's, 284.
    Florida, 284.
    Maryland, 283.
    Rio Grande, 284.
    Western, 284.
Yphantes, 208.

ZENAIDA, 121.
    zenaida, 121.
Zenaidura, 121.
    macroura, 121.
Zonotrichia, 230.
    albicollis, 231.
    coronata, 231.
    leucophrys, 230.
    leucophrys gambeli, 231.
    leucophrys intermedia, 230.
    querula, 230.

www.ingramcontent.com/pod-product-compliance
Lightning Source LLC
Chambersburg PA
CBHW030344230426
43664CB00007BB/522